WITH
FIRMNESS IN THE RIGHT

American Diplomatic Action Affecting Jews,

1840–1945

By

CYRUS ADLER

and

AARON M. MARGALITH

NEW YORK
THE AMERICAN JEWISH COMMITTEE
1946

PRINTED IN THE UNITED STATES OF AMERICA
PRESS OF THE JEWISH PUBLICATION SOCIETY
PHILADELPHIA, PENNA.

PREFACE

There seems to be a general misconception in this country that the action by the American Government in recent years to secure cooperation among democratic countries in aid of refugees from Germany marked a new turn in the foreign policy of our nation. It is hoped that the present volume will serve to dispel this and similar misconceptions. The student of the history of the foreign policy of the United States knows that this action was in complete harmony with the policies developed during an earlier period by a number of great American statesmen. When for example, in 1938, the Department of State invited thirty other States to discuss measures for helping persons forced to flee from a country in which they were being persecuted, because of their religious faith or political affiliations, or because of their ancestry, the Department was following a policy which had been practiced by this country for many generations, long before the pronouncements of the Four Freedoms and The Atlantic Charter. This practice conforms with principles which constitute the moral basis of the American nation.

In fact, the championship of humanitarianism, freedom of conscience and civil liberties is enunciated again and again in our diplomatic correspondence with other nations. The United States, conceived in freedom, gave assistance, in word and in deed, to oppressed minorities everywhere.

But, while the administration of the late President Franklin D. Roosevelt (and, it would seem also, that of his successor, President Harry S. Truman) did not blaze new trails in American foreign policy, the Roosevelt Administration did, by its championing at every opportunity the cause of religious freedom and racial equality, and, especially, by sponsoring the refugee plan, bring to an end the period of reactionary isolationism which began with the rejection of President Wilson's plans for world cooperation. The voice

iii

of President Franklin D. Roosevelt who, like many presidents and secretaries of state before him, acted as the spokesman and true agent of the American people, had a welcome and encouraging sound at a time when the world suffered from moral depression and suicidal nationalisms, when the nations of the world were divided into weak and wicked ones, and barbarism threatened to come upon us with all the fury of modern science and invention. During the few months that President Truman has been in office he has proved himself to be a good disciple of his great predecessor by continuing the latter's liberal foreign policies both in spirit and in action.

"No class of people," said Oscar S. Straus, "have been compelled more often to invoke the humanitarian diplomacy of civilized states than the Jews, because no people have, since time immemorial, by reason of race hatred and religious persecution, suffered as they have from inhumanity and oppression in every form and degree." It is natural, therefore, that Jews should have been the chief beneficiaries of the humanitarian policies of the United States. The persecution and maltreatment of human beings on account of their belonging to a particular race or religion have always been obnoxious to the spirit of the American people. Whenever and wherever anti-Jewish feelings have expressed themselves in oppressive measures against Jews, the voice of outraged America has always been raised in protest, and there were times when the American people, directly or through its elected governments, chose more specific action to communicate its disfavor.

Dr. Cyrus Adler made the first attempt to organize and publish that part of American diplomatic correspondence which concerns itself with Jews. At the thirteenth annual meeting of the American Jewish Historical Society, in 1905, Dr. Adler delivered the presidential address which was based on his researches in this field. This address was later published as Volume 15 of the *Publications* of that Society. This monograph consisted of excerpts from the diplomatic correspondence of the United States which affected Jews and was entitled "Jews in the Diplomatic Correspondence of the United States." Some of this correspondence concerned itself with Jews in foreign countries and was based on general and humanitarian grounds. Most of it, however, dealt with cases affecting Jewish Americans and was based on legal and constitutional grounds. Dr. Adler's monograph included chapters on Turkey, Switzerland, Morocco, Rumania, Russia, and Persia.

In 1935, Dr. Adler asked me to bring the record of American diplomatic action affecting Jews up to date. Because of the tremendous amount of new material accumulated since 1905, it was decided to recast the structure followed in Dr. Adler's monograph and write what practically amounted to a new book. Chapters dealing with Austria, Germany, Italy, Palestine and Poland, countries not dealt with in the earlier monograph, are included. In 1905, Palestine was a part of the Ottoman Empire and was treated under Turkey, while Poland was then divided among Russia, Germany and Austria-Hungary. The material on Russia has more than trebled, and it was found necessary to divide it into three chapters. In a number of cases, too, material other than the official publications of the United States has been used.

Much new material was made available, especially for the chapter on Russia, by research conducted at the National Archives Building and in the Archives of the Department of State in Washington. The full utilization of the additional material already accumulated and that which is still to be studied at these sources, would go far beyond the scope of the present book.

This book appeared originally under the title "American Intercession on Behalf of Jews in the Diplomatic Correspondence of the United States, 1840–1938," and was published as Volume 36 of the *Publications* of the American Jewish Historical Society, in 1943. In the present enlarged edition, two new chapters are added. The first is an introductory chapter which discusses the main principles that guided American foreign policy in the subjects treated in the book;

it also gives a summary review of the whole subject matter according to countries. The second new feature is the last chapter which deals with the years 1938 to the conclusion of the United Nations Conference on International Organization held in San Francisco in 1945. In this chapter geographical treatment was discarded in favor of treatment by subject.

Since the completion of the manuscript of this book my revered collaborator has died. His passing, on April 7, 1940, not only deprived me of his valuable advice and counsel in the further steps of the publication of the book, but was also a grievous personal loss to me. Fortunately, my esteemed friend Mr. Harry Schneiderman, editor of the *American Jewish Year Book*, who read the book in all its stages and generally gave the authors the benefit of his knowledge of this phase of American history, was good enough to offer me his aid in the final revision of the manuscript and of the proofs. In the pre-publication stages, I was benefited also by the valuable assistance of Rabbi Isidore S. Meyer, the able librarian of the American Jewish Historial Society. I am grateful also to Mrs. Rose G. Stein of the staff of the American Jewish Committee for her conscientious and painstaking work in the revision of the proofs. Mr. Sidney Liskofsky deserves special thanks and appreciation for the valuable assistance he gave in the writing of the last chapter.

It is hoped that this book will encourage the American people to remain true to its established traditions and its future destiny, by continuing to spread its ideals to all the benighted corners of the world. History has rarely, if ever, offered a greater opportunity to a mighty and liberal nation than that which it presents to the American people of this generation. We look to the future with the confidence that in facing the many problems which victory on the battlefield has brought in its wake, American statesmen will carry forward the humanitarian traditions, encouraged by the noble precedents set by their high-minded predecessors.

AARON M. MARGALITH

CONTENTS

about value of intercession.— Cooperates with European ministers to save Jewish lives.— Jews of Arzila thank Felix A. Mathews, new American Consul at Tangier, for his aid.— Mathews communicates with Grand Vizier.— Board of Delegates of American Israelites sends agent to Tangier.— U. S. Minister Fairchild offers aid.— Visits Morocco and reports to Secretary Blaine.— King of Spain offers refuge to German and Russian Jews.— U. S. representative intercedes in behalf of Jews of Morocco at Algeciras conference, 1906.— Text of motion adopted at Algeciras.

Early American interests in Palestine.— Turkish Government informs U. S. Minister that Jews may settle in Turkey but not in Palestine.— Turkish attempted distinction between native and naturalized American citizens disputed by Minister Wallace.— American Minister Straus interests himself in plight of American Jews in Palestine.— Protests to Turkish Foreign Office.— Straus action followed by British and French ministers.— Strong protest by Chargé King results in freeing of three American Jews.— Straus visits Jerusalem.— B'nai Brith lodge presents testimonial to Straus.— New Turkish restrictions protested by Secretaries Gresham and Hay.— Ambassador Morgenthau sends relief to Jews of Palestine, 1915.— Secretary Bryan expresses fear for security of Jews in Syria and Palestine.— Morgenthau secures permission for American cruisers to stay in Turkish waters.— American cruisers rescue Jewish refugees and transfer them to Egypt.— American officials assist in bringing relief to Palestine Jews.— British and American views on relief conflict.— Jewish medical unit recognized.— Frankfurter-Morgenthau Mission.— Madrid conference with Dr. Weizmann and M. Weyl.— Mission ends abortively.— Secretary Lansing inquires about the "Jewish State" promised in Balfour Declaration.— Lord Robert Cecil expresses hope that U. S. will become trustee of an "internationalized" Palestine.— Crane-King commission to Syria and Palestine.— President Wilson on Palestine.— U. S. government insists on equality of rights and privileges.— American claim disputed by Great

PART TWO

RUMANIA AND POLAND

PART THREE

RUSSIA

Part Four

CENTRAL EUROPE

Contents.

zation of former German nationals.— Ambassador White's famous report on condition of Jews in Germany.— Jews granted full equality by Weimar Constitution, 1919.— Points affecting Jews in the Nazi program, 1920.— Anti-Jewish riots begin.— American Ambassador makes representation on instructions from President Hoover and, later, Secretary Hull.— Secretary Hull meets Jewish representatives.— Acting Secretary Phillips takes steps to facilitate entry of German Jews into U. S.— American public condemns German anti-Jewish policy.— House and Senate pass resolutions requesting the President to do everything possible to improve conditions of Jews in Germany.— League of Nations takes up problem of refugees.— Office of High Commissioner for German refugees created.— Secretary Hull and President Roosevelt rebuke Germany.— Secretary of Interior Ickes expresses President's distress at condition of Jews in Germany.— The *Bremen* flag incident.— Magistrate Brodsky in dismissing arrested persons likens swastika "to "black flag of piracy".— Germany protests and Hull expresses regret, September 1935.— Germany again protests against utterances by Mayor Fiorello H. La Guardia, March 5, 1937.— Hull's apology contains indirect rebuke to Germany.— Another statement by La Guardia becomes a subject of diplomatic exchange, March 15, 1937.— U. S. protests against application to American Jews of German anti-Jewish financial measures, May 11, 1938.— President Roosevelt invites twenty-nine governments to discuss facilitation of emigration of refugees from Germany and Austria, March 24, 1938.— International Conference on Refugees at Evian, July 1938, establishes Intergovernmental Committee.—The anti-Jewish riots of November 10, 1938.— Ambassador Hugh R. Wilson recalled.— American embassy and German Foreign Office exchange notes on application of German anti-Jewish laws to American Jews.— Acting Secretary Sumner Welles rejects German protest against remarks by Secretary Ickes.

German "racial experts" visit Italy.— Pure "Aryan" lineage of Italian people established by Italian "scientists".— First anti-Jewish decree, November 15,

Neutral nations warned against harboring Nazi criminals.— The Three Power statement on atrocities, Moscow, October, 1943.— Hungary invaded by Nazis, March, 1944.— Hungarian Jews deported for extermination or slavery.— President Roosevelt appeals to Hungarians to help Jews.

Latin America: Anti-Semitism in Argentina.— Argentina rebuked by President Roosevelt.— Inter-American conference at Chapultepec.— Declaration for the international protection of rights of man.

Intergovernmental Committee on Refugees: Conference on refugees at Evian, 1938.— Special meeting of Committee at White House, October 1939.— Santo Domingo project.— Negotiations with Vichy.

Anglo-American Conference, Bermuda, March 1943: State Department note reviews American aid to refugees.— Secretary Hull's figures on immigration disputed.— Result of conference disappointing.

"Free Ports": Thousand refugees settled at Fort Ontario, N. Y.

United Nations Relief and Rehabilitation Administration (UNRRA): Herbert H. Lehman elected Director General.

International Protection of Human Rights: Human rights at Dumbarton Oaks Conference.— Minorities treaties proved inadequate.— President Roosevelt favors an international bill of rights.— Possible grounds for opposition by leading powers.— Consultants at UNCIO petition American delegation to press for charter provision for human rights.— Proposal gains support of conference.— Provisions of charter relating to international protection of human rights.— Comments of Secretary Stettinius and President Truman.

APPENDIX

INTRODUCTION

American diplomatic interpositions in the interests of Jews have been of two sorts. They have been, first, interpositions in behalf of American citizens abroad and, second, interpositions on purely humanitarian grounds in behalf of Jews who were not American nationals. The largest part, by far, of this type of diplomatic activity has been of the first sort.

Most instances of interposition in behalf of American citizens of Jewish faith occurred in the latter half of the nineteenth century, the years of rapidly growing Jewish immigration to the United States. Many of the recent arrivals would return to their native lands to arrange for the emigration of families which they had left behind, or to revisit for purely sentimental reasons the towns or villages where their youth had been spent. Other Jews would return for business purposes.

Under American law, these persons were entitled to the protection of the President of the United States, and the Department of State was required to take immediate action whenever the rights of any American citizen were violated or threatened.

This protection is specifically accorded such persons by an act of Congress of July 27, 1868, which provides that:

Whenever it is made known to the President that any citizen of the United States has been unjustly deprived of his liberty by or under the authority of any foreign government, it shall be the duty of the President forthwith to demand of that government the reason for such imprisonment; and if it appears to be wrongful and in violation of the rights of American citizenship, the President shall forthwith demand the release of such citizen, and if the release so demanded is unreasonably delayed or refused, the President shall use such means not amounting to acts of war, as he may think necessary and proper to obtain or effectuate the release; and all facts and proceedings relative thereto shall as soon as practicable be communicated by the President to Congress.[1]

[1] Act of July 27, 1868, c. 249, 15, *Stat.*, 224.

This law makes no distinction between a native or a naturalized citizen of the United States. Both are equally entitled to the protection of the government. This was emphasized even earlier, in 1859, in an opinion of Attorney General Jeremiah S. Black:

In regard to the protection of our citizens in their rights at home and abroad, we have no law which divides them into classes or makes any difference whatever between them. A native and a naturalized American may therefore go forth with equal security over every sea and through every land under heaven, including the countries in which they were born.[2]

Nor does the law make any distinction between American citizens on the ground of religious faiths. In the words of Secretary of State Lewis Cass, it is the object of the United States "not merely to protect a Catholic in a Protestant country, a Protestant in a Catholic country, a Jew in a Christian country, but an American in all countries."[3]

This attitude was reiterated by Secretary of State James G. Blaine in the following quotation from a long letter to Mr. John W. Foster, United States Minister at St. Petersburg:

I need hardly enlarge on the point that the government of the United States concludes its treaties with foreign states for the equal protection of all classes of American citizens. It can make absolutely no discrimination between them, whatever their origin or creed. So that they abide by the laws at home or abroad it must give them due protection and expect like protection for them. Any unfriendly or discriminatory act against them on the part of a foreign power with which we are at peace would call for our earnest remonstrance whether a treaty existed or not.[4]

These principles were applied most prominently in American relations with Tsarist Russia. Diplomatic negotiations with Russia relating to recognition of the American passport by that Government were carried on for a number of years.

---

[2] Right of Expatriation, 9. Opinions of Attorney General, 360.

[3] Secretary Cass, quoted in J. B. Moore, "American Diplomacy," New York, 1905, page 135.

[4] Foreign Relations, 1881, page 1033.

In its oppressive laws against Jews, the Government of Imperial Russia made no distinction as to their citizenship. Thus, American citizens of the Jewish faith were refused the permission to establish themselves, to visit or even to pass through certain regions of Russia. From 1873 to 1911, American secretaries of state and diplomatic representatives at St. Petersburg, with patience and persistence protested to the Russian Government against the application of its anti-Jewish laws to American citizens. But these efforts were in vain. The persistence by the Russian Government in discriminating against American Jews solely on the basis of their religion created such a violent reaction in this country that the termination by the United States, in 1912, of its 1832 commercial treaty with Russia met with universal approval.

American correspondence with pre-Hitler Germany also include a number of cases involving American Jews, in which their religion was a factor operating to their disadvantage. These, however, were the exception rather than the rule. Most of the correspondence was concerned with the question of military service of naturalized American citizens. Germans who emigrated prior to fulfilling the required period of military service, and who returned to Germany for any purpose, were arrested and impressed into military duty despite their American citizenship. This thorny problem was eventually settled by a naturalization treaty.[5]

---

[5] One of the most interesting features of this correspondence is the very illuminating analysis of anti-Semitism in Germany sent to the State Department by the famous American educator, author and diplomat, Andrew D. White, then serving as United States Minister to Germany. The report, dated Berlin, April 29, 1881, is given in full on pages 354–362 of this book. A similar report on the condition of the Jews in Russia was written by Mr. White twelve years later, when he was United States Minister to that country. The full text of this lengthy and interesting essay is given in the appendix of this book, pages 389–402. These and similar reports by American diplomats abroad are a valuable source of information for the history of the Jews in a number of countries and throw an interesting light upon the understanding by some of our diplomats of the duties and the opportunities offered them by their missions abroad.

Like Tsarist Russia, but with much graver implications, Nazi Germany several decades later discriminated against American citizens of the Jewish faith. Actually it was not the faith but the "race" of the Jew that made him the object of Nazi wrath. Adhering rigidly to their racial theories, the Nazis treated all Jews under their jurisdiction alike, irrespective of their national allegiance.

Adhering to the principles previously applied in their relations with Tsarist Russia and pre-Hitler Germany, the American government, in a note presented to the German Ministry of Foreign Affairs on December 14, 1938, demanded assurances from the German Government that American citizens of the Jewish faith would not be subjected to discriminatory treatment because of their race or creed. The note pointed out that such discrimination against American Jews would be contrary to the fundamental principle of American law, which did not permit any distinction among citizens on the basis of their race or creed. It added that, in its relations with other nations, the United States had always refused them the right to apply such discrimination as between American citizens.

The German Government, in reply, contended that the American principle of non-discrimination on the basis of race and creed could not be made to apply to American citizens residing in countries where such discrimination is practised. For this and other well-known reasons, diplomatic relations with Germany were terminated, and the American Ambassador to Berlin recalled.

In its diplomatic relations with the Government of Austria-Hungary, the United States added a significant chapter to its tradition of religious liberty. The famous Keiley case is unique in that the Government of the United States refused to send another minister to Vienna after its minister-designate was declared *persona non grata* by the Government of Austria-Hungary for the sole reason that his wife was allegedly born a Jewess. This interesting episode is discussed fully in a later chapter, but, for our present purpose, it will suffice to quote a short passage from the remarkable correspondence between the two governments, in which Secretary Thomas F. Bayard expressed in eloquent words the American view of religious liberty and the part it plays in our constitutional democracy.

Religious liberty is the chief cornerstone of the American system of government, and provisions for its security are imbedded in the written charter and interwoven in the moral fabric of its laws.

Anything that tends to invade a right so essential and sacred must be carefully guarded against, and I am satisfied that my countrymen, ever mindful of the sufferings and sacrifices necessary to obtain it, will never consent to its impairment for any reason or under any pretext whatsoever—.

It is not believed by the President that a doctrine and practice so destructive of religious liberty and freedom of conscience, so devoid of catholicity, and so opposed to the spirit of the age in which we live, can for a moment be accepted by the great family of civilized nations or be allowed to control their diplomatic intercourse.

Certain it is, it will never, in my belief, be accepted by the people of the United States nor by any administration which represents their sentiments.[6]

Another brilliant chapter in the struggle by American diplomats to have American citizens abroad treated with complete equality, irrespective of their race or creed, was written by Theodore S. Fay, United States Minister to Switzerland from 1853 to 1861.

The Switzerland of the time was a loosely governed confederation. Not only was each canton free from federal control in important internal matters and even foreign relations, but even within each canton every commune enjoyed similar liberties. Treaties entered into by Switzerland with other nations were often ignored by some of the cantons, and the federal government was without power to coerce them into adherence. The Swiss Federal Council was willing to interpret liberally the treaty of 1850 between the United States and Switzerland and to extend to American Jews the same rights and privileges granted American Christians. Some of the cantons, however, persisted in their discrimina-

[6] Foreign Relations, 1885, page 50.

tion and refused to permit American Jews to establish themselves within their jurisdiction.

Mr. Fay, becoming absorbed in the whole problem of anti-Jewish prejudices, made a thorough study of the condition of the Jews in Switzerland and neighboring countries. As a result of these studies, he wrote the famous "Israelite Note," which he circulated among the respective cantons. This note, in turn, created a strong pro-Jewish agitation in a number of cantons, and the anti-Jewish laws were repealed. There is no doubt, too, that the efforts of Mr. Fay in behalf of the Jews in Switzerland, contributed to the change of the Swiss constitutional system. According to the new constitution, all discrimination on the basis of race and religion was eliminated, and the treatment of aliens made a federal matter.

Thus, the Government of the United States has gone far in its efforts to protect the rights and interests of its citizens of the Jewish faith. It should be noted that, although in the cases just mentioned moral considerations strongly motivated the actions of the Government, they were nevertheless primarily based on legal and constitutional grounds. International, as well as national, law recognizes the right and duty of a nation to protect the interests of its nationals when they are threatened by other nations. However, in American diplomatic history there are many cases where the Government came to the aid of persons who were not citizens of the United States, who lived in foreign lands, and in whose situation the interests of the United States were not involved in any manner. The motives in these cases were clearly humanitarian.

In a number of cases, American representatives abroad interceded, on their own initiative, in behalf of persecuted Jews, and later received the full approval of their superiors in Washington. Sometimes, too, the initiative was taken by the Government in Washington even before interested parties had brought the case to their attention. A notable instance of this kind is the famous Damascus case, which occurred in 1840. Mr. Forsyth's dispatch in the case, quoted in the first chapter of this book, is the first representation relating to Jews made by the United States to any foreign power. American intercession was instrumental in freeing a number of Jews who had been accused of ritual murder. This accusation, it was soon discovered, was political in origin but, before the end of the affair, a number of Jews had been tortured imprisoned, or put to death.

American consuls on other occasions also came to the aid of the "scattered remnants of God's ancient people," as the Jews were termed by one American consul in Turkey.

In Persia and in Morocco, American intercession was on purely humanitarian grounds. In connection with these cases, no treaty provisions were violated, nor did any American complain of an unjust discrimination. The American consuls in these countries, because they possessed extraterritorial rights, were very helpful to the local Jews who were chronically exposed to inhuman treatment at the hands of the native population and rulers. On one urgent occasion, an American consul in Morocco was instructed by the Secretary of State to overlook technicalities. The letter of instruction to the consul contained the following passage:

No official interposition in behalf of Israelites who are Moorish subjects can be sanctioned, as this would be improper in itself, and would be a precedent against us which could not be gainsaid. Still, there might be cases in which humanity would dictate a disregard of technicalities, if your personal influence would shield Hebrews from oppression.[7]

The American diplomatic correspondence relating to the Jews of Tsarist Russia includes instances of intercessions on behalf, not merely of American citizens, but of persecuted Jews in general.

The new Poland, reconstituted in 1918, contained within its boundaries large groups of religious or national minorities,

[7] Letters of Secretary Evarts to Mr. Mathews, March 20, 1878, "Moore's Digest," *op. cit.*, page 349.

including Jews who constituted a considerable proportion of the population.

During the Peace Conference, reports of anti-Jewish outbreaks in several places in Poland reached the outside world. American public opinion was shocked, and the Department of State was urged to exert its influence to bring about the cessation of anti-Jewish attacks. One early result of the pressure of public opinion was the dispatch, in 1919, by President Wilson, of a special mission to investigate the reported excesses. This mission was headed by Henry Morgenthau, Sr., former American ambassador to Turkey. The British Government sent a similar commission of inquiry. This action by the two governments effectively halted the excesses which, the commissions ascertained, had in fact taken place. However, during the ensuing years, up to World War II, the Jews of Poland were subjected to both official discrimination and to outbreaks of violence.

In the treaty with Poland, signed at Versailles on September 28, 1919, Poland undertook to assure to all Polish nationals "without distinction as to race, language or religion," equality before the law and enjoyment of "the same civil and political rights." Poland also undertook to regard those provisions of the treaty which dealt with the protection of minorities as "fundamental laws" and as "obligations of international concern . . . placed under the guarantee of the League of Nations." Poland failed to observe the provisions of this treaty insofar as Jews were concerned, and on the eve of World War II repudiated the agreement. This course, and the violation by Austria, Hungary and Rumania of similar treaties, were important factors in calling forth a demand, during World War II, for the international protection of human rights by means of an international bill of rights whose observance would be the responsibility of a proposed international security organization.

In no European country in modern times, with the exception of Nazi Germany, were the Jews exposed to greater suffering and degradation than in Rumania. Long before

Rumania became an independent state, the American Government had occasion to interpose on humanitarian grounds in behalf of the Rumanian Jews.

Attacks on Jews in the principalities of Moldavia and Wallachia prompted President Ulysses S. Grant to appoint Mr. Benjamin F. Peixotto, grand master of the order of B'nai B'rith, as United States Consul to Rumania. In the words of President Grant, Mr. Peixotto undertook the duties of Consul as "a missionary work for the benefit of the people he represents." In spite of his intense efforts, in which he was aided by the consular and diplomatic representatives of the leading powers, Mr. Peixotto was not able to improve the conditions of the Jews in the principalities.

In 1878, when the Congress of Berlin established the kingdom of Rumania, the United States Government, though not a party to the Congress, exerted its influence towards making the recognition of Rumania contingent upon definite promises to emancipate the Jews and grant them civil equality. Although the promises were exacted, they were never kept.

One of the most striking items in American diplomatic correspondence is the famous note written by Secretary of State John Hay on July 17, 1902. Mr. Hay was prompted to write this lengthy note by the Rumanian refusal to sign a naturalization treaty with the United States, on the ground that such a treaty might result in benefits to American Jews of former Rumanian allegiance. The note discusses in detail the background of the Jewish problem in Rumania and contains direct and indirect censure of the maltreatment of the Jews in that country. In this note, Secretary Hay advances the important principle that the American Government has the right to concern itself with the situation of the Jews in Rumania on the ground that the oppressive conditions under which they are forced to live makes them involuntary emigrants. This kind of immigration, the note argues, "lacks the essential conditions which make alien immigration either acceptable or beneficial."

All efforts by the American and by other governments

which supported the United States in its endeavor to ameliorate the situation of the Jews in Rumania, failed. Rumania, which was on the side of the Allies in World War I, gained new territories after 1918, and as a result the number of Jews under her yoke was increased to almost a million.

Palestine, until 1918 a part of the Turkish Empire, is also mentioned frequently in American diplomatic correspondence. On the whole, the nature of the diplomatic action in pre-1918 Palestine in behalf of Jews who claimed United States protection, differs little from American activity elsewhere, but there is no doubt that the peculiar status of the Holy Land gave American efforts there a special prominence.

Mandated Palestine, in which, according to the Balfour Declaration, a Jewish National Home was to be established, early gained the sympathy and support of the American people and Government. This sentiment was expressed by leading American statesmen on many occasions. On October 14, 1938, for example, Secretary of State Cordell Hull issued s statement saying: "The American government and people have watched with the keenest sympathy the development in Palestine of a National Home, a project in which American intellect and capital have played a leading role."

Aside from the sentimental and humanitarian interest in Palestine, the Anglo-American Convention of 1924 which provided (article 7) that any modification of the mandate which would affect the interest of American citizens must first receive the assent of the United States, furnished a legal basis for American intercession when, in May 1939, the British Government issued a White Paper limiting Jewish immigration and land purchase. It was argued that the new policy discriminated against American Jews on the sole ground that they were Jews and that it had been issued without the previous assent of the United States.

The White Paper of 1939 intensified American interest in the Palestine question and resulted in numerous discussions in Congress and in many pronouncements and statements by high government officials.

Because of the absence of published official documents regarding it, there is no description in the body of this book of the Mortara affair which, in 1858, aroused world-wide discussion and protest. The case grew out of the abduction by Papal guards of Edgar Mortara, the six-year old son of Jewish parents, residing in the city of Bologna, at that time within the Papal States over which the Vatican ruled. The explanation given by the papal authorities was that, four years earlier, the child had been secretly baptized at the request of a Catholic maid-servant of the Mortaras.

In the United States, Jewish community leaders approached both Secretary of State Lewis Cass and President James Buchanan, with the request that the administration intercede with the Vatican on behalf of the parents of the abducted child. In the course of the interview with these community leaders, President Buchanan declined to take any action on the ground that "it is the settled policy of the United States to abstain from all interference .... as they expect other nations to abstain from all interference in the internal affairs of our country."[8]

In a statement on refugees issued by the late President Roosevelt, on March 24, 1944, the opening paragraph reads as follows:

"The United Nations are fighting to make a world in which tyranny and aggression cannot exist — a world based upon freedom, equality and justice; a world in which all persons, regardless of race, color or creed, may live in peace, honor and dignity."

Decent people everywhere hope that this ideal will be given effective realization by those who are called upon to decide the shape of things to come.

[8] See article "Mortara Case" in the *Jewish Encyclopedia*. For correspondence relating to this case and an account of the interview with the President and the Secretary of State, see *Occident*, Vol. XVI, 1858, pages 536–542, and *The Jewish Messenger*, Vol. IV, 1858, pages 138–140, 154, and Vol. V, page 68.

PART ONE

THE NEAR EAST AND MOROCCO

I. TURKEY

Most of the diplomatic correspondence between the United States and pre-War Turkey regarding the Jews who lived there was concerned with Jews who settled in Palestine, and will therefore be treated in a separate chapter.

The correspondence with Turkey is notable for the fact that, barring occasional scattered references to Jews in connection with affairs in the Barbary States, the first representation made by the United States to any foreign government in which Jews were concerned was to the Ottoman Government in connection with the so-called Damascus Affair.

In 1840, the charge of ritual murder was brought against the Jews of Damascus at the instance of the French Consul of that city. He utilized the accusation tor political purposes and was actively supported by the Franciscan order. Many Jews were imprisoned and tortured, and of these a number died.

In Europe, it was Sir Moses Montefiore of England, and Adolphe Crémieux of France, who aroused public opinion about the infamous historic lie. In the United States, Secretary of State John Forsyth, by direction of President Van Buren, addressed a dispatch on this subject to John Gliddon, American Consul at Alexandria, Egypt, urging him to use his good offices to the end that justice and humanity be extended to the Jews of Damascus. It is to be noted that this dispatch was sent before the Department of State had received any communication about this case from the leaders of any Jewish community in the United States. This dispatch, the first of its kind from the United States, is here given in full:[1]

---

[1] "Persecution of the Jews in 1840," by Jacob Ezekiel, in *Publications of the American Jewish Historical Society*, No. 8, 1900, page 143.

[*Mr. Forsyth to Mr. Gliddon*]

Washington, August 14, 1840

John Gliddon, Esq.,
   United States Consul at Alexandria, Egypt.

SIR:— In common with all civilized nations, the people of the
United States have learned with horror, the atrocious crimes imputed to the Jews of Damascus, and the cruelties of which they
have been the victims. The President fully participates in the
public feeling, and he cannot refrain from expressing equal surprise and pain, that in this advanced age, such unnatural practices
should be ascribed to any portion of the religious world, and such
barbarous measures be resorted to, in order to compel the confession of imputed guilt; the offenses with which these unfortunate
people are charged, resemble too much those which, in less enlightened times, were made the pretexts of fanatical persecution or
mercenary extortion, to permit a doubt that they are equally
unfounded.

The President has witnessed, with the most lively satisfaction,
the effort of several of the Christian Governments of Europe, to
suppress or mitigate these horrors, and he has learned with no
common gratification, their partial success. He is moreover
anxious that the active sympathy and generous interposition of
the Government of the United States should not be withheld from
so benevolent an object, and he has accordingly directed me to
instruct you to employ, should the occasion arise, all those good
offices and efforts which are compatible with discretion and your
official character, to the end that justice and humanity may be
extended to these persecuted people, whose cry of distress has
reached our shores. I am, sir,

Your obedient servant,
JOHN FORSYTH

Meetings of protest against the barbarous treatment of
innocent Jews in Damascus and the isle of Rhodes, where
a similar accusation had been raised against local Jews, were
held in a number of communities in the United States, and
petitions were sent to President Van Buren praying that he
instruct the appropriate representatives of the United States
to co-operate with those of other powers in behalf of the
persecuted Jews of Damascus and elsewhere.

From the letter of acknowledgment which Secretary Forsyth sent to a resolution adopted at a meeting in New York City, we learn that the Department of State was first informed of the "heart-rending scenes which took place at Damascus" by a dispatch from the American consul at that city. It was this dispatch which caused the foregoing letter to be written to John Gliddon. Also, at about the same time, the American Chargé d'Affaires at Constantinople was instructed "to interpose his good offices in behalf of the oppressed and persecuted race of Jews in the Ottoman Dominions, among whose kindred are found some of the most worthy and patriotic of our citizens."

A brief series of dispatches which passed between Mr. David Porter, United States Minister at Constantinople, and the State Department followed. Mr. Porter adopted the attitude of the Department, somewhat against his will, and was instrumental in having the Sultan issue a *firman* to the judges of Constantinople ordering them to free all Jews accused of ritual murder, as these accusations were false, pure calumnies and absurd slanders.

The American Minister sent a copy of the *firman* to Washington, expressing his hope that, in the future, it would not be necessary for him to take any steps when the interests of the United States are not immediately affected. Yet, he adds: "But I shall always be alert in everything when my interference will prevent humanity from being outraged. I shall be governed by the benevolent and philanthropic views of the President, as communicated in your instructions."

Nothing further occurred in connection with Turkey until 1867, when under date of April 19, Myer S. Isaacs, on behalf of the Executive Committee of the Board of Delegates of American Israelites, called the attention of Secretary Seward to the fact that in the recently organized government of Serbia severe laws and a painfully proscriptive administration of them had rendered the condition of the Jewish population deplorable in the extreme. The Department was petitioned to forward instructions to the Minister of the

United States at Constantinople to the end that he might investigate the subject and, if the occasion were deemed fitting, make suitable representations to the Serbian Government. The Department forwarded the letter of Mr. Isaacs to Mr. Edward Joy Morris, the Minister at Constantinople, instructing him to cause inquiries to be made at the earliest opportunity and report to the Department. His report, dated Constantinople, May 31, 1867, is a most unsympathetic document. Based on the explanation of the political agent of Serbia at Constantinople, it declares that the Jewish population is but 1300, and charges them with usury, non-assimilation, and lack of patriotism.

The question of the Jews of Serbia arose again in 1879 in connection with the recognition by the United States of the now independent state of Serbia. The Union of American Hebrew Congregations had interceded with the State Department in Washington in behalf of the Jews of Rumania and Serbia, asking that religious and civil equality be guaranteed to them in the new constitutions of these "two countries."

Mr. John A. Kasson, United States Minister at Vienna, sent to Washington the following dispatch:[2]

[*Mr. Kasson to Mr. Evarts*]

Legation of the United States
Vienna, March 31, 1879

SIR:

..... The Jewish question in Servia presents no longer a reason for delay in the full diplomatic recognition of her independence. Prior to the annexation of territory, secured to her by the congress of Berlin, the number of Jews in Servia was about 1,200. The annexations brought in about 800 more. The former Jewish population (1,200) was chiefly composed of the descendants of an old colony of Spanish Jews, who still preserve the Spanish language among themselves. They have long enjoyed full political rights; but their right of residence has always been confined to four towns along the Danube; and they were not allowed to hold real estate. The new Jewish population (say 800), coming with the annexed Turkish territory, were, on the contrary, free from this restriction.

[2] Papers Relating to the Foreign Relations of the United States (hereinafter referred to as Foreign Relations), 1879, page 60.

It was easy, therefore, for the Servians to determine that their old population of this race must not have less right than the aliens just brought into their jurisdiction. Pursuant to the provisions of their constitution, an amendment of that instrument requires the sanction of two ordinary *skuptschinas*, and final adoption by the *grand skuptschina*, specially assembled therefor. The first two sanctions have already been given, and for the third the *grand skuptschina* will be summoned probably in the early summer. This body is four times as numerous as the ordinary legislative body; and there is said to be in Servia no building large enough to serve them as a hall for meeting. So the government, must, at least accommodate them in the open air with a favorable season. No doubt at all is entertained of their ratification of the act abolishing the discriminations against the Jews.

* * * * *

JOHN A. KASSON

In the treaty of recognition negotiated by Mr. Kasson, with Serbia, the United States secured for Americans of all faiths protection of person and property equally with that given to natives, full rights of trade and full liberty for the exercise of the rights of religious faith and public worship.

The case of Rabbi Hyman L. Sneersohn is mentioned in the correspondence of 1877. The facts in his case were as follows: Rabbi Sneersohn, a citizen of the United States, while on a visit in Tiberias, Palestine, in November, 1874, was attacked by lawless persons, robbed of a considerable sum of money and shamefully maltreated. The rabbi first applied to the British consul at Beirut for intervention because his attackers claimed to be under British protection. The British consul, however, did not deem it his duty to interfere.

The rabbi then brought his case before the American consul in the same city who went in person to Tiberias to plead for the rabbi. Though the consul succeeded in bringing the culprit to court, it was not for long, for the marauder was soon rescued from the hands of the Turkish authorities and finally fled from the country.

Rabbi Sneersohn made many attempts to recover damages. He even went to Constantinople where he enlisted the help of Mr. Horace Maynard, the United States Minister to

Turkey. But even the latter proved to be of no assistance. Reporting on this case to Washington, Mr. Maynard said:[3] "... the rabbi, wearied and impoverished by the delay, seems to have abandoned all hope of redress, and to have gone, I believe, to France; possibly he returned to America. Nothing further has been done in his case; indeed, in his absence, nothing could be done."

Though the intervention of American officials was not fruitful in this particular case, it cannot be said to be a typical one. American consuls in Turkey were eager to come to the aid of the "scattered remnant of God's ancient people," as our consul put it, even when the Jews were not citizens of the United States. Minister Maynard found it necessary to warn all consuls not to extend American protection to non-citizen Jews; but at the same time he ordered them "to observe carefully the condition of the Hebrews within their consular districts, and any instance of persecution or other maltreatment to report without delay to the legation, calling attention to them unofficially of the governors or other Ottoman authorities."

Another reference to Turkey occurs in a dispatch of June 27, 1877, which Mr. Maynard sent to Secretary Evarts. This dispatch dealt mainly with Rumania which at that time was still under the sovereignty of the Sublime Porte. In the quotation given below the American minister compares the treatment of the Jews in Rumania with that of their coreligionists in Turkey. His statement is an accurate description of the situation of the Jews in Turkey, before the World War.[4]

Justice to the Turks requires me to say they have treated the Jews much better than have some of the western powers of Europe. When banished from Spain, for instance, they found an asylum in Turkey, where their descendants remain to this day, distinguished from the others of the same faith by the use of the Spanish tongue. An impression prevails that under Turkish rule the treatment of the Jews is better than that of the Christians. They are recognized

[3] Foreign Relations, 1877, page 593.
[4] *Ibid.*, page 594.

as an independent religious community, with the privilege of
possessing their own ecclesiastical rule, and their chief rabbi
(*chacham-bashi*) possesses, in consequence of his functions, great
influence.

Yesterday, during my weekly call upon the Minister of Foreign
Affairs, I introduced the subject. His excellency protested that
where the Turkish rule obtained the Israelites had always enjoyed
every privilege and immunity accorded by the laws to Ottoman
subjects. His language in this sense was very emphatic. For their
treatment in the provinces the Sublime Porte could not justly be
held responsible. Yet, even then, in the late treaty with Servia,
they had exacted from her a promise of justice to these much-
injured people.

The Peace Treaty negotiated between Turkey and the
Allies, signed at Lausanne on July 24, 1923, which reduced
Turkish territory to a mere fraction of the former Turkish
Empire, contained articles for the protection of minorities
similar to those included in the treaties between the Allied
and Associated Powers and other countries. Turkey agreed
that these articles constituted "obligations of international
concern and shall be placed under the guarantee of the
League of Nations."

In August of 1926, however, the Jewish National Assembly
of the republic of Turkey, claiming to speak for the Jewish
community in Turkey, voluntarily surrendered all rights and
privileges accorded to them under the minority provisions
of the Treaty of Lausanne. The decision to renounce all
minority rights was passed unanimously by the Assembly
which was composed of seventy Jewish "notables," headed
by Jacques Bey Nahmias. The Assembly also resolved to
submit the regulation of Jewish communal institutions to
the ordinances of the Turkish Government, thus sacrificing
the cultural autonomy guaranteed to the Jews under the
minority provisions.[5]

It should be noted that from a legal point of view this
renunciation of minority rights by the alleged leaders of the
Jewish community in Turkey is of no legal validity. The
Jews of Turkey were not a party to the treaty and had

[5] *American Jewish Year Book*, 1927–28, page 429.

therefore not the legal power to cancel any of its provisions.

There is no doubt, however, that this act of voluntary renunciation was a mortal blow to the principle of minority rights. The danger was thus created that this act might become a precedent soon to be followed by similar acts in other countries whose governments could then point out that the minority provisions were an anachronism and should therefore be repealed.

Mr. Louis Marshall, then president of the American Jewish Committee, protested vigorously against this act. Mr. Marshall, who took an active part in the framing of the minority treaties during the Peace Conference in 1919, described in a press statement of August 10, 1926, the renunciation as "utterly futile and at the same time unspeakably cowardly and disgraceful." The minority treaties, said Mr. Marshall, were "the outcome of the most careful thought and study of conditions which have brought misfortune to millions of human beings for centuries past, and especially to the Jews," and should they be eliminated, the minorities would then be exposed to very positive and dangerous discriminations.

II. PERSIA

The Persian correspondence is very meager owing to the fact that no rights of American Jews were involved, and that, for centuries, the Persian Jews had been kept at such a low condition as to have become inarticulate. They did not dare complain against the ruling authorities for fear of aggravating a condition already bad enough.

As late as 1894 the Jews of Persia had to wear a patch on their clothes to signify their origin. Jews who, as a result of continuous persecution, changed their religion and were converted either to Mohammedanism or Christianity, soon discovered that their situation did not improve because of their conversion. And it is because of the continued discrimination against Jewish converts that the Jewish question in Persia first appeared in the United States diplomatic correspondence.

In July, 1894, Mr. John Tyler, vice consul general of the United States at Teheran, capital of Persia, wrote a note to Mr. W. Q. Gresham, Secretary of State, about the renewal of persecutions against the Jews of Hamadan. There, under the leadership of Akhund Mullah Abdullah, a fanatical ecclesiastic dignitary, the home of Mr. Hawkes, an American missionary, had been invaded and a man who sought refuge there had been forcibly removed.

At that time it seems a number of Jews were converted to Christianity and Akhund Mullah Abdullah considered it a reflection on himself, as well as the Moslem religion, that Jews turned to Christianity, and not to his faith.

The above matter formed the subject of a number of letters exchanged between Mr. Tyler, Mr. Hawkes, and Dr. Holmes, the American medical missionary at that station. It was Mr. Hawkes especially who was anxious to protect the life and property of Jews. Though, as a missionary, his main interest lay in protecting the rights of converts, nevertheless it must be said that he was equally insistent when unusual acts of oppression were perpetrated against Jews.

In an interview with the civil and religious heads of Hamadan, Mr. Hawkes and Dr. Holmes insisted that, while they had nothing to say about the relation of the ruling authorities with the Jews of this city, they reserved the right to report to the American and other governments any violence or indignities which might be imposed upon them.

As we see in this letter to Dr. Holmes, Mr. Tyler took a very serious attitude concerning the situation when informed of the invasion of the home of Mr. Hawkes by Mohammedan fanatics:[1]

[*Mr. Tyler to Dr. Holmes*]

Legation of the United States
Teheran, July 10, 1894

Dear Sir:

I wrote a few lines on the 3d instant to inform you that Mr. Hawkes's letter of the 28th and yours of the 29th ultimo had just arrived; and I have now to acknowledge receipt of yours of the 6th instant.

It appears from what you report concerning the persecution of the Jews of Hamadan, and the forcible removal from Mr. Hawkes's premises of a former pupil and teacher of your school, that these are matters requiring serious consideration. They may not be of a very grave import in themselves, but it is possible that if they are allowed to go on unchecked and unredressed, time after time, they may eventually assume alarming proportions.

．．．．．

I have already communicated Mr. Hawkes's report to the English legation, where, I have no doubt, it will receive due attention.

I remain, etc.,

John Tyler

[1] Foreign Relations, 1894, page 496.

The American Secretary of State, however, in a letter of acknowledgment to Mr. Tyler took a diametrically opposite point of view.[2]

[*Mr. Gresham to Mr. Tyler*]

Department of State
Washington, August 18, 1894

Sir:

I am in receipt of your No. 113 of the 12th ultimo, inclosing correspondence relating to renewed persecution of Jews at Hamadan and the forcible removal of a man who had taken refuge in the house of the Rev. James Hawkes, an American missionary at that place.

With regard to the invasion of Mr. Hawkes's premises by the Persian authorities and the forcible arrest of a fugitive therein, it is regretted that this act should have been brought about by an untenable assertion of asylum for a Persian subject. This Government does not claim that its official agents have the right to afford asylum.

By the seventh article of the treaty of 1856 between the United States and Persia, it is stipulated that —

> The diplomatic agent or consuls of the United States shall not protect, secretly or publicly, the subjects of the Persian Government, and they shall never suffer a departure from the principles here laid down and agreed to by mutual consent.

The domiciliary rights of citizens of the United States in Persia may not be expanded to embrace the protection by them of Persian subjects, when such protection is explicitly disclaimed by the Government of the United States, and when its assertion by their diplomatic and consular representatives is positively inhibited.

I am, etc.,

W. Q. GRESHAM

The crime with which this "fugitive" (a Jew who had been converted to Christianity) was charged, was failure to wear a patch on his dress.

The efforts of the American missionaries and Mr. Tyler bore fruit, and, on August 29 of the same year, Mr. Tyler was able to report to Mr. Gresham that information had

[2] Foreign Relations, 1894, page 497.

been received from Rev. Hawkes that the Shah had ordered his governor at Hamadan to preserve order and to prevent further molestation of Jews and Christians, and that "no occasion be given to the U. S. legation to make representations of this character."

Acknowledging this note, Mr. Gresham commended Mr. Tyler's action in the matter of the religious persecution in Hamadan.

However, the occasional interventions of the American missionaries and the promises they extracted from the Persian officials could not change a condition inherently unfavorable to Jews. The lawless spirit of the people, the failure of the ruling authorities to control the situation, and the cupidity of the populace, all combined to make the Jews the most available outlet for the lowest passions of men.

Again it must be pointed out that those Jews who had forsaken the religion of their fathers with the hope of securing safety for themselves and their property failed utterly to achieve their aims. In a letter to Mr. Tyler, dated September 25, 1896, Dr. Holmes refers to the condition of the Moslem converts as follows:[3]

The fact that the man charged with the crime was a Moslem and had forsaken the religion of his fathers makes no difference at all in the eyes of the people who are after loot and not justice. There has been much pressure brought upon the Jews in the past to make Moslems of them; but it seems they have to bear the curse of their nationality and responsibility even for those who have turned away from their faith.

Dr. Holmes refers here specifically to a case that happened at Hamadan when personal enemies trumped up charges against a Jew who, after the disturbances of 1892, had entered the Moslem faith. At the trial, a large crowd of Moslems appeared and threatened the Ameer that unless the accused was put to death instantly, the whole Jewish community would be massacred. The innocent Moslem Jew was executed, and his home and those of his neighbors were broken into, pillaged and burnt. Only the efforts of Mr. Hawkes and

[3] Foreign Relations, 1896, page 484.

his Moslem servants saved the homes of the other Jews from the same fate.

When informed by Dr. Holmes of these events, Mr. Tyler wrote to the Sadr Azem. From Mr. Tyler's reply to Dr. Holmes, we learn the interesting fact that in Persia, as was not the case in other countries, the central government in Teheran welcomed intercession by a foreign government in behalf of a persecuted minority. The agents of the central government had let their power slip from their hands, and irresponsible ecclesiastics were not slow to take advantage of this fact to advance their own interests. As a result the Teheran government, afraid to act with open authority and determination, was glad to have its hands strengthened by the influence of a foreign power.

The following letter to Dr. Holmes which Mr. Tyler, the American consul, enclosed in his dispatch to Mr. Gresham on October 7, 1896, brings out this point:[4]

[*Mr. Tyler to Dr. Holmes*]

Legation of the United States
Teheran, October 6, 1896

DEAR SIR:

I have to acknowledge the receipt of your letter of the 27th ultimo, reporting the execution of a Jew in and the disturbed state of the city of Hamadan.

The story you have to tell is a sad one, and reflects great discredit and incapacity on the part of the authorities. They have allowed their power to slip out of their hands, and the irresponsible ecclesiastics have not been slow to take it up and to use it with advantage to further their own interests. This is a position it will be difficult to upset or even to neutralize. It appears that the Central Government is afraid to act with open authority and determination. In such case it is a question of considerable difficulty as to how far and in what sense the legation can interfere without aggravating the circumstances. When a request is addressed to the Government by the official representative of the United States, whatever it may be, they can not ignore it without assuming a very grave

---

[4] Foreign Relations, 1896, page 485.

responsibility. And I think I can, so far as my experience goes, say that attention has been given to my representations. The Government would, I feel sure, welcome the pretext of a complaint from a foreign legation to make their power felt, if they were confident of their ability to do so. But as this is more than doubtful, I feel it necessary to act with care and prudence, lest in invoking their interference on behalf of their own subjects I make matters more complicated and threatening. I can always demand the intervention of the Government when your lives, work and property are in danger, and can also make this an occasion for reporting the condition and invoking the protection of the authorities for the persecuted and oppressed of other creeds and nationalities.

On receipt of your letter I addressed a communication to the Sadr Azem, of which the inclosed is a copy, and I hope it will have the effect intended. I have not hesitated to use your name, for I know that the Shah has great respect for your judgment, prudence, and transparency of character.

I remain, etc.,

JOHN TYLER
Vice-Consul-General in Charge

On May 17, 1897, Mr. Alexander McDonald, United States Minister to Persia, wrote to Secretary Sherman that he had interposed unofficially in behalf of the Jews of the city of Teheran, who were being subjected to mob outrages by the Mohammedans. He reported that he had told the chief of the Shah's ministers that, without any authority in the matter, he had come to him in the interest of humanity to ask that immediate steps be taken for the protection of the assaulted people; they were a race without a country or government of their own to defend them, and, as a whole, were harmless and inoffensive, and in the emergency he felt like speaking strongly for them in behalf of his government and his country, where so many were domiciled. This personal interview does not seem to have resulted satisfactorily, for on the same day Mr. McDonald sent a letter to the Shah's chief minister, the Amin-ed-Dowlah, in which he again recited the facts.[5]

[5] Foreign Relations, 1897, page 430.

[*Mr. McDonald to the Amin-ed-Dowlah*]

Legation of the United States
May 17, 1897

YOUR EXCELLENCY:

In the conversation which I had with you yesterday morning, I was given to understand that the persecution and ill treatment which was being inflicted upon the Jews had ceased. I regret to state to you, however, that I have just been informed that there has been a renewal of the maltreatment, and that many have been subjected to ill usage and indignities, while the government *ferashes* (police) sent, I presume, to restore order, have forcibly taken money, and left without effecting anything for the preservation of the peace of the district. I have not the remotest desire to interfere or to make any suggestions as to the administration of the affairs of this city, but from motives of humanity and of sympathy with those who are called upon to suffer, I appeal to you to put an end to this molestation and interference with the liberties of this loyal, intelligent, and industrious section of His Majesty's subjects.

I have, etc.,

ALEX McDONALD

It must be added that, in addition to the above-stated motives, Mr. McDonald was interested in the Jews of Teheran, because, as he wrote in a note of May 20, 1897, to Secretary of State John Sherman, the American missionaries maintained schools in the Jewish quarter, and disturbances there were therefore doubly unwelcome.

Mr. Sherman acknowledged the various messages from the American consul at Teheran, and complimented him for his good offices in the interest of common humanity and civilization, in the note which follows:[6]

[*Mr. Sherman to Mr. McDonald*]

Department of State
Washington, July 8, 1897

SIR:

Your dispatches Nos. 294 and 296, dated, respectively, May 17 and 20 last, in which you report that you have tendered your good offices in behalf of the Jews of Teheran who were being subjected

[6] Foreign Relations, 1897, page 431.

to mob violence at the hands of the Mohammedans of that place, have been received.

In reply I have to say that your good offices in this somewhat delicate question seem to have been discreetly used in the interest of common humanity and in accordance with the precepts of civilization.

Respectfully yours,
JOHN SHERMAN

The next time that references to Persian Jews appear in American diplomatic correspondence is in 1918, in connection with the relief activities of the American Jewish Joint Distribution Committee. The State Department as well as the American diplomatic representatives abroad were very helpful to the Committee in distributing funds, food and other necessities to the starving Jews everywhere.

On May 10, 1918, Secretary of State Lansing sent a telegram to John L. Caldwell, American Minister at Teheran, asking him to report on the situation of Jews throughout all Persia. On May 13, Mr. Caldwell wired the Secretary that needy Jews in Persia were estimated to number between thirty and forty thousand, twenty-five per cent of them being in a starving condition and in dire need.

Mr. Caldwell was then empowered by Secretary Lansing, in a telegram of May 29, 1918, to draw on the Secretary of State up to $15,000.00, which had been deposited with the State Department by the Joint Distribution Committee; the funds were to be used to relieve Jews in distress. Mr. Caldwell was asked to seek the advice of the Comité de Bienfaisance Israélite, Teheran, the Alliance Israélite, Hamadan, the British consul at Ispahan, and especially the leaders of the Jewish community, regarding the distribution of the relief funds, and to send at the earliest opportunity a detailed report from local Jewish committees for the Joint Distribution Committee.[7]

It is relevant here to note that Rabbi Joseph Saul Kornfeld of Toledo, Ohio, served as United States Minister to Persia during the years 1921–25.

[7] Foreign Relations, 1918, Suppl. 2, page 567.

III. MOROCCO

The intercession of the government of the United States in behalf of maltreated Jews of Morocco was based mainly on humanitarian motives. Here there was not a question of violation of treaty agreements or discrimination against American citizens of the Jewish faith. The consuls of the American Government in Morocco often came to the aid of the Jews of that country because, as representatives of a civilized nation, they felt it their duty to protect a minority specially subject to outrages at the hands of barbarous tribes, ruled by a weak and conscienceless government.

It should be noted that, because in Morocco as in other countries in the Near and Far East, European and American consular agents possessed exterritorial rights, they were often instrumental in mitigating the barbarities of the ruling administration against foreigners as well as against members of minority groups in Morocco.

The Jews quite frequently had occasion to ask protection, for, in accordance with the customs of the land, a Jew who in self-protection raised his hand against a Moor had his hand cut off, and a Moor could not be put to death for having killed a Jew.

In the midst of the Civil War in the United States, the Department of State turned its attention to the wretched condition of the Jews in Tangier. Innocent Jews, falsely accused of the most fearful crimes, had been barbarously tortured and many executed, in response to the cruel mandate of the Sultan of Morocco. When the news of these outrages reached Great Britain, the Jewish Board of Deputies of that country commissioned Sir Moses Montefiore, the famous philanthropist, personally to visit Morocco and, with the co-operation and sympathy of the British representatives there, of which he had been assured, seek to secure justice for the unoffending Jews.

19

In a memorial, dated November 25, 1863, the Board of Delegates of American Israelites called the attention of Mr. William H. Seward, Secretary of State, to the renewal of atrocities and barbarities against the Jewish population of Tangier.[1]

The American Board asked the Department of State to convey instructions to the United States consul in Tangier "that he cooperate with the British authorities in measures which may be taken to further the mission of Sir Moses Montefiore, authorizing him (the consul) to proceed to as great an extent as may be consistent with the relations of this government and the Barbary States, in securing justice to the unfortunate people and preventing the general persecution apprehended." The case of 1840, when the United States intervened on behalf of the Jews in Turkey, was cited as a precedent.

Two weeks later, December 9, 1863, Mr. Seward, who in a letter to the Board of Delegates had expressed surprise and regret that "in this comparatively enlightened age, any class of people in any country should be persecuted on account of their religious tenets," dispatched a note to Mr. Jesse H. McMath, the American consul in Tangier, authorizing him "to exert all proper influence to prevent a repetition of the barbarous cruelties to which Israelites in the Moorish Empire have on account of their religion been subjected," adding that such a course was dictated by common humanity.

Mr. McMath was also approached directly by the president of the Hebrew Congregation of Tangier, but he observed the rule of non-interference not because of indifference, but because he was of the opinion that intervention would make a bad condition worse. In a letter to Mr. Seward, dated

---

[1] Tangier at that time was part of the larger Moroccan Empire, nominally an independent state under the rule of the Sultan of Morocco. Actually the penetration of European countries, especially France and Spain, in Morocco had already begun and was soon to culminate in reducing "independent" Morocco to a protectorate, or rather to two protectorates under French and under Spanish influence. At present Tangier enjoys a peculiar international status, that of an "international zone."

November 5, 1863,[2] Mr. McMath asserted that representations made by Jewish representative bodies of Great Britain and France had aggravated rather than alleviated the condition of the Jews in Morocco. Mr. McMath enclosed a number of extracts from London newspapers in which it was stated that a great share of the blame for the sudden revival of anti-Jewish feelings and its evil concomitants lay at the door of the Spanish consul in Morocco, who, it was alleged, acted in a manner remindful of the Inquisition of an earlier century, the infliction of the bastinado being one of the less cruel means of physical torture which he had employed.

To the complaint of the English, French and Italian representatives in Morocco against this barbarous action, Señor Merry, the Spanish consul, replied that he had acted under orders from his superiors. The intercession of Baron James de Rothschild, the elder brother of the famous Baron Edmond de Rothschild, with the Spanish Government saved the remaining Jews, still in the hands of Señor Merry, from sharing the fate of their brethren. The Spanish Government failed, however, to prosecute its guilty official, and must therefore share in the blame for and the shame of his acts.

In a communication from Tangier, dated January 12, 1864, Mr. McMath reported to Secretary Seward of another intervention with the government of Spain.[3] With the sanction of Earl Russell, British Prime Minister, Sir Moses Montefiore had visited Madrid and had been instrumental in the liberation of two Jews, held in prison for a crime they had not committed. The British consul in Morocco had accompanied Sir Moses as interpreter.

In the meantime, later cruel occurrences in Morocco had moved some of the European nations to send their representatives instructions on how to act in the event of future maltreatment of Jews. These atrocities had also led Mr. McMath to change his opinion about outside intervention, for in the same letter he tells Mr. Seward that, "after the terrible occurrences which took place at Saffi, resulting in the

[2] Foreign Relations, 1864, Part IV, page 414.
[3] *Ibid.*, page 425.

execution of two of their race, without the least shadow of proof of guilt or that a crime had been committed, they [the Jews] were clearly justified, in my opinion, in appealing to the liberal nations of Europe, and to our own, for an amelioration of their unfortunate condition in this country."

Mr. McMath closes his dispatch by saying: "In view of all the circumstances and upon the authority of your late instructions, at the same time exercising the greatest care for the just rights of all concerned, I believe it to be my duty, in the name of humanity, to exert my influence with His Majesty's government to prevent any injustice to this race."

Very soon, too, Mr. McMath had opportunity to become active "in the name of justice and humanity." In a dispatch dated May 15, 1865, he reports how, in conjunction with the British and other European ministers, he had been able to save four Jews from the arbitrary punishment of a local Basha. From the same note we also learn that the Sultan of Morocco was constantly being misled about the Jews and their actions by his advisors and ministers. According to Mr. McMath, "the Sultan is well disposed toward this part of his subjects [the Jews], but his officers, wishing to show their authority, frequently manufacture the most unfounded accusations against them, and impose upon the Sultan by representations that have no foundation of fact."

But the Jews of Morocco suffered not only at the hands of officials. In August, 1878, bands of thieves and murderers infested the town of Arzila and made the Jews their special victims. Fear of robbery and assassination by these bandits prevented the Jews of Arzila from earning their daily bread at the various markets; many of them had been plundered and one Jew had been killed by the marauders. The story of these outrages is given in the following letter written by Mr. W. L. Benshiton, on behalf of the Jewish community of Arzila, to Mr. Felix A. Mathews, American consul at Tangier.[4]

---

[4] Foreign Relations, 1878, page 691.

[*Mr. Benshiton to Mr. Mathews*]

Arzila, August 11, 1878

Sir: I have the honor to inform you, with much regret, that yesterday the Moors killed a Hebrew, by the name of David or Jacob Ederhy, quite close to this town, and that all the environs and gardens of this town are infested with thieves and assassins getting ready to enter and plunder the Israelites, who already do not risk to go out of town for fear of being assassinated and robbed. Thus they are prevented from earning their daily bread at the various markets, and consequently their sufferings on these days of famine, sickness, and misery are great.

For several days past these highwaymen and evil-doers have attempted to scale the town walls; also they tried to break its gates; and all this is taking place for the want of government and police.

In vain we have appealed to the governor of Laraiche for help; and now all the Hebrews of Arzila have come to me to appeal to you in the name of humanity, that, with your influence and good-will you may speak on our behalf with the Moorish Government, and obtain for us some troops that may drive the malefactors away from this neighborhood and protect our lives and properties, now in the most imminent danger; and this act of yours will be a favor which God Almighty will reward you with his blessing and much happiness.

I remain, etc.,

W. L. Benshiton

From a second letter to Mr. Mathews from the same source, we learn that the American consul had made effective representations to the Moroccan Minister of Foreign Affairs:

[*Mr. Benshiton to Mr. Mathews*]

Arzila, August 22, 1878

Sir: I have the honor and great satisfaction to inform you that at nine o'clock this morning 50 soldiers, with their chief, entered the town from Laraiche, sent by the governor of that city for the purpose of defending the lives and property of the Jewish inhabitants of this town, according to your request to the minister of foreign affairs of Morocco.

The inhabitants of Arzila, in the name of whom I have the honor to address you, are full of gratitude toward you for the amiability and prompt attention you have shown in their hour of peril, and implore of the Almighty God that he may reward you with much happiness and prosperity in union of your children, whom may God preserve for infinite years.

I remain, etc.,

W. L. BENSHITON

Mr. Mathews had acted before receipt of a note from Mr. Evarts, Secretary of State, dated July 2, 1878, requesting him to intervene and "to take such steps toward accomplishment of the end desired as may be consistent with your international obligations, and the efficiency of your diplomatic relations with the Government of Morocco." From Mr. Mathews' reply to Mr. Evarts,[5] we learn further details of the outrages which his prompt action had succeeded in bringing to an end.

[*Mr. Mathews to Mr. Evarts*]

Consulate of the United States
Tangier, September 20, 1878

SIR: I have the honor to acknowledge the receipt of your dispatch No. 132, dated July 2, 1878, together with its accompaniments, relative to the request of the president and vice-president of the board of delegates of American Israelites, New York, requesting that I should be instructed to inquire into the condition of the Jews in this empire, and to consult for the amelioration of their status, and to take such steps toward the accomplishment of the end desired, consistent with my international obligations with this government.

I am happy to state that my relations with this Government of Morocco are such that I can exercise my unofficial friendly offices on behalf of the Israelites in this country with good result when required, as it has been the case lately, when a Jewish family was murdered near Laraiche, and another Israelite near Arzila, and the town itself menaced by the Kabyles, who were preparing to murder and plunder all the Israelites in the place. Having received a letter to this effect from the elders of the Hebrew community of Arzila, I lost no time in communicating the same personally to the Moorish minister of foreign affairs, who at once dispatched a messenger to the governor of Laraiche, who, on receipt of our letters, immediately ordered a Kaid and fifty soldiers to Arzila, there to protect the Jewish population, who were in great consternation.

[5] Foreign Relations, 1878, page 691.

The murderers of the Jewish family are now in prison, and the minister for foreign affairs has assured me that their punishment will be such as to deter others from committing similar acts of violence in the future.

I beg to inclose herewith copies of the two letters addressed to me by Mr. M. L. Benshiton, chief of the Israelites of Arzila, requesting my intercession on their behalf, and acknowledging the result of the same.

I shall avail myself of all proper opportunities to accomplish in the manner you have been pleased to indicate, the ends desired by the board of delegates of American Israelites.

I have, etc.,

FELIX A. MATHEWS

Mr. Mathews was again useful to the Moroccan Jews in 1880, when, as a result of the withdrawal of foreign protection from some Jews, atrocities were committed against them by the natives who saw in the withdrawal an invitation to attack the unprotected Jews. Mr. Mathews informed Mr. Evarts of the developments in the following dispatch:[6]

[*Mr. Mathews to Mr. Evarts*]

Consulate of the United States of America
Tangier, March 8, 1880

SIR: I have the honor to inclose herewith a translation of an unofficial letter addressed to me by the Sultan, through his prime minister, on the subject of the recent atrocities committed on the Jews of Morocco, with the object of ameliorating their present condition.

The withdrawal of foreign protection from several Israelites, natives of Morocco, who had enjoyed the same, unfortunately was understood by various Moorish officials in the interior and by the populace as a sign for them to commit their excesses and ill-treatment upon the Jews.

I beg to cite an instance of the unwise predisposition of the Moorish authorities on the occasion of the Spanish minister withdrawing his protection from an elderly Jewish merchant called Isaac Amar. The latter was at once seized by the Moorish authorities, who, in their eagerness to pounce upon their prey, quickly devised an accusation of murder against the man, who was im-

[6] Foreign Relations, 1880, page 794.

prisoned, loaded with irons, and would have been summarily executed, and his property confiscated, but for the timely interference of a member of the Anglo-Jewish Association, who happened to be at Tangier, and who at once proceeded to Casablanca, where the prisoner was confined, with the object of being present should a trial have taken place. At the request of several Jewish delegations, some of the foreign vice-consuls at Casablanca were instructed by their ministers at Tangier to be present at the trial. I also instructed our consular agent, Captain Cobb, to be present and watch the proceedings. The Moorish authorities, receiving intelligence that their proceeding was going to be witnessed by foreign officials, and having no evidence whatsoever that could be brought against the prisoner, the latter was released after suffering four months of close confinement in irons.

Simultaneously with the news of the withdrawal of foreign protection from some Jews reaching the interior towns, we received information of several Jews having been murdered, flogged to death, and lately, at the capital Fez, an old man, aged seventy, was burned to death in the street.

A committee of the "Alliance Israélite de Maroc" called on me, begging my intervention on behalf of their coreligionists in the interior; upon which I addressed my letter to the Sultan, and, I am happy to state, with apparently the most beneficial effect; an express courier arriving this morning from the court with news that the Sultan, on receipt of my letter, at once issued strict orders to the effect that any Moor found insulting or in any way offending a Jew would be at once severely punished and imprisoned.

Intelligence reached Tangier from Morocco that the governor of that city, on hearing of the withdrawal of the protection from the Jews, immediately gave orders that all the Jewish houses in the Ghetto having a second story from which the Kashbah (Basha's residence) could be seen were to be demolished at once. It is further stated that fifteen Jews, having remonstrated against this arbitrary order, were flogged and imprisoned, and subsequently released on payment each of $30.

It is hoped that, should the International Congress at Madrid take place, to regulate the protectorate of foreign nations over subjects of Morocco, provision will be made to put an end to the excesses against the Israelites of this empire in future.

The Moorish government could easily do away with all foreign protections over its own subjects by protecting them itself, by simply administering equal justice to all.

My friendly intervention on behalf of the Jews of Morocco in this instance is in conformity with the request of the president of the board of delegates of American Israelites to you on the 15th of

June, 1878, and to your dispatch No. 132, dated July 2, 1878, to me (see Foreign Relations, 1878, p. 685), and I hope it will meet with your approval.

I have, etc.,

Felix A. Mathews

Mr. Mathews enclosed a translation of the Arabic letter which he had sent to the Grand Vizier of the Sultan of Morocco. The letter itself is rather long, and the western reader will sense at once that it was addressed to an Eastern potentate. The following quotations will prove relevant, even today:

Centuries past, a nation expelled from their soil Moors and Jews, and these took refuge in this empire, where the reigning Sultan at the time received them with kindness and induced them to make Morocco their home, offering them protection and assistance. The country thus prospered and became rich and powerful, the Jews introducing, in large scale, commerce and arts, and in those days the Sultans always had for counsellor in their foreign intercourse a Jew, who was a member of his court, and the empire thus flourished. But of late years the persecution and ill-treatment to which the Israelites are subjected is attracting the attention and sympathy of foreign nations, and this state of affairs cannot continue without great prejudice and injury to the Empire of Morocco . . . .

You should be aware that in the greatest nations the Jews are found in large numbers, and many of them occupying the highest positions in the management of the government affairs, and they prosper and flourish, they having the same rights and enjoying the same protection as the other subjects or citizens, no matter how high be their standing and position.

The Hebrews when they rise united are capable of doing much. The Hebrews bring commerce and wealth to the countries where they establish themselves; they are the most pacific, religious and hospitable people in the world; they never shed blood, and you are aware that they are the most industrious subjects; these are facts that every one knows, and it is also a fact that the nation that continually ill-treats them brings its own ruin, as it is proved by history. God placed the Jews in the world on a level with the rest of mankind, having the same form and propensities as other men; they live and die the same as the Christians and Mohammedans; then why should they be ill-treated and partially dealt with in law? This is against God's will. It is pretending to be able to do more than God Himself, for the Almighty makes them equal to all other men, and no one has the right to take away from them that equality without being exposed to its consequences as it is proved in our days . . . .

After reminding the Grand Vizier that Jews in other countries would protest against injustice to their Moroccan coreligionists, Mr. Mathews goes on to say:

. . . . Should you properly protect your own subjects they will never seek for any other protection, and when your subjects shall be protected and supported in their rights they will be prosperous and happy, and the prosperity of your subjects will undoubtedly make the country prosperous and happy, as the subjects of various creeds are the body or what compose a nation, and should they flourish and become wealthy, then the nation itself is rich and fortunate, and in this consists the great secret.

The Sultan replied to the American consul through his vizier who referred to an atrocity of that year, the burning of a Jew, 85 years of age, in a street of Fez, capital of Morocco. The vizier justified this atrocity on the alleged ground that the old Jew had insulted and threatened a crowd of Moors. He further charged that a Moor had previously been killed by another Jew.

Reporting on this event on April 17, 1880, Mr. Mathews gave indirectly his opinion about the vizier and his letter, as will be seen from the following quotation:

The well known timid character of all Moorish Jews who are obliged to walk barefooted and never permitted to ride any kind of an animal through the streets of Fez, makes it ludicrous to learn from a Sultan's minister that an old Jew, eighty-five years old, insulted and threatened a crowd of Moors at the fanatical city of Fez, when they are pent up in a ghetto, in constant fear of their lives. I have the most reliable evidence of the fact that no Moor died, nor even was wounded at the hands of a Jew, and that the story is a fabrication got up to extenuate the magnitude of the crime.

The "most reliable evidence" to which Mr. Mathews referred was furnished by Captain John Cobb, American consular agent at Casablanca, who happened to be in Fez at the time of the alleged affair.

It became obvious that Mr. Mathews, while fulfilling the duties of American consul in Morocco, could not devote the necessary time and attention to the discovery and punishment of the many wrongs to which the Jews of Morocco were then subjected. The Board of Delegates on Civil and Religious Rights of the Union of the American Hebrew Congregations therefore designated a Mr. Levi A. Cohen as its accredited agent at Tangier and informed Mr. Evarts, Secretary of State, of this fact in the following letter:[7]

[*Mr. Sanger to Mr. Evarts*]

Union of American Hebrew Congregations
Board of Delegates on Civil and Religious Rights
New York, October 18, 1880

Sir: I have the honor to inform you that this board has designated Mr. Levi A. Cohen as its accredited agent at Tangier, Morocco, to look after the interests of our Israelitish brethren in that locality, and with a view to his presenting to the United States consul at Tangier, authenticated facts in relation to any wrongs done them, so that the perpetrators thereof may be speedily punished and proper reparation made.

I have been requested to communicate this action to the Department of State of the United States, with the view that Mr. Mathews may be officially advised of the facts and his co-operation invited.

In support of our action we find the within statement.

I am, with assurances of regard, very respectfully, yours,

ADOLPHE L. SANGER
Secretary

Ten days later, Oct. 28, 1880, Mr. Evarts sent to Mr. Mathews the following dispatch:[8]

[*Mr. Evarts to Mr. Mathews*]

Department of State
Washington, October 28, 1880

Sir: This Department is in receipt of a communication from Mr. Adolphe L. Sanger, secretary of the board of delegates of the Union of American Hebrew Congregations in New York, acquainting it with the designation of Mr. Levi A. Cohen as the accredited agent of that board at Tangier, Morocco, to look after the interests of

[7] Foreign Relations, 1881, page 1043.
[8] *Ibid.*, 1880, page 805.

Hebrews in that locality. It is one of the purposes of Mr. Cohen's appointment that he should present to you authenticated facts in relation to any wrong which may be done to Hebrews in Morocco, in order that the perpetrators thereof may be punished and reparation made in proper cases. The board of delegates in communicating this information desires that you may be officially advised of the capacity with which Mr. Cohen, who resides at Tangier, is invested, and that your co-operation with him may be invited.

Your earnest and urgent intercessions in behalf of this persecuted race in Morocco have for some time past commanded the cordial sympathy and approval of this Department. In view of this it seems unnecessary to do more than acquaint you with the mission undertaken by Mr. Cohen as the representative of the large and influential Hebrew organizations of this country; and in the interest of humanity and civilization you will doubtless upon any future occasion continue your good offices in behalf of the Jewish race.

I am, etc.,

Wm. M. Evarts

Mr. Lucius Fairchild, United States Minister to Spain, was also informed of Mr. Cohen's appointment in the following note:[9]

[*Mr. Evarts to Mr. Fairchild*]

Department of State
Washington, November 12, 1880

Sir: The accompanying copy of a letter from Mr. Adolphe L. Sanger, the secretary of the board of delegates on civil and religious rights of the Union of American Hebrew Congregations, will explain the circumstances under which this Department has instructed Mr. Mathews, the United States consul at Tangier, to extend all proper countenance and support to Mr. Levi A. Cohen, as the accredited agent of that board to watch over the interests of Hebrews in Morocco, and to present to the consulate authentic facts in relation to wrongs done them.

Mr Mathews's instructions, requiring the communication to you of all that he may trustworthily learn respecting the ill-treatment of Jews in Morocco, will cover the transmission to the legation of such facts as he may obtain from Mr. Cohen.

I am, sir, etc.,

Wm. M. Evarts

[9] Foreign Relations, 1881, page 1043.

Mr. Fairchild's reply already gives us an inkling of what baneful influence intolerance in Europe may have on conditions in backward countries.[10]

[*Mr. Fairchild to Mr. Evarts*]

Legation of the United States
Madrid, December 2, 1880

Sir: I have the honor to acknowledge receipt of your instruction No. 80, inclosing copy of a letter from Mr. Sanger to Mr. Evarts relating to the Jews in Morocco. I shall be much pleased if at any time I can be of service to that unfortunate people in that unhappy country.

It is to be hoped that the Sultan of Morocco is not well informed of all that is taking place in Europe; for if he should learn of the anti-Jewish agitation which now exists in Germany, as stated in the newspapers of the day, he may feel encouraged to increase, rather than diminish, the oppressions of the same race in his dominions. We cannot expect to find a more enlightened liberality in Morocco than exists among the highly educated people of Europe.

I, have etc.,

Lucius Fairchild

In the summer of 1880, an international conference for the protection of the non-Moslem population of Morocco was held in Madrid. To this conference, the Sultan of Morocco sent a communication, which was to be dispatched to all the cabinets of the nations represented at the conference, in which he promised amelioration of the conditions of the Jews.

This amelioration did not, however, come to pass. In fact, conditions went from bad to worse. Mr. Fairchild continued to receive information from Mr. Mathews of numerous attacks on Jews who were unjustifiably imprisoned, heavily fined, and even whipped to death. At the same time, the perpetrators of these outrages went unpunished. In conjunction with other representatives, the American Minister sent a joint note to Sid Mohamed Bargash, the Prime Minister of Morocco, in which they complained of the very

[10] Foreign Relations, 1881, page 1044.

loose manner in which order and security were maintained in the Shereefian Empire.

A description of the political conditions in Morocco, which in large part accounted for the precarious situation of the Jews, is given in a dispatch dated April 20, 1881, in which Mr. Fairchild reports to Secretary James G. Blaine on a trip to Morocco which the American Minister had voluntarily undertaken in order to make a personal investigation of the condition of the Jews there.[11]

[*Mr. Fairchild to Mr. Blaine*]

Legation of the United States
Madrid, April 20, 1881

SIR: . . . I have now the honor to report that I proceeded to Tangier, Morocco, where I arrived on the 22d of last month.

Keeping constantly in mind that the object of the visit was to learn all I could of the present condition of the Jews and other non-Mohammedan subjects of the Sultan, I embraced every opportunity to converse with and make inquiries of residents of Tangier on the subject. I had before leaving Madrid provided myself with letters to certain Jews in Tangier who were well known to their prominent co-religionists here and in Paris, so that the very best facilities were offered me for obtaining information from unofficial sources. I also conferred freely with several of the diplomatic corps resident in that city.

I will not attempt to describe the condition of the people in whose well-being the Government of the United States takes so great an interest. The files of the Department of State, through our energetic consul at Tangier, and from many other sources, contain all that can now be said on the subject by any one. That the treatment of the Jews is not now in any perceptible degree better or more humane than it was before the writing of the letter of the Sultan to the Madrid conference on affairs in Morocco last summer, is a melancholy fact, notwithstanding the far-reaching promises made in that communication.

While the Jews are subjected constantly to the greatest humiliation because of their religious belief, murders of and brutal behavior towards them by Mohammedans are not of daily occurrence; still, at brief intervals, such sad events happen, and the protection of the victims often enlists the earnest sympathy and active efforts

[11] Foreign Relations, 1881, page 1054.

of the official representatives of foreign countries at Tangier. Without such protection as those officials can give by interceding in behalf of the oppressed, and by urgent demands for the punishment of the guilty ones, the situation of the Jews would be an hundred-fold worse.

However, it is believed by many who have had much experience in Morocco, that the Sultan would be glad to see a greater measure of liberty granted to all of his non-Mohammedan subjects; but that should he endeavor to enforce official decrees to that effect he would be met by such resistance from his Mohammedan subjects as would endanger his throne. Of rebellions and civil wars His Majesty has on his hands more than a comfortable supply at all times, and his anxiety to avoid one which would seriously jeopardize his government cannot be wondered at. The bright side of the picture is the fact that most of the important governments of the world have representatives at Tangier, all of whom are unflagging in their endeavors to lessen the burdens of the oppressed in that unhappy land, and I am proud to know that my own country stands well to the front in this good work, and that our consul, Mr. Mathews, loses no opportunity to effectively contribute his full share in that direction.

All that can be done in the near future is to continue to protect the suffering people by intercession in individual cases, and by constant appeals to the Sultan to do all that he can, or dare, towards the uplifting of those who are now in such a down trodden condition. European complications may arise which will be of vast benefit to Morocco, and I look forward with pleasure to the day, which possibly we will see, when some one or more of the European nations will have gained such ascendancy over it as to be able to compel, by force if necessary, a more enlightened and liberal administration of affairs. Thus the people of Morocco can be relieved, and I see at present no other hope.

While I am unable, because of this visit to Tangier, to add much to the information already in the possession of the Department, I have the advantage of having ascertained on the spot that the reports which have for years been published of the sad situation of the people there, have not been in the least exaggerated, and I have the greatest satisfaction in knowing more of the philanthropic efforts in their behalf by the official representatives of foreign countries — the United States not being behind any other. And these efforts of the Government of the United States are most highly appreciated by those in whose behalf they are put forth, as well as by their brothers in religion in the United States and in Europe. As an indication of that feeling, I beg to quote from a letter to me from one of the most prominent Israelites (a citizen of the United States) in Europe, who learned of the object of my journey to Morocco. He writes:

> It does one's heart good to belong to a government which is as strong and mighty as it is humane and philanthropic, and which from motives of pure humanity sends one of its ministers to a far off country to alleviate the sufferings of a people and a race which is quite foreign to it.

Confident that my government will in the future, as in the past, be one of the foremost of nations in such good works, I shall always esteem it a high privilege, whether as one of its officials or as a private citizen, to contribute thereto my very best efforts.

I have, etc.,

LUCIUS FAIRCHILD

Mr. Blaine was very much impressed by this report and the spirit which permeated it, and sent to Mr. Fairchild the following note:[12]

[*Mr. Blaine to Mr. Fairchild*]

Department of State
Washington, June 13, 1881

SIR: I must express to you my appreciation of your admirable dispatch No. 140, of the 20th of April last, conveying your personal observations in regard to the condition of the Jews in Morocco. The confidence I have reposed in your discretion in this relation is abundantly justified, and I feel that I can safely leave to you the correct interpretation, now as in the past, of the sentiments of humanity which prompt the friendly action and counsel of the United States in the direction of endeavoring to procure toleration and personal security for this unhappy race in their chief African asylum.

I am, etc.,

JAMES G. BLAINE

Before he received this note, Mr. Fairchild had sent, on June 20, an unusually interesting report to Mr. Blaine. The American Minister must have had the Jewish question constantly in mind and, evidently was giving much thought to its solution. Anything that might lead to even a partial solution of it was apparently of great interest to him. Hence, he promptly informed Mr. Blaine when some Spanish news-

[12] Foreign Relations, 1881, page 1056

papers reported in their columns the willingness of the Spanish Government to allow Jews from Germany and Russia, who were at that time subjected to religious persecutions, to settle in Spain, where they would be assured shelter, protection and full freedom of religion. This proposition, it was stated, had the sanction even of His Majesty, the King of Spain. Quite appropriately, Mr. Fairchild observes that "truly the world moves, when His Catholic Majesty the King of Spain publicly gives to the people of Germany a lesson in religious liberty." That Mr. Blaine was highly pleased by this news is evident from his letter to Mr. Fairchild requesting him to express the satisfaction of the government of the United States:[13]

[*Mr. Blaine to Mr. Fairchild*]

Department of State
Washington, July 8, 1881

SIR: I have to acknowledge the receipt of your No. 164, by which you apprise me of a recent offer of protection extended by the Government of His Majesty the King of Spain to persons of the Jewish race in Germany and Russia, who had originally appealed for such protection to foreign representatives at Constantinople; and, in reply, to request that you will profit by the first suitable occasion to convey to the Spanish Government an expression of the lively satisfaction which has attended the reception of this intelligence by the Government of the United States.

The liberal and humane spirit which has inspired this act of noble hospitality is naturally appreciated by the people of this country, the laws of which are based on the same enlightened sentiment, and extend alike protection to the oppressed of every race, faith, and condition, from whatever country they may come.

I am, etc.,

JAMES G. BLAINE

As late as 1905, the Jews of Morocco were still subject to many restrictions because of their religion. These restrictions were especially severe in interior towns. Jews had to live in *mellahs* or ghettos, the gates of which had to be closed at night. They had to wear a peculiar garb, and when

---

[13] Foreign Relations, 1881, page 1059.

outside of the *mellah* had to go barefoot and bareheaded as a sign of submissiveness. Jewish provision dealers were forced to offer their goods free to all officials. Jews were not permitted to testify in court, and the punishment for the murder of a Jew was a mere money fine. These are only a few of the many restrictions which the Jews of Morocco had to suffer and against which they dared not protest.

In 1906 the world's leading powers met at Algeciras, Spain, to discuss the political fate of Morocco.[14] President Theodore Roosevelt, who had been instrumental in the calling of this conference, appointed Mr. Henry White, United States Ambassador at Rome, head of the American delegation; Mr. Lewis Einstein, then an assistant secretary at the American Embassy in London, served as its secretary. Mr. Samuel Gummeré, Minister to Morocco, was the other member of the delegation.

The conference met at Algeciras on the 16th of January, 1906.

The instructions of Secretary of State Elihu Root to Ambassador White touching on the question of the situation of the Jews in Morocco and suggestions for its improvement are contained in the following dispatch:[15]

[*Mr. Root to Mr. White*]

Department of State
Washington, November 28, 1905

SIR: Supplementing my instructions of even date, and in connection with your functions as a representative of the United States at the Moroccan conference, it is desired that in all proper ways you shall urge upon the conference the consideration of guaranties of religious and racial tolerance in Morocco.

Concurrent testimony positively affirms the intolerance of the Mohammedan rule in that country toward non-Mussulmans in all that concerns their lives, avocations, and creeds. Jews, especially, appear to suffer from painful and injurious restrictions. I have been furnished by Mr. Jacob H. Schiff with a statement of the

---

[14] See the chapter "Secret History of the Algeciras Conference," in the official biography of President Roosevelt, "Theodore Roosevelt and His Time," by Joseph B. Bishop, Vol. 1, pages 467–505.

[15] Foreign Relations, 1905, page 680.

existing restrictions upon Moroccan Jews living in other than the harbor towns, the details of which appear well-nigh incredible and utterly at variance with any sound theory of the relation between the governing and governed classes. Were an American citizen, Jew or gentile, to suffer a tithe of such proscriptions in Morocco it would be impossible for this government to shut its eyes to their existence; and it is equally hard now to ignore them when we are called upon to enter, with Morocco as with other powers, upon the examination of schemes for bettering the relations of the Shereefian Empire with the countries to which it is bound by treaty engagements. It is alike the part of prudence and goodwill, on the one side as on the other, to restrain the spirit of intolerance and preclude the development of its effects into antagonism between all Mohammedans and non-Mohammedans. The powers are, it would seem, interested in seeking equality of privilege for their nationals and national interests in Morocco — not in emphasizing by the contrast of treaty discriminations in their favor, the class restrictions which weigh upon natives. To do so would but fan the popular prejudice and increase the spirit of resentment toward aliens. It is moreover, evident that these restrictions operate to contract the field of commercial intercourse by barring a notable part of the population of Morocco from the open door of equal intercourse which we are so anxious to see established and by hampering the channels of barter and the opportunities of consumption and supply.

It is also evident that reform in this regard is of equal importance from the point of view of internal order and security, a matter provided for in the programme submitted for consideration by the conference. The first subject concerns the adequate policing of the interior of Morocco through an international agreement. Effective policing means and requires such change in internal conditions as will smooth away the class and caste impediments to a beneficial intercourse, remove the prejudices that exist against aliens, and render the people of Morocco receptive to the broad influences of friendly international intercourse. If on no other ground, the measures advocated in this instruction should necessarily commend themselves to the good judgment of the conferees because essentially contributory to the success of any practical scheme of interior police in Morocco.

I inclose for your information copy of a letter from Mr. Schiff communicating the statement above mentioned. It is the President's wish that you give this subject your earnest attention and endeavor in all proper ways to impress its importance upon your colleagues in the conference.

I have, etc.

ELIHU ROOT

Mr. Schiff's letter recited a long list of restrictions, political, legal, and social, in trade, commerce, and even in lodging and dress, some of which have been mentioned above, to which Moroccan Jews were subjected, especially in the interior.

As secretary of the American delegation, Mr. Lewis Einstein went over to Tangier to study at first hand the condition of the Moroccan Jews. In his report[16] he declared that the restrictions referred to by Mr. Schiff were *de jure* restrictions and not *de facto*. It would further seem, according to Mr. Einstein's report, that while the efforts of foreign representatives in Morocco had succeeded in ameliorating many abuses which once oppressed the native Jews, yet, at the same time, "almost unknown to the outside world, a peaceful humanitarian reform has silently been accomplished, and the Jews of Morocco are well-nigh emancipated from the oppressions which formerly burdened their lot." Most of the restrictions had either been abolished altogether or had fallen in abeyance. Thus, while concentration of Jews in the *mellahs* or ghettos continued, it was not as an imposition by the Moors but rather by the free choice of the Jews themselves who may leave it and build homes for themselves in any part of the cities. Legal restrictions, too, were of no moment, Mr. Einstein reported. "As justice in our sense of the word is a thing unknown in Morocco, as bribery counts alone in influencing the judge's decision, the real position of the Jew before the law is little different from that of the Mussulman." Furthermore, there would be no use of legislation wherever restrictions do exist, because "laws occupy a very subordinate place in Morocco."

Mr. Einstein concluded: "Moroccan Jews stand thus today in no need of especial solicitude. When once security has been established in the country, when roads have been built and policed, they will be the first to profit from the establishment of law and order in the new era which will then have opened in Morocco. Their present desire is only for an ex-

---

[16] Foreign Relations, 1906, page 1472.

pression of interest in their welfare as an acknowledgment on the part of a great power that the enlightened policy of toleration pursued by the Sultan has met with its full approval."

Fearing that a mere statement, as suggested by the leading Jews of Morocco, would be "inadequate and unsatisfactory to our Jewish fellow-citizens," Mr. White asked for definite instruction from Secretary Root. Mr. Root instructed him to follow the advice of the Moroccan Jewish leaders.

So, on April 8, Mr. White asked the conference to express a *vœu* (which is stronger than the English word "hope") in favor of equitable treatment of the Jews particularly, as well as other non-Mussulman subjects of the Sultan of Morocco.

The text of the motion or *vœu* follows:[17]

The Government of the United States has always considered it as a duty to associate itself to all that can contribute to the progress of humanitarian ideas and that can secure the respect due to all religious beliefs. Animated by these sentiments and by the friendship that has so long subsisted between it and the Moroccan Empire, whose development it follows with profound interest, my Government has charged me to invoke the support of this conference at the moment when it is going to end its labors, in order to express a vœu for the welfare of the Jews in Morocco.

I am happy to notice that the conditions of the Jewish subjects of His Shereefian Majesty has been much ameliorated during the reign of the late Sultan Mouley-el-Hassan and that the present Sultan appears, as much as it has been possible for him, to have treated them with equity and kindness. But the agents of the Maghzen in the parts of the country far removed from the central power, are not always sufficiently inspired with the feelings of tolerance and justice that animate their sovereign.

The American delegation therefore begs the conference to be pleased to express the vœu that His Shereefian Majesty continue the good policy inaugurated by his father and maintained by His Majesty himself as regards his Jewish subjects, and that he should see that his Government neglects no opportunity to make known to its functionaries that the Sultan insists that the Jews of his Empire and all his subjects, without any distinction or belief, be treated with justice and equity.

[17] Foreign Relations, 1906, page 1493.

Though the British and French delegation had asked **Mr.** White, if possible at all, not to bring the subject of Jewish disabilities before the conference because they deemed it undesirable to discuss any matter not strictly within the programme, the response to Mr. White's motion was unanimously favorable. Every chief delegate, except the Moorish, expressed approval and support of the proposals; some even made short speeches. The Moorish delegate declared that the Sultan "would be happy to keep up the system inaugurated by his father of treating the Jews with fairness."

Mr. White received the following letter of thanks from the representatives of the Alliance Israélite Universelle, dated April 9, 1906:[18]

[*Alliance Israélite Universelle to Mr. White*]

Mr. Ambassador: The whole of the Jewish World is profoundly grateful to you for the motion ("vœu") in favor of the Israelites of Morocco which you presented at the Algeciras Conference. No one will be surprised that the initiative in this manifestation of tolerance and of lofty liberalism was taken by the delegate of the great country which receives with so magnificent a generosity the victims of religious persecutions and which has intervened, on many an occasion, to cause liberty of conscience and unrecognized rights of humanity to be respected. The Moroccan Israelites have been able, for many years past, to appreciate the value of the protection which the United States bestows upon them. Through you your noble country gives them a new magnificent evidence of her precious benevolence.

The Alliance Israélite Universelle, which has occupied itself for nearly fifty years past with the uplifting of the Moroccan Israelites, has the honor to address to you in their behalf, in the name of the Israelites of the whole world, the expression of its most profound gratitude for the great service which you have just rendered to the cause of civilization and progress.

Pray, accept, Mr. Ambassador, the assurance of our profound respect.

N. Leven, President
L. Bigart, Secretary

Under the Algeciras Act, signed on April 7, 1906, the "independence" of Morocco was recognized, though the whole

---

[18] Foreign Relations, 1906, page 1494.

economic structure of the country, as well as its police force, were put under international control. In 1912 Morocco became a protectorate of France. In a treaty with Spain, signed on November 27, 1917, France recognized the Spanish protectorate over a small part of Morocco, comprising a twelfth of Moroccan territory and a tenth of its population.

Since the establishment of these two protectorates the question of religious minorities has ceased to be an international question and there is no further mention of it in the published diplomatic correspondence of the United States, up to the time of writing.

IV. PALESTINE

The Government of the United States showed its interest in Palestine long before it became a distinct governmental territorial unit. When Palestine was still an integral part of the Turkish Empire and known as the Province of Southern Syria, the people of the United States always recognized the sentimental connection of the Jewish people with its ancient home. In a letter to Major Mordecai Manuel Noah, President John Quincy Adams said: "I really wish again in Judaea an independent nation."[1]

In the year 1891, the American public was outraged by the treatment extended to the Jews in Russia, and the commiseration with the Jew rose to a very high pitch. This righteous anger and generous sympathy expressed itself in a petition which was sent to President Harrison on March 5, 1891. In this historical document, the petitioners asked the President to use the good offices of the United States and call an international conference "to consider the condition of the Israelites and their claims to Palestine as their ancient home, and to promote, in all other just and proper ways, the alleviation of their suffering condition."

It is interesting to note that the petition was conceived, subscribed to and executed wholly by American Christians, the originator of the whole plan being a clergyman, Reverend William E. Blackstone.

The petition, in part, reads as follows:

... Why not give Palestine back to them [the Jews] again? According to God's distribution of nations it is their home — an inalienable possession from which they were expelled by force. Under their cultivation it was a remarkably fruitful land, sustain-

---

[1] "Some Early American Zionist Projects," by Max J. Kohler, in *Publications of the American Jewish Historical Society*, No. 8, 1900, page 75.

ing millions of Israelites, who industriously tilled its hillsides and valleys. They were agriculturists and producers as well as a nation of great commercial importance — the center of civilization and. religion.

Why shall not the powers which under the treaty of Berlin, in 1878, gave Bulgaria to the Bulgarians and Servia to the Servians now give Palestine back to the Jews? . . . If they could have autonomy in government, the Jews of the world would rally to transport and establish their suffering brethren in their time-honored habitation. For over 17 centuries they have patiently waited for such a privileged opportunity.

We believe this is an appropriate time for all nations, and especially the Christian nations of Europe, to show kindness to Israel. A million of exiles, by their terrible sufferings, are piteously appealing to our sympathy, justice and humanity. Let us now restore to them the land of which they were so cruelly despoiled by our Roman ancestors.

Outstanding personalities of the time appended their signatures to this petition, including Melville W. Fuller, Chief Justice of the United States, Cyrus H. McCormick, J. Pierpont Morgan, Speaker Thomas B. Reed, Representative, later President, William McKinley, Chauncey M. Depew, John D. Rockefeller, Cyrus W. Field, Russell Sage, Cardinal Gibbons, and many other men famous in both public and private life.

That the United States had been and continued to be a haven of refuge for persecuted Jews and that its government was always ready to use its influence in behalf of Jews in a number of less civilized countries must have become common knowledge among Jews and their leaders everywhere. It is, therefore, no surprise that Jews who were forced to leave Russia and found themselves stranded in Constantinople, then capital of Turkey, homeless and starving, should appeal to the American minister for aid. Mr. Lawrence Oliphant, an English author, and some of the Jewish leaders acquainted General Lewis Wallace, author of "Ben-Hur," then serving as United States Minister at Constantinople, with the wretched condition of these refugees.

On July 11, 1882, Gen. Wallace, in a note to Secretary of State Frederick T. Frelinghuysen, reported that, as a consequence of the Jewish exodus from Russia, some of the refugees had reached Constantinople and were starving in the streets, that his sympathy was excited in their behalf, and that he had received a petition asking that his services be rendered unofficially to secure to Jews the privilege of colonizing in such districts of Syria as contained localities available for the purpose. Gen. Wallace goes on to state that, at the instance of Mr. Oliphant and Mr. Alexander, he had visited the Minister of Foreign Affairs, who had informed him that the matter had been before the Council of Ministers who had decided that Jews from whatever parts could come and settle in Turkey, that they could settle on any unoccupied lands in Mesopotamia, in Syria, about Aleppo, or in the region of the Orontes River, but that they could not establish themselves in Palestine, and that every colonist was bound to become an Ottoman subject. Gen. Wallace concluded his dispatch, which was accompanied by documents that had passed between him and the Minister of Foreign Affairs, with the following sentences: "In conclusion, there is nothing to prevent all the Israelites on the earth from settling in Asiatic Turkey. They shall not settle in Palestine — that is the only prohibition." It should be remarked here, again, that the persons on whose behalf General Wallace visited the Minister of Foreign Affairs were not American citizens and his action was, therefore, taken solely upon the grounds of humanity.

A delicate legal question arose, a few months later, between Gen. Wallace and the Turkish Foreign Office, which involved the fate of a number of Jews who lived in Jerusalem and claimed the protection of the American consul there as citizens of the United States. These Jews, thirty-five or forty in number, were, in the words of General Wallace in his dispatch of January 24, 1884, "mostly old men, and quite poor, who have betaken themselves to Palestine as the most sacred of places, thinking that if they behaved themselves and lived orderly lives, they might be permitted to die and be quietly buried there." Some of them had originally been Russian subjects.

The Turkish officials aimed to differentiate between two

classes of American citizens, those who were born in the United States and those who became naturalized there. It was of the latter group that the Turkish Government wished to take eventual jurisdiction. This was to be accomplished by making them automatically Turkish subjects as soon as they had lost their adopted nationality.

In a note of January 22, 1884, to General Wallace, phrased in vague terms, Aarifi Pasha, Minister of Foreign Affairs, wrote of a number of Russian subjects who had left their country five years before to live in Palestine and had succeeded in having themselves admitted as American citizens. The Imperial Government, the Turkish Pasha continued, could not recognize such naturalization as legitimate and valid, for "in principle and strict right, any foreigner established in the Empire who should lose his rights to his original nationality, must be considered an Ottoman subject."

In a reply of January 24, 1884, General Wallace regretted that the communication from the Foreign Office was not definite in its terms, and stated that the American consul at Jerusalem was instructed to protect only those who had taken out their first papers and renounced their previous allegiance to another Government. Of course, there should be no question as to the rights to American protection of those who had perfected their naturalization as citizens of the United States. Those who did not belong to either of these two classes could not claim any rights appertaining to American citizenship. But the distinction between these classes of persons is to be made by the American consul, for "the United States have never admitted the right of a foreign government to decide upon and nullify in any manner the franchise conferred under its naturalization laws." General Wallace added that the consul was instructed to protect naturalized citizens, that "he must exhaust the means usually of resort on such occasions; failing in them, he must close his consulate and come away, if possible bringing the threatened people with him."

What was gained for American citizens in Palestine, at that time mainly Jews, was an agreement that any person presenting a certificate, under the official seal, given to him by a consul or consular agent, had *prima facie* evidence that he was an American citizen and his citizenship could not be questioned by any Turkish official.

A more or less organized movement of Russian Jews to settle in Palestine and establish agricultural colonies there started in the latter half of the nineteenth century. The Ottoman rulers became alarmed lest the Jews eventually gain too strong a hold on the country and endanger the territorial and political integrity of the Empire. In order to combat the movement, various obstacles were put in the way of any Jew who showed an interest in the country to the extent of wishing to settle there. One of the decrees (*iradeh*) limited the time for Jews who came to Palestine "to perform their pilgrimage" to one month, after the expiration of which they were to be expelled.

In 1887, the Governor of Jerusalem addressed a note to Mr. Henry Gillman, American consul at Jerusalem, complaining to him that the foreign consuls did not lend the police department in Jerusalem the necessary assistance in causing the foreign Jews to leave Palestine after the expiration of the temporary period assigned to them. Mr. Gillman forwarded the note to Washington and requested specific instructions. Secretary of State Thomas F. Bayard, in turn, sent Mr. Gillman's note to Mr. Oscar S. Straus, our minister at Constantinople, asking further information about the expulsion of American Jews from Palestine.

In answer to Mr. Straus, Mr. Gillman reported that, while a number of foreign Jews had been expelled from Palestine, the Turkish officials receiving the full support of the respective consuls, no American citizens had been expelled during the time he was connected with the consulate. Furthermore, he could never agree to such a thing happening as in all communications with the local officials he had consistently held the position that the American Government forbade any discrimination for or against American citizens on account of their race or creed. In fact, Raouf Pasha, Governor of Jerusalem, had complained to the American consul that he alone of all the ten foreign consuls in Jerusalem had not promised to assist in carrying out this *iradeh.* Even the British consul was surprised to see the American consul so friendly to Jews. Later, however, the British Government sent direct orders to their consul forbidding him to lend aid to the Turkish police in expelling British Jews from Palestine. It is very probable that this change came about as a result of a talk which the British Ambassador at Constantinople had with Mr. Straus.

Meanwhile Mr. Straus called at the Porte a number of times with the intention of counteracting any decision to prohibit American Jews, recently arrived in Palestine, from settling there. Mr. Straus was informed at one of these interviews that the reason the Jews were forbidden to stay in Palestine more than three months — the Council of Ministers had, in the meantime, changed the limit of the stay from one month to three months — was because, at a recent Easter celebration in Jerusalem, religious fanaticism had risen to such a pitch that the Jews residing in the city were compelled to remain within their homes in order to avoid attack, or even murder, at the hands of Christians; it was really for the protection of Jews that the Turkish Government had issued this regulation.

Realizing, perhaps, that this explanation was not sufficient, and that from the same situation quite an opposite decision could just as logically be drawn, representatives of the Ottoman Government added another reason. This was, in the words of Mr. Straus, "the report that has spread abroad that the Jews throughout the world intended to strengthen in and around Jerusalem with a view, at some future time, of re-establishing their ancient kingdom there."

Mr. Straus was not quite satisfied with either of the two reasons. As to the first, racial disorders could easily be avoided by a stronger police force, and as to the second reason, Mr. Straus could not see that the Jews of the world were actuated by any such ideas as those which had caused such great fear to Turkish officials in Constantinople and Jerusalem. But in any case, the American Government could not allow any foreign power to distinguish as between its citizens on the basis of their faith. The interview ended with an assurance given to Mr. Straus that due consideration would be given to the American attitude on this question, and the proper officials would be instructed accordingly.

All these facts were reported by Mr. Straus in the following dispatch to Secretary Bayard:[2]

[*Mr. Straus to Mr. Bayard*]

Legation of the United States
Constantinople, January 28, 1888

Sir: In answer to your instruction No. 51, of October 31, 1887, I have the honor to report:

Shortly after the receipt of your instruction, I called at the Porte and had an interview with the Grand Vizier on the subject in question. He informed me that a regulation had been communicated by the Porte to the Imperial authorities at Jerusalem to limit the stay of foreign Jews at Jerusalem to the period of one month. At a second interview he further informed me that the council of ministers was about amending the regulation so as to make the period three months. He gave as a reason for such a regulation, that the spirit of religious fanaticism rose to such a high pitch at Jerusalem that at certain seasons of the year, during Easter, the Jews were compelled to remain within their houses to avoid coming in contact with the Christians, who would attack them and perhaps murder them.

The purpose of the regulation was to avoid the possibility of such conflicts.

Another reason was also given by the Grand Vizier as the cause of this regulation, namely, the report that had spread abroad that the Jews throughout the world intended to strengthen themselves in and around Jerusalem with a view, at some future time, of re-establishing their ancient kingdom there.

I explained as to the first contingency, that it could be avoided by a strong force of police. As to the second, the re-establishment of a Jewish kingdom, I informed his highness that if the Porte would make inquiry it could easily satisfy itself that no such purpose actuated the Jews throughout the world. I informed him also that so far as concerned American citizens, naturalized or native, it is one of the fundamental principles of my Government to make no distinction as to its citizens based upon creed or race,

[2] Foreign Relations, 1888, Part II, page 1559.

and that, uniformly in its relation with foreign nations, it had emphatically denied their right to make such discriminations against American citizens. I quoted to him several passages from your correspondence and instructions bearing upon this principle, and referred to the ancient capitulations and the provisions of our treaty with the Ottoman Empire.

His Highness assured me should the authorities threaten to expel any American citizen he would give due weight to the foregoing consideration, and give instructions accordingly.

Shortly thereafter the Right Honorable Sir William A. White, the British ambassador, asked me what position my Government had taken in reference to discriminations made against its citizens who were of Jewish faith. He said that he desired to know in view of several cases before him arising under the aforesaid regulation of the Porte. He stated that the foregoing principles fully coincided with his own sense of duty and convictions, and that he would be guided accordingly.

About the same time I sent a dispatch to our consul-general here requesting him to instruct our consul at Jerusalem, Henry Gillman, esq., to make report whether any American citizens had been expelled or were threatened with expulsion; also to report such other facts relative to the subject as he might deem important. A copy of his dispatch in reply of December 31, 1887, I herewith enclose.

I have, etc.,

O. S. STRAUS

In reply to this dispatch, Mr. Straus received from Mr. Bayard a short note, dated February 21, 1888, approving the action of Mr. Straus as discreet and proper.

About two weeks later, Mr. Bayard sent Mr. Straus the following extremely significant dispatch firmly refusing to accede to the claim of the Ottoman Government to discriminate as between American citizens on the ground of creed or race.[3]

[*Mr. Bayard to Mr. Straus*]

Department of State
Washington, March 5, 1888

SIR: I transmit herewith for your information copy of a note addressed to me by Mavroyeni Bey on the 2d instant, and of my

[3] Foreign Relations, 1888, page 1566.

reply, both having relation to the treatment of foreign Jews resorting to Palestine.

These notes continue, and importantly enlighten, the subject to which my instruction No. 51, of 31st of October, 1887, and your report No. 57, of 28th January last, had reference.

It appears from Mavroyeni Bey's statement that the regulation of which the Grand Vizier spoke to you, amendatory of the previous iradeh and extending the term of permitted sojourn of foreign Jews in Palestine to three months (instead of one month, as reported in Consul Gillman's No. 26, of September 28, 1887), is coupled with a most obnoxious condition, by prescribing that such alien Israelites shall only be permitted to enter Palestine when bearing passports setting forth "that they are going to Jerusalem in the performance of a pilgrimage and not for the purpose of engaging in commerce or taking up residence there;" which passports, so drawn up (*ainsi libellés*) are to be visaed by the consuls of Turkey. A further *permis de séjour* is also prescribed to be issued by the Imperial authorities, and although not so stated explicitly, it is inferred that the permission in question is only granted on production of the passport itself; the declarations of which the *permis de séjour* is stated to repeat.

It is regarded as strange that so important a condition as this should not have been communicated to you by his excellency. Had it been brought to your notice, it is conceived that you would have considerably amplified and emphasized your declaration to the Grand Vizier that it is one of the fundamental principles of your Government to make no distinction as to its citizens based upon "creed or race," and that you would have made instant and earnest protest against a requirement which would not only involve a declaration by this Government, expressed or inferential, in its formal passports, of the creed of the citizens to whom they are issued, but would further infringe the laws and practice in the matter whereby this Department and its agents are governed, and which preclude giving to citizens of the United States preparing to go abroad any certificate as to their purpose in so going.

To require of applicants for passports, which under our laws are issued to all citizens upon the sole evidence of their citizenship, any announcement of their religious faith or declaration of their personal motives in seeking such passports, would be utterly repugnant to the spirit of our institutions and to the intent of the solemn proscription forever by the Constitution of any religious test as a qualification of the relations of the citizen to the Government, and would, moreover, assume an inquisitorial function in respect of the personal affairs of the individual, which this Government can not exert for its own purposes, and could still less assume to exercise with the object of aiding a foreign Government in the enforcement of an objectionable and arbitrary discrimination against certain of our citizens.

Our adherence to these principles has been unwavering since the foundation of our Government, and you will be at no loss to cite pertinent examples of our consistent defense of religious liberty, which, as I said in my note to Baron Schaeffer of May 18, 1885, in relation to the Keiley episode at Vienna, "is the chief corner-stone of the American system of Government, and provisions for its security are embedded in the written charter and interwoven in the moral fabric of its laws."[4]

In case a copy of the Keiley correspondence should not be on file in your legation, I inclose the printed document herewith for your convenience.

It may be well for you to ascertain as discreetly as may be the views of your colleagues in respect of this remarkable requirement of the iradeh in question, of which you should also endeavor to secure a copy for examination; but under any circumstances the impossibility of this Government's acceding to any such require-ment should be distinctly made known to the Government of the Sublime Porte.

T. F. BAYARD

Mr. Straus thereupon approached the British and French ambassadors in order to ascertain their views on the subject, and learned that, although they had received instructions from home similar to those he had received, they were not yet ready to take any action. Mr. Straus, however, thought it advisable not to wait for the others to act, and dispatched a strongly-worded protest to Saïd Pasha incorporating the main points and arguments raised by Mr. Bayard. The note follows:[5]

[Mr. Straus to Saïd Pasha]

Legation of the United States
Constantinople, May 17, 1888

EXCELLENCY: Respecting the recent instructions placed by the Imperial Ottoman authorities upon foreign Jews going to Pales-tine, the Secretary of State has referred to me, with definite instruc-tions, a note addressed to him by his excellency Mavroyeni Bev.

---

[4] For full account of this episode, see pages 323–46.
[5] Foreign Relations, 1888, page 1589.

imperial minister at Washington, bearing date the 2d day of March, 1888, whereby he informs the Government of the United States that, in order to put an end to the immigration of Jews into Palestine, "the Sublime Porte has decided only to authorize free access into Palestine to Israelites coming from foreign countries under the following conditions: Their passports should expressly state that they are going to Jerusalem in the performance of a pilgrimage and not for the purpose of engaging in commerce or taking up their residence there. As regards their sojourn in Palestine, instead of one month, it can not in any case exceed the space of three months. They must have their passports so drawn up (*libellés*) viséd by the Ottoman consuls, and on their arrival they will be bound to supply themselves with a *permis de séjour* issued by the Imperial authorities and couched in the same terms."

I am instructed to inform your excellency that under any circumstances the impossibility of my Government acceding to any such requirement should be distinctly made known to the Sublime Porte.

To require of applicants for passports, which under our laws are issued to all citizens upon the sole evidence of their citizenship. any announcement of their religious faith or declaration of their personal motives in seeking such passport would be utterly repugnant to the spirit of our Constitution and to the intent of the solemn proscription by the Constitution of any religious test as a qualification of the relations of the citizens to the Government, and would, moreover, assume an inquisitorial function in respect of the personal affairs of the individual, which our Government cannot exert for its own purposes and could still less assume to exercise with the object of aiding a foreign government in the enforcement of an objectionable and arbitrary discrimination against certain of our citizens.

I am informed that these restrictive regulations are being very cruelly enforced, not only in Palestine but at the various ports along the Syrian coast, and that foreign Jews upon their arrival at these ports, in addition to the foregoing restrictions, are compelled to furnish security to the local authorities that they will again leave the country when the period of three months has expired, and in default of their being able to furnish such security they are thrown into prison.

The foregoing considerations are submitted with the hope that the Sublime Porte will cause these restrictions to be modified or annulled in accordance with the broad principles of toleration that were proclaimed throughout the Ottoman Empire first among the nations of Europe and the Old World, that are embodied in the grand charters of liberties, the Hatti-Scheriff and Hatti-Humayoun, and secured to all races and creeds under the capitulations, and under treaties with the United States and other nations.

Accept, excellency, etc.,

O. S. STRAUS

A week after Mr. Straus had sent the above note to the Imperial Minister of Foreign Affairs, the French and British ambassadors sent similar notes, demanding the abrogation of the discriminatory regulation against foreign Jews desiring to settle in Palestine. The British Government found these regulations derogatory to the rights and privileges of British subjects in the Turkish Empire. The French Ambassador emphasized the fact that France having given full religious and legal equality to Jews, there would not be any likelihood that French Jews would emigrate *en masse* to Palestine, and he must, therefore, insist that French Jewish nationals enjoy everywhere in Turkey all the rights and liberties given to all French citizens.

During the year of 1888 there arose a specific case which put the theoretical discussion in the above exchange of notes to a practical test. Three American Jews arrived at Jaffa, Palestine, on August 20, 1888. They bore American passports which had not been viséed by a Turkish consul. The police authorities at Jaffa were ordered to have them expelled from the country, but held them meanwhile incarcerated until the next steamer should leave the port of Jaffa.

With great difficulty the American consul at Jerusalem, Mr. Henry Gillman, and his consular agent in Jaffa, Mr. Ernest Hardegg, succeeded in having the execution of the order of expulsion postponed; this, however, was to take place on September 6.

Two of the three Jews were over 70 years of age and had come to Palestine to live there the few remaining years of their lives and be buried in the holy soil. The Turkish officials were willing to free them on the condition that the American consul sign an assurance that they would leave the country after the expiration of three months. This the consul rightfully refused to do, and, instead, cabled to the American legation in Constantinople as follows:

> Three Americans, with unvisaed passports, threatened with expulsion. Protest.

Mr. Pendleton King, Chargé d'Affaires during the absence from the capital of Mr. Oscar S. Straus, corresponded with Saïd Pasha on this subject, calling his attention to the declaration of American principles by which the United States Government is guided in reference to religious differences contained in Mr. Straus's note of May 17, 1888. Mr. King described the detention and expulsion of the three American Jews as a violation of long-established right, and threatened that "their expulsion might lead to disagreeable complications."[6]

---

[6] This language may seem rather strong in a note to a Minister of Foreign Affairs by an official in charge of a foreign legation. But what may be strong and tactless in any other place was not so in the old Turkish Empire. Diplomatic phraseology of the usual run would have had no effect there and would only have invited contempt and a hardened opposition. The efficacy of strong language was brought out by Mr. Straus, in 1911, at a hearing before the House Committee on Foreign Affairs on the termination of the treaty of 1832 with Russia. Mr. Straus related how, during his second mission to Turkey, a number of American instructors in the American schools and colleges in Turkey were refused a *teskere*, or internal passport. Without a *teskere* their lives enroute to their posts would be endangered. Mr. Straus then asked for an interview with the Sultan, and when this was granted made the following statement to the Sultan: "If you will not give our citizens an internal passport to travel in your Empire, I will give it to them, and if any harm befalls them, I give you notice now that no effort on my part will be spared to induce my Government to go to the fullest extreme to protect her citizens in this Empire."

The Turkish Minister of Foreign Affairs had based his refusal on the Russian precedent, generously supplied to him by the Russian ambassador at Constantinople. This, however, failed to move Mr. Straus from his position, and at one o'clock in the morning, after the meeting with the Sultan, Mr. Straus received a note from a messenger sent by the Sublime Porte saying that the Council of Ministers had just sent out instructions to officials of the various provinces through which the American teachers were to pass ordering them to accord the Americans all possible protection.

These representations apparently resulted favorably, as is evidenced by the following note:[7]

[*The Ministry of Foreign Affairs to the Legation of the United States*]

Sublime Porte
Ministry of Foreign Affairs
October 4, 1888

In answer to the *note verbale* that the legation of the United States of America kindly addressed to the ministry of foreign affairs on the 17th of May last (No. 27), the ministry of foreign affairs has the honor to inform the United States legation that the measure concerning the Israelites going to Palestine shall not be applied, except to those who emigrate in number (*en nombre*), and that no obstacle shall be opposed to the sojourn of those who are not of this class.

Instructions of this sense have already been sent to the governor of Jerusalem.

The entire incident formed the basis of the following dispatch from the Department of State to our consul at Jerusalem:[8]

[*Mr. Rives to Mr. Gilman*]

Department of State
Washington, October 12, 1888

SIR: Your dispatches, Nos. 62 and 65, dated, respectively, August 30 and September 10, ultimo, have been received. They relate to the attempted expulsion from Palestine of three citizens of the United States — Meyer Freeman, Isaac Gliechman, and Jacob Reichman — who having arrived at Jaffa on the 20th of August last by steamer from Port Said, were prevented from continuing their journey to Jerusalem on the grounds that they were Hebrews, and that their passports, issued by the Department of State in July last, did not bear the visa of some Ottoman consul abroad.

It appears that their passports were taken from them (although subsequently returned), and they were notified that they would be required to leave Palestine by the first steamer. Through the efforts of the consular agent at Jaffa, Mr. Hardegg, their attempted

[7] Foreign Relations, 1888, page 1619.
[8] *Ibid.*, page 1617.

expulsion was deferred until September 6. One of these persons in question, Jacob Reichman, escaped, on August 27, from Jaffa, while Meyer Freeman and Isaac Gliechman (the latter accompanied by his wife) succeeded in evading the vigilance of the Jaffa police, reached Jerusalem on the 5th of September, and were at once placed under police restraint and threatened anew with expulsion. They were, however, offered their liberty on condition of your signing an assurance that they would remain in Palestine only three months, which you very properly refused to do. They were subsequently released in consequence, as would appear, of a perfunctory and irresponsible guaranty, on the part of a resident of Jerusalem, that they would quit Palestine as required. You had reported the case to our legation at Constantinople, and were awaiting the result, the persons in question remaining at liberty, and the date of their notified expulsion, September 6, having passed without steps being taken to effect their removal.

A report in their case has been received from Mr. King, chargé d'affaires *ad interim* at Constantinople, who writes, under date of the 24th ultimo (No. 115), that he had actively intervened with the Porte, and caused telegraphic orders to be sent the authorities at Jerusalem by the minister of foreign affairs and the Grand Vizier, which he hoped would stop the attempted expulsion.

Your course on the whole seems to have been proper, and the language employed by you to the Ottoman authorities, although very emphatic, may not have been unduly so in view of the slight amenability of the Turkish provincial officers to temperate reasoning or even to superior orders.

The question out of which this incident grows is not a new one. Under date of 2d March last, Mavroyeni Bey, the Turkish envoy at this capital, informed the Department that in view of the alleged inconvenience of the resort of numerous alien Israelites to Palestine for the purpose of business and residence, the Sublime Porte had decided to authorize the entrance of such persons only on the condition that they bear passports which shall "expressly state that they are going to Jerusalem in the performance of a pilgrimage and not for the purpose of engaging in commerce or taking up their residence there," that the passport so drawn up shall be duly *visaed* by Ottoman consuls, and that on arriving the holders shall be bound to provide themselves with "permits of sojourn" (*permis de séjour*) issued by the imperial authorities and couched in the same terms as the passports — the duration of such permitted sojourn not to exceed three months.

Mr. Straus was promptly directed to protest against such a measure. As you will see by the inclosed copies of our correspondence, stress was laid upon the total repugnance of the measure to the principles upon which our Government rests and which necessarily determine our treatment of citizens at home or abroad.

The impossibility of making any distinction as to our citizens based upon creed or race precludes any recognition of any curtailment of their treaty rights abroad on such grounds, and in entering into reciprocal stipulations for the mutual advantage and protection of our citizens abroad and aliens of the United States, no qualifications of the sole condition of citizenship could be implied or imposed by the other contracting party without being expressly consented to by us.

No treaty has been entered into between the United States and Turkey to curtail the personal rights or liberty of our citizens, and no such curtailment can now be introduced into our conventional obligations at the will of one of the parties thereto. Still less can Turkey claim, as she has appeared to do, our assistance in enforcing a regulation in execution of her claim to apply a discriminatory treatment, the right to which we absolutely deny.

As explained in the Department's reply to Mavroyeni Bey and its instructions to Mr. Straus, the passports we issue can contain no declaration, expressed or inferential, of the creed of the citizens to whom they are issued, or certification of their purpose in going abroad. It is equally incompetent to the Department's agents abroad to make such statements, and still more so to limit the personal freedom of our citizens within their jurisdiction except by due process of law. The guaranty you were asked by the local authorities to give in respect of Freeman and Gliechman would have been expressly and inferentially obnoxious to all objections recited and therefore unlawful. Your refusal to comply with such a request is entirely approved. You can assume no inquisitorial functions in regard to the private and personal affairs of our citizens within your jurisdiction, and so far as their passports are concerned, your official duty is limited to affixing your *visa* as good for your consular district, and to endeavoring to secure for them, without discrimination, the treatment to which law-abiding citizens are entitled by treaty.

A copy of this instruction will be sent, with transcripts of your dispatches, to Minister Straus, for his information.

I am, etc.,

G. L. Rives,
Acting Secretary

In 1889, when Mr. and Mrs. Straus visited Jerusalem, they were presented by the Jerusalem Lodge of the Order B'nai B'rith, with a memorial written in English and Hebrew, engrossed in gold and rubric, as a token of its appreciation of Mr. Straus' activities in behalf of the Jewish immigrants to Palestine. In a note to Secretary Blaine, April 20, 1889, referring to the memorial, Mr. Straus said with great modesty that "considerable allowance must be made for the extravagant language in which the memorial is couched, after the manner of the East."[9]

[*Memorial from Jerushalaim Lodge of the Independent
Order of B'nai B'rith*]

HONORABLE SIR:

Deeply touched by feelings of gratitude for your generous exertions in behalf of our Russian brethren, who, in consequence of dire persecutions, were seeking a refuge in this country, the Jerushalaim Lodge of the Independent Order of B'nai B'rith, at their meeting of the 2nd instant, unanimously and enthusiastically resolved to tender you these expressions of their feelings.

The efficient way in discharging your official duties of the high post you fill will secure you forever the admiration and gratitude not only of your countrymen but also of the Jewish nation throughout the universe. For, if we can boast of merchant princes and renowned names in the field of art and science, you, honorable sir, are the first who shed glory upon the Jewish name as a statesman.

It will always be remembered with deep satisfaction in the annals of the Jewish history that a man, chosen by the enlightened Government of the great American Republic to represent her important interests at the Sublime Porte, never forgot his suffering brethren. You not only came to Jerusalem, accompanied by your noble lady, to pay homage to the sacred memories of our glorious past, but having become acquainted with the restrictive measures taken against foreign Jewish emigrants, you used all your influence with your colleagues and with the well-intentioned Turkish Government, and succeeded in having the exceptional law repealed. It is to you that we owe no more to witness the heartrending scenes of the unhappy emigrants being mercilessly driven from our shores, and therefore our lodge only follows the commands of simple duty in expressing to you their appreciation of your noble deeds and their lasting esteem and gratitude.

DR. HERSBERG, President
EPHRAIM COHEN, Vice-President
BEN ZENUDA, Secretary

[9] Foreign Relations, 1889, page 717.

The right of American Jews to purchase and sell land in Palestine was brought up in the case of Hyman J. Roos in 1893. On March 21, 1893,[10] Mr. Roos sent a complaint to Secretary Gresham against a Turkish proclamation which forbade to Jews all transactions in real estate. It seems that he owned some real estate in Jerusalem and wished to sell it, but was prevented from doing so by the law just mentioned. Mr. Roos's note posed the following two questions: "Has the Government of the United States of America official knowledge of this arbitrary discrimination against citizens of the United States of America on account of their religious belief?" "Is the Government of the United States willing to try inducing the Turkish Government to stop abridging the rights of American citizens?"

Mr. Selah Merrill, American consul at Jerusalem, received instruction from the Department of State in Washington to investigate the matter and see whether this was a proper case for his intervention. Mr. Gresham's dispatch ended with these words: "No religious test can be recognized by this Government, and equal rights under treaties are claimed for all American citizens regardless of the faith they profess."

Mr. Gresham's interest in the case was very much aroused because of Mr. Merrill's note of May 8, 1893. Mr. Merrill reported that he was able to do very little for Mr. Roos. According to the Real Estate Protocol of 1874 between the United States and Turkey, all matters pertaining to land were beyond the jurisdiction of the consulate, so that if there was an order against Jews buying or selling land, he was not aware of it. Should he ask the governor about the existence of such an order, the question would be regarded as an impertinent one, for the Turkish officials were very jealous of the rights of foreigners which treaties with foreign powers gave to them exclusively. Still the treaty did not warrant discrimination against an American citizen because of his religion. There was only one way of finding out whether such an order of discrimination, open or secret, actually existed. That was by putting a specific case to a

[10] Foreign Relations, 1893, page 640.

test. But, complained Mr. Merrill, in the note of May 8, 1893, to Washington, no American Jew was willing to make a trial case. As a result, he had no ground for action, rumors alone being palpably insufficient.

The case was finally referred by Mr. Gresham to Mr. A. W. Terrell, United States Minister at Constantinople, who was directed "to ascertain in such discreet way as suggests itself to you the position of the Turkish Government with regard to this matter, and to report to the Department the result of your inquiry."

The incident closed in a manner favorable to the contention of Mr. Roos. The Turkish Government modified its attitude in the matter of refusing permission to American Jews to buy or sell land in Palestine. It would seem from the final dispatches on this case that the Turkish Government's main objections were against the acquisition of land by non-residents for speculative purposes, with no intention to reside upon the property after the purchase.

In 1894, the Turkish Government again put difficulties in the path of Jews, including American Jews, visiting Palestine. This time the Turkish officials demanded that Jews should deposit a guarantee that they would leave the country within thirty days. Besides, Jews were subjected to all sorts of annoyances, such as having their baggage unnecessarily delayed, being deprived of their passports, and many similar inconveniences and indignities. In a dispatch to Consul General Luther Short, on October 3, 1894, Consul Edwin S. Wallace declared that his complaints to the Turkish Governor against abuse of American Jews had led to no result and that "something more should be done or the indignity will be repeated." He, therefore, begged that the matter be brought before the higher authorities in Constantinople. He urged speed as "any delay on our part in taking note of them will but aggravate the indignity."

In Constantinople, Minister Terrell discovered that the Porte had sent instructions to its consuls in the United States not to visé the passports of Jews who intended to stay in Palestine for more than 90 days, and that their baggage was seized in Jaffa in order to assure their return within that period. His Excellency Saïd Pasha, Turkish Minister of Foreign Affairs, in all seriousness gave to Mr. Terrell the reason for the policy of preventing a large number of Jews from settling in the Holy Land, in the following words:

We believe that Jesus Christ was a great prophet, and if the Jews get control of Jerusalem they will steal the sepulcher of Christ and destroy everything that can remind people of him.

Apprised of the situation by the American minister, Secretary of State Gresham sent the following note to Mr. Terrell:[11]

[*Mr. Gresham to Mr. Terrell*]

Department of State
Washington, November 7, 1894

SIR: Your dispatch No. 324, of the 16th ultimo, relative to the harsh treatment of Jews temporarily resorting to Jerusalem, has been received.

The restriction of the sojourn of visiting Jews in the ancient capital of their race has been enforced for several years past. Mr. Straus, in his No. 57, of January 28, 1888, touches upon the ostensible reasons for this limitation, which was originally fixed at one month and was about that time prolonged to three months. Extended correspondence in regard to the effect of this measure upon American Jews going to Jerusalem is printed in the second volume of Foreign Relations for 1888.

The arbitrary interferences with this class of voyagers which your dispatch reports, such as the detention of their personal effects at Jaffa in order to make their prolonged sojourn in Judea impossible or difficult, should properly call forth urgent remonstrance in the event of injuring any citizen of the United States; and should your surmise that the intolerant course of the Turkish officials in that quarter is prompted by corrupt motives be verified, those unworthy agents will doubtless be severely rebuked by the high authority of the Porte itself — which cannot be supposed to countenance extortion in any form.

As regards the duration of the period during which law-abiding American citizens of the Jewish faith may propose to visit Jerusalem, this Government neither draws nor admits any presumption of intended permanent domicile there from the mere fact of resorting

[11] Foreign Relations, 1894, page 752.

thither. Abandonment of American residence and consequent loss of the right to protection due to bona fide citizens can only be determined by the facts of each case as it may arise. As the records of your legation and of the consulate at Jerusalem will show, this Department has heretofore had occasion to deal with such cases on the facts, and has not hesitated to withdraw protection when permanent domicile in Judea was shown without evident intent to return to this country.

I am, etc.,

W. Q. GRESHAM

In 1901, the Turkish Minister of the Interior issued an order requiring foreign consuls in Palestine to be called upon to compel their subjects to leave the country after the expiration of the 90 days allowed under the passport. It was usual for Jews who entered Palestine and who desired to remain there to refuse to leave the country on the ground of having no money to pay for the return passage. This new Turkish order was intended to put the responsibility for their leaving the country on the shoulders of the foreign consuls.

In answer to a request for instructions as to how American consuls should comply with the new order, Secretary John Hay sent instructions to the American consuls in the following note to Mr. Lloyd C. Griscom, Chargé d'Affaires at Constantinople:[12]

[Mr. Hay to Mr. Griscom]

Department of State
Washington, February 28, 1901

SIR: I have to acknowledge the receipt of your dispatch No. 316 of the 31st ultimo, reporting that you are advised by the United States consul at Jerusalem that the Ottoman minister of the interior has issued a new order respecting the sojourn in Palestine of foreign Jews who go there as pilgrims or visitors.

You state the provisions of the order and request instructions in the premises.

Setting aside the objectionable feature whereby a racial or religious distinction is made in regard to Jews, and of which feature this Government finds difficulty in taking official cognizance, in

---

[12] Foreign Relations, 1901, page 517.

view of our constitutional inhibition against any disability founded
on creed, the Turkish order now reported appears to establish the
rule of three months' permitted sojourn of American visitors to
Palestine, for which we have always contended. See instructions
to Mr. Straus, No. 13, dated October 14, 1898, and subsequent
correspondence, on the subject of the Ottoman regulations respecting the entrance of foreign Jews into Palestine.

It should, however, be made clear to the Turkish authorities
that the consuls of the United States in Turkish jurisdiction are
neither directed nor permitted by law to assist the Turkish officers
in their execution of municipal laws or regulations, and therefore
could not intervene to constrain the departure of an American
citizen from Turkish jurisdiction. Neither can the consul be called
upon to forego the performance of his duty in case an American
citizen should be harshly dealt with in contravention of treaty or law.

As the consul is without authority to compel a visiting American
citizen to deposit his passport and citizen papers in the consulate
it would seem that he is not in a position to contest the Turkish
requirement that such papers be surrendered to the Ottoman
officers during the time of sojourn in Palestine.

I am, etc.,

JOHN HAY

Not until the outbreak of the World War is there another
mention of Jews or Jewish interests in the diplomatic correspondence between the United States and the former Turkish
Empire. Early in the War, the Turks joined the Central
Powers and declared war against Russia, Great Britain and
France, and immediately, as a result, the position of the
American ambassador and the American consuls in Turkey,
as protectors of Jewish life and property, became more important. For the American consul had now to protect the
interests of the nationals of countries at war with Turkey
who, especially in the case of Palestine, were mostly of the
Jewish faith. It would be no exaggeration to say that, had
it not been for the humanitarian activities of the American
Government in Palestine and in other parts of Turkey, many
thousands of Jews, both native and foreign, would have per-
ished in Turkish prisons or have met death by starvation.
It was the American cruisers which helped transport foreign

Jews, nationals of the Allied Powers, from Palestine to Egypt, thus saving them from the wrath of the Turkish officials. The medical and food supplies brought into the country by the cruisers greatly reduced the mortality among Jews, which had risen to abnormally high rates owing to a serious lack of these essentials in Palestine while it was under the rule of the Turkish army.

At the end of August, 1914, the American Jewish Committee received a number of cablegrams from Ambassador Henry Morgenthau urging that the sum of $50,000 be sent immediately to avert the threatened destruction of the Jewish colonies and to relieve the pitiable situation then faced by the Jews of Palestine.[13]

The sum asked for was soon sent to Mr. Morgenthau. The American Jewish Committee contributed $25,000, Mr. Jacob Schiff, $12,500, and the remainder was contributed by the Federation of American Zionists. The Standard Oil Company was helpful by making available to Mr. Morgenthau the sum of $50,000 in gold currency, which otherwise could not have reached its destination. Mr. Otis A. Glazebrook, United States consul in Jerusalem, supervised the relief activities in Palestine.

In 1915, foreign Jews of allied citizenship were given the alternative of either becoming Ottoman subjects or leaving the country. In the majority of cases, the Jews chose the latter. To live in Turkey under a war regime and with no right to appeal to any outside power would have made life insufferable, as was the bitter experience of those Jews who lost foreign protection. Especially difficult was the position of the Jews in Palestine, it being near the war zone and, later, the center of hostilities.

On February 18, 1915, Secretary of State William J. Bryan sent the following telegram to Ambassador Morgenthau:[14]

[13] *American Jewish Year Book*, 1915–16, page 359.
[14] Foreign Relations, 1915, Suppl., page 979.

[Mr. Bryan to Mr. Morgenthau]

[Captain] Decker telegraphed Department through Navy Department that sentiment of people in Syria and Palestine is very strong against Jews, and danger at any moment of outbreak that may destroy life and property. You are instructed to attempt to secure from Turkish Government order to civil and military officials throughout Palestine and Syria that they will be held responsible for lives and property of Jews and Christians in case of massacre or looting. This is required immediately.

Ambassador Morgenthau communicated this telegram to Talaat Pasha, Minister of Interior, who declared that there was no reason for apprehension, and that Jews and Christians were properly protected. However, it was Mr. Morgenthau's unpleasant duty, very soon after, to report by cable about Turkish atrocities against Armenians and that there was reason to believe that this movement against the Armenians would be followed by action against Zionists. On April 2, Secretary Bryan cabled Mr. Morgenthau: "Urge Turkish Government to protect both Armenians and Zionists." Mr. Morgenthau's intercession this time was successful and he was able to cable on May 2 that "we have succeeded in suspending movement against Zionists and secured permission for their representative Jacobson to leave Turkey instead of being expelled."

Ambassador Morgenthau saw that there was great danger for the lives of subjects of the powers engaged in war against Turkey and obtained special permission from the Sublime Porte to have the American cruisers *Tennessee* and *North Carolina* stay in Turkish waters. Very soon, in fact, they were put to good use. Later they were assisted by the *Des Moines* and *Chester*. Most of the foreign Jews chose to leave Palestine rather than become Ottoman subjects. July 14, 1915, was set as the final date, and if they had not by that date assumed Turkish nationality they were to be expelled. After many and great difficulties, the American ships rescued the refugees and transferred them to Alexandria, Egypt.

In a long dispatch of July 27, 1915, reporting on his activities for the relief of the foreign subjects, Ambassador Morgenthau praised the officers and crews of the American ships in the following words:[15]

In this connection I also wish to speak in the highest terms of the service rendered earlier in the year by the *Tennessee* to the Jewish and other refugees which it transported from Jaffa to Alexandria. Many expressions of grateful appreciation of what was done for these people have since reached me, and I cannot speak too highly of the kindly assistance given them by Capt. Benton C. Decker and his officers and men. The use of our cruisers for this purpose has meant much extra work and inconvenience for their officers and crews. But they have satisfied an urgent need, and in their ready and gracious help to those in anxiety and distress will long be remembered by their grateful beneficiaries.

More evidence that the Ottoman Government was eager to use all means to reduce the Jewish population of Palestine appeared very soon. The following month, Ambassador Morgenthau sent the following telegram to Secretary Bryan:[16]

[*Mr. Morgenthau to Mr. Bryan*]

Constantinople, August 16, 1915

There are about 30 British Jews, 420 French Jews, 180 Russian Jews and 200 other belligerent Jews whose respective nationalities unreported and 310 neutral Jews such as Greek, Roumanian, Spanish, and American at Haifa, Jerusalem, Jaffa, and Beirut. The Turkish Government states that unless they are bound to some other country they will intern all of them that are belligerents. Egypt and Rhodes refuse to receive any more Jews. I am trying to obtain reconsideration of Egyptian Government. The Turkish Government refuses permission for any Christian neutral to be transported unless each ship taking neutrals will take three times as many belligerent Jews. Will you kindly communicate with British and French Governments and have them arrange to what port or ports these are to be sent. Glazebrook [American Consul at Jerusalem] telegraphs they are suffering great hardship at the harbors as they have disposed of their homes and are destitute.

[15] Foreign Relations, 1915, Suppl., page 958.
[16] *Ibid.*, page 977.

The Turkish Government's decision has frustrated plans to transport Italian subjects and may lead to an open rupture between Italy and Turkey.

MORGENTHAU

Later, Djemal Pasha, Commander of the Fourth Turkish Army in Syria, laid down the rule that all Jews of belligerent countries should be expelled before other refugees could be taken away. The expelled Jews were saved from the grave danger which faced them in Palestine, namely, internment in special camps for the duration of the war, by the Egyptian Government, which opened its gates and granted them a haven of refuge. The *Des Moines* and the collier *Chester* thereupon called at Jaffa and took away the Jewish and other refugees. This was in December, 1915. After that date no American naval vessels were allowed to call at Syrian ports.

As the Turkish ports were blockaded by an Allied fleet, and Turkey could not produce the needed medical supplies, the civil population was suffering greatly from lack of essential medicines as well as expert medical help. The American Red Cross, with the help of the State Department, attempted to obtain permission to bring those necessities to American hospitals in Beirut, but the Turkish Government would not permit any ship to enter that port, although the British and French were willing to let them pass the blockade. The only route open for the Red Cross party would be through Constantinople.

On February 4, 1916, Secretary Robert Lansing cabled to Consul Glazebrook at Jerusalem as follows:[17]

[Mr. Lansing to Mr. Glazebrook]

Red Cross planning send about February 15 on United States collier about two tons medical supplies for Jewish hospital Jerusalem. Telegraph whether agent Jaffa can arrange send small boat meet collier beyond mined area and land supplies.

Chargé d' Affaires Philip wired back from Constantinople that the Turkish Government would permit landing of these

[17] Foreign Relations, 1916, Suppl., page 925. The United States Embassy was also used as an agency through which money was sent for the relief of the Jewish poor and needy in the Holy Land.

supplies on the condition that no member of the crew went ashore and that no one, not even an American consular official, was to go on board the collier.

But now it was the French Government which stood in the way of landing the supplies. Secretary Lansing communicated by wire with the American ambassadors at Paris and London, asking them to ascertain from the respective Governments to which they were accredited, whether they would relinquish the blockade in favor of landing medical supplies for Jewish hospitals in Jerusalem. And though the Turkish Government again assured the American chargé at Constantinople that the supplies would go directly to the Jewish hospitals and none of it would be requisitioned by Turkish officials, the French and British governments refused to modify the blockade "for very serious military reasons."

Secretary Lansing persisted in his demand upon the French Government and the latter finally agreed to the delivery of hospital supplies for Jerusalem "under certain conditions," to be formulated by Admiral de Spitz, in command of the French blockading squadron, with whom the American consul at Alexandria, where the supplies were stored, was directed to consult. Eventually these supplies reached their destination, but not until Southern Palestine was occupied by the British army under General Allenby. It was then that all relief work was organized, largely through the efforts of Hampson Gary, the American agent and consul general at Cairo, and of the "Special Committee for the Relief of Jews in Palestine." Mr. Gary brought about the co-operation between the relief agencies of the American and Egyptian Jews, as will be evident from the following report which he sent to the Secretary of State:[18]

[*Mr. Gary to Mr. Lansing*]

Cairo, August 24, 1918

SIR: Believing that it would prove of interest to the Department to have a report on some of the work I have performed the past seven months growing out of the British occupation of Palestine I have the honor to submit a *résumé* of same.

[18] Foreign Relations, 1918, Suppl. 2, page 563.

RELIEF WORK

Soon after my arrival in Egypt last January various Jewish organizations in America became active in their endeavor to send financial relief to Palestine (Jerusalem having been captured by the British forces), and I was called upon to investigate and report upon the condition of the people and the measures of relief most needed. At the same time the Jews in Egypt were making similar plans and finally organized the "Special Committee for the Relief of Jews in Palestine." I think I may say that it was largely due to my efforts that cooperation between American and Egyptian Jews took place and that general relief work became centralized in the local Committee. This tended to bring about systematic organization and effective control, and brought the work into more harmonious touch with the military authorities who exercise, of course, absolute authority over all matters in the Holy Land.

When the "Special Committee" in Cairo with its subcommittees in Palestine became organized, I notified the Joint Distribution Committee in New York, and thereafter American relief funds commenced to flow into Palestine through the intermediary of this office.

Upon the arrival in Egypt of the International Zionist Commission, headed by Dr. Weizmann, all Jewish work was absorbed by the Commission. Dr. Weizmann called at the Agency with the members of his Commission to confer with me on the subject of relief in Palestine and other matters, and it was finally decided to establish an office in Cairo to represent the Commission in relief matters with Mr. Jack Mosseri in charge thereof.

I have continued to act as the intermediary for the transmission of all relief funds from America to Palestine — both for general purposes and for individual cases. Many tens of thousands of dollars have been and are being handled by this office for such relief.

AMERICAN ZIONIST MEDICAL UNIT TO PALESTINE

A few days ago there arrived in Egypt the American Zionist Medical Unit to Palestine, a party composed of some 38 members of whom 33 are citizens of the United States. They stopped in Cairo only a brief time on their way to Jerusalem. Mr. Moses Baroway of Baltimore, Md., secretary attached to the Unit, who remained a few days in Cairo, called on me here at the Agency. He told me that there were 20 nurses and 18 physicians in the Unit headed by Miss Alice Seligsberg. He further stated that the Chairman of the Unit, Mr. E. W. Lewin-Epstein, was ill in London but hoped to proceed to Palestine in the near future. In response to his request I gave Mr. Baroway such data and information about Jerusalem and the situation there as I thought might prove helpful to him and told him to write or telegraph me whenever I could further serve him and the American Zionist Medical Unit.

* * * * *

As was the case in connection with relief activities on behalf of the Jews of Poland, the United States and Great Britain differed in their policies toward relief of the Jews of Palestine. Two American Jewish agencies were interested in the latter effort: the American Jewish Joint Distribution Committee and the Provisional Executive Committee for General Zionist Affairs. The State Department was always ready to be helpful in this direction, by lending its services to the relief agencies, and whenever it could not do so itself it approached another friendly government to achieve the same humanitarian aims. It should be remembered that these privileges were extended at a time when the United States had already joined on the side of the Allies and assistance to residents of Turkey was of indirect help to the cause of the enemy. Thus, individual remittances not exceeding $125 per person per month, as well as relief funds in bulk, could be transmitted through a specified bank. It was soon found necessary to qualify this permission by excluding enemy subjects in Turkey. But Jews, Syrians and Armenians who were subjects of the Ottoman Empire were not considered to be "enemy subjects," in this connection. Also, the $125 allowed to an individual was interpreted to include his dependents. It is interesting to note that Ambassador Sir Cecil Spring-Rice, in a letter to Assistant Secretary of State William Phillips, of date December 3, 1917, declared the British policy to be that "*all* subjects of the Ottoman Empire, of whatever race or religion, are enemy subjects, and that funds transmitted to these people will eventually tend to help Turkey to prolong the war." The American point of view was best expressed by the following paragraph taken from the reply of Assistant Secretary Phillips to the above British note:[19]

The grounds upon which we have based our policy in this respect seem to us to be sound, not only from the humanitarian point of view, but from that of expediency as well. We feel that

[19] Foreign Relations, 1918, Suppl. 2, page 550.

the material benefit to the Turkish Government is insignificant compared to the moral and political advantage to our own cause which must result from helping these starving races within reasonable limits.[20]

However, after the British armies had victoriously entered Jerusalem and had also occupied the whole southern part of Palestine, the British Ambassador's view on relief changed somewhat. On December 26, 1917, Sir Cecil Spring-Rice sent the following letter to Mr. Frank L. Polk, Counselor for the Department of State:[21]

[*Sir Cecil Spring-Rice to Mr. Polk*]

Washington, December 26, 1917

MY DEAR MR. COUNSELLOR:

I noticed in the newspapers that the Jews of this country with their usual generosity were sending money to be used in the relief of their co-religionists in the Holy Land, and I was, indeed, approached on the matter by one of them.

In reply to enquiries which I made at London by telegraph, I have been informed that it is proposed to send the eminent Doctor Wise [*Weizmann*] at the head of a small committee to organize relief measures, but that in the meantime there does exist a body named the "Special Committee" under the leadership of Mr. Jack [*Mossui?*] which has its offices at the British Headquarters in Cairo, and that this is the best channel through which at the present time assistance may be rendered: the amounts forwarded ought to be limited, it was added, to such sums as are absolutely indispensable for the most pressing necessities.

[20] The United States and Turkey severed relations in April 1917, but war between them was never declared. Moukhtar Bey, Turkish Under Secretary for Foreign Affairs, stated that American institutions and schools were not to be disturbed. Djavid Bey, Acting Minister of the Interior, sent a telegraphic circular to all provincial authorities, instructing them that "the rupture of diplomatic relations was not a declaration of war, that American citizens and institutions should be treated by the authorities as heretofore, without, however, having any official relations with the American consuls." However, before evacuating Jerusalem, the Turkish authorities arrested all American-Jewish citizens in that city and transported them to Damascus. These deportations were carried out under such intolerable conditions as to cause widespread sickness among refugees, resulting fatally in a number of cases. The American Government took up their cause with the Turkish Government and the cases are still pending at the time of writing.

[21] Foreign Relations, 1918, Suppl. 2, page 550.

I should be greatly obliged if you would bring these facts to the knowledge of the parties concerned, and if you would lend me your assistance, so that the desires of the British authorities, who are doing all that is in their power to cope with the situation, may be duly heeded and their work accordingly facilitated.

Believe me [etc.]

CECIL SPRING RICE

Secretary Lansing duly transmitted the information to the Joint Distribution Committee and the Provisional Committee for General Zionist Affairs.

Early in 1918, there was a movement among American Zionists to dispatch a medical unit to Palestine under the leadership of Mr. E. W. Lewin-Epstein. Lord Reading, British Ambassador on Special Mission, took cognizance of this movement and through his secretary, T. B. Hohler, informed Mr. Lansing that the British Government would not object to such a mission provided it was recognized by the United States Government and the information be further given to the enemy as required by the provisions of the Geneva Convention. Under date of May 17, 1918, Secretary Lansing sent the following memorandum to Lord Reading, extending official recognition to the Jewish Medical Unit as a "society authorized to lend the services of its sanitary personnel and formations to the British Government":[22]

[*The Department of State to the British Embassy*]
Memorandum

The United States of America pursuant to the practice outlined in Article 2 of the convention for the amelioration of conditions of the armies in the field, signed at Geneva, July 6, 1906 (which the United States does not consider as binding on it in the present war), hereby officially recognizes the American Zionist Medical Unit of Palestine as a society authorized to lend the services of its sanitary personnel and formations to the British Government, and consents to its doing so.

Since the United States is not at war with Turkey where the Zionist Unit is to be employed, the society is to be regarded as a society of a neutral state whose function in accordance with existing

[22] Foreign Relations, 1918, Suppl. 2, page 558.

practice is merely to recognize officially the said Unit and to consent to its use. It is presumed that the British Government which is the belligerent to accept the assistance of this Unit, will desire to notify the enemy before making any use of the Unit.

Washington, May 17, 1918

In the summer of 1917, President Wilson sent former Ambassador Henry Morgenthau and Professor Felix Frankfurter of the Harvard Law School abroad as a commission for purposes that were not very clear. As stated, the aim of this commission was to ameliorate the condition of the Jews in Palestine. However, the impression gained ground that the real purpose of the Morgenthau-Frankfurter commission was to break Turkey away from the side of the Central Powers. The story of this commission, whose life was short and shrouded in mystery, may be inferred from the following facts.

On June 21, 1917, Secretary Lansing sent the following telegram to Mr. Arthur Garrels, United States consul at Alexandria, which he was to transmit to Hoffman Philip, Counselor of the Embassy at Constantinople.[23]

[*Mr. Lansing to Mr. Garrels*]

In an effort to ameliorate the Jewish conditions in Palestine the President has sent abroad former Ambassador Henry Morgenthau and Prof. Felix Frankfurter of the Harvard Law School.[24] Mr. Morgenthau will reach Egypt in July, and has asked that you remain to consult with him. Department would be glad to have you assist Mr. Morgenthau in every way.

On the very same day Mr. Morgenthau sailed on the steamship *Buenos Aires* for Cadiz, Spain. A few days later, Secretary Lansing cabled to Ambassador Walter Hines Page in London to inform Mr. Balfour, British Secretary of State for Foreign Affairs, of Mr. Morgenthau's movements, and asked him to arrange that Professor Chaim Weizmann meet Mr. Morgenthau at Gibraltar, "as it is considered most important that Mr. Morgenthau see Mr. Weizmann."

[23] Foreign Relations, 1917, Suppl. 2, Vol. 1, page 108.

[24] Professor Frankfurter was at that time serving as Assistant Secretary of War.

Joseph E. Willard, United States Ambassador to Spain, was also informed that Mr. Morgenthau would reach Cadiz on July 1, in a cabled message which concluded with the following words: "Please telegraph in special red code strictly confidential to the Consul to meet Mr. Morgenthau and tell him that British and French representatives will meet him at Gibraltar. Also that Department understands that Monsieur Weyl will go to Gibraltar, and French consul will have his address."

Presumably the "British and French representatives" of this cable referred to Dr. Weizmann and Monsieur Weyl. But from the first report of the special agents (Morgenthau and Frankfurter) to the Secretary of State, we learn that the announced purpose of the commission, "to ameliorate the Jewish conditions in Palestine" might have been a mask to hide its main task.

The report to the Department of State was signed not only by the American special agents, but also by Dr. Weizmann and Monsieur Weyl. At the Madrid conference of these four agents, which lasted two days, July 4–5, 1917, the Americans stated that President Wilson had received intimations that Turkey was wearying of the war and that some of its leaders, notably Talaat Pasha, Minister of the Interior, and Djavid Bey, the Minister of Finance, would be ready to enter negotiations with the Allies for a separate peace. The President desired to do all that was possible to help detach Turkey from her Allies, and, after sounding out the opinion of England and France, had decided to send a special mission to look into the possibilities of accomplishing it, and at the same time, to meet representatives of the British and French Governments and exchange opinions and information on the subject. It was not thought expedient to make these aims public, for publicity could accomplish nothing, but might hurt and even destroy every possibility of success. But "contemporaneous concern in the United States about the Jews in Palestine furnished a ready instrument for the appointment of a mission and to dispatch it abroad."

At the time this conference took place, conditions on the

various battlefields were unfavorable to the Allies. On the Western Front the Allies had suffered a number of serious reverses, and events as they developed in Russia tended to weaken the influences of those Turkish leaders who were chafing under the control of Germany and who would have liked to break away from that country. In consideration of these facts the conclusion was reached that the time was not ripe to open channels of communication with Turkish leaders but that such a development must await success on the military field.

Dr. Weizmann's suggestion that an American force should participate in the eastern campaign was countered with the statement that the United States was not at war with Turkey.

Reading this report one might conclude that the special agents Morgenthau and Frankfurter were quite sure what the purpose of their mission was, and assumed that the Department of State also possessed the same knowledge. For in the report of July 8, the agents said that in view of the present military situation and the resulting optimism in Turkey "it is useless therefore to proceed to Egypt; Philip's stay there unnecessary." Mr. Morgenthau therefore took advantage of his stay in Europe and went to Aix-les-Bains, France.

It seems, however, that the Department of State was not of the same opinion. On July 13, the Department inquired by telegraph of Ambassador Willard: "By what route is Morgenthau proceeding to Cairo, and at what places may he be reached en route?" On July 14, the Acting Secretary of State, Mr. Polk, sent a dispatch to Mr. Morgenthau through the American Embassy in Paris which read:[25]

[*Mr. Polk to Mr. Morgenthau*]

Department surprised and disturbed by your 670 [the report of July 8] as text of statement set out in cable seems to indicate a belief that you have been authorized to enter into negotiations looking toward separate peace with Turkey.

[25] Foreign Relations, 1917, Suppl. 2, Vol. I, page 129.

Department desires to remind you that your final instructions were to deal solely with conditions of Jews in Palestine. This Government has been most careful not to express any opinion as to terms of peace, and the President hopes that no opinion was expressed at the conference which purported to be the views of this Government. Please report in detail as to purpose of conference and reason for stating views as coming from this Government.

The President requests that you and Frankfurter proceed to Cairo to carry out announced purpose of the mission, and that under no circumstances should you confer, discuss, or carry messages on any subject relating to the international situation in Turkey or bearing upon a separate peace.

Mr. Morgenthau cabled in reply that he had done nothing which in the remotest degree exceeded instructions and that, therefore, neither the President nor the Department of State had any cause to feel disturbed. Professor Frankfurter returned to the United States, and Mr. Morgenthau decided to stay at Aix-les-Bains and await new instructions from the President after he had heard Professor Frankfurter's oral report.

The following month, August 30, 1917, the State Department received a telegram from Ira Nelson Morris, the American Minister in Sweden, as follows:[26]

[*Mr. Morris to Mr. Lansing*]

Stockholm, August 30, 1917

Swedish Chargé d'Affaires, Constantinople, states that—

It appears that the activity of the commission of which ex-Ambassador Morgenthau is the head has created a feeling of uneasiness in Ottoman Government circles as well as among the Jews in this country. It is rumored that the said commission is endeavoring to obtain the political independence of Palestine for the Jews. The local press has published statements from the various Jewish committees and organizations in [Turkey] to the effect that the Jews of Ottoman nationality remain loyal to the local government and that they have always been faithful to their duties as loyal subjects of the Empire. It is possible

[26] Foreign Relations, 1917, Suppl. 2, Vol. 1, page 181.

that these rumors unless denied may have unpleasant results in so far as Americans in Turkey are concerned.

The foregoing is submitted to the Department of State for such action as it may deem necessary.

MORRIS

The whole incident ended with the following telegram of Mr. Lansing to Mr. Morris:[27]

[*Mr. Lansing to Mr. Morris*]

You may inform Swedish Government that there is not the slightest foundation for the report that Morgenthau was proceeding to Europe to obtain political independence of Palestine for the Jews. He is now on his way back to the United States.

In 1917, there arose an agitation in Congress for the declaration of war against Turkey by the Government of the United States. In a confidential memorandum to Senator William J. Stone, chairman of the Foreign Relations Committee, we find this argument against the proposal: "As a final observation, it may be added that if we should declare war against Turkey, the Turks would be likely to retaliate by fresh massacres on the Christians and Jews in the Turkish Empire."

But while the United States never declared war against Turkey, it allowed the recruitment of American Jewish citizens for service with the British army in Palestine. A considerable number of Jews did so enlist and performed valuable service on that front.[28]

---

[27] Foreign Relations, 1917, Suppl. 2, Vol. 1, page 194.

[28] See "With the Zionists in Palestine," by Colonel John Henry Patterson. Here is the place to mention the flag incident which formed the subject of an interesting exchange of telegrams between the United States diplomatic agent in Cairo and the Department of State. On the 20th of July, 1918, a Jewish battalion marched through the principal streets of Cairo carrying with them American, British and Zionist flags, all of equal size. Reporting on this event, Mr. Hampson Gary, the agent, said, "In view of the acute political situation here in connection with Zionist and Arab movements and also the fact that the United States has not declared war on Turkey, feel that this open display of the American flag should be called to the Department's attention." Mr. Polk replied that he had made representation

The discussion for a separate peace with Turkey was revived in the early winter of 1917, as a result of the British victories in Palestine. In a dispatch under date of November 23, 1917, to Secretary Lansing, Ambassador Page advised from London against the conclusion of a separate peace with Turkey. Among the number of reasons advanced by Mr. Page are the following:[29] "Mr. Balfour's letter to Lord Rothschild regarding the future of Palestine has awakened great hopes among the Zionist Jews of this country and press dispatches indicate that it has been read with great interest by the Jews of America. The Zionist feeling should no doubt be kept in mind." Mr. Page's dispatch concluded with the following inquiry: "I should be glad of an intimation of your views on this subject for discreet use in the proper quarter should occasion arise."

On December 15, 1917 Secretary Lansing dispatched the following crisp telegram to Ambassador Page:[30] "Investigate discreetly and report fully and promptly to Department reasons for Balfour's recent statement relative to Jewish State in Palestine." The words "Jewish State" in Mr. Lansing's cable proved that even he himself was not quite clear as to what the British Government aimed at in its declaration.

Mr. Page's reply to Mr. Lansing, cabled from London on December 21, 1917, follows in full:[31]

[Mr. Page to Mr. Lansing]

Lord Robert Cecil, in charge of Foreign Office while Mr. Balfour is ill, informed us that the British Government has an understanding with the French Government that Palestine shall be international nationalized. Mr. Balfour's letter, printed in the *Times* of November 9 merely [stated] that the British Government pledges itself to put

to the British authorities and to the Jewish battalion to prevent the recurrence of such display. It later became known that the American flag was used without authority and even "without the knowledge of the commanding officer of the battalion concerned."

[29] Foreign Relations, 1917, Suppl. 2, Vol. 1, page 317.

[30] *Ibid.*, page 473.

[31] *Ibid.*, page 483.

[apparent omission] the Jews in Palestine on the same footing as other nationalities. No discrimination shall be made against them. This is as far the British Government has yet gone.

Then followed an informal conversation. An internationalized Palestine must be under the protection of some great power. Lord Robert speaking only for himself feared that the continental powers would not agree that any one of them should hold the protectorate and some of them would object even to England's holding it. Still speaking informally and only for himself he hoped that the United States would consent to be the protecting power when the time comes, and he felt sure that all the powers would gladly agree.

At the Peace Conference, and after the mandatory principle was already adopted for the administration of those territories which were taken from Germany and her allies, President Wilson sent Messrs. Charles R. Crane and Henry C. King as a commission to Syria and Palestine to sound out the desire of the population as to who should be their Mandatory Power. The Crane-King Commission subsequently reported that their first choice would be the United States of America, Great Britain being second. In a confidential part of the same report, "for the use of Americans only," the commissioners advised modification of the extreme Zionists' program for Palestine so as to make it clear that "a national home for the Jews in Palestine is not equivalent to making Palestine into a Jewish state."

President Wilson and other members of the United States mission to the Peace Conference at Versailles were very helpful to the Zionist cause whenever occasion arose. In his one visit to the United States, during the course of the Conference, the President made the following statement to a Jewish committee composed of Judge Julian W. Mack, Dr. Stephen S. Wise, Louis Marshall and Bernard G. Richards:

As to your presentations touching Palestine, I have before this expressed my personal approval of the declaration by the British Government regarding Palestine. I am moreover persuaded that the Allied nations with the fullest concurrence of our own Government and people are agreed that in Palestine there shall be laid the foundation of a Jewish commonwealth.

Though not a member of the League of Nations, the United States demanded the same rights and privileges, notably the provisions for the open door and equal opportunity in the matter of concessions in mandated territories, including Palestine, which the mandate accorded to all League members. A long series of letters was exchanged over a number of years between the Governments of the United States and Great Britain.[32] The latter Government was of the opinion "that the terms of the mandates can only properly be discussed at the Council of the League of Nations by the signatories of the Covenant."[33] In other words, according to this view, as given by Lord Curzon, British Secretary of State for Foreign Affairs, to Mr. John W. Davis, the United States Ambassador to the Court of St. James, citizens of the United States would enjoy in the mandated territories a status inferior to that of nationals of members of the League.

Mr. Bainbridge Colby, Secretary of State, objected strenuously to the British point of view, and in a letter to Lord Curzon, of November 20, 1920, he claimed equality for the United States as a matter of right, saying:[34]

Such powers as the Allied and Associated Nations may enjoy or wield in the determination of governmental status of the mandated areas accrued to them as a direct result of the war against the Central powers. The United States as a participant in that conflict and as a contributor to its successful issue cannot consider any of the Associated powers, the smallest not less than itself, debarred from the discussion of any of its consequences, or from participation in the rights and privileges secured under the mandates provided for in the treaties of peace.

In a note to the President and members of the Council of the League of Nations, Secretary of State Colby reiterated the American attitude on the same question, and insisted that draft mandates be communicated to the United States for its consideration before their submission to the Council, in order "that the Council might thus have before it an expression of the opinion of the Government of the United

---

[32] See "Mandate for Palestine," prepared by the United States Department of State, Division of Near Eastern Affairs, 1927.

[33] *Ibid.*, page 35.

[34] *Ibid.*, page 39.

States on the form of such mandates, and a clear indication
of the basis upon which the approval of this Government,
which is essential to the validity of any determination which
may be reached, might be anticipated and received."[35] Otherwise, he continued, the Government of the United States
would not regard itself bound by the terms and provisions
of such mandates.

In reply, Mr. Gastao da Cunha, President of the Council
of the League, declared that no conclusion with regard to
"A" Mandates will be reached "until the United States has
had an opportunity to express its views."

In a memorandum to the British Foreign Office the position
of the United States with regard to the Mandate for Palestine
was clarified. Specifically, the United States demanded
that it be given capitulatory rights, that provision be made
for American consular tribunals in Palestine, that American
citizens be not subjected to any sort of discrimination, and
that American missionaries be allowed to practice in
Palestine. From a letter of Eyre A. Crowe, British Under
Secretary of State for Foreign Affairs, to Ambassador George
Harvey, December 24, 1921, in reply to the American memorandum, the following statement is quoted which, incidentally, throws some light on how the British Government
of that time viewed the development of the Palestine
mandate.[36]

His Majesty's Government regret that they cannot see their
way to adopt the suggested introduction into the Palestine mandate of the provision of Article 7 of the "B" mandate for East Africa
on the subject of concessions quoted in your memorandum of
August 21. The suggestion appears to His Majesty's Government
to overlook the peculiar conditions existing in Palestine and especially the great difference in the natures of the tasks assumed in
that country and undertaken by them in East Africa. So far as
Palestine is concerned, Article 11 of the mandate expressly provides that the administration may arrange with the Jewish agency,
mentioned in Article 4, to develop any of the natural resources of
the country in so far as these matters are not directly undertaken
by the administration. The reason for this is that, in order that

[35] "Mandate for Palestine," page 42.
[36] *Ibid.*, page 56.

the policy of establishing in Palestine a national home for the Jewish people should be successfully carried out, it is impracticable to guarantee that equal facilities for developing natural resources of the country should be granted to persons or bodies who may be actuated by other motives. The general spirit of the Palestine mandate in the view of His Majesty's Government, seems to render unnecessary the insertion of an especial provision preventing the Mandatory from developing the natural resources of the country for his own benefit.

The United States succeeded, however, in winning over the British Government to its own point of view. While Lord Arthur Balfour was on a special mission to the United States serving as head of the British delegation to the Washington Conference of 1921–22, he exchanged letters with Mr. Charles E. Hughes, then United States Secretary of State, concerning the Mandate for Palestine. On behalf of his Government, he accepted the proposals of the United States as expressed in the American memorandum, but suggested that they be incorporated in a separate treaty and not in the Mandate itself. Article 8 of the Palestine Mandate, which deals with the rights and immunities of foreigners, was modified as a direct result of the intervention of the United States, and a new paragraph was added providing that the privileges and immunities of foreigners, including the benefits of consular jurisdiction and protection formerly enjoyed by capitulation or usage in the Ottoman Empire, should be re-established immediately after the expiration of the Mandate.

Lord Curzon was anxious that the convention between the United States and Great Britain regarding Palestine should contain "a specific allusion to the policy of establishing a national home for the Jewish people in Palestine." At his suggestion, the preamble of the convention incorporated the preamble and the full text of the Mandate for Palestine.[37]

[37] The Preamble of the Mandate for Palestine, after reciting the Balfour Declaration of November 2, 1917, in favor of a national home for the Jews in Palestine, declares that "recognition has thereby been given to the historical connection of the Jewish people with Palestine and to the grounds for reconstituting their national home in that country." ("Mandate for Palestine," page 109.)

Article 1 of the convention itself declares that "subject to the provision of the present convention, the United States consents to the administration of Palestine by His Britannic Majesty pursuant to the mandate recited above."

Other pertinent articles are Articles 2 and 7:

Article 2. The United States and its nationals shall have and enjoy all the rights and benefits secured under the terms of the mandate to members of the League of Nations and their nationals, notwithstanding the fact that the United States is not a member of the League of Nations.

Article 7. Nothing contained in the present convention shall be affected by any modification which may be made by the terms of the mandate, as recited above, unless such modification shall have been assented to by the United States.

In other words, according to Article 7, Great Britain cannot change or propose a change in the status of Palestine unless it has first received the consent of the Government of the United States to that change.

In April, 1922, the Foreign Affairs Committee of the House of Representatives held public hearings on the following resolution which had been introduced by Representative Hamilton Fish, Jr., of New York:

[*Resolution by Representative Hamilton Fish, Jr.*]

Whereas the Jewish people have for many centuries believed in and yearned for the rebuilding of their ancient homeland; and whereas owing to the outcome of the World War and their part therein the Jewish people, under definite and adequate international guarantees are to be enabled, with due regard to the rights of all elements of the population of Palestine and to the sanctity of its holy places, to recreate and reorganize a national home in the land of their fathers: Therefore be it

Resolved by the House of Representatives (the Senate concurring,) that the Congress of the United States hereby expresses its profound satisfaction in the outcome of the victorious war which promises the building up of a new and beneficent life in Palestine, rejoices in this act of historic justice about to be consummated, and on behalf of the American people commends an undertaking which will do honor to Christendom and give to the House of Israel its long-denied opportunity to reestablish a fruitful Jewish life and culture in the ancient Jewish land.

Subsequently, this resolution was replaced by a joint resolution, introduced simultaneously in both Houses, by Representative Fish and Senator Henry Cabot Lodge. The Fish-Lodge Resolution, which was passed unanimously, and was signed by President Harding on September 21, 1922, reads as follows:[38]

Joint Resolution favoring the establishment in Palestine of a national home for the Jewish people.

Resolved, etc. That the United States of America favors the establishment in Palestine of a national home for the Jewish people, it being clearly understood that nothing shall be done which may prejudice the civil and religious rights of Christians and all other non-Jewish communities in Palestine, and that the holy places and religious buildings and sites in Palestine shall be adequately protected.

The people of the United States expressed on a number of occasions their sympathies with the Jewish aspirations in their ancient homeland and their interest in the development of the Jewish national home. President Wilson and all American presidents since have publicly and often expressed themselves in full sympathy with these aspirations.

The policies pursued by the Mandatory Power have been the target for much adverse criticism. Although the number of Jews in Palestine had grown from 80,000 in 1920 to about 425,000 in 1939, and in spite of the greater achievements in agricultural and urban enterprises by Jewish individuals and organizations, many Jews in Palestine and elsewhere still felt that the development of the Jewish national home in Palestine was consistently hampered by the British administration.

The Arab population in Palestine, still the overwhelming majority, on the other hand, fear their own eventual displacement in the life of the country by an ever-growing Jewish immigration. The Arab leaders refused and still refuse to recognize the Mandate because it embodied the recognition of the Jewish rights in Palestine created in the Balfour Declaration and in the Mandate itself.

There thus developed a feeling of antagonism between the

[38] *Congressional Record*, 67th Congress, 2d Session, Part 10, page 10210.

two portions of the population which brought many disturbances that at times reached major proportions, causing the loss of many lives and the destruction of much valuable property.

This antagonism reached its climax in the disturbances of 1936, which lasted for over two years and seriously hampered the economic life of the country. The weakness and indecision of the Palestine Administration helped aggravate the situation, and the British Government was forced to take action.

A commission of six, headed by Viscount Peel as chairman, was sent to Palestine for the purpose of inquiring into the manner in which the Mandate had been conducted, of discovering the grounds for complaints or grievances by Jew and Arab, and, finally, of recommending a possible solution.

The investigation was opened in Jerusalem on November 12, 1936. The Commission held meetings, public and secret, at which testimony from many sources was heard. Members of the Commission also visited the troubled areas in the country. Further hearings were held in London.

In its report the Commission recommended that the present Mandate be replaced by the partition of Palestine into a Jewish State, an Arab State and a British Mandate. By far the largest part would go to the Arab State. Less than one-third of the country would go to the proposed Jewish State; the city of Jerusalem, the corridor to the port of Jaffa, the "Holy Cities"— Nazareth, Bethlehem, etc. — would go to the British Mandate; and the Port of Haifa would virtually remain under the British Mandate for the "present." The city of Tel-Aviv and most of the colonies near the Mediterranean would be in the Jewish zone, but the great potash works at the Dead Sea, the Ruthenberg power plant at Dagania, and possibly Tiberias would be in the Arab zone.

The British government accepted the partition plan in principle but this plan was not approved by the House of Commons. The government was authorized to present the plan to the Council of the League of Nations. This action did not lessen but seemed rather to heighten the disturbances in Palestine.

The American Government took official recognition of the British plan for the division of Palestine as established by the Anglo-American convention of 1924. There was an exchange of notes between the British Foreign Office and the United States Embassy in London.

Ambassador Robert W. Bingham, in a note to the British Foreign Office, referred to the convention of 1924, and reminded Mr. Anthony Eden that no change in the Government of Palestine can take place without the previous consent of the Government of the United States.[39]

[Note of July 6, 1937, from the American Ambassador at London to the Foreign Office]

The American Ambassador presents his compliments to His Majesty's Principal Secretary of State for Foreign Affairs and has the honor to inform Mr. Eden that the United States Government would be glad to receive at the earliest possible moment a detailed elucidation of the official British position, having regard to the terms of the American-British Convention of December 3, 1924, on the question of consulting the United States Government with respect to any changes that may be proposed in Palestine as the result of the report of the Royal Commission.

In a response to this note the British Government gave a rather restricted interpretation to the terms of the British American convention:

[Note of July 7, 1937, from the Foreign Office to the American Ambassador at London]

With reference to Your Excellency's memorandum No. 2662 of the 6th July, I have the honor to inform you that, in the view of His Majesty's Government in the United Kingdom, the rights of the United States Government and their nationals in regard to Palestine depend on the terms of the "Convention between the United Kingdom and the United States of America respecting the rights of the governments of the two countries and their respective nationals in Palestine," which was signed in London on the 3d December, 1924, and of which the ratifications were exchanged in

[39] *The New York Times*, August 14, 1937, page 2.

London on the 3d December, 1925. The rights of the United States Government and their nationals as regards Palestine are those recited in Articles 2 to 6 of the Convention, and in Article 7 of the Convention these rights must remain intact whatever changes may be made in the mandate for Palestine, unless the United States assent to such a change.

2. In the view of His Majesty's Government, however, these rights are limited to those specified in the articles of the Convention referred to above, and the consent of the United States Government will, therefore, not be required to any change in the Palestine mandate unless the specific rights in question are thereby affected.

Indeed, the United States having assented, by Article 1 of the Convention, to the mandate as a whole, it follows that the United States Government has accepted the provision in Article 27 of the mandate which lays down that the mandate may be altered with the consent of the Council of the League of Nations.

His Majesty's Government in the United Kingdom proposes to seek the consent of the Council of the League at its September session for any changes in the mandate of Palestine which may be required as the result of the Royal Commission's report; but, should any such changes affect any of the United States rights laid down in Articles 2 to 6 of the Convention referred to above, His Majesty's Government will immediately inform the United States Government and seek its consent thereto.

3. While the foregoing represents the views of His Majesty's Government as to its legal obligations toward the United States Government in the matter, they fully appreciate, and indeed welcome, the interest taken by the United States Government in the question of the solution of the Palestine problem, and it is their intention to keep the United States Government fully informed of any proposals which they may put forward to the Council of the League for the modification of the mandate.

The American note of August 4 reiterated the American claim that the views of the Government of the United States be given, as a matter of right, full consideration before any modification of the Mandate for Palestine takes place.

*[Note of August 4, 1937, from the American Ambassador
at London to the Foreign Office]*

I have the honor to acknowledge the receipt of your note of July 7, 1937, concerning the rights of the United States and its nationals in Palestine, as determined by the American-British Convention of December 3, 1924.

Since the receipt of the above-mentioned note, the report of the Royal Commission of Inquiry on Palestine has been published and my Government has noted that the commission proposes that the mandate for Palestine should terminate and be replaced by a treaty system in accordance with the precedent set in Iraq and Syria.

In this general connection, His Majesty's Government will recall that at the time of the termination of the special relations between the United Kingdom and Iraq in 1932, the United States Government set forth in some detail its views regarding its rights relating to the termination of mandatory regimes. At the request of my Government, which was anxious to have its views in this matter receive wide publicity, His Majesty's Government was good enough to transmit copies of that correspondence to the League of Nations, and the text of the correspondence was reproduced in the League of Nations Official Journal for January, 1933.

The attitude of the American Government, as revealed by this correspondence, was summed up in two paragraphs, one of which appeared in a letter dated March 1, 1932, from the first secretary of this embassy to the head of the Eastern Department of the Foreign Office and the other in an aide-memoire, dated July 8, 1932, left at the Foreign Office by this embassy. For convenience of reference these paragraphs are quoted below:

> Since the termination of a regime in a mandated territory necessarily involves the 'disposition' of the territory and affects the interests of American nationals therein, the right of the United States to be consulted with respect to the conditions under which the territory is subsequently to be administered is on precisely the same basis as its right to be consulted with regard to the establishment of a mandatory regime.
>
> Accordingly, the American Government desires| to |make a full reservation of its position in this matter and, with a view to avoiding any possible misconception which may arise in the future, to make clear that its action in refraining from insisting upon a fulfillment of its rights in the case of Iraq is not to be construed as an abandonment of the principle established in 1921 that the approval of the United States is essential to the validity of any determination which may be reached regarding mandated territories.

The views of my Government as set forth in the above-mentioned correspondence are, of course, fully applicable to the proposed termination of the Palestine mandate, and it is pertinent to add that those views were brought to the attention of the French Government in August, 1936, during the negotiations between the French Government and a Syrian delegation looking to the termination of the Syrian mandate. It is hardly necessary, however, to repeat the assurances heretofore communicated to His Majesty's Government that the position of my Government as set forth in the quoted correspondence is based exclusively on its obligation and purpose to provide for the protection of American interests in Palestine on a basis of equality with those of other governments and their nationals.

In expressing satisfaction and appreciation for the assurances furnished that His Majesty's Government intends to keep the United States Government fully informed of any proposals which may be made to the Council of the League of Nations for the modification of the Palestine mandate, I am instructed to request that these proposals may be communicated to my Government in ample time to enable it to determine what, if any, observations it may desire to make with a view to the preservation of American rights in Palestine.

Meanwhile protests against the partition of Palestine were heard in the Congress of the United States. Perhaps the most notable of these was that of Senator J. Hamilton Lewis of Illinois, who had been against the Balfour Declaration in its original phrasing, and now objected to the proposed division of Palestine. From his speech of July 22nd, we quote the following passages:[40]

What I beg to call to the attention of the Senate is the situation of the American Jew who has settled in portions of that country in compliance with the charitable and generous opportunity given by his own people. In that connection, recall that our American Jews have expended millions of American money in the Holy Land for the settlers . . . I deny the right of any land or any nation to have removed this American without consideration of America or representatives of the American Jew . . . .

I respectfully insist that we recognize the sacred history and the sacred established fact that as to Jerusalem the Jews have had so long a claim and so long a rightful privilege that we recognize it as sacred. Today we may turn to the sacred law and repeat the claim of the children of Abraham that this home should belong to Jews, as should the well, because their father had digged the well and set the landmarks of the sacred habitation.

Early in January, 1938, the British Government published a White Paper on Palestine in which it stated that it did

---

[40]*Congressional Record*, 75th Congress, 1st session, Vol. 81, Part 8, page 7363.

not consider itself committed to the Partition Plan, and that another commission would be sent to further investigate the condition prevailing in Palestine. The situation in Palestine from a political and economic point of view continued unhealthy. Acts of Arab terrorism, after a short recession, were revived with greater intensity. These outbreaks were now turned against the British as well as against the Jews; nor were the lives and property of moderate Arabs safe from these attacks. The weak and vacillating policy of the Palestine Administration helped the influence of the rebels in almost every corner of the country. Eventually London was forced to send a small army to Palestine and "reconquer" many towns and villages which for a time were held by the rebels.

But what the Arab rebels were not able to gain by force of their arms, the British now seemed willing to grant them as a gesture of goodwill, incidentally endangering the very existence of the Jewish national home. Reports from London clearly indicated that the British Government was now ready to change its Palestinian policy in such a way as to amount to practical surrender to the maximum demands of the extremist Arab leaders.

Even before this change of policy was officially announced, the President of the United States and the Department of State were flooded with letters and telegrams protesting against the betrayal of the Jewish cause in Palestine. These protests came from almost every corner of the land from gentiles as well as Jews. President Franklin D. Roosevelt was asked to take action in a petition signed by 51 Senators, 194 Representatives and 30 Governors. The President expressed his sympathy and promised to do "all in his power" to prevent curtailment of Jewish immigration to Palestine.

The official attitude to the proposed change in the government of Palestine was expressed in a statement issued by Secretary of State Cordell Hull on October 14, 1938, in response to a petition presented to him by a delegation representing every section of organized Jewish life in the United States.

In this petition the Jewish spokesmen appealed to the Department of State to take suitable action to urge upon the British Government a reaffirmation and a fulfillment of its pledge to facilitate the establishment of the Jewish national home and to assist and encourage immigration of Jews into Palestine. The petition pointed out that the Government of the United States possesses an indisputable right to intercede both on legal grounds, since the consent of the American Government is required before any change in the international status and political structure of Palestine can be effected, and also on humanitarian grounds, since the abolition of the Mandate would further aggravate the indescribable plight of the refugees from lands of oppression who could no longer find a haven in their ancient homeland.

In his statement Secretary Hull declared that while the American people and its government have on a number of occasions manifested their sympathy and interest in a Jewish homeland, the United States cannot, on the basis of the Anglo-American convention of 1924, prevent the modification of the terms of the Mandate. The full text of the statement is as follows:[41]

[*Statement by Mr. Hull*]

Within the past few days this government has received a large number of telegrams and letters from individuals and organizations in the United States concerning the Palestine situation, with particular reference to the reported possibility of the application by the British Government of a new policy with respect to that country. It is obviously impracticable to reply separately to the many communications which have been received and this statement is therefore being issued in lieu of individual answers.

As is well known the American people have for many years taken a close interest in the development of the Jewish National Home in Palestine. Beginning with President Wilson each succeeding President has on one or more occasions expressed his own interest in the idea of a National Home and his pleasure at the progress made in its establishment. American sympathy in a Jewish homeland in Palestine was further manifested by the joint resolution of Congress signed by the President on September 21, 1922, recording the favorable attitude of the United States toward

[41] *The New York Times*, October 15, 1938, page 1.

such a homeland. In submitting the resolution the House Committee on Foreign Affairs reported that it "expresses our moral interest in and our favorable attitude toward the establishment in Palestine of a National Home for the Jewish people. It commits us to no foreign obligation or entanglement."

It is in the light of this interest that the American Government and people have watched with the keenest sympathy the development in Palestine of the National Home, a project in which American intellect and capital have played a leading role.

On several occasions this government has brought its views regarding the rights of the United States and its nationals in Palestine to the attention of the British Government. As recently as 1937, a formal exchange of correspondence took place and the following self-explanatory paragraph is quoted from the concluding note dated August 4, 1937, communicated by the American Ambassador in London to the British Foreign Office:

> In expressing satisfaction and appreciation for the assurances furnished that His Majesty's Government intends to keep the United States Government fully informed of any proposals which may be made to the Council of the League of Nations for the modification of the Palestine Mandate, I am instructed to request that these proposals may be communicated to my government in ample time to enable it to determine what, if any observations it may desire to make with a view to the preservation of American rights in Palestine.

It is expected, therefore, that this government will have an opportunity to submit its views to the British Government with respect to any changes affecting American rights which may be proposed in the Palestine Mandate. These rights, which are defined by the American-British Mandate Convention or Treaty of December 3, 1924, comprise non-discriminatory treatment in matters of commerce, non-impairment of vested American property rights, permission for American nationals to establish and maintain educational, philanthropic and religious institutions in Palestine, safeguards with respect to the judiciary, and, in general, equality of treatment with all other foreign nationals.

The rights of the United States in connection with any changes in the terms of the Palestine Mandate are set forth in Article 7 of the above-mentioned treaty, which reads as follows:

> Nothing contained in the present Convention shall be affected by any modification which may be made in the terms of the Mandate, as recited above, unless such modification shall have been assented to by the United States.

This Article is substantially identical with corresponding articles included in eight other existing agreements concluded by this government with respect to the mandated territories of Syria and the Lebanon, former German islands in the North Pacific; French Cameroons, French Togoland, Belgian East Africa, British Cameroons, British East Africa and British Togoland.

None of these articles empower the Government of the United States to prevent the modification of the terms of any of the mandates. Under their provisions, however, this government can decline to recognize the validity of the application to American interests of any modification of the mandates unless such modification has been assented to by the Government of the United States.

It is the department's understanding that the Palestine Partition Commission, which was appointed some months ago to make recommendations with respect to partition, will make its report to the British Government at the end of this month, and that no decision will be reached by that government on the subject until after an opportunity has been had to give consideration to that report.

In reply to a question in the House of Commons on October 6, 1938, Mr. MacDonald, British Colonial Secretary, is reported to have stated that the House of Commons would not be in the position of having to confirm or reject a decision already taken and put into operation, but would have an opportunity of considering the policy before it was adopted and put into operation by the British Government.

The department will, of course, continue to follow the situation closely and will take all necessary measures for the protection of American rights and interests in Palestine.

Despite many protests against a new policy, the British Cabinet, on November 9, 1938, published a statement declaring that, after a careful study of the Whitehead Report, it had reached the conclusion that the creation of independent Arab and Jewish states in Palestine is impracticable, that the surest foundation for peace and progress would be an Arab-Jewish understanding, and that the government is prepared to make a determined effort to bring about such an understanding.

The British soon called a Round Table Conference on Palestine to which Jews and Arabs were invited to send delegations. Most of the Arab delegation belonged to the extreme faction, and insisted on complete independence of

Palestine and the immediate establishment of an Arab State. The Arab delegation, to which were added representatives from neighboring Arab countries, refused to meet the Jews in conference, denying that the Jews had any legal right to participate in the parleys.

As the Jewish delegation was unwilling to consider any plan which would involve curtailment of Jewish immigration into Palestine, and insisted on adherence to the Balfour Declaration, the conference was bound to fail even before it started. Thus, though the parleys which began on February 7, 1939, did not adjourn until March 17, they failed of their purpose. On the latter day, both the Jewish and Arab delegations submitted their formal rejection of the Government proposals. The British Government thereupon proceeded to impose its own solution on the country, which, in the main, paralleled its previous proposals at the Round Table parleys.

On May 17, the British Government published a White Paper which embodied the new plan for the government of Palestine. It declared the Government's desire "to see established ultimately an independent Palestine State. It should be a state in which the two peoples in Palestine, Arabs and Jews, share authority in government in such a way that the essential interests of each are secured." This new state would be established ten years after peace has been restored in the country. In the future Palestine, the Jews, according to this plan, would be a permanent minority, never to rise to more than a third of the population of the country.

The White Paper was approved by both houses of Parliament only after a bitter debate in which the Government was accused of betraying the Jewish cause in Palestine. Many Conservatives abstained from voting as a protest and expression of their dissatisfaction with the Government's plan.

In the United States, too, fifteen members of the House Foreign Affairs Committee urged the State Department to protest Britain's Palestine policy, and termed the White Paper a "clear repudiation" of the 1924 Anglo-American Convention, in spite of the fact that the White Paper promised to see to it that "the interests of certain foreign countries in Palestine, for the preservation of which they [the British Government] are at present responsible, are adequately safeguarded." That the British Cabinet itself felt that its proposed solution for the future of Palestine was not based on the merits of the case but rather on political expediency of the moment is evidenced from a statement reputedly made by Lord Halifax, Secretary of State for Foreign Affairs, that there are times when ethical considerations must yield to practical necessity.

It is generally believed that this so-called proposed solution is not the final word on Palestine. Its future fate will rather depend upon the turn of events and decisions reached in larger fields of the international political and military arena.

The outbreak of the second world war brought to an end the civil strife between the Jews and Arabs in Palestine. The two communities even tended to co-operate along many lines as Palestine was threatened again and again with becoming a military battleground. At the time of writing,* the danger is more acute than ever before.

As for the British policy regarding Palestine, it may well be said that, owing largely to the exigencies of war, this policy has, in practice, undergone many changes, though officially it has not been altered.

The fate of Palestine must await the decision to be reached at the coming Peace Conference when the question of Palestine will undoubtedly be on the agenda. At this conference, the voice of the United States will have a decisive influence on the outcome.

*June 1942.

PART TWO

RUMANIA AND POLAND

V. RUMANIA

The treatment of Jews in Rumania has been the subject of international diplomatic intervention for almost a century, beginning long before Rumania was recognized by the nations of the world, first, as the Government of the Principalities, Moldavia and Wallachia, and then as the kingdom of Rumania. While in most countries of Europe the period of enlightenment initiated by the French Revolution brought about the extension to Jews of religious, civil and political equality, in Rumania the Government not only retained its medieval laws but in the early nineteenth century passed new ones aimed directly against the personal liberty and economic security of the Jewish population. When, after the Crimean War, the European concert of powers met at Paris in 1856 and in 1858, the status of Jews in Rumania was among the subjects discussed. Though the reference to equality in the Convention of Paris was mainly to the extension of equality to Protestant Christians among the Moldavians and Wallachians, who were mainly of the Greek Orthodox Church, the Convention also provided that "the enjoyment of these rights may be extended to other religions by legislative arrangement." Though "other religions" referred to Jews, the latter derived no benefit from this clause. Their situation in the Principalities changed if anything for the worse. It proved to be an example of the practice subsequently followed by Rumania in all international negotiations with regard to her treatment of her Jewish inhabitants, of giving them promises which she did not fulfill. The same procedure was followed many times later and it explains why to this day the condition of the Jews in Rumania, now greatly enlarged in territory, and having a Jewish population of approximately a million souls, is far from satisfactory, despite the pledges of equality of treatment to which Rumania subscribed in the minorities treaty with the Allied and Associated Powers which followed the World War.

As far back as June 14, 1867, the Board of Delegates of American Israelites brought to the attention of the Department of State the wrongs to which the Jews of Rumania were being subjected, and requested the good offices of our Government in behalf of their coreligionists in the Danubian principalities. Edward Joy Morris, United States Minister to Constantinople, reported to Mr. Seward, under date of July 12, 1867, that Mr. Golesco, the agent of the Danubian principalities, had denied that there had been any real persecution and that the action of the government was of purely defensive character. Mr. Morris reported himself as replying that whatever might be the object of the Government, its acts had all the appearance of religious persecution, and that the confidence of the Government of the United States in the Government of Bucharest would be impaired unless the proscriptive measures against the Jews were discontinued.

Reference to the Jews in Rumania appeared again in 1870 when attacks on Jews were renewed. In the House of Representatives Mr. Boyd Winchester of Kentucky offered the following resolution[1] on June 1, 1870:

Resolved, that the House of Representatives of the United States learns with profound regret and disapproval, of the gross violations of the great principle of religious liberty by some of the people of the province of Roumania, in Turkey, in their late persecutions and outrages against the Israelites, and hereby express the earnest hope that they will speedily cease.

In the same month President Grant appointed Mr. Benjamin F. Peixotto, Grand Master of the Order B'nai B'rith, to serve as United States consul at Bucharest, and, at his request, without remuneration.

President Grant gave Mr. Peixotto the following letter of introduction written in his own handwriting to Prince Charles, the ruler of Rumania:[2]

---

[1] *Congressional Globe*, 41st Congress, 2nd Session, Part 5, page 4062.
[2] *The Jewish Times*, Vol. II, page 250.

Executive Mansion
Washington, D. C.
December 8, 1870

The bearer of this letter, Mr. Benjamin Peixotto, who has accepted the important though unremunerative position of United States Consul to Rumania, is commended to the good offices of all representatives of this Government abroad.

Mr. Peixotto has undertaken the duties of his present office more as a missionary work for the benefit of the people he represents than for any benefit to accrue to himself — a work in which all citizens will wish him the greatest success. The United States, knowing no distinction of her own citizens on account of religion or nativity, naturally believes in a civilization the world over which will secure the same universal view.

U. S. GRANT

Mr. Peixotto, who, as consul, addressed his diplomatic notes to William Hunter, the Second Assistant Secretary of State, sent copious dispatches on the Rumanian situation. His reception by the Prince was most gracious, and Mr Peixotto was pleased to inform Mr. Hunter in the dispatch given below, that the act of the United States Government in appointing him exercised a great moral influence.[3]

[*Mr. Peixotto to Mr. Hunter*]

Consulate of the United States of America
Bucharest, October 6, 1871

SIR:

... Concerning the persecution of the Jews, I am pleased to say that the action of our Government has realized, thus far, the moral influence it was hoped my appointment and acceptance of the position would exercise.

My official reception by the prince, as I have already communicated, was most gracious. The sentiments of humanity he was pleased to express have been practically carried out in a more jealous regard for, and protection of, the rights of the oppressed Israelites. While it has been impossible to restrain prejudices fostered by designing men, mostly for political ends and in many instances for the purposes of robbery, every attempt at open violence has been promptly quelled and effective measures taken to prevent outrage.

[3] Senate Executive Documents, No. 75, 42nd Congress, 2nd Session, 1872.

The actual cabinet of His Highness are in perfect accord with his humane and enlightened sympathies, while no previous legislature has exhibited such marked appreciation of a question which affects in so vital degree the moral and material interests of the land. The best hopes are cherished by the friends of order and stability for the realization of the emancipation of the Jews, and of a more just and enlightened policy towards strangers.

I am, sir, etc.,

BENJ. F. PEIXOTTO
United States Consul

But not very much later Mr. Peixotto had a totally different story. In February 1872, he reported from Bucharest very deplorable scenes in a number of Bessarabian towns, where the population had rushed upon the Jews and hundreds of families were beaten and robbed, and "blood has been shed."

Because of the many protests these unfortunate events evoked in almost all European chancelleries and, incidentally, because it also throws some light on what justice could mean in Rumania, the story of the riots at Ismail, Vilcov, and Cahul deserves to be told in some detail.

On January 5th, 1872, a rumor was spread in the city of Ismail that some money and some holy vessels had been stolen from a church, which had been profaned by the robbers. Jacob Silberman, a baptized Jew, was immediately suspected of having perpetrated the robbery. This Silberman was a deserter from the Russian Army. He had come to Ismail some three months previous and was working in a Jewish tailor's shop. When arrested, he implicated his master. Though, after a search in the latter's home, nothing implicating him in the robbery was found, the tailor was nevertheless arrested. Subsequently and for reasons best known to himself Silberman made a second declaration, this time implicating Mr. D. Goldschlaeger who allegedly had told him, "Go to the church, steal the holy objects, bring them to me and I shall make you the richest man in the city and you shall be a saint with the Jews." Goldschlaeger, a prominent merchant with an excellent reputation, was thrown into prison in spite of evidence which proved that Goldschlaeger could not have talked to Silberman at the time he had received the alleged instructions. Besides Goldschlaeger, the local rabbi was also arrested. As a consequence of the publicity given the arrests, many homes were plundered and even demolished. The rioters who were arrested were set free on the same day.

There was reason to believe that the whole matter was instigated by agents of the Russian Government and that Silberman himself may have been sent into Bessarabia for that very purpose. Additional support for this claim may be gathered from a statement in a letter by Mr. Peixotto to Mr. Hunter of February 7, 1872, which reads as follows: "The Austrian and English Consuls and agents report that the Russians and Bulgarians, who form the principal part of the inhabitants, were the chief promoters."

More cruel and damaging were the events in the city of Cahul which followed those of Ismail. The Commissioner of Police was criminally negligent and even the soldiers of the garrison did not fulfill their obvious duties. The authorities did nothing to prevent the excesses. It is interesting to note that in Cahul too, the Russians seem to have been the instigators and consequently claimed that they had received orders from the government to kill all the Jews. A number of Jewish delegations from Ismail and Cahul visited Mr. Peixotto beseeching his intercession in behalf of their still suffering and imperiled condition. "In depth of despair they presented themselves to representatives of a government distinguished the world over by its justice, enlightenment, and humanity, believing that their unhappy condition might be alleviated should an effort be made in their behalf." Mr. Peixotto had to reply that, though his government was anxious to see the inhabitants of every land protected in their lives and property, he could not properly interfere in the internal affairs of the country. "Nevertheless," he continued, "there are certain principles which all governments are bound to respect and when these were outraged nations were concerned to see the barbaric land brought within the pale of civilization."

Mr. Peixotto did all he could do to help these delegations

by presenting their condition to the responsible ministers in Bucharest, and he also addressed himself directly to them in his capacity as United States consul. The Government had assured him again and again that they would take stringent measures to punish the guilty persons. The Procuror-General, who went to Ismail to investigate conditions on the spot, returned and made a report in which he completely exonerated every Jew of any participation whatsoever in the alleged theft and desecration of the church. All evidence tended to show that the outrage had been committed by a renegade from the Russian army, an apostate, who by his own confession, made in open court, had been three times convicted of crime in Russia.

In spite of this report the five Jews arrested, among them a rabbi and the president of the community, were still confined in prison and committed to stand trial as common felons. Later, these five Jews were tried and condemned to three years imprisonment as accomplices of the thief Silberman. This verdict was delivered in the face of the most positive evidence of their innocence. The Attorney General declared that he, although public prosecutor, must abandon the accusation because there was absolutely no case against them, and that he must ask for their acquittal. At the same time, forty-six of the principal rioters of Cahul were set free. Reporting on April 5, 1872, to Washington on these developments, Mr. Peixotto came to certain conclusions which he expressed as follows: "It seems to be every day more apparent that nothing but the direct intervention of the powers who have the right under the Treaty of Paris will put an end to the eternal disorders resulting from the serious persecution of the Hebrews."

Protests against the barbaric abuses aimed at the lives and property of Jews were heard all over Europe. In the Congress of the United States resolutions were adopted requesting President Grant to protest "against the intolerant and cruel treatment of the Jews in Rumania." In a message to the Senate, dated May 14, 1872, the President transmitted copies of the correspondence between Mr. Peixotto and the Department of State relative to the persecution and oppression of the Jews in the principality of Rumania.

In the meantime, Hamilton Fish, Secretary of State, had sent the following note to Mr. Peixotto, as well as to the American ministers at Paris, Berlin, Rome, London, St. Petersburg and Constantinople:[4]

[*Mr. Fish to Mr. Peixotto*]

Department of State
Washington, April 10, 1872

SIR:

Among the large number of Israelites in this country, there are probably few whose sympathies have not been intensely excited by the recent intelligence of the grievous persecutions of their co-religionists in Roumania. This feeling has naturally been augmented by the contrast presented by the position of members of that persuasion here, who are equals with all others before the law, which sternly forbids any oppression on account of religion. Indeed, it may be said that the people of this country universally abhor persecution anywhere for that cause, and deprecate the trials of which, according to your dispatches, the Israelites of Roumania have been victims.

This Government heartily sympathizes with the popular instinct upon the subject, and while it has no disposition or intention to give offense by impertinently interfering in the internal affairs of Roumania, it is deemed to be due to humanity to remonstrate against any license or impunity which may have attended the outrages in that country. You are consequently authorized to address a note to the minister of foreign affairs of the principalities, in which you will embody the views herein expressed, and you will also do anything which you discreetly can, with a reasonable prospect of success, toward preventing a recurrence or continuance of the persecution adverted to.

HAMILTON FISH

Meanwhile, the consuls in Rumania of Germany, Austria-Hungary, France, Great Britain, Greece and Italy, joined by the American consul, sent the following collective note to

[4] Senate Executive Documents, No. 75, 42nd Congress, 2nd Session, 1872.

the Government, in which they protested against the delay in publishing the result of the official investigation, and expressed their regret at the action of the court assizes at Buzéo which freed all individuals who were charged with having participated in excesses and crimes against the Jewish population. It is worthy of note that the name of the Russian consul is missing.[5]

[*Consuls' Note to Rumanian Government*]

Bucharest, April 18, 1872

The undersigned deem it their duty to address to the government of the Prince, collectively, and in the most formal manner, the verbal observations which most of them have been ordered by their governments to present to it in relation to the Israelitish question. They cannot, in the first place, help expressing their astonishment that the result of the investigation, ordered in Roumanian Bessarabia more than two months since, has not yet been communicated to them, notwithstanding the assurance contained in the note of the minister of foreign affairs, bearing the date of the 7–19th of February last.

They have, moreover, learned with profound regret that, after having condemned several Israelites to severe penalties, the prosecution of whom was abandoned by the public ministry itself, the court assizes at Buzéo has acquitted all the individuals who were charged with having committed the gravest excesses and crimes against the Jewish population of the town of Vilcova. The undersigned see, in this double verdict, an indication of the dangers to which Israelites are exposed in Roumania, the imminence of which, at the approach of the Easter holidays, justified the steps recently taken by them simultaneously near the government of the Prince.

The governments of the undersigned will judge whether the impunity which has been enjoyed by the assailants of the Jews is not of a nature to encourage a repetition of scenes of violence quite unworthy of a civilized country, which, as such, ought to insure freedom and security to all religious denominations.

Upon the receipt of a copy of the above note, Secretary Fish sent the following dispatch to Mr. Peixotto:[6]

---

[5] Senate Executive Documents, No. 75, 42nd Congress, 2nd Session, 1872.
[6] *Ibid.*

[*Mr. Fish to Mr. Peixotto*]

Washington, May 13, 1872

SIR:

The Department has received your dispatch, No. 30, of the 19th ultimo, accompanied by a copy of a remonstrance addressed by the representatives of foreign governments at Bucharest, to that of the principalities, against recent maltreatment of Israelites there.

The Department approves your taking part in that remonstrance. Whatever caution and reserve may usually characterize the policy of this Government in such matters, may be regarded as inexpedient when every guarantee and consideration of justice appear to have been set at defiance in the course pursued with reference to the unfortunate people referred to. You will not be backward in joining any similar protest, or other measure which the foreign representatives there may deem advisable, with a view to avert or mitigate further harshness toward the Israelite residents in, or subjects of, the principalities.

I am, sir, etc.,

HAMILTON FISH

In a note of June 24, 1872, Mr. Peixotto informed Mr. Fish of the results of the trials in the towns of Rumanian-Bessarabia when anti-Jewish riots took place. Not only were all the accused persons set free, but all claims for indemnification of the sufferers were outlawed. This dispatch closes with the suggestion that a note be addressed to the American ministers to the Powers signatory to the Treaty of Paris of 1856 and 1858, instructing them to use all moral efforts to advance the solution of a question the importance of which is already recognized by them.

Following the suggestion of Mr. Peixotto, Mr. Fish dispatched the following note simultaneously to the United States representatives in Austria-Hungary, France, Germany, Great Britain, Italy, Russia and Turkey asking them to request the governments to which they were accredited, signatories of the Treaty of Paris of 1858, to intervene on behalf of the Rumanian Jews. It will be observed that this action was taken despite the fact that, not having been a party to that treaty, the United States had no legal basis on which to remonstrate with the Government of the Principalities.[7]

[*Mr. Fish to United States Representatives*]

Washington, July 22, 1872

SIR:

It has been suggested to this Department, and the suggestion is concurred in, that if the sympathy which we entertain for the inhumanly persecuted Hebrews, in the principalities of Moldavia and Wallachia, were made known to the government to which you are accredited, it might quicken and encourage the efforts of that government to discharge its duty as a protecting power, pursuant to the obligations of the treaty between certain European states. Although we are not a party to that instrument, and, as a rule, scrupulously abstain from interfering, directly or indirectly, in the public affairs of that quarter, the grievance adverted to is so enormous, as to impart to it, as it were, a cosmopolitan character, in the redress of which all countries, governments and creeds are alike interested.

You will consequently communicate on this subject with the minister for foreign affairs of the Austro-Hungarian Empire in such way as you may suppose might be most likely to compass the object in view.

I am, etc.,

HAMILTON FISH

Not all the replies received from the United States representatives in Europe were encouraging. Mr. John Jay, United States Minister at Vienna, reported that the Austro-Hungarian Government was somewhat doubtful whether the Treaty of Paris offered ground for intervention; besides, he was fearful that foreign intervention might result in diminishing the ability of the government to restore order and subject the Jews to increased prejudice and further persecution; the Austro-Hungarian Government, however, hoped that, since the attention of the civilized world was aroused against the ill-treatment of the Jews in Rumania, there was reason to believe that this would not be repeated and that there would be an amelioration of their condition.

[7] Foreign Relations, 1872, page 55.

Mr. Elihu B. Washburne, American Minister at Paris, reported that the French Government would, when the occasion presented itself, insist that equal protection be accorded in Rumania to residents of all creeds. Similar sentiments were expressed to George Bancroft, American Minister at Berlin, by the German Government. The British Government, which had already made a number of representations to the government of Rumania and had initiated similar steps, now taken by Mr. Fish, "would be most happy," in the words of Lord Granville, Secretary of State for Foreign Affairs, to Robert C. Schenck, American Minister to Great Britain, "to communicate freely on this matter with the Government of the United States as to anything which could be done and which might have practical effect." George H. Boker, American Minister at Constantinople, belittled the issues involved, while the American Minister at Rome, George W. Wurts, advised the Government of the United States to make representations in St. Petersburg whence alone any improvement in the condition of the Rumanian Jews could be obtained.

The Rumanian rioters, and the juries who found the Jews guilty while freeing the rioters, received the greatest moral support from the Russian Government. Mr. Eugene Schuyler, Chargé d'Affaires *ad interim* in St. Petersburg, was told by the Russian Government that according to the information received by the Imperial Government there had been no persecution of the Hebrews in Rumania. Quarrels had taken place, but for these both parties were equally to blame. There had been no infraction of the Convention of Paris and, besides, nothing in that instrument gave the Hebrews the right to ask the intervention of the signatory powers. The Russian Government officially accepted the verdict of the Rumanian juries who, against all evidence to the contrary, had found the Jews guilty of something they had not done. In the communication to Mr. Schuyler, Mr. Westmann, Russian Acting Secretary for Foreign Affairs, justified the position taken by Russia, by putting the whole blame on the Jews:[8]

[8] Foreign Relations, 1872, page 497.

"It is true that regrettable disorders have occurred in certain localities of Rumania, but these disorders were provoked, as is unanimously admitted, by some Israelites, who gave themselves up to acts odiously sacrilegious in the eyes of the Christians. Besides, these matters have been regularly submitted to the courts of justice, which have pronounced their final judgment." Mr. Westmann's letter concluded with the following statement: "As regards systematic and notorious persecutions in Roumania against the Israelite population, our official agents in the principalities made no mention of any in their reports. The imperial government has no reason to doubt their impartiality."

Though Peixotto was a Jew, it would be difficult to discern this fact from his dispatches. Any American would have acted in the same manner, and most likely might have used even stronger words. His objectivity is further shown by the fact that he forwarded to Mr. Fish a confidential circular note to the Rumanian agents abroad, sent out by Mr. Costaforo, Rumanian Minister of Foreign Affairs. Peixotto questioned the propriety of transmitting this note to Washington, inasmuch as he was not officially furnished a copy. Yet being desirous of presenting to Washington both sides of the question, he decided to send the note, satisfying himself with the remark that he did not doubt that Mr. Fish would appreciate the point at issue and that the attempted denial and belittling of the riots were in consonance with a policy which had always been followed by the Rumanian Government in this question.

The Costaforo note is an apologetic, incoherent, and dishonest document. The first conclusion one comes to is that it was *not*, as Costaforo states, the Rumanian ignorant masses alone who hated the Jews to such an extent as to ignore the elementary principles of humanity and justice. An appreciable part of the blame must rest upon the shoulders of the executive and administrative branches of government as well. In trying to weaken the impression which the riots in Ismail, Vilcov, and Cahul had made upon the nations of Europe and their Governments, Mr. Costaforo tried to belittle the extent of these outrages. Though he admitted that the Rumanian juries might have been prejudiced in their decision, he yet accepts these decisions as being the established truth, ignoring the findings of his Attorney General, who after having investigated on the spot, came to the conclusion that none of the Jews were implicated in the theft from, and desecration of, the Church.

Enclosed with the above circular note, Peixotto also sent a translation of a leading editorial and an article in the *Neue Freie Presse* of Vienna in which this note is thoroughly analyzed and its true nature brought to light. It was, in the opinion of the writer, nothing short of an insult to the foreign ministers of the respective European Governments to be fed with material such as this. As to the opinion of Mr. Costaforo, himself, on the Jews of Rumania and their sufferings at the hands of their oppressors, it was sufficient only to quote a remark which he made in a careless moment to a journalist:[9] "The damned filthy Jews deserve what has been done to them; had I been at Ismail at the time of the sacrilege, I would have joined the mob; the agents make a great fuss, but the more they will cry the less will I listen to them." In the face of such an attitude towards Jews and towards the protests of the agents of the signatory powers, nothing useful to the Jews could be accomplished. However, Peixotto had tried his best to mitigate the evils here and there, first, in his capacity as consul of the United States, and secondly, as a distributing agent of relief monies collected in Europe and the United States for the benefit of the sufferers. He was also instrumental in calling together a Jewish conference in Brussels for discussion of the situation of the Rumanian Jews, where the ground was laid for the future presentation of the Jewish case in that country whenever the occasion should present itself. This occasion did arrive a few years later when the Balkan question was again before the European concert of powers at the Congress of Berlin.

[9] Foreign Relations, 1872, page 696.

In 1877, another war broke out between Russia and Turkey, the former announcing that it was fighting for the liberation of the Christian provinces in the Balkans from Turkish rule. The Russians were victorious, and in the Treaty of San Stefano were able to impose rather harsh terms upon Turkey. The European powers were not willing to accept this treaty as final, and called a Congress to meet in Berlin where the whole Balkan situation would be reopened.

Early in May, 1877, Mr. Myer S. Isaacs, President of the Board of Delegates of American Israelites, addressed a letter to Mr. William M. Evarts, Secretary of State, calling his attention to the dangers to which Rumanian Jews were being exposed during the War. Some attacks on the Jews had already taken place and he, therefore, asked that the United States ministers in Vienna and Constantinople be asked to co-operate with their colleagues "in such measures as may be devised for the relief of the persecuted Hebrews in Rumania."[10] In his answer to Mr. Isaacs of May 26, 1877, Mr. Evarts informed him that, although all ordinary diplomatic protests would not avail in a time of war, still he would forward his letter to the United States Minister in Constantinople with instructions to take such action in the matter, as would in his own judgment, be best calculated to secure an amelioration of the condition of the oppressed people. In his note to Horace Maynard, United States Minister to Constantinople, transmitting the above correspondence, Mr. Evarts said:[11] "You will give such instructions to our Consular representatives in the Provinces as will be in your judgment, in view of the peculiar exigencies of the situation at present, best adapted to secure to the Israelites the desired protection."

With the reopening of the Balkan question, it was generally expected that the status of the Jews in Rumania would be discussed, though, at first, it was not known who

[10] "Jewish Disabilities in the Balkan States," by Max J. Kohler and Simon Wolf, in *Publications of the American Jewish Historical Society*, No. 24, 1916, page 34.

[11] *Ibid.*, page 33.

would present it to the Congress. A number of Jewish delegations, notably those representing the Alliance Israélite Universelle of France, and the Board of Deputies of British Jews, exerted all the pressure they could to make Rumanian independence conditional upon granting the Jews religious and civil equality with the rest of the Rumanian population. It is interesting to note that the American Minister in Vienna, Mr. John A. Kasson, first brought to the attention of the Government in Washington the opportunity offered by the Congress of Berlin to settle once and for all the troubled question of the Jews in Rumania. He felt sure that such action on behalf of the American Government would greatly gratify the American people, and evoke especial gratitude from that race which had found in the United States absolute legal equality and security. His letter follows:[12]

[*Mr. Kasson to Mr. Evarts*]

Vienna, June 5, 1878

SIR: The United States Government has on different occasions interested itself in the question of protecting American Jews traveling or residing in Roumania, and has expressed its sympathy with the oppressed condition of the race in that country. Preliminary to a report which I am preparing respecting the establishment of treaty relations between the United States and Roumania, whose independence, it is expected, the congress about to assemble will recognize, I beg leave to bring to your attention the question of securing the object in which so many of our compatriots take a deep interest.

In anticipation of Roumanian independence, Germany commenced negotiations with the Roumanian Government for a commercial treaty. According to information received here, the hostility of the latter to the recognition of equal rights for Jews of a foreign nationality with those of other citizens or subjects of the same nationality would have practically proscribed a portion of the German subjects. For that reason the proposed treaty was not accepted by Germany.

There is little conception in America of the tenacity of the prejudice against that race in Roumania, and of the contempt and occasional violence and wrong to which this prejudice leads, as well as to the legal deprivation of the ordinary privileges of good citizenship.

[12] Foreign Relations, 1878, page 42.

It would be to the honor of the United States Government if it could initiate a plan by which at once the condition of American Hebrews resident or traveling in Roumania, and the conditions of natives of the same race, could be ameliorated and their equality before the law at least partially assured.

The European congress is about to assemble, and will be asked to recognize the independence of Roumania. Would there be any just objection to the United States Government offering on its part, if the European powers would on their part make the same condition, to recognize the independence of that country, and to enter into treaty stipulations with its government, only upon the fundamental preliminary agreements:

1. That all citizens or subjects of any such foreign nationality shall, irrespective of race or religious belief, be entitled to equal rights and protection under the treaty and under their laws.

2. That all subjects or citizens under the jurisdiction of the Roumanian Government shall, irrespective of their race or religious belief, have equal rights of trade and commerce with the citizens or subjects of the foreign governments making such treaty; equal rights in the purchase, consumption, barter, or sale of the products of such foreign country, and in sales of Roumanian products to such aliens; equal rights to make contracts with the citizens or subjects of such foreign government, and to be equally protected by the laws in the exercise of the rights so secured.

To this extent, at least, it seems foreign governments would be justified by international law and the law of self-interest; while they would at the same time give effect to the humane instinct of all truly civilized and Christian nations. The persecuting and oppressive spirit is so strong in Roumania against the Jews that it requires united action by liberal and constitutional governments, as well as an appeal to the strongest desires of the Roumanian people, which are just now to be permitted to enter the family of nations, to bring relief and emancipation to this proscribed race.

Your own judgment will improve, doubtless, the form of action above suggested; but it will be sufficient, I hope, to attract your attention to a question, the favorable solution of which would greatly gratify the American people, and evoke especial gratitude from that race which has found in the United States absolute legal equality and security, and the occasion of the congress is most favorable for giving it effect, if approved.

I have, etc.,

JOHN A. KASSON

The United States was not a party to the Congress of Berlin, but Mr. Kasson, its minister in Vienna, was present, and in a number of cases was helpful to the Jewish delegations there. In a letter of August 3, 1878, he optimistically informs Mr. Evarts that the hopes of the Jews were realized in that Congress. In Article V of the Treaty of Berlin absolute freedom and equality of religious faith and professions for all forms of faith and worship and of persons adhering to these different forms of faith, were stipulated in all the new countries of the Balkan Peninsula, including Rumania. Mentioning Rumania specifically, Article XLIV of the Treaty of Berlin provides that, "In Roumania, the difference of religious creeds and confessions shall not be alleged against any person as a ground for exclusion or incapacity in matters relating to the enjoyment of civil and political rights, admissions to public employments, functions, and honors, or the exercise of the various professions and industries in any locality whatsoever." In identical phraseology, Mr. Kasson concluded his letter with the following paragraph: "You will observe in reading the model article (V) how completely that equality of religious right is expressed. I wrote you before the meeting of the congress in respect to the propriety and possibility of ameliorating the condition of the Jews in these principalities, by coming to accord with European Governments upon some clause of a treaty in which this could be secured as a condition of the recognition of their independence. This result has been attained by the great powers in the Berlin Treaty; but it remains to give effect to it by a change of the laws in the several principalities. Unless and until this is done, it would be wise to incorporate the provision in substance in any treaty made with the principalities; and especially so in the case of a government which is not a party to the Berlin Treaty."

Resistance to the demands for equality for Jews was so great in Rumania, that there was agitation to refuse independence on these terms. However, the Rumanian delegates were not able to break the united front of the representatives of Germany, France, Great Britain, and even Russia, who

insisted that such equality be granted to the Jews. But that
Rumania did not expect to abide by her signature of acceptance is seen from a letter written by Prince Karl Anton,
father and chief advisor of the Rumanian ruler, in which he
said that the provisions with respect to the Jews were
merely "humane generalities." He went on to say: "It is
left for the legislative board alone, to phrase them, and I
am convinced that later on, with the exception of the Alliance ·
Israélite, not another rooster will crow over the form in which
these provisions will be phrased."

In 1879, Mr. Balatshano, the Rumanian Minister in
Vienna, approached Mr. Kasson with the view of establishing diplomatic relations between the governments of the
United States and Rumania. Mr. Kasson reports on this in
the following note:[13]

[*Mr. Kasson to Mr. Evarts*]

Legation of the United States
Vienna, February 16, 1879

Sir: Mr. Balatshano, the envoy and minister of Roumania, who
is accredited to this court and has already been received, yesterday
verbally communicated to me the wish of his government to enter
into diplomatic relations with the Government of the United
States. Whether the representative of the American Government
should be an envoy of the first rank or of any inferior diplomatic
grade, his royal highness Prince Charles would commission one of
the same grade to represent his government at Washington. He
wished this communication to be considered as "official."

So accepting it, I have now the honor to advise you of the same,
and to await instructions from you touching the fitting response
to be made.

In the course of conversation, I alluded to the preliminary
requirements of the Berlin treaty in respect to the Jews. He replied
that the necessary changes would be made in their laws to give
satisfaction on this point, and to establish for the Jews the basis
of absolute equality with other races. He estimated the number
of Jews in Roumania at 600,000, of whom less than one-tenth
were native-born, and he thought Roumania had a right to protect
her own native race from being overwhelmed by a foreign incursion
of this character which did not wish to submit to the duties and
responsibilities which are borne by natives of the Roumanian race.

[13] Foreign Relations, 1879, page 49.

He referred with politeness, and not without a point which I
appreciated, to the law just passed by one House of our Congress
for the suppression of Chinese immigration to the United States,
although the proportion of that race present in the United States
to the native population is minute in comparison with that of the
Jewish immigrants to native Roumanians. He, however, repeated
the assurance that they would be placed on a basis of equality
before the law.

I have, etc.,

JOHN A. KASSON

Negotiations for recognition of Rumania by the United
States were then undertaken, and the following correspondence was exchanged between Mr. Kasson and Mr. Evarts:[14]

[*Mr. Evarts to Mr. Kasson*]

Department of State
Washington, November 28, 1879

SIR: Your dispatch No. 256 of the 31st ultimo, inclosing the
reply of His Highness the Prince of Roumania to the letter which
the President addressed to him on the 15th of August, 1878, has
been received. In connection with the subject of Roumanian
recognition, I inclose for your consideration a copy of a letter
under date of the 30th ultimo, from Mr. Myer S. Isaacs, president,
and other officers of the board of delegates on civil and religious
rights of the Hebrews, asking that the Government of the United
States may exert its influence towards securing for the Hebrew
subjects and residents in Roumania the equality of civil and religious rights stipulated in Article XLIV of the treaty of Berlin.

As you [are] aware, this government has ever felt a deep interest
in the welfare of the Hebrew race in foreign countries, and has
viewed with abhorrence the wrongs to which they have, at various
periods, been subjected by the followers of other creeds in the East.
This Department is therefore disposed to give favorable consideration to the appeal made by the representatives of a prominent
Hebrew organization in this country in behalf of their brethren in
Roumania, and while I should not be warranted in making a compliance with their wishes a *sine qua non* in the establishment of
official relations with that country, yet any terms favorable to the
interest of this much-injured people which you may be able to
secure in the negotiations now pending with the Government of
Roumania would be agreeable and gratifying to this Department.

I am, etc.,

WM. M. EVARTS

[14] Foreign Relations, 1880, page 35.

In answer to this letter, Mr. Kasson, in a dispatch of December 24, 1879, informed the Secretary of State that Italy, Austria and France had recognized Rumanian independence, thereby implying that they were satisfied with the action Rumania had taken in fulfilment of her engagement in Berlin. So far, Germany had not yet recognized her, but the delaying of German recognition was based upon an altogether different consideration. Mr. Kasson had interested himself in the condition of the Jews in the principalities and he was convinced that much progress has been made, that the only branch of civil rights which still gave just cause of anxiety was that relating to the extent and mode of granting to the Hebrews the rights of citizenship; and it seemed to Mr. Kasson that, outside of this exception, Jews in Rumania already enjoyed full civil equality. In a letter of February 25, 1880, Mr. Kasson further urges recognition of Rumania, noting that Germany and Great Britain also had recognized Rumanian independence. Great Britain's recognition did not come without an expression of the inadequacy of Article VII of the Rumanian Constitution. The British note announcing recognition also contained the following paragraph: "Her Majesty's Government cannot consider the new constitutional provisions which have been brought to their cognizance and particularly those by which persons belonging to a non-Christian creed in Rumania and not belonging to any foreign nationality, are required to submit to the formalities of individual naturalization as being a complete fulfillment of the views of the powers signatories of the Treaty of Berlin." Enclosed in that letter was a translation of a note which Baron Haymerle of Austria had sent to the governments of Germany, France, and Great Britain. It reads in part as follows:[15]

If we consider the situation of Roumania, and take note of the difficulties, political and social, by which the government of the prince was unquestionably surrounded, in the accomplishment of its task, we cannot avoid acknowledging that by the law upon the

[15] Foreign Relations, 1880, page 52.

revision of Article VII of the constitution, as well as subsequently by the naturalization of a certain number of Israelites, the Roumanian legislation has taken an important step in advance, and that the princely government has given evidence of its sincere intention to satisfy the unanimous desire of Europe.

After Washington had been notified that the Kingdom of The Netherlands, too, had recognized Rumania as an independent power, the Government of the United States took the required action and established direct diplomatic relations with Rumania.

The most notable action taken by the Government of the United States in behalf of the Jews in Rumania occurred in 1902 when John Hay, Secretary of State, at the direction of President Theodore Roosevelt, dispatched the famous Rumanian note to the diplomatic representatives of the United States Government at the capitals of the signatory powers of the Berlin Treaty. The immediate cause for this note was the refusal of the Rumanian Government to conclude a naturalization treaty with the United States. The United States had approached the Rumanian Government a number of times, pointing out the great advantages which would accrue to both governments if such a treaty should be signed. The reason given for refusal was that "it would complicate the already troublesome Jewish question in that country." The Rumanian Government was afraid that a large number of Rumanian Jews would leave for America with the express purpose of becoming naturalized there, and then return to Rumania and claim protection as American citizens. The Hay note gives a thorough discussion of the whole background of the Jewish problem in Rumania and the exceptions of the American Government both to the treatment of Jews in Rumania and to the large immigration to the United States resulting from this treatment.

In the note, the United States came again, as it had before in a number of other cases, to the defense of the civil rights of its naturalized citizens, emphasizing especially the right of expatriation of every individual and insisting that the American Government could never assent "that a foreign state, of its own volition, can apply a religious test to debar any American citizen from the favor due to all."

As to immigration into the United States, it had always welcomed the immigration of Jews who as a group possessed high moral and mental qualifications for conscientious citizenship. The Jews of Rumania, however, due to the fact that for centuries they had been treated as "aliens not subject to foreign protection," were rendered incapable of lifting themselves from the enforced degradation which they endured, and therefore would not make good immigrants.

Mr. Hay believed that the United States, being the only country of refuge for these cruelly mistreated Jews, had a right to remonstrate against the acts of the Rumanian Government. This remonstrance was based not solely upon the fact that Rumanian mistreatment of Jews caused injury to the United States, but is also advanced "in the cause of humanity."

As the United States itself was not a signatory to the Treaty of Berlin, it could only appeal to the principles of international law and eternal justice, hoping that they would be applied in practice.

The original note was sent to Mr. Charles S. Wilson. The full text of the note follows:[16]

[*Mr. Hay to Mr. Wilson*]

(Confidential)

Department of State
Washington, July 17, 1902

Sir: Your legation's dispatch No. 19, of the 13th February last, reported having submitted to the Roumanian Government, through its diplomatic representative in Greece, as the outcome of conferences had by Mr. Francis with him on the subject, a tentative draft of a naturalization convention, on the lines of the draft previously submitted to the Servian Government, and Mr. Francis added that his excellency the Roumanian minister had

[16] Foreign Relations, 1902, page 910.

informed him of his hearty approval of the project, which he had forwarded to his Government with his unqualified indorsement. Minister Francis was instructed on March 4 that his action was approved. No report of progress has since been received from your legation, but it is presumed that the matter is receiving the consideration due to its importance.

For its part the Government of the United States regards the conclusion of conventions of this character as of the highest value, because not only establishing and recognizing the right of the citizens of the foreign state to expatriate themselves voluntarily and acquire the citizenship of this country, but also because establishing beyond the pale of doubt the absolute equality of such naturalized persons with native citizens of the United States in all that concerns their relation to or intercourse with the country of their former allegiance.

The right of citizens of the United States to resort to and transact affairs of business or commerce in another country, without molestation or disfavor of any kind, is set forth in the general treaties of amity and commerce which the United States have concluded with foreign nations, thus declaring what this government holds to be a necessary feature of the mutual intercourse of civilized nations and confirming the principles of equality, equity, and comity which underlie their relations to one another. This right is not created by treaties; it is recognized by them as a necessity of national existence, and we apply the precept to other countries, whether it be conventionally declared or not, as fully as we expect its extension to us.

In some instances, other governments, taking a less broad view, regard the rights of intercourse of alien citizens as not extending to their former subjects who may have acquired another nationality. So far as this position is founded on national sovereignty and asserts a claim to the allegiance and service of the subject not to be extinguished save by the consent of the sovereign, it finds precedent and warrant which it is immaterial to the purpose of this instruction to discuss. Where such a claim exists, it becomes the province of a naturalization convention to adjust it on a ground of common advantage, substituting the general sanction of treaty for the individual permission of expatriation and recognizing the subject who may have changed allegiance as being on the same plane with the natural or native citizens of the other contracting state.

Some States, few in number be it said, make distinction between different classes of citizens of the foreign State, denying to some the rights of innocent intercourse and commerce which by comity and natural right are accorded to the stranger, and doing this without regard to the origin of the persons adversely affected. One country in particular, although maintaining with the United States a treaty which unqualifiedly guarantees to citizens of this country the rights of visit, sojourn, and commerce of the Empire, yet assumes to prohibit those rights to Hebrew citizens of the United States, whether native or naturalized. This Government can lose no opportunity to controvert such a distinction, wherever it may appear. It can admit no such discrimination among its own citizens, and can never assent that a foreign State, of its own volition, can apply a religious test to debar any American citizen from the favor due to all.

There is no treaty of amity and commerce between the United States and Roumania, but this Government is pleased to believe that Roumania follows the precepts of comity in this regard as completely and unreservedly as we ourselves do, and that the American in Roumania is as welcome and as free in matters of sojourn and commerce and legal resorts as the Roumanian is in the United States. We hear no suggestion that any differential treatment of our citizens is there imposed. No religious test is known to bar an American from resorting to Roumania for business or pleasure. No attempt has been made to set up any such test in the United States whereby any American citizen might be denied recourse to the representatives of Roumania in order to authenticate documents necessary to the establishment of his legal rights or the furtherance of his personal interests in Roumania. And in welcoming negotiations for a convention of naturalization Roumania gives proof of her desire to confirm all American citizens in their inherently just rights.

Another consideration of cognate character presents itself. In the absence of a naturalization convention, some few states hold self-expatriation without the previous consent of the sovereign to be punishable, or to entail consequences indistinguishable from banishment. Turkey, for instance, only tacitly assents to the expatriation of Ottoman subjects so long as they remain outside Turkish jurisdiction. Should they return thereto their acquired alienship is ignored. Should they seek to cure the matter by asking permission to be naturalized abroad, consent is coupled with the condition of nonreturn to Turkey. It is the object of a naturalization convention to remedy this feature by placing the naturalized alien on a parity with the natural-born citizen and according him due recognition as such. This consideration gives us added satisfaction that negotiations on the subject have been auspiciously inaugurated with Roumania. If I have mentioned this aspect of the matter, it is in order that the two Governments may be in accord as to the bases of their agreement in this regard, for it is indispensable that the essential purpose of the proposed convention should not be impaired or perverted by any coupled condition of banishment imposed independently by the act of either contracting party.

The United States welcomes now, as it has welcomed from the foundation of its Government, the voluntary immigration of all aliens coming hither under conditions fitting them to become merged in the body politic of this land. Our laws provide the means for them to become incorporated indistinguishably in the mass of citizens, and prescribe their absolute equality with the native born, guaranteeing to them equal civil rights at home and equal protection abroad. The conditions are few, looking to their coming as free agents, so circumstanced physically and morally as to supply the healthful and intelligent material of free citizenhood. The pauper, the criminal, the contagiously or incurably diseased are excluded from the benefits of emigration only when they are likely to become a source of danger or a burden upon the community. The voluntary character of their coming is essential; hence we shut out all immigration assisted or constrained by foreign agencies. The purpose of our generous treatment of the alien immigrant is to benefit us and him alike — not to afford to another state a field upon which to cast its own objectionable elements. A convention of naturalization may not be construed as an instrument to facilitate any such process. The alien, coming here voluntarily and prepared to take upon himself the preparatory and in due course the definitive obligations of citizenship, retains thereafter, in domestic and international relations, the initial character of free agency, in the full enjoyment of which it is incumbent upon his adoptive State to protect him.

The foregoing considerations, whilst pertinent to the examination of the purpose and scope of a naturalization treaty, have a larger aim. It behooves the State to scrutinize most jealously the character of the immigration from a foreign land, and, if it be obnoxious to objection, to examine the causes which render it so. Should those causes originate in the act of another sovereign State, to the detriment of its neighbors, it is the prerogative of an injured State to point out the evil and to make remonstrance; for with nations, as with individuals, the social law holds good that the right of each is bounded by the right of the neighbor.

The condition of a large class of the inhabitants of Roumania has for many years been a source of grave concern to the United States. I refer to the Roumanian Jews, numbering some 400,000. Long ago, while the Danubian principalities labored under oppressive conditions which only war and a general action of the European powers sufficed to end, the persecution of the indigenous Jews under Turkish rule called forth in 1872 the strong remonstrance of the United States. The treaty of Berlin was hailed as a cure for the wrong in view of the express provisions of its forty-fourth article, prescribing that "in Roumania the difference of religious creeds and confessions shall not be alleged against any person as a ground for exclusion or incapacity in matters relating to the enjoyment of civil and political rights, admission to public employments, functions, and honors, or the exercise of the various professions and industries in any locality whatsoever," and stipulating freedom in the exercise of all forms of worship to Roumanian dependents and foreigners alike, as well as guaranteeing that all foreigners in Roumania shall be treated, without distinction of creed, on a footing of perfect equality.

With the lapse of time these just prescriptions have been rendered nugatory in great part, as regards the native Jews, by the legislation and municipal regulations of Roumania. Starting from the arbitrary and controvertible premise that the native Jews of Roumania domiciled there for centuries are "aliens not subject to foreign protection," the ability of the Jew to earn even the scanty means of existence that suffice for a frugal race has been constricted by degrees, until nearly every opportunity to win a livelihood is denied; and until the helpless poverty of the Jew has constrained an exodus of such proportions as to cause general concern.

The political disabilities of the Jews in Roumania, their exclusion from the public service and the learned professions, the limitations of their civil rights, and the imposition upon them of exceptional taxes, involving as they do wrongs repugnant to the moral sense of liberal modern peoples, are not so directly in point for my present purpose as the public acts which attack the inherent right of man as a breadwinner in the ways of agriculture and trade. The Jews are prohibited from owning land, or even from cultivating it as common laborers. They are debarred from residing in the rural districts. Many branches of petty trade and manual production are closed to them in the overcrowded cities where they are forced to dwell and engage, against fearful odds, in the desperate struggle for existence. Even as ordinary artisans or hired laborers they may only find employment in the proportion of one "unprotected alien" to two "Roumanians" under any one employer. In short, by the cumulative effect of successive restrictions, the Jews of Roumania have become reduced to a state of wretched misery. Shut out from nearly every avenue of self-support which is open to the poor of other lands, and ground down by poverty as the natural result of their discriminatory treatment, they are rendered incapable of lifting themselves from the enforced degradation they endure. Even were the fields of education, of civil employment, and of commerce, open to them, as to "Roumanian citizens," their penury would prevent their rising by individual effort. Human beings so circumstanced have virtually no alternatives but submissive suffering or flight to some land less unfavorable to them. Removal under such conditions is not and cannot be the healthy, intelligent emigration of a free and self-reliant being. It must be, in most cases, the mere transplantation of an artificially produced diseased growth to a new place.

Granting that in better and more healthful surroundings the morbid conditions will eventually change for good, such emigration is necessarily for a time a burden to the community upon which the fugitives may be cast. Self-reliance and the knowledge and ability that evolve the power of self-support must be developed, and at the same time avenues of employment must be opened in quarters where competition is already keen and opportunities scarce. The teachings of history and the experience of our own nation show that the Jews possess in a high degree the mental and moral qualifications of conscientious citizenhood. No class of emigrants is more welcome to our shores when coming equipped in mind and body for entrance upon the struggle for bread and inspired with the high purpose to give the best service of heart and brain to the land they adopt of their own free will. But when they come as outcasts, made doubly paupers by physical and moral oppression in their native land, and thrown upon the long-suffering generosity of a more-favored community, their migration lacks the essential conditions which make alien immigration either acceptable or beneficial. So well is this appreciated on the Continent that, even in the countries where antisemitism has no foothold, it is difficult for these fleeing Jews to obtain any lodgment. America is their only goal.

The United States offers asylum to the oppressed of all lands. But its sympathy with them in nowise impairs its just liberty and right to weigh the acts of the oppressor in the light of their effects upon this country, and to judge accordingly.

Putting together the facts now painfully brought home to this Government, during the past few years, that many of the inhabitants of Roumania are being forced by artificially adverse discriminations to quit their native country; that the hospitable asylum offered by this country is almost the only refuge left to them; that they come hither unfitted by the conditions of their exile to take part in the new life of this land under circumstances either profitable to themselves or beneficial to the community, and that they are objects of charity from the outset and for a long time — the right of remonstrance against the acts of the Roumanian Government is clearly established in favor of this Government. Whether consciously and of purpose or not, these helpless people, burdened and spurned by their native land, are forced by the sovereign power of Roumania upon the charity of the United States. This Government cannot be a tacit party to such an international wrong. It is constrained to protest against the treatment to which the Jews of Roumania are subjected, not alone because it has unimpeachable ground to remonstrate against the resultant injury to itself, but in the name of humanity. The United States may not authoritatively appeal to the stipulations of the treaty of Berlin, to which it was not and can not become a signatory, but it does earnestly appeal to the principles consigned therein, because they are the principles of international law and eternal justice, advocating the broad toleration which that solemn compact enjoins and standing ready to lend its moral support to the fulfillment thereof by its cosignatories, for the act of Roumania itself has effectively joined the United States to them as an interested party in this regard.

Occupying this ground and maintaining these views, it behooves us to see that in concluding a naturalization convention no implication may exist of obligation on the part of the United States to receive and convert these unfortunates into citizens, and to eliminate any possible inference of some condition or effect tantamount to banishment from Roumania, with inhibition of return or imposition of such legal disability upon them by reason of their creed, as may impair their interests in that country or operate to deny them judicial remedies there which all American citizens may justly claim in accordance with the law and comity of nations.

I am, sir, your obedient servant,

JOHN HAY

In this note, Secretary Hay, in the words of Oscar S. Straus, formulated "with a logic and force as has never been done before, the ethical principle that when wrongs extend beyond national boundaries, so also does the right for their redress."

Mr. Hay sent his famous note to the American representatives in London, Berlin, St. Petersburg, Paris, Rome and Constantinople, with the following accompanying letter:[17]

[*Mr. Hay to U. S. Diplomatic Representatives*]

Department of State
Washington, August 11, 1902

SIR: In the course of an instruction recently sent to the minister accredited to the Government of Roumania in regard to the bases of a negotiation begun with that Government looking to a convention of naturalization between the United States and Roumania, certain

[17] Foreign Relations, 1902, page 42.

considerations were set forth for the minister's guidance concerning the character of the emigration from that country, the causes which constrain it, and the consequences so far as they adversely affect the United States.

It has seemed to the President appropriate that these considerations, relating as they do to the obligations entered into by the signatories of the treaty of Berlin of July 13, 1878, should be brought to the attention of the Governments concerned and commended to their consideration in the hope that, if they are so fortunate as to meet the approval of the several powers, such measures as to them may seem wise may be taken to persuade the Government of Rumania to reconsider the subject of the grievances in question. [This dispatch continues to the end in the same wording as that of Mr. Hay's dispatch to Mr. Wilson of July 17, 1902, omitting the last paragraph and putting in its place the following:]

You will take an early occasion to read this instruction to the minister of foreign affairs and, should he request it, leave with him a copy.

I have the honor, etc.,

JOHN HAY

On the whole, the United States diplomatic representatives could but report noncommittal answers which they had received from the respective foreign offices. Only Mr. Joseph H. Choate, American Ambassador at the Court of St. James, reported the receipt from the British Foreign Office of the assurance that "His Majesty's Government will place themselves in communication with the other powers signatories of the Treaty of Berlin, with a view to joint representation to the Rumanian Government on the subject." Meanwhile, Charles S. Wilson, Chargé d'Affaires *ad interim* in Athens, was replaced by John B. Jackson, Minister to Greece, who also had charge of United States affairs in Rumania. In March 1903, Secretary Hay again pressed the point in the following letter to Mr. Jackson:[18]

[Mr. Hay to Mr. Jackson]

Department of State
Washington, March 5, 1903

SIR: The Department's instruction No. 14 of July 17 last (Roumanian series), to your predecessor, presented for his guidance in

---

[18] Foreign Relations, 1903, page 702.

the negotiation of a naturalization treaty with Roumania, certain considerations having special reference to the Jews in that country.

The refusal of the Roumanian King, reported in Mr. Wilson's unnumbered dispatch of August 6 last (Roumanian series), to consider the project of a naturalization treaty with the United States, made that instruction ineffective.

With its No. 15, of August 23 last, same series, the Department inclosed, for the legation's information, a copy of a circular instruction which it addressed, on August 11, 1902, to the diplomatic representatives of the United States, to the governments parties to the treaty of Berlin of July 13, 1878, and which they were directed to bring to the attention of the governments concerned and to commend to their consideration, in the hope that they would take such measures as to them might seem wise to persuade the Government of Roumania to reconsider the subject of the grievances of Jews in that country.

It is the President's desire that you should, on your first visit to Roumania, discreetly and cautiously endeavor to learn whether the considerations so presented to them have resulted in any representations to the Roumanian Government by the powers, either separately or jointly, looking to the amelioration of the oppressed conditions of the Roumanian Jews and the observance of the principles of the Berlin treaty.

The matter is one in which the President has deep interest, and the Department would be pleased to have you furnish it with all information in this regard which you may be able to confidentially gather.

I am, etc.,

JOHN HAY

In reply, Mr. Jackson, in a letter dated Athens, March 21, 1903, reported that so far as he was aware no action had been taken by any of the powers signatory to the Treaty of Berlin; and that the Rumanian Government never had been notified formally of the contents of the circular, because, assured by the Rumanian minister to Athens that neither the King nor his cabinet was willing, at that time, to consider an extradition treaty with the United States, Mr. Wilson had not found it necessary to communicate directly with the Rumanian Minister for Foreign Affairs.

In the same note, Mr. Jackson volunteers some observations about the Jews in Rumania, obviously based on information which had been given to him by prejudiced sources.

The American Minister, whose main duties demanded that he spend most of his time in Athens, could not give enough time to study the Jewish problem as it unfolded itself in Rumania. As long ago as 1878, he tells us, a commission of deputies, appointed to study the question, reported that Rumanian Jews never existed, but only indigenous Jews — that is to say, Jews born in Rumania but not, for that reason, resembling Rumanians either in language, manners, customs, or aspirations. Though this attitude should have been changed by the Treaty of Berlin, Jews even now could become citizens only when they individually proved their acceptability to the legislative body. Very little had been accomplished in this matter during the previous twenty years, especially since the governments which took a real interest in the Jews had refrained from exerting any real pressure. An intimation to the State Department not to be too persistent on behalf of the Jews of Rumania is readily inferred from a concluding paragraph of Mr. Jackson's note, which reads as follows:[19]

Practically, it is hardly to be expected that the powers will show any more zeal than they did twenty-odd years ago, and it is not probable that success would accompany an effort to introduce into Roumania, by means of foreign pressure, legislative changes which are unacceptable to the country itself. Neither the King nor the Government has the power to change existing conditions, legislative action being necessary in the case of the naturalization of any "foreigner," no matter of what race or religion and I have heard it stated that foreign interference has already had an unfavorable effect.

The following month, April, 1903, after a visit to Bucharest, Mr. Jackson did not find it necessary to make any direct reference to the Jewish question, but he talked freely about the same question with his diplomatic colleagues and others. These "others" must have convinced him that "the prejudice is neither against the race nor the individual, but is based upon the genuine fear as to what would result from general naturalization." He was also careful to point out that in

[19] Foreign Relations, 1903, page 702.

Moldavia, where sixty percent of the population is Jewish, the Jews "it is said" use the Yiddish language and speak but little Rumanian.

Minister Jackson, at least as far as Rumania is concerned, based his reports on what "others" told him, and on what "is said." Later in the fall of 1903 he did have a talk with Mr. Sturdza, Rumanian Prime Minister, about the circular "note" (August 11, 1902) and the Jewish question. Mr. Sturdz agave the American Minister a "lecture" on Jewish anthropology. In the following dispatch, Mr. Jackson reports on this conversation, and also states that in the course of his travels in Rumania, in the summer of 1903, he had found that "the general feeling is that the naturalization of Jews must be a gradual matter as they become educated up to being Roumanians." The full text of this dispatch follows:[20]

[*Mr. Jackson to Mr. Hay*]

Legation of the United States
Sinaia, Roumania, September 7, 1903.

Sir: I have the honor to report that in conversation yesterday Mr. Sturdza, the Roumanian prime minister, spoke at length about the circular "note" of August 11, 1902, and the Jewish question. He said that there were two kinds of Jews in Roumania, the Spanish Jews, who are of a higher class, and the Jews who are principally found in Moldavia (and the neighboring parts of Austria and Russia), who he claimed are not Israelites at all, but Mongols, who were converted many centuries ago. There were few of this kind in what is now Roumania prior to 1828, and most of those who were in the country up to that time enjoyed either Austrian or Russian protection. Before the treaty of Paris no Jew, Turk, or Armenian could own real estate in the country. In the meantime, however, the Armenians had become Roumanianized, and there was no objection to the change, which was made in 1856, which enabled any Christian to do so. Later, at the time when the country became independent, a further change was made and any "Roumanian" obtained the right to hold land. Ultimately, after the treaty of Berlin of 1878, the complete independence of Roumania was recognized by the European powers. At that time there were practically no American interests in the country, yet the United States saw fit to recognize its independence of its own accord in

[20] Foreign Relations, 1903, page 704.

1880 and to send a diplomatic representative (Mr. Eugene Schuyler) to reside in Roumania. This action was greatly appreciated at the time, and it has not been forgotten. Since that time, however, Roumania has no longer been under the tutelage of the treaty powers, and now she does not recognize their right to intervene.

* * * * *

Mr. Sturdza said that now that I had seen something of Roumania and the Roumanians and now that they had become acquainted with me he was ready to inform me as to his position. He said at first that Roumania had not liberated herself from Turkish sovereignty in order to accept that of the Jews; that she had powerful neighbors and must do everything possible (compare dispatch No. 7) to maintain and develop her own nationality. He said that to grant political rights or to naturalize the Jews en masse, even if this were considered advisable, would necessitate a change in the constitution, and he was not in favor of frequent changes in a thing which should be of a permanent and more or less sacred character. He said that absolutely no question of religious prejudice was involved and cited a number of instances where Jews who had become Roumanians and been naturalized had attained political prominence under both liberal and conservative governments. He referred to one instance where he and other ministers had attended a wedding in the synagogue at Bucharest "in dress clothes and with decorations because of respect for the man whose daughter was being married." He said, however, that the mass of the Jews did not regard themselves as Roumanians; that they spoke of belonging to the "Jewish nation" and considered themselves as of a superior race to the Christians, and that they had their own customs, language, and ambitions, and neither would nor could assimilate with the native Roumanians. They wanted to become naturalized, or rather naturalization was wanted for them, in order that they might secure political rights and own land. Moreover, it is not merely a question of the Jews already in Roumania, as for many reasons their position here is much better than that of their coreligionists in Austria and Russia, and if existing restrictions were to be removed there would be a great influx from those countries. In Roumania there is not the least religious persecution, there have been no massacres, and passports are not necessary to enable one to travel inside the country. Jews generally are not allowed to live in rural districts, because experience has shown that they rarely if ever become actual farm laborers, but wish to exploit such laborers, as overseers, etc. or to keep inns and drinking places.

After this general statement Mr. Sturdza went on to describe the special circumstances which led to the increased emigration of Jews a few years ago. He said that the Government had never favored such emigration and it had no wish to drive the Jews out of the country. The emigration, he said, was due to bad times, which prevailed for various reasons, but principally on account of drought and the failure of the crops. For more than a year the laboring population of Roumania was unable to support itself. The Government and the owners of private estates did all that was possible, but there was a great deal of suffering. The bad times were felt particularly in the cities, as building practically stopped, and as the people had no money to spend in the shops. Naturally many people thought of emigrating, especially among the Jews who had few local attachments, and soon this emigration was given a political character. Instead of going by rail the Jews began making demonstrative marches through the country, singing and otherwise disturbing the peace. Many of them were not permitted to go further than Budapest and Vienna, and many suffered greatly, but more or less unnecessarily. In the case of those who were turned back, however, the Roumanian Government repatriated them at its own expense, spending several hundred thousand francs for the purpose. The country was in financial straits at the time and certain foreign influences were brought to bear in order to discredit it generally. Had it been forced to grant political rights to the Jews, many Roumanians would have been forced to sell their mortgaged estates, but the situation of the Jews in Roumania, especially the poorer classes, would not have been materially improved.

During the last summer I have traveled more or less about the country and have visited Jassy, Berlad, Galatz, Braila, and other cities and done my best to inform myself as to the exact situation. . . . The general feeling is that the naturalization of the Jews must be a gradual matter — as they become educated up to being Roumanians.

I have, etc.,

John B. Jackson

The speed with which Jews became "educated up to being Roumanians" is indicated in the following note, sent in 1906, by Mr. J. W. Riddle, United States Minister at Bucharest, to the Secretary of State:[21]

[*Mr. Riddle to Mr. Root*]

American Legation
Bucharest, July 2, 1906

Sir: It may be of interest to know that during the last parliamentary session (November, 1905 — May, 1906) twenty-seven

[21] Foreign Relations, 1906, page 1248.

Roumanian Jews were naturalized by vote of the Senate and Chamber of Deputies and thus admitted to all the rights enjoyed by Roumanian subjects.

I have, etc.,

J. W. RIDDLE

In the meantime, in May 1904 Mr. Charles S. Wilson had reported that there had been a distinct improvement in the situation of Jews in Rumania.[22]

[*Mr. Wilson to Mr. Hay*]

American Legation
Athens, May 5, 1904

SIR: I have the honor to report that under the title of "New attitude of the London Israelites," the semiofficial "Indépendence Roumaine," publishes extracts in French from certain Jewish newspapers of London, which speak of the better relations now existing in Roumania between the Jews and the Christians; the increase in the number of Jews naturalized; the more humane manner of enforcing the anti-Jewish laws, as well as the fact that no further laws of this nature have been proposed; and also the almost complete cessation of the expulsion of Jews from the rural communes.

The report of Major Evans-Gordon to the Alien Immigration Commission is referred to, and in view of the improved condition of things the Jewish newspapers advise against any measures from outside in behalf of the Roumanian Jews.

I have, etc.,

CHARLES S. WILSON

In an earlier dispatch, November 15, 1903, Mr. Wilson had already referred to the report of Major Evans-Gordon, a member of a royal commission sent to investigate into the causes of immigration to England from the various countries. Major Evans-Gordon's report on the condition of the Jews in Rumania contains the following statement:[23]

The expulsive force is undoubtedly the intolerant attitude of the Government toward the Jews and the series of oppressive measures which, contrary to treaty engagements, have appeared upon the statute books of that country.

[22] Foreign Relations, 1904, page 706.
[23] *Ibid.*, 1903, page 707.

The Jewish question has been a burning one ever since Roumanian independence was granted, and even long before. At the time of the Berlin conference, in 1878, an attempt was made to place the Jewish subjects of Roumania upon a footing of equality with the other classes of the population.

The evident intention of the powers throughout the negotiations was to establish a complete religious and civil equality for the Jews. The policy of the Roumanian Government was then and is still directly opposed to this intention. Rightly or wrongly, they have always asserted that such equality, if given to the Hebrew race, would end in the subjugation of their country by an alien people, and far from complying with the conditions laid down by the great powers, their policy tends toward the suppression, political extermination, and expulsion of the Jews.

Mr. Wilson belittles the importance of this report and doubts whether it represents the actual condition. His attack on the report concludes with a telling observation, indirectly verifying the very report he attacks; he says that "the report does not take into consideration at all that, in the opinion of Roumanians of all classes, as well as of most foreigners who understand the conditions of the country, the restrictions placed upon the Jews in Roumania are absolutely necessary for their national preservation."

No further reference is made on the situation of Jews in Rumania for a number of years. The conditions, however, did not improve, and when next an international conference considered the Balkan situation, the United States again came forward to exert its influence with the nations of the world in behalf of the Rumanian Jews. This conference, which took place in London in the summer in 1913, had for its purpose the termination of the war which the Balkan states were then waging among themselves after they had previously concluded a successful war against their common enemy, Turkey. As a result of these wars almost a quarter of a million Jews, formerly Turkish subjects, became nationals.

In January 1913, Mr. Louis Marshall, President of the American Jewish Committee, wrote a letter to President Taft urging him to use the influence of the United States, through the signatory powers of the Berlin Treaty, to include

in the peace treaties to be concluded at the close of the
Balkan Wars, a clause guaranteeing life, liberty and equality
to all inhabitants of the countries involved, irrespective of
race and creed. Mr. Marshall pointed out in his letter that
mass immigration to the United States would follow, should
equality be refused.

Meanwhile there occurred a change of administration in
Washington, Woodrow Wilson becoming the head of the
government. Dr. Cyrus Adler, with Dr. Herbert Friedenwald,
met the new president and acquainted him with the Rumanian situation. There then ensued an exchange of letters between John Bassett Moore, Counselor of the Department of
State and Acting Secretary of State, and Dr. Adler, representing the American Jewish Committee.[24] In a letter of
July 24, 1913, Mr. Moore informed Dr. Adler that the Department had found it possible to instruct the American Ambassador in London "that it desires the Ambassador to
take occasion to express to the British Foreign Office the
satisfaction with which the United States would regard the
inclusion, in any such agreement as may ultimately be concluded in regard to these questions, of a provision assuring
the full enjoyment of civil and religious liberty to the inhabitants of the territories in question without distinction of
creed." However, in a letter of July 30, Mr. Moore informed
Dr. Adler that the conference was not expected to deal with
the domestic questions of the several Balkan States, but that
Sir Edward Grey, British Secretary of State for Foreign
Affairs, would be willing to lay before the conference the
suggestions of the United States on this matter, should
occasion arise. In another letter, dated August 6, 1913, Dr.
Adler was informed that the Department had given similar
instruction to the representatives of the United States
in Greece, Montenegro, Bulgaria, Rumania and Serbia.

The question was taken up by the conference but nothing
was accomplished. Three days later, Mr. Moore wrote

[24] The full text of these letters will be found in "Jewish Disabilities in the
Balkan States," by Max J. Kohler and Simon Wolf, in *Publications of the
American Jewish Historical Society*, No. 24, 1916, pages 89–92.

to Dr. Adler telling him that the conference decided that "it would be superfluous to include in the treaty of peace a special provision of the nature contemplated inasmuch as the constitutions of all the states involved guaranteed civil and religious liberty." The Minister of Rumania took occasion to declare the view that in accordance with the principles of international law all citizens without distinction of race or religion become citizens of the annexing state. The American Minister in Rumania was further assured by the Rumanian Government that "the Jewish inhabitants of the territory about to be transferred to Rumanian sovereignty will be accorded the same rights and privileges as are given to persons of other races and religions."

Again the signatory powers of the Berlin Conference failed in their obvious duty to the Jews of Rumania. There was no doubt that there was ample ground for them to intervene to persuade Rumania to abide by her international engagements, in respect of her Jewish population, but, alas, in vain did the United States exert her influence in an attempt to alleviate Jewish sufferings in Rumania.

Persecution of the Jews continued unabated in Rumania. On October 10, 1913, Representative Howard P. Chandler spoke in favor of the following resolution, introduced by him in the House of Representatives:[25]

[Resolution by Mr. Chandler]

Whereas, the Government of Roumania accepted the terms of said articles of said treaty as a condition precedent to the recognition of her independence; and

Whereas it is a matter of certain knowledge that the Jews of Roumania, numbering about 250,000, have been the barbarized and impoverished victims of Roumanian discriminatory legislation and of Roumanian riots and massacres for a period of more than 30 years in violation of both the letter and the spirit of the treaty of Berlin: Therefore be it

Resolved by the Senate and House of Representatives of the United States of America, in Congress assembled, that it is the

[25] *Congressional Record*, 1913, 63rd Congress, 1st Session, Vol. 50, Part 6, page 5541.

sense of the American Congress that the interests of civilization, the rights of humanity, the principles of eternal justice, and the dignity and sanctity of international law demand that the signatory powers of the treaty of Berlin compel Roumania to observe the stipulations of the treaty of Berlin in the matter of the treatment of the Jews.

Resolved, that the Secretary of State be requested to transmit a copy of this resolution to the Governments of Great Britain, Germany, Austria, Russia, France, Italy and Turkey.

From the body of his speech we quote the following paragraphs:

But why should we do all these things for the Jews, you ask? The reply is that these things are not to be done primarily for the Jews. They are to be done to promote and maintain civil liberty and religious freedom, among men; to prevent offenses against international morality and to uphold the dignity and sanctity of international law; and above all things, to compel respect for the laws of humanity and regard for the principles of eternal justice. These are the primary objects of action to be taken against Roumania.

But if you challenge me to open declaration I will candidly say to you that I am in favor of doing all manner of good things at all times for the Jews simply because they are Jews. And in this declaration is no sickly sentimentality, no maudlin sentiment. . . .

The marvelous contributions of the Jewish people to the spiritual and intellectual wealth of the world entitle them to the gratitude and homage, not the hatred and persecution, of mankind. If gratitude were a supreme virtue of nations, as it should be of individuals, there would never be any organized governmental persecution of Jews. The civilized nations of this earth are too deeply and everlastingly indebted to the Jews to be able ever to cancel the obligation. They should at least treat them with humanity and accord them those considerations which are the absolute essentials of happiness in a civilized state. . . .

If her [Roumania's] sense of national honor and international obligation does not incline Roumania to deeds of justice and righteousness, then let the strong arm of force be used and the wrath of nations be visited upon her.

Unfortunately, the signatory powers failed to respond to such appeals. The attitude of the Rumanian Government itself is best learned from a pronouncement of M. Take Jonescu, Rumanian Minister of Interior, who in 1913 declared:

As for the other question of the manner in which Roumania may have carried out the provisions of the Treaty of Berlin, that problem ceased to be a part of international law on the day on which the powers subscribing to the Treaty of Berlin recognized the independence of Roumania. The question of the Jews in Roumania became a question of internal law.

But in spite of this opinion, the question of the Jews in Rumania again became a question of international law when the nations of the world met after the World War to conclude the various peace treaties.

In the treaties of the Allied and Associated Powers (of which Rumania was one) with Austria and Hungary, Articles 60 and 47 respectively, the Government of Rumania agreed, much against its will, "to embody in a treaty with the Principal Allied and Associated Powers such provisions as may be deemed necessary by these Powers to protect the interests of inhabitants of that State who differ from the majority of the population in race, language or religion."

Such a treaty was later concluded between the Principal Allied and Associated Powers and Rumania.[26] It provided that Jews as well as other persons belonging to racial, linguistic and religious minorities were to be treated as equals of the majority population; that due recognition be given to the language of minorities; that they be allowed to use their mother tongues as languages of instruction in primary schools and that such schools be entitled to a portion of government funds for the education of the people. Jews formerly citizens of Austria-Hungary and who live permanently in the territories now ceded to Rumania should become *ipso facto* Rumanian citizens without the necessity of a formality.

One article, the seventh, deals with Jews only, and reads: "Roumania undertakes to recognize as Roumanian nationals *ipso facto* and without requirement of any formality Jews inhabiting any Roumanian territory, who do not possess another nationality."

---

[26] For the full text of the minority treaties see "History of the Peace Conference of Paris," edited by H. W. V. Temperley, Vol. V, pages 437–46; also "The Jews and Minority Rights 1898–1919," by Oscar Janowsky.

These and other provisions of the treaty for the protection of minorities Rumania recognized as "fundamental laws, and that no law, regulation or official action shall conflict or interfere with these stipulations, nor shall any law, regulation or official action prevail over them." In fact they could not be modified without the assent of a majority of the League of Nations.

Unfortunately, the condition of the Jews in Rumania has not improved materially as a result of the minorities treaty. This treaty, as well as the Rumanian constitution, contains liberal provisions, but they are not applied in practice. With the internal condition growing worse and international help not forthcoming, the Jews of Rumania were subjected during the succeeding years, up to the outbreak of the second world war, to the same persecutions as had been their lot during the fifty years preceding the signing of the minorities treaty.

The situation of the Jews during the Hitler war has been a veritable chapter of horrors. They have been made the first and chief victims of civil strife, and have been plundered, expropriated, deported in large numbers, subjected to the ravages of concentration camps and to mass murder,— all at the hands of the government of the country in which they lived.

VI. POLAND

Poland is one of the new states in Europe which owes its existence to the Peace Treaty of Versailles. Twice before there existed a Polish State in Eastern Europe. But helped by internal dissension, Austria, Prussia and Russia, the neighbors of Poland, divided various portions of the monarchy among themselves. The last partition, in 1795, resulted in the total disappearance of the Polish State. In 1807 Napoleon revived Polish sovereignty by |creating the duchy, which in 1815 became the second Kingdom of Poland. This new kingdom also disappeared in 1830.

Diplomatic correspondence with the new government centered mainly around the disturbances of 1919, which caused the governments of the United States and of Great Britain to send special commissions to investigate them. The United States Government, in conjunction with the Allied Powers, was instrumental in obtaining minority rights for the Jews of Poland and elsewhere when the question was before the Peace Conference at Versailles.

However, Poland figured in the foreign relations of the United States even before it was reconstituted as a nation. Russian Poland, that part of modern Poland which before the World War was part of the Russian Empire, was, during the latter part of the War, under the military occupation of the German armies. As a consequence of the severance of this portion of Poland from Russia, and the ravages of a cruel war, the population of the occupied region was suffering from starvation aggravated by the dictatorship of an army, which, of course, was interested only in the prosecution of the war, and cared nothing for the people of the occupied provinces.

Equally with the other noncombatants, the Jews of Poland hungered and suffered, and many would have per-ished had it not been for the humanitarian response of American Jews to the cry of their Polish brethren.

It must be said to the eternal credit of the Government of the United States and their representatives abroad that, before and after the entry of the United States into the World War, Washington was always ready to co-operate with the American Jewish Joint Distribution Committee. This was the agency of the Jewish community of the United States charged with the conduct of relief activities on behalf of Jews abroad.

The first time Polish relief was mentioned in the diplomatic correspondence of the United States was in the middle of February, 1917,[1] when the declaration of war against Germany was imminent. Before that time, relief monies gathered in the United States for distribution in Poland were sent through M. M. Warburg & Co., Hamburg. On February 16, 1917, Secretary of State Lansing sent a cable to Joseph E. Willard, the American Ambassador at Madrid, asking him, at the request of the Joint Distribution Committee of Funds for Jewish War Sufferers, to ascertain from the Spanish Government whether its Ambassador in Berlin would undertake to receive funds cabled to him, for the purpose of purchasing foodstuffs for noncombatants, inhabitants of Poland, and transmit the same to local relief committees which were in Vilna and Warsaw. The Central Berlin Committee would give guaranties to the Spanish Ambassador that the funds were properly distributed at their destination.

Mr. Willard's reply was received on February 17, 1917. In it, he informed Mr. Lansing that the Spanish Ambassador was willing to handle the money for the Jewish war sufferers in Poland, but that it would be impossible for him, or the Central Committee in Berlin, to purchase foodstuffs in Germany.

However, after giving careful consideration to the question of continuing the relief work of the Joint Distribution Committee, the Department of State reached the conclusion that the method of sending this relief through the Spanish Ambas-

[1] Foreign Relations, 1918, Suppl. 2, page 498.

sador in Berlin was not wholly desirable, but that the relief work should be done by a committee in a neutral country. This conclusion was communicated to Herbert H. Lehman, Treasurer of the Joint Distribution Committee, on April 21, 1917, by William Phillips, Assistant Secretary of State, in the following letter:[2]

[*Mr. Phillips to Mr. Lehman*]

Washington, April 21, 1917

SIR: The Department has given careful consideration to the question of continuing the relief work which is being carried on by your Committee among the Jews in that part of Russian Poland now occupied by the Germans, and has reached the conclusion that the method of sending this relief through the Spanish Ambassador in Berlin is not wholly desirable, and that a neutral committee should be formed in a neutral country with entirely new machinery for carrying on this work.

Realizing, however, the great suffering among the people to whom your Committee has been extending relief, the Department will raise no objection to the Spanish Ambassador here transmitting to the Spanish Ambassador in Berlin directly, $100,000, to be distributed by the Spanish Ambassador in Berlin directly to the Russian committees in occupied Poland. In future, however, the relief funds should be transmitted through a committee in a neutral country, and I beg that you will take immediate steps to create this new machinery of distribution.

I am [etc.]

For the Secretary of State
WILLIAM PHILLIPS
Assistant Secretary

The attitude of Washington towards relief in occupied enemy territories was totally different from the attitude taken in London. Frank L. Polk, Counselor for the Department of State, inquired of Sir Cecil Spring-Rice, the British Ambassador at Washington, whether relief was being sent from the United Kingdom to Russian Jews in enemy-occupied districts of Poland, and if so, through what channels. After addressing an inquiry by cable to London, the British Ambassador told Mr. Polk that His Majesty's Government had

[2] Foreign Relations, 1918, Suppl. 2, page 499.

been compelled to discourage proposals to forward such relief owing to the impossibility of insuring that it would reach the desired quarter.

The State Department, taking a more humane attitude, sent the following telegram to Marshall Langhorne, Chargé d'Affaires in the Netherlands:[3]

[*Mr. Lansing to Mr. Langhorne*]

Washington, May 16, 1917

Please ascertain whether the Netherlands Government would be willing to cause limited distribution under active supervision of Dutch Consul at Warsaw of relief funds to destitute Russian and Polish Jews and Russian Poles in Russian Poland under German occupation. Since it is a matter of prime importance that the funds should not reach German hands, or those of her allies, a method of distribution would have to be devised which could be considered as a guarantee to that end. Should the proposal be favorably received, we would be glad to learn the view of the Consul in this regard.

LANSING

The Dutch Minister at Berlin communicated with the Netherlands consul at Warsaw regarding the possibility of obtaining assurances that the German authorities would not interfere with the distribution of the funds by the consul.

Owing to the fact that these districts were under military occupation, and also that there were bureaucratic delays, it was not until October, 1917, that the State Department was informed, through the Foreign Ministry in Madrid, that the Oberrabbiner (Chief Rabbi) had told the Spanish Ambassador in Berlin that the German Government had no objection to the distribution, through the consular representatives of Holland, of funds to Jews in territories occupied by Germany; in fact, Germany was disposed to facilitate such distribution through nationals of any neutral country.

Thereupon, Mr. Max Senior and Dr. Boris Bogen, European agents for the Joint Distribution Committee, as a test, requested the German authorities for permission to transmit

[3] Foreign Relations, 1918, Suppl. 2, page 500.

$40,000.00 to Warsaw. This permission was duly granted, and arrangements were made for similar distribution in all German-occupied territories. On October 22, 1917, John W. Garrett, the United States Minister to the Netherlands, cabled Mr. Lansing that "the Dutch Government gladly co-operated and no further difficulty was expected on the part of Germany."

On November 14, 1917, Minister Garrett was asked by Mr. Lansing to draw on the Secretary of State for such amounts as Messrs. Bogen and Senior might request on account of the Joint Distribution Committee. The amount, however, was not to exceed $300,000.00. Messrs. Bogen and Senior were authorized to distribute the relief money through the Netherlands consul at Warsaw, and were asked to obtain receipts and forward them through the Department.

In addition to the lack of food, the war sufferers in occupied Poland were in great need of clothing. Winters in that part of Europe are very severe, and many faced death from exposure. To remedy this evil, Mr. Lansing, at the suggestion of the Polish and Jewish relief societies, contemplated permitting relief societies to purchase second-hand or inexpensive new clothing in countries adjacent to Germany for shipment and distribution in Poland.

Accordingly, Secretary Lansing cabled the following to Mr. Garrett, United States Minister at The Hague, asking him to repeat to American Ministers in Berne, Copenhagen, and Stockholm:[4]

[*Mr. Lansing to Mr. Garrett*]

Washington, March 21, 1918

For your information. After April 1 amount of relief remittances permitted by this Government to go to Poland monthly for relief all nationalities will not exceed $300,000 of which $200,000 general relief, and $100,000 individual remittances. To supplement this, Department is contemplating permitting relief societies to purchase second-hand clothing or inexpensive new clothing in countries adjacent to Germany for shipment to and distribution in Poland.

[4] Foreign Relations, 1918, Suppl. 2, page 529.

Please ascertain and report by cable if local representatives of relief societies can obtain adequate written guarantees from German authorities that such shipments to Poland will be permitted and will not be seized and that distribution in Poland by neutral agents of relief societies will be carried out unmolested by German authorities, civil or military; also that German authorities will not seize in Poland a stock of clothing to offset such quantities as may be forwarded to Poland by American relief societies. Report in detail terms of guarantees of German authorities.

LANSING

This benevolent plan was not realized. In a letter to the Joint Committee, dated June 3, 1918, Mr. William Phillips informed the Committee with regret that the State Department had received unfavorable replies from the American legations at The Hague, Berne, Copenhagen and Stockholm, regarding the purchasing and forwarding of clothing to Poland. Clothing being scarce in these countries, there appeared no immediate possibility of obtaining permission from local authorities for the exportation of wearing apparel to Poland. A check for $15,000.00, which was to be used for the purchase of old clothing, was returned to the Joint Distribution Committee.

In a memorandum dated November 2, 1917, which, under direct instruction from Mr. Arthur James Balfour, British Secretary of State for Foreign Affairs, the British Ambassador sent to Mr. Lansing, the British Government opposed the forwarding of condensed milk for starving babies of Poland. Among the reasons which the memorandum gave for this opposition, was the following:[5]

The large and influential Jewish element in Poland is to a great extent actively pro-German, and its members are often employed as German agents in collecting food-stuffs for export to Germany.

One of the weapons which the Allies used against Germany was that of a financial blockade, whereby they attempted to depress the value of German money. Obviously, the sending of relief funds to German-occupied territory was incon-

[5] Foreign Relations, 1918, Suppl. 2, page 518.

sistent with such a plan. It was estimated that in one year, a sum of from three hundred thousand pounds to five hundred thousand pounds passed from England to Poland alone. Representatives from various British offices gathered at London on November 6, 1917 to discuss thoroughly the entire question of relief.

The following plan was suggested:[6]

1. No general relief to be allowed.
2. No general licenses for sending remittances to be granted.
3. No licenses for any remittances directly or indirectly to any others than a subject of the remitting country to be granted, except with the sanction in each case of the Government of that country at war with the Central Powers of which the beneficiary was a citizen, the Government of the remitting country to retain full discretion as to the granting and conditions of licenses, and remittances to be sent via England, and only channels of communication under control of British censorship were to be used.

It was also suggested that the Government of the United States and the Dominion of Canada be invited to adopt similar procedure.

Walter Hines Page, United States Ambassador at London, reporting at the request of the State Department, upon this conference, asked for an expression of opinion from Mr. Lansing on this plan.

On November 14, 1917, Mr. Lansing replied that, while the Department fully approved the principle involved in the suggestions of the British Government and itself intended to limit relief remittances to the lowest reasonable amount, and to have even those remittances under the strict control of the Government, it could not cut off all relief activities:[6a]

... not only on account of the consideration it owes to the views of the loyal Jewish and Polish elements in this country who desire to prevent the starvation of their relatives in Poland, but also from the broader viewpoint of humanity.

As for the inconsistency of sending money into Germany, while at the same time trying to enforce a financial blockade

---

[6] Foreign Relations, 1918, Suppl. 2, page 521.
[6a] *Ibid.*, page 522.

against it, the Department reached the conclusion, after careful and thorough investigation, that the sums sent to Poland would result in inappreciable advantage to the enemy, certainly not enough to warrant complete discontinuance of relief work in Poland.

Pressure from London to limit further remittances to Poland continued and grew more insistent. In March, 1918, Secretary Lansing addressed a letter to President Wilson, at whose request monetary relief to the destitute in occupied Poland was continued, asking him for a new expression of his views on this question. Mr. Lansing was of the opinion that it had become desirable to limit the monthly remittances, that the sum of $700,000.00 which the Polish Relief Committee and the Joint Distribution Committee were sending as a monthly average to Poland, was altogether too high; and that $300,000.00 per month should be fixed as a maximum amount to be sent to Poland, of which $200,000.00 be assigned for general relief, and $100,000.00 for individual remittances. Mr. Lansing concluded by asking the President whether, in the event he approved these suggestions, the limitation should be made retroactive and include the sum of $1,500,000.00, which had not yet gone forward, but for which licenses had been granted by the War Trade Board.

President Wilson's reply follows:[7]

[*President Wilson to Mr. Lansing*]

Washington, March 16, 1918

MY DEAR MR. SECRETARY: It is a most distressing decision to be forced to, but I fear I must concur in your judgment that these amounts must be limited, and I have no doubt that you are in a much better position than I to say to what figures they should be restricted. I think, however, that it would not be wise or just to make the restriction retroactive.

Faithfully yours,
W. W.

Mr. Lansing's suggestions were then made the policy of the Department, and American Ministers at Berne, The

[7] Foreign Relations, 1918, Suppl. 2, page 528.

Hague, Copenhagen and Stockholm were informed to the effect that after April 1, 1918, the amount of remittances permitted by this Government to go to Poland would be limited to $300,000.00 monthly, for the relief of all nationalities. Furthermore, this amount was to be restricted to Poland, and was not to include inhabitants of Lithuania. Upon advice from American diplomatic representatives in Russia, Sweden and Denmark, it was suggested that the cause of the Allies would best be served if inhabitants of enemy-occupied territory other than Poland were excluded from the benefits and privilege of relief activities. It was hoped that this policy would increase the antagonism of the population towards Germany, and correspondingly create sympathy for the Allies. The provinces of Grodno, Vilna and Kovno, where many Jews lived, were thus left to their own fate, and deprived of the little help which their brethren in the United States were only too willing to extend to them. After the Armistice relief for the Jews in Poland was broadened, and became increasingly constructive as time went on. This effort which was actively carried on from Paris in 1919 was greatly aided by the American Relief Administration of which Mr. Herbert Hoover was then the head, by Mr. Lewis L. Strauss, his secretary, and by Mr. Louis Marshall and Dr. Cyrus Adler who were then in Paris.

Meanwhile Poland became an independent state, and diplomatic correspondence was now carried on directly between the Government of the United States and the Government of the new Poland.

One of President Wilson's famous fourteen points concerned itself with the condition of Poland and the Polish people. President Wilson, and all America with him, felt that a great historic wrong against the Polish people had been committed when Poland was divided as spoils for her stronger neighbors. One of the aims sought to be achieved by the Peace Conference was to re-establish Poland as an independent republic.

After the Armistice, the Poles organized a government with General Josef Pilsudski as Chief of State, and Ignace

Paderewski, the famous pianist, as Premier and Minister of Foreign Affairs. The Provisional Government of Poland was quickly recognized by the United States. Because President Wilson and Secretary of State Lansing were very eager to extend immediate recognition to the Provisional Government, the regular procedure in such matters was not observed, and instead of the formal note of recognition, which comes from the State Department in Washington, Secretary of State Lansing, then in Paris, sent the note to Paderewski, who was then Chief of the Polish Delegation to the Peace Conference.

The notification of recognition contained the following paragraph, which expressed fully the sentiment of the American people towards new Poland:[8]

Mr. Lansing wrote:

It is my privilege to extend to you at this time my personal greetings and officially to assure you that it will [be] a source of gratification to enter into official relations with you at the earliest opportunity. To render to your country such aid as is possible at this time as it enters upon a new cycle of independent life, will be in full accord with that spirit of friendliness which has in the past animated the American people in their relations with your countrymen.

Mr. Hugh Gibson was then given a recess appointment as Minister to Poland. Mr. William Phillips, Acting Secretary of State, was notified both of the recognition and the appointment as facts accomplished. Poland, in turn, sent Prince Casimir Lubomirski as Envoy Extraordinary and Minister Plenipotentiary of Poland at Washington. Mr. Phillips recognized him as appointed Minister until such time as the President might be able to receive him in formal audience.

Beside these formal notes, couched in polite diplomatic phraseology, other notes of a less pleasing nature were exchanged between the Administration in Washington and the Polish National Committee in Paris. Some of these notes, most of which were transmitted by wire, arrived prior to

[8] Foreign Relations, 1919, Vol. II, page 741.

the formal recognition of the Polish Provisional Government.

On December 2, 1918, Secretary Lansing sent the following cable to Mr. William G. Sharp, United States Ambassador at Paris:[9]

[*Mr. Lansing to Mr. Sharp*]

Washington, December 2, 1918

For Polish National Committee.

Department of State has received information through various sources of pogroms conducted against Jews in Poland. If these reports are true the sympathy of the American people for Polish aspirations will undoubtedly be affected.

Two days later, Mr. Polk, Acting Secretary of State, sent another telegram to Ambassador Sharp, in which he complained that additional information received at the State Department indicated that the pogroms were on the increase, and the situation had become quite alarming. Mr. Sharp was asked to take up the matter with the Polish National Committee, and cable their reply.

Mr. Sharp communicated at once with Roman Dmowski, head of the Polish National Committee in Paris, and in a long telegram of December 6, 1918, reported their conversation. According to Mr. Dmowski, reports of the massacres of Jews in Poland were greatly exaggerated, and he could prove that organized propaganda of the Jews in Poland and Russia was responsible for these stories, which had little foundation in fact; but Mr. Dmowski conceded that outrages were committed, and for these, the Polish people themselves were not only blameless, but unfortunately quite helpless to prevent them. Owing to the anarchical condition of the country, and also to the fact that many German prisoners were crossing Poland on their way from Russia to Germany, much pillaging and even murder took place. The Polish troops, numbering in all 20,000 men, were not able to cope with the situation.

Moreover, Mr. Dmowski stated, the scarcity of food, and

---

[9] Foreign Relations, 1919, Vol. II, page 746.

the practice of some proprietors of stores to hoard supplies for a rise in prices, caused the population in some places to plunder the food stores, and in many cases, the food store owners were killed. The fact that the owners of these stores were in many cases Jews was, according to Mr. Dmowski, only incidental. Much of the blame for the disorders was laid by Mr. Dmowski at the feet of a few Russian Jews, who, he alleged, had come to Poland, as representatives of the Bolshevist government in Russia, for the sole purpose of initiating there the same form of government as was practiced in Russia.

Mr. Dmowski, who was known, even at that time, as an arch anti-Semite, absolved himself and the Polish Government of anti-Semitism; he averred that being composed of Socialists, the Polish Government could never be anti-Semitic.

Mr. Gibson was appointed Minister to Poland early in April, and his commission was issued April 16, 1919. Even before he left Paris for Warsaw, he received the following telegram from Acting Secretary of State William Phillips:[10]

[*Mr. Phillips to Mr. Gibson*]

Washington, April 25, 1919

Certain Jews have furnished Department with reports that at Pinsk on April 5th, Jews were massacred by Poles while passover bread was being distributed. Another report received by Department states persons killed were Bolshevists attempting to start insurrection. Upon arrival Poland investigate very carefully truth of matter and report promptly to Department.

PHILLIPS

Minister Gibson cabled back that both reports were inaccurate, and that a committee composed of Poles and Jews had gathered some four hundred pages of testimony on the spot where the disturbances occurred; he promised to forward a full report as soon as he received that of the committee.

The State Department was not satisfied with this reply, and cabled Minister Gibson again as follows:[11]

[10] Foreign Relations, 1919, Vol. II, page 748.
[11] *Ibid.*, page 749.

[*Mr. Phillips to Mr. Gibson*]

Washington, May 21, 1919

Department much concerned with matter which is being widely discussed in American newspapers. Conflicting statements being constantly issued by Poles and Jews. Important Department know real truth earliest possible moment. Cable synopsis testimony to Department promptly as possible.

The following cable was sent only two days later.[12]

[*Mr. Polk to Mr. Gibson*]

Washington, May 23 [1919] 4 PM

Referring to Department's No. 9, May 21. Fifteen thousand Jews held meeting May 21, Madison Square Garden, New York City, to protest against atrocities charged to have been perpetrated against Jews in Poland, Galicia, Lithuania and other countries in Eastern Europe. Charles E. Hughes spoke and stated in part:

> If America stands for anything in her service to humanity, then let America speak. America owes it to herself that this time her people should act with one accord and because they are Americans should unite in this effective protest. These sad reports of Jewish massacres are well authenticated and must be accepted, and therefore I say if we mean aught when we talk of liberty and of the cause for which we have been fighting, if in all these days we have not simply been mouthing words, if America stands for anything in her service to humanity, then now let America speak.

Question will undoubtedly continue to be violently agitated this country and in all probability will be discussed in Congress. It is very essential that you keep Department very fully and promptly informed exact truth treatment Jews by Poles including question of religious toleration and also attitude Jews toward Poles.

The newspapers are carrying special reports of a Jewish massacre at Vilna.

POLK

The report of this meeting of May 23 was transmitted in a cable of some two thousand words by Mr. Jacob H. Schiff, Mr. Louis Marshall, President of the American Jewish Com-

[12] Foreign Relations, 1919, Vol. II, page 749.

mittee, and Dr. Cyrus Adler, Chairman of its Executive
Committee. The two latter, who were then in Paris, immediately sought and obtained an interview with President Woodrow Wilson, who stimulated the Department
of State and other officials into full activity.

Thereafter, Mr. Polk sent telegrams almost daily to the
American Minister in Warsaw and, as he received no immediate answer, concluded his telegram of May 28 with the
following admonition:

Agitation in this matter continues and Department must know
whole truth of situation at once. You are requested to give investigation treatment Jews by Poles and attitude Jews toward Poles
precedence over other matters in order to furnish Department
complete report without delay.

Acting under these instructions Mr. Gibson undertook to
make as thorough a study of the Jewish question in Poland
and of the disturbances and their causes as it was possible
in a brief time, and frequently without access to first hand
information, and as it is not unnatural, based to a certain
extent upon statements made to him by Polish officials.

In a cablegram dated June 2, 1919, which contained about
eighteen hundred words, Mr. Gibson submitted his observations on the Polish-Jewish problem, which, according to him,
must always be kept in mind, whenever the questions affecting Jews in Poland were discussed.[13]

Though Mr. Gibson did not base his observations on first-
hand study, as such a thing would have been impossible,
considering the speed in which he was urged to produce his
report, he made the best use of all available sources of information. He consulted representatives of the American Relief
Administration, of the American Red Cross, and of other
allied missions; the local press, both Jewish and Polish;
agents of the American Jewish Joint Distribution Committee,
as well as Jewish delegations and representatives of Jewish
organizations, to whom Mr. Gibson was always accessible,
and who talked frankly with him concerning the whole scope
of the situation of the Jews in Poland.

[13] Foreign Relations, 1919, Vol. II, pages 756–60.

According to Mr. Gibson, "The Jews should not for all purposes be considered as a whole." A large Jewish element considered the Jews to be a distinct nationality, totally different in culture and civilization from that of the majority groups. Jewish press and the Jewish representatives in the Diet continually stressed this distinction, and the Polish press, in return, kept emphasizing the same conditions, and as a result great ill-feeling prevailed.

The Jews had always formed the middle group, or ground between the peasant and the landowners in Poland. Most of the merchants and tradesmen were Jews and, in some parts of the country, the Jews had a practical monopoly of all trade, particularly in foodstuffs. With the price of food high and the majority of the populace too poor to purchase foodstuffs in the open market, temptation to plunder was sometimes too strong to resist. And, said Mr. Gibson: "If a Jew is injured, it is called a pogrom; if a Christian is mobbed, it is called a food riot."

Mr. Gibson would not trust all news published in the European and American press about alleged massacres in Poland. Most of the news, he said, originated in Kovno, which at the time was in German hands. These rumors were spread for German political reasons, and certainly not for the altruistic purpose of helping the Jews. Mr. Gibson took the American aim in this matter to be to "exert any proper effort to prevent violence and discrimination against the Jews, and to contribute so far as may be to a better understanding between the races." To achieve this aim, he suggested that the local press, Jewish and Polish, be urged to moderate its tone. (He himself had already taken the initiative in this direction.) Representative Poles and American and English Jews, Mr. Gibson recommended, should exchange visits and study the Jewish question along constructive lines. Though not very optimistic, Mr. Gibson did not believe the situation was entirely hopeless.

A great problem which is the product of time and circumstances requires both patience and good will for its solution. Solution is deferred by agitation which is productive of ill will on both sides. The Polish Government is [well intentioned] but lacks power and experience in authority. It is amenable to suggestion to an extent that is surprising. I should be glad therefore, to receive ideas from the Department or from anybody sincerely interested in the problem.

Mr. Gibson experienced great difficulties in accumulating the necessary data from the various places where outrages against Jews were committed. The Department of State, under pressure of public opinion as expressed in the newspapers, and in many other public forums, continually pressed him for more detailed information.

On June 2, 1919, he cabled the Acting Secretary of State, in Washington, that he had received no reports of atrocities perpetrated against Jews in Poland, Galicia, or Lithuania, with the exception of the Pinsk and Vilna affairs. The more cruel of these two was the former, in which thirty-five Jews had been stood up against a wall and shot without even the ceremony of a court martial.

Reports of these executions at Pinsk were received originally through Mr. Hoover in Paris, who was then in charge of the American Relief Administration, and were at his direction reported by the then Lieutenant James Becker to Oscar S. Straus, Louis Marshall and Cyrus Adler, who at once undertook to secure further information. It appeared that Baruch Zuckerman, who was a representative of the Peoples' Relief Committee, had called a meeting in Pinsk to arrange with the local committee for the distribution of flour at Passover. After having made this arrangement he left, and the military authorities held that this meeting was called without permission and they suspected it of being called in the interests of the Bolsheviks. This was the reason given for the execution of these thirty-five Jews who came together on an errand of mercy. A Polish commission appointed by the Diet to investigate the causes of the anti-Jewish riots asserted that though the action of military authorities was precipitate, their suspicions towards certain portions of the Jewish population were well founded.

Upon suggestion from the United States State Department, Mr. Gibson, accompanied by Lieutenant Colonel Walter G.

Bailey, Director for Poland of the American Red Cross, and
Dr. Boris Bogen, Director for Poland of the Jewish Joint
Distribution Committee, paid a personal visit to Vilna, where
sixty-four Jews had been shot and many more arrested, and
reported on their visit in a long telegram to Washington,
dated June 17, 1919. Conclusions reached as a result of this
visit and with which Dr. Bogen was in full agreement were
as follows:[14]

1. In view of the lack of any contemporary record, we doubt
whether the exact truth of [occurrences] can ever be ascertained.

2. The events described took place during the fighting of the
first three days, and before the authorities obtained control.

3. At the time the Polish troops entered Vilna there was such
a wide spread feeling among the Polish population and among the
soldiery against Jews believed to be allies of the Bolsheviki, war
profiteers and enemies to Poland that a hostile sentiment prevailed
against the Jews as such.

4. On entering Vilna the troops were fired upon from private
houses throughout the town and some of these houses were occupied
by Jews. Searches disclosed fuses, machine guns, and other
weapons.

5. The troops during these three days made wholesale arrests,
ransacked dwellings, and shops, and summarily executed a number
of persons.

6. At the end of three days the military and civil authorities
issued orders against pillaging and took effective control. Since
that date no cases of serious violence were reported.

7. At the present time the laws, so far as the protection of life
is concerned, are maintained.

8. The Jews are apprehensive; a general under current of anti-
Jewish feeling still exists and gives cause for some concern.

9. The Jewish population expresses confidence in the fairness of
the Chief of State, the Commissioner at Vilna, and General Szep-
tycki commanding on the Bolshevik front.

The American Minister had a frank talk with General
Pilsudski, Chief of State, on which he reported to Washington in the following telegram:[15]

[14] Foreign Relations, 1919, Vol. II, page 767.
[15] *Ibid.*, page 752.

[Mr. Gibson to Mr. Lansing]

Warsaw, May 31, 1919, 8 P.M.

Have had long frank talk with Chief of State regarding Jewish situation in general and situation at Chenstokhov in particular.

1. He states that he has given positive instruction for the maintenance of order and protection of the Jews at Chenstokhov.

2. That he is issuing peremptory orders to the Polish army stating that he will not tolerate anti-Jewish acts; that punishment will be severe and that the officers will be made responsible for the behavior of their men.

[3.] The minister of the Interior has been in Chenstokhov to investigate and with a free hand to take such steps as may be necessary. He is expected back tonight and his report is promised me without delay. General Pilsudski was evidently alarmed and indignant. He said that [to persecute] the Jews brought shame upon the name of Poland and could not but harm the country, that no matter what might be said these millions of Jews are in Poland; they are not going to leave Poland and the Poles have got to live in close contact with them. "The Government as well as all good Poles are strongly opposed to any persecution for we know that we cannot settle down to peaceful development while there is discord among elements of our own population. For the good of the country the Government is determined to put down any anti-Jewish activities with an iron hand."

Confidential. He told me that until the last few days he had felt that anti-Jewish persecution pretty well at an end but that the troops newly arrived from France had shown a disposition to make life miserable for the Jews, chasing them through the streets, cutting off their beards, et cetera. That this was causing a recrudescence of such acts by the civil population and this is confirmed by statements made to me this afternoon by reliable American-Jewish informant before I saw General Pilsudski.

[GIBSON]

Reports of much more serious riots against Jews reached the United States, and American Jews clamored for more effective action by the State Department. In the Senate, the following resolution was introduced by Senator William F. Calder, of New York on May 26, 1919:[16]

[16] *Congressional Record*, 66th Congress, 1st Session, Vol. 58, Part 1, page 246.

[*Resolution by Senator Calder*]

Whereas it is reported that innocent men, women, and children, particularly of the Jewish faith, are being outraged and massacred in Poland, Roumania, and Galicia:

Therefore be it *Resolved* that the Department of State be, and hereby is, directed to communicate such reports to the President of the United States, and request that he confer with the representatives at the peace conference of the countries where such outrages and massacres are reported to occur and inform them that this body and the American people generally deeply deplore acts of violence and cruelty committed against men, women, and children because of race or religion.

President Wilson must have had this matter before him, even before this resolution was introduced in the United States Senate, but the task of ascertaining all facts and interpreting them required more time and attention than Mr. Gibson was able to give to it. He felt that no one could honestly give an opinion on these events based upon such investigations as he could make while under constant pressure of other official duties; he asked, therefore, that a commission be appointed, which should devote its entire attention to an investigation of the relations between the Jews and the Poles.

Mr. Gibson's work in this connection is well summarized in the following cablegram, which he sent to the Acting Secretary of State:[17]

[*Mr. Gibson to Mr. Polk, Acting Secretary of State*]

Warsaw, June 20, 1919

Since our arrival here we have devoted most of our efforts to Jewish questions. We have discussed the matter at length with Jews of varying opinions and with Poles, both in and out of the Government. I feel that we have been successful in impressing the Government with the seriousness of the situation and they have already acted upon some of our suggestions. The friendly declarations of General Haller, and the Minister of the Interior and governmental pressure enable the press to modify its tone. They realize the friendly spirit which prompts our interest, show a

[17] Foreign Relations, 1919, Vol. II, page 768.

readiness to follow our advice and I believe that other steps will be taken soon.

The various excesses, which have taken place since last November, appear to be due chiefly to abnormal conditions. I attach greater importance to the state of public opinion which is undoubtedly bad and may have serious consequences. We are trying to improve the situation in this respect by exerting our friendly influence with the Polish Government to adopt obvious measures such as moderating tone of press, controlling actions of troops, issuing strict instructions to officials throughout the country, etc.

I shall be glad to receive any suggestions as to specific action that the Department may be disposed to offer either as its own views or those of people interested in the question.

GIBSON

Mr. Gibson came to Paris for consultation with the State Department authorities there and learned of the decision of the President to appoint a special commission to proceed to Poland and investigate the entire situation on the spot. Then he cabled to Mr. Polk:

I am informed that the President contemplates sending to Poland a Mission to investigate Jewish matters. In case this is decided upon it would seem futile for me to make further investigation.

The idea of sending a commission to investigate conditions in Poland was mentioned for the first time on December 10, 1918, when Mr. Pleasant A. Stovall, the United States Minister in Switzerland, wired to Mr. Phillips that the Polish Chargé d'Affaires in Berne had informed him on behalf of the Polish Government, that it had taken official cognizance of the request of a number of Jewish organizations, that the Allied and Associated Governments send a mission into Poland for the purpose of investigating the alleged pogroms. The Polish Chargé d'Affaires added that his Government would be gratified to see that such a step be taken and would accord to such a mission all possible facilities.

The investigation, undertaken at the request of the State Department by Mr. Gibson in conjunction with Col. Bailey and Dr. Bogen, may also be viewed as the work of a neutral commission. The assignment for this commission was specific and expired soon after its first investigation was concluded. It was felt in this country that what was required was a commission which would be able to devote its whole attention, for as long a time as was necessary, to the pursuance of its mission. The same feeling prevailed in England where the Investigating Commission was headed by Sir Stuárt Samuel. President Wilson appointed Mr. Henry Morgenthau, former United States Ambassador to Turkey, as chairman of the Mission of the United States Government to Poland. The other members were Mr. Homer H. Johnson and Brigadier General Edgar Jadwin. Major Arthur Goodhart, who had been detached from his command in the Judge Advocate General's department, was assigned to this mission as a legal adviser. Incidentally his stay in Poland resulted in a very interesting book entitled "Poland and the Minority Races."

The terms of reference for this mission are given in the following statement which Secretary of State Lansing made to its members on June 30, 1919:[18]

[*Terms of Reference to U. S. Mission to Poland*]

It is desired that the Mission make careful inquiry into all matters affecting the relations between the Jewish and non-Jewish elements in Poland. This will, of course, involve the investigation of the various massacres, pogroms, and other excesses alleged to have taken place, the economic boycott, and other methods of discrimination against the Jewish race. The establishment of the truth in regard to these matters is not, however, an end in itself. It is merely for the purpose of seeking to discover the reasons lying behind such excesses and discriminations with a view to finding a possible remedy. The American Government, as you know, is inspired by a friendly desire to render service to all elements in the new Poland — Christians and Jews alike. I am convinced that any measure, that may be taken to ameliorate the conditions of the Jews will also benefit the rest of the population, and that, conversely, anything done for the community benefit of Poland as a whole will be of advantage to the Jewish race. I am sure, that the members of your Mission are approaching the subject in the right spirit, free from prejudice one way or the other and filled with a

[18] Foreign Relations, 1919, Vol. II, page 774.

desire to discover the truth and evolve some constructive measures to improve the situation which gives concern to all the friends of Poland.

The mission worked from July 12 to September 13, visiting towns and villages, all places where excesses had occurred, and also all institutions, such as libraries, hospitals, museums, asylums and prisons. The Commissioners visited the latter in order to appraise the social and cultural conditions of the population. The mission took all possible means to establish contact with representatives of all classes in order to obtain a correct impression of what had occurred, and to have a correct idea of the mental state of the people, and the attitude of the various groups towards each other.

For a number of reasons, it was impossible for the members to embody their findings in one report. As a result two reports were submitted, one by the chairman, Mr. Morgenthau, and the second by the other two members.[19]

Mr. Morgenthau began his report with a short history of the Jews in Poland, when the Jews migrated from Germany and other countries, as the result of severe persecution. At the end of the war, the general conditions in Poland were chaotic and provided good ground for social unrest. The outbursts against Jews were ascribed to the fact that "the chauvinistic reaction created by the sudden acquisition of a long-coveted freedom, ripened the public mind for anti-Semitic or anti-alien sentiment."

Both reports avoided the use of the term "pogrom," because it had no fixed definition and had come to be applied to everything disorderly, from petty outrages to premeditated and carefully organized massacres.

Mr. Morgenthau reported that there had been eight principal excesses, the first at Kielce, on November 11, 1918, before the Polish Republic came into being, in which four Jews had been killed and many more wounded. Much more serious had been the excesses in Lemberg during the 21st, 22nd and 23rd days of November, 1918. The Ukrainians

[19] For full text of reports see Foreign Relations, 1919, Vol. II, pages 774–800.

and Poles of Lemberg had fought for the control of the city. The declaration of neutrality by the Jews had been of little help to them; in fact, it enraged both sides and they had suffered equally from both factions. Sixty-four Jews had been killed, a large number injured, and a considerable amount of property belonging to Jews had been destroyed.

The most outrageous of all excesses had taken place in Pinsk on April 5, 1919. This was purely a military affair. In less than an hour after their arrest, thirty-five Jews had been lined up against the wall of the Cathedral and shot; this outrage was illuminated by the headlight of an automobile. At the time of the arrest these Jews were holding a meeting to discuss the distribution of relief sent by the American Jewish Joint Distribution Committee. Three of the men who were found still alive the next morning were shot a second time. Major Luczynski, the town commander, had held no trial whatsoever, and had made no conscientious effort to investigate the charges of Bolshevism against the prisoners. It is relevant to note that the committee sent by the Polish Diet to investigate the Pinsk affair did not publish its findings.

In Lida, thirty-nine Jews had been killed, soon after the capture of the city from the Russians. Many Jews had been arbitrarily arrested, kept without food, or had been impressed into service for forced labor without respect to age or infirmity.

In Vilna, fifteen Jews had lost their lives. Over two thousand Jewish stores and houses had been entered by Polish soldiers and civilians during the 19th, 20th and 21st days of April, 1919, and the inhabitants had been robbed and beaten; the material losses were estimated at over ten million rubles. Without trial or investigation old men and children had been seized and deported in box cars, in many cases, without food or water for four days.

The excesses in Minsk had occurred on August 8, while the American Mission was in town. Thirty-one Jews had been killed by Polish soldiers, although only one of the Jews had been in any way connected with the Bolshevists.

Besides these six and two other major excesses, there had been many sporadic cases of murder and robbery in a number of places. All excesses had been both political and anti-Semitic in character. Mr. Morgenthau held that the responsibility for them lay chiefly on the undisciplined Polish recruits, and their timid officers, who had regarded the Jews as aliens, and had sought to profit at their expense. In most cases, little, if anything, had been done to punish the perpetrators or compensate the victims. Mr. Morgenthau did not condemn the Polish nation as a whole for the violence committed by uncontrolled troops or local mobs. The murder of the Jews had not been premeditated, otherwise the number of the victims might have run into the thousands, instead of totaling two hundred and eighty.

Mr. Morgenthau discussed also the anti-Jewish discrimination, as manifested in the economic boycott against the Jewish population. The Jews had come to feel that there was an invisible rope around their necks, and that they were gradually being strangled to death. In this discrimination the Government itself had been an active partner. Government-owned railways had discharged Jewish employees for the sole reason that they were Jews; Jewish co-operatives also had been discriminated against in the distribution of government-controlled supplies.

In considering the causes for this anti-Jewish feeling, Mr. Morgenthau found that the desire of some Jews to establish cultural autonomy, financially supported by the State, and the insistence of Jews that the Treaty of Versailles guarantee their protection, had created a strong resentment against them. The Jews were looked upon as aliens because they had a culture of their own, wore distinctive dress, spoke their own language, and generally lived by themselves in separate quarters in almost every city in Poland.

The American Mission was not able, as a result of its short stay in Poland, to formulate a solution of the Jewish problem. Mr. Morgenthau suggested that the League of

Nations, or the larger nations interested in the problem, should send to Poland a commission of experts, "which should remain there as long as necessary to examine the problem at its source." To the Polish Government, the following remark was addressed:

Poland must promptly develop its full strength, and by its conduct first merit and then receive the unstinted moral, financial and economic support of all the world, which will insure the future success of the Republic.

The Jewish minority, fourteen percent of the entire population of Poland, was encouraged to participate with their whole strength and influence in making Poland a great united country.

The concluding observation of Mr. Morgenthau reads:

All citizens of Poland should realize that they must live together. They cannot be divorced from each other by force or by any court of law. When this idea is once thoroughly comprehended, every effort will necessarily be directed toward a better understanding and the amelioration of existing conditions, rather than toward augmenting antipathy and discontent. The Polish nation must see that its worst enemies are those who encourage this internal strife. A house divided against itself can not stand. There must be but one class of citizens in Poland, all members of which enjoy equal rights and render equal duties.

The report of General Jadwin and Mr. Johnson emphasized the separatism of the Jews, who still remembered that during the Middle Ages and much later they had enjoyed almost complete internal autonomy. The report of Messrs. Jadwin and Johnson stated further that the alleged sympathies of the Jews, first for the German invaders, and then for the Bolshevists, had aggravated an already bad situation. The program of the Bund, the Jewish Socialist Party, was likened by the Poles to that of the Bolshevists in Russia, though, as a matter of fact, the Bund had allied itself with the Mensheviks, the moderate element among the Russian Socialists. Then, there was "a sensitive Polish nationalism," which had been "resentful of any self-assertion from a minor-

ity whose very language recalls the hand of the oppressor."
The Jew who does not declare himself Polish is regarded as
an ally of any visible alien factor.

Both reports expressed doubt as to the advisability of
maintaining separate schools for Jewish children.

This report put Poland in a more favorable light by
pointing out that within that part of Poland which had
formerly been part of the Russian Empire and was generally
called Congress Poland only eighteen Jews had lost their
lives, whereas, in the other territories which had formerly
been parts of Germany and Austria-Hungary, most of the
serious excesses had occurred. Much ground for hope was
seen in the working of the minority treaty and the improvement of the economic conditions of the country.

The President communicated both reports to the Senate,
and they were subsequently published as a Senate Document.[20]

Poland, like Rumania and other countries, was persuaded
to sign a special treaty with the Principal Allied and Associated Powers for the protection of persons belonging to racial,
religious and linguistic minorities among its inhabitants. This
persuasion was exerted mainly through the famous letter
which Georges Clemenceau, President of the Council of the
Peace Conference, wrote to Ignace J. Paderewski, head of the
Polish delegation to the Peace Conference, on June 20, 1919.
After pointing to the long established international practice
which usually imposed certain principles of government upon
the new state before formal recognition was extended, and
after reminding the Polish people that it owed the recovery
of its independence to the endeavors and sacrifices of the
Principal Allied and Associated Powers, Mr. Clemenceau
urged upon Mr. Paderewski the immediate acceptance of
the minority provisions.

From this long and interesting letter we give the following
two pertinent quotations:[21]

[20] Senate Document No. 177, 66th Congress, 2nd Session.
[21] *American Jewish Year Book*, 1920–1921, page 107.

The situation with which the powers have now to deal is new, and experience has shown that new provisions are necessary. The territories now being transferred both to Poland and to other States inevitably include a large population speaking languages and belonging to races different from that of the people with whom they will be incorporated. Unfortunately, the races have been estranged by long years of bitter hostility. It is believed that these populations will be more easily reconciled to their new position if they knew that from the very beginning they have assured protection and adequate guarantees against any danger of unjust treatment or oppression. The very knowledge that these guarantees exist will, it is hoped, materially help the reconciliation which all desire, and will indeed do much to prevent the necessity of its enforcement.

Clauses 10 and 12 deal specifically with the Jewish citizens of Poland. The information at the disposal of the Principal Allied and Associated Powers as to the existing relations between the Jews and the other Polish citizens has led them to the conclusion that, in view of the historical development of the Jewish question and the great animosity aroused by it, special protection is necessary for the Jews in Poland. These clauses have been limited to the minimum which seems necessary under the circumstances of the present day, viz., the maintenance of Jewish schools and the protection of the Jews in the religious observance of their Sabbath. It is believed that these stipulations will not create any obstacle to the political unity of Poland. They do not constitute any recognition of the Jews as a separate political community within the Polish State.

The provisions of this Treaty are practically the same as those of the Roumanian treaty, except that in the Polish treaty there are two articles which mention Jews specifically and which are absent in the Roumanian treaty. These articles are:[21a]

ARTICLE 10: Educational Committees appointed locally by the Jewish communities of Poland will, subject to the general control of the State, provide for the distribution of the proportional share of public funds allocated to Jewish schools in accordance with Article 9, and for the organisation and management of these schools.

The provisions of Article 9 concerning the use of languages in schools shall apply to these schools.

[21a] *Protection of Linguistic, Racial and Religious Minorities.* League of Nations, Geneva, 1927, page 44.

ARTICLE 11: Jews shall not be compelled to perform any act which constitutes a violation of their Sabbath, nor shall they be placed under any disability by reason of their refusal to attend courts of law or to perform any legal business on their Sabbath. This provision, however, shall not exempt Jews from such obligations as shall be imposed upon all other Polish citizens for the necessary purposes of military service, national defence or the preservation of public order.

Poland declares her intention to refrain from ordering or permitting elections, whether general or local, to be held on a Saturday, nor will registration for electoral or other purposes be compelled to be performed on a Saturday.

Here, too, international protection proved inadequate to solve the many difficulties the Jews experienced in Poland.[22] In fact, owing to the development of the Polish economy and to the ever-increasing anti-Semitic agitation by certain political groups in that country, the condition of the Jews was going from bad to worse. Thousands of Jewish families were able to subsist only from the proceeds of charity generously supplied by Jews of other countries more happily situated. Many other thousands emigrated from their homeland.

The Nazi invasion of Poland in September 1939 has temporarily destroyed the Polish Republic. Poles and Jews have become alike the victims of degradation and despotism. It is to be hoped that the new republic, which will undoubtedly rise from the ashes of the old, will be a truly democratic state, in which all inhabitants will be equal, regardless of their religion or their ancestry.

[22] In October, 1934, Foreign Minister Josef Beck announced that Poland would no more feel herself bound by the minority treaties.

PART THREE

RUSSIA

VII. RUSSIA

1873–1881

The most considerable correspondence between the Government of the United States and that of any foreign power about Jews was with Russia. Though the main subject of the correspondence was the passport question, other phases of the Jewish problem in Russia were also treated. Over and over again attempts were made by American diplomats, through patient counsel and moral suasion given orally or through the written word, to convert the Russian Government to a liberal view of the Jewish question in Russia. Of special note is the fact that United States ministers and ambassadors to Russia used to send to Washington, at frequent intervals, detailed reports on the legal and social status of the Jews of that vast Empire.

American intervention with the Russian Government in behalf of American citizens of the Jewish faith is important also because of the fact that the commercial treaty concluded in 1832 between the two countries was terminated by the Government of the United States mainly because its Jewish citizens were not recognized by Russia as equals in every respect with American citizens of other faiths. In no other case in history did any government ever take such a serious step in behalf of Jews who chose to make their home under its jurisdiction.

The history of the Jews in Russia is a recital of a long series of attacks on Jews, individually and as a people. Pogroms, in which thousands of innocent Jews lost their lives and many more all their earthly belongings, were an all too frequent occurrence.

The Government of the United States, of its own initiative as well as in response to the request of representative Jews and liberal non-Jews, did its utmost to mitigate the evils to which the Jews of Russia were subjected. However, very little could be accomplished with a government to which truth and justice, elementary decency and respect for the opinion of other nations made no appeal. It was with disgust that the Treaty of 1832 was terminated by the United States, with all liberal elements everywhere hoping for the day when the life of the corrupt Czarist government would be ended.

The case of Bernard Bernstein,[1] a native of Isbica, Russian Poland, was the first instance in which a Jew appeared as a subject in the Russo-American diplomatic correspondence. Bernstein, who had become an American citizen by naturalization, was arrested in October, 1864, in his native town while on a visit to his parents, taken under military escort to Wloclawek and thrown into prison as an outlaw. He communicated with the American legation in St. Petersburg, and with the State Department in Washington. Though Bernstein was soon released, it was believed because of his American citizenship, he claimed to have lost a large amount of money as a direct result of his imprisonment. Several noted lawyers of that time took up his case with Secretary of State William H. Seward, but the latter did not press it with the Russian Government. The fact that, on leaving Russia in 1845, Bernstein was owing military duty to his native country, was a factor in his disfavor.

It should also be noted that Poland was at that time in a very unsettled state. The American Minister, Cassius M. Clay, recommended to Secretary Seward, that all naturalized American citizens born in Russia should stay away, as several revolutionists in that country used American passports to escape detection. This practice by some of the Polish revolutionaries, too, brought Mr. Bernstein under the suspicion of being engaged in re-

[1] House Executive Document 197, 42nd Congress, 3rd Session.

volutionary activities against the Russian State.[1a] This case also formed the subject of a presidential report to Congress in reply to a demand for all correspondence in his case; but this step was likewise of no avail. There was a similar incident several years later when Benjamin Goldberg, a naturalized citizen of the United States, was arrested while on a visit in Poland and held for military service.[2]

In 1867, Mr. Seward inquired of the Russian Government whether it would negotiate a treaty which should regulate the treatment of citizens of the United States of Russian nativity, who wished to visit their native country. Prince Gortchakov, then Russian foreign minister, refused to negotiate such a treaty, declaring that Russia forbade the return of subjects who chose to abandon her protection and to escape from her allegiance. Mr. Hamilton Fish, who followed Mr. Seward in the office of secretary of state, gave out this statement in 1869 in reply to an inquiry concerning the treaty relations between the United States and Russia and the treatment by Russia of American naturalized citizens of Russian nativity:[3]

We have no special treaty with Russia on this subject, nor is this Department informed as to her laws or practice in such cases. The friendly disposition manifested by Russia towards this Government would lead it to entertain the hope that its citizens, who conduct themselves properly in that country, would be allowed to travel therein without molestation.

He, however, warned that the United States Government could not protect an American citizen, a native of Russia or Poland, if he owed military service to his native country before he emigrated to the United States.

At the same time Secretary Fish instructed Andrew G. Curtin, our minister to St. Petersburg, to make a diligent but careful inquiry about a report that an obsolete *ukase* against the Jews had been revived and that many Jews were

[1a] Dispatches, Russia, Vol. 20, No. 66, Dec. 17, 1864, The National Archives, Washington, D. C.

[2] Diplomatic Correspondence, 1866, Part 1, page 391.

[3] Moore's Digest, Vol. III, Sec. 453, page 623.

banished from their homes. The Department wanted a report on the subject so that further instructions might be given.[3a]

In accordance with this instruction, Mr. Curtin, assisted by Eugene Schuyler, then United States consul at Revel, investigated, and in a dispatch to Secretary Fish, enclosing a memorandum on the question, Mr. Curtin stated that "from the facts therein set forth it would seem to me that no action on the part of the United States would change the policy of the Russian Government in this matter."[3b]

Acknowledging the dispatch and the interesting memorandum, Mr. Fish expressed the hope that "the Government of Russia will find it consistent with its policy to grant the additional privileges [to Jews] which they now have under discussion."

Our experience shows that the removal of restrictions of a sectarian character elevates the class relieved and advances the common good and social organization.

The first in a series of reports on the legal and social status of the Jew in the Russian Empire was sent by Mr. Eugene Schuyler, Chargé d'Affaires *ad interim*, in September, 1872. The report, under the title "Memorandum on the Legal Position of the Hebrew in Russia" is rather lengthy, and shows that Mr. Schuyler went to some pains to understand the peculiar position of the Jew in Russia,[4] which he summarized in the following paragraph:

The present position of the Hebrews in Russia, so far as it is regulated or affected by the laws, is substantially this: The Hebrews are an alien race, living in Russia and owing allegiance to the imperial government, subject to all the burdens and endowed with few of the privileges of Russian subjects. On the assumed theory of their being hurtful to the population at large, they are under the special supervision of the government, and are restricted in their place of abode, their occupations, acquisition of property, mode of life, dress, education, and manner of worship.

[3a] Instructions, Russia, Vol. 15, No. 14, Dec. 17, 1867, The National Archives, Washington, D. C.

[3b] Dispatches, Russia, Vol. 22, No. 20, Jan. 6, 1870, The National Archives, Washington, D. C.

[4] Foreign Relations, 1872, page 498.

This observation is then discussed in great detail under the headings of civil rights and religious rights. Mr. Schuyler's valuable report concludes with the following paragraph:

The spirit of modern Russian legislation is to fuse together the different races that inhabit the empire and to make them all Russians. It is obvious that this object cannot be attained, so far as the Hebrews are concerned, while laws exist which render them a separate and distinct body, and, by casting a slur on them, cause them only to shut themselves still more, and to resist all attempts to draw them into normal relations with the rest of the body politic.

About three years later, March 15, 1875, Mr. Schuyler transmitted to Mr. Fish an extract from a report by Professor V. Grigorieff, a member of a commission for the improvement of the life of the Hebrews. His extract deals with the specific question of granting permission to the Jews to reside freely in all parts of the Empire. Professor Grigorieff's opinion was that this permission should not be extended to the Jews. In spite of the stated aim of the commission, as expressed clearly by its name, Grigorieff, the referee of the commission on the question of the Pale of Settlement, stated frankly: "What is important in this question is not whether the Jews will fare better when granted the right of residence all over the Empire, but rather the effect of this measure upon the economic well-being of an enormous part of the Russian people." He concluded that the Jews should not be given the right to settle freely outside the Pale.[5] The arguments which he presents in support of his conclusions are the same arguments as Russia and its officials had always used against the Jews and against any attempts to ameliorate their condition. Professor Grigorieff concludes: "The Hebrews were not always such as we see them now in the western provinces and are not such everywhere now. The great cause of their present position is chiefly owing to their selfish, ignorant and fanatical leaders."[6]

[5] See "History of the Jews in Russia and Poland," by S. M. Dubnow, Vol. II, page 196.

[6] Foreign Relations, 1875, page 1054.

In presenting the report, Mr. Schuyler says that it is hoped that the Commission for the Improvement of the Life of the Hebrews would devise some method for relieving the ignorance and distress which certainly exist among the Hebrews of the eastern provinces. The memorandum itself is highly intolerant and prejudicial, and one can hardly see why it should have been forwarded with but the slight comment he made, and why it should have been preserved in our Foreign Relations. It is interesting to note that, though there is no mention of it in the diplomatic correspondence with Russia, there was another report submitted by a minority of the Commission which differed fundamentally from the Grigorieff report. The minority report advised complete emancipation of the Jews, in the name of morality and justice as well as for the benefit of the "original" population. The separatism of the Jews and their one-sided economic activity were, in the opinion of the signatories of the minority report, the results and not the causes of anti-Jewish discrimination.[7]

In the meantime, in 1879, Mr. Wickham Hoffman, Chargé d'Affaires at St. Petersburg, had sent to Mr. William M. Evarts, Secretary of State, a dispatch concerning the case of Herman Rosenstraus,[8] a naturalized citizen of the United States of Russian birth, who had returned to Kharkoff, purchased some real estate there, and paid for it, but had been prohibited by the local government from holding it on the ground that Jews were not permitted to hold real estate in that territory unless they belonged to the first guild merchant class. The American representatives were not very enthusiastic in their support of the claim to his right as an American citizen to own real estate, under the terms of the Russo-American Treaty of 1832. The correspondence between Mr. Rosenstraus, his agents, and the various American agents in Russia as well as in Washington, continued from 1873 to 1879, and during all this time he apparently paid no taxes, performed no militia or jury duty, and made no return whatever for the protection he claimed from the United States.

[7] See Dubnow, Vol. II, page 197.
[8] Foreign Relations, 1879, page 921.

One American consul, Mr. Marshall Jewell, while intervening in his behalf, disclaimed any privileges for Mr. Rosenstraus which were not extended to native Jews. Another consul, Mr. William H. Edwards, answered Mr. Rosenstraus that "the treaty in force between Russia and the United States concedes to you no rights in addition to those enjoyed by Russian subjects of like faith."

Altogether, this case was not a favorable one, but it is noteworthy because the House of Representatives regarded the case of Theodore Rosenstraus, brother of Herman, who had suffered from the same difficulties, flagrant enough to warrant the passage of a resolution demanding presidential action, even though the Secretary of State had expressed doubt of his ability to grant relief to the claimant under existing treaty stipulations.[9] The volume of letters, dispatches, instructions and reports about the case of Theodore Rosenstraus, his brother Herman, and their relatives, which began in 1866, and lasted for over a generation, is very large, and touches on almost every possible point of conflict between the United State and Russia. A fair-sized book could be written on this case alone. The Rosenstrauses had continual difficulties with the Russian authorities, but managed, with the aid of American consular and diplomatic representatives, to stay on and prosper.

In the Russo-American diplomatic correspondence of 1880, we find an interesting dispatch from Secretary Evarts to John W. Foster, then United States Minister to Russia. In sending this dispatch Mr. Evarts was not moved by the appeal of American citizens of the Jewish faith for equality of treatment abroad, but solely by a desire to employ the good offices of the United States Government in the interests of humanity. The dispatch, dated April 4, 1880, referred to the letter of Messrs. Simon Wolf and Adolphus S. Solomons, representing the Board of Delegates on Civil and Religious Rights of the Union of American Hebrew Congregations, which reported that the Jews in Russia had been subjected

[9] House Resolution 77: *Congressional Record*, 46th Congress, 1st Session, Vol. IX, Part 2, page 1891.

by the government there to extreme hardships. The view of the Department is expressed in the following instructions to Mr. Foster:[10]

[*Mr. Evarts to Mr. Foster*]

Department of State
Washington, April 14, 1880

SIR: I have received a letter from Messrs. S. Wolf and A. S. Solomons, of this city, representing the "Union of American Hebrew Congregations," in which they refer to newspaper statements indicating that the Jews in Russia have recently been subjected by the government there to extraordinary hardships, and expressing a desire that the minister of the United States to St. Petersburg may be instructed to "make such representations to the Czar's government, in the interests of religious freedom and suffering humanity, as will best accord with the most emphasized liberal sentiments of the American people." The writers of the letter observe at the same time that they are well "aware of the impropriety of one nation interfering with the internal affairs of another in matters of a purely local character."

You are sufficiently well informed of the liberal sentiments of this government to perceive that whenever any pertinent occasion may arise its attitude must always be in complete harmony with the principle of extending all rights and privileges, without distinction on account of creed, and cannot fail, therefore, to conduct any affair of business or negotiation with the government to which you are accredited, which may involve any expression of the views of this government on the subject, in a manner which will subserve the interests of religious freedom. It would, of course, be inadmissible for the Government of the United States to approach the Government of Russia in criticism of its laws and regulations, except so far as such laws and regulations may injuriously affect citizens of this country, in violation of natural rights, treaty obligations, or the provisions of international law, but it is desired that the attitude of the minister, as regards questions of diplomatic controversy, which involve an expression of view on this subject, may be wholly consistent with the theory on which this government was founded.

I am, sir, etc.

WM. M. EVARTS

[10] Foreign Relations, 1880, page 873.

Mr. Evarts emphasized treaty obligations undertaken by Russia under the Treaty of 1832 because he was of the belief, later adopted as the official interpretation of the American Government and its diplomatic agents, that this Treaty guaranteed American citizens of the Jewish faith equality of treatment with other American citizens. Mr. Foster, on the other hand, adopted the Russian interpretation according to which Jews were excepted by Article I of that Treaty and were, therefore, a class by themselves.

It was this radical difference in the interpretation of the treaty that was the crux of the dispute between the respective Governments, and led to the termination of the treaty by the Government of the United States in 1912. This important question will be met with later in this study. But a more immediate reason why Mr. Evarts desired to limit the points of conflict with the officials of the Russian Government may be discovered in the difficult experience American representatives had with these officials in the celebrated cases of Henry Pinkos and Marx Wilczynski.

The facts in the Pinkos case were as follows: In 1879, as was true many a year before and after, the Russian police unearthed a number of plots against the Czar and his government. In a number of provinces attempts had been made on the lives of the governors. In St. Petersburg itself, an attempt had been made to assassinate Czar Alexander II. It was alleged by the Russian authorities that among the plotters against the state there was a very high percentage of Jews, a number of whom were suspected to be of foreign allegiance. The prefect of police of the capital, therefore, had ruled that all foreign Jews should leave the capital as well as a number of other metropolitan cities.

Among those affected by this regulation was Henry Pinkos, an American Jew who had established a business in St. Petersburg and had been living there for a number of months with his wife and children. Pinkos was ordered to leave the city but, through the intercession of Mr. Edwards, the American consul, and Wickham Hoffmann, Chargé d'Affaires of the American Legation, he was granted a number

of delays in the execution of the order for his expulsion.
Some of the dispatches bearing on this case are well worth
quoting. In one of these communications to the American
Minister to Russia, the Secretary of State expressed his un-
willingness to accept the Russian view that the religion of an
American citizen has any bearing whatsoever on his rights
in another country, and dissatisfaction with the attitude
taken by Mr. Hoffmann, who was inclined to let the whole
matter drop.[11]

[*Mr. Evarts to Mr. Foster*]

Department of State
Washington, September 4, 1880

SIR: I have to acknowledge the receipt of Mr. Hoffman's No. 23
of the 11th ultimo in the Pinkos case.

Notwithstanding the tenor of your No. 9 and of your note to
the department of July 24 last, as to the inexpediency of pres-
ently appealing to the Government of the Czar in the sense of the
instruction of June 28 last, touching the expulsion of citizens of
the United States from Russia (or certain cities thereof) by reason
of their religious convictions, the statements of Mr. Hoffman's
No. 23, of August 11 last, are such that the Government of the
United States would seem indifferent to the cause of its citizens
in Russia did it neglect to make immediate remonstrance as set
forth in said instructions of June 28. Mr. Hoffman's inference
from the facts connected with Mr. Pinkos' departure from Russia
is that Mr. Pinkos had made up his mind that Russia "was no
place for one of his creed."

If the meaning of this is that a citizen of the United States has
been broken up in his business at St. |Petersburg, simply for the reason
that he is a Jew rather than a believer in any other creed then it
is certainly time for this government to express itself as set forth
in the instruction above mentioned. It should be made clear to the
Government of Russia that in view of this government the religion
professed by one of its citizens has no relation whatever to that
citizen's right of the protection of the United States, and that in
the eye of this government an injury officially dealt to Mr. Pinkos
at St. Petersburg on the sole ground that he is a Jew, presents the
same aspect that an injury officially done to a citizen of Russia in
New York for the reason that he attends any particular church
there would to the view of His Majesty's Government.

[11] Foreign Relations, 1880, page 880.

It is evident that the losses incurred by the abandonment of his business in St. Petersburg will afford Mr. Pinkos ground for reclamation, if no other cause can be shown for the official breaking up of his said business than the religious views he entertained.

The direct application to have Mr. Pinkos indemnified, however, may be deferred until he shall make it appear what those losses were.

I am, sir, etc.,

WILLIAM M. EVARTS

The Secretary of State was somewhat impatient with the view of the Chargé d'Affaires, Mr. Hoffmann, who, because Mr. Pinkos had, in the meantime, left the country, expressed the view that "there appears to be no necessity for my communicating with the Russian Government."

Mr. John W. Foster, newly-appointed United States Minister at St. Petersburg, shared the broader view of the State Department on this interesting case, rather than the particularistic view of Mr. Hoffmann. As soon as he had acquainted himself with the facts and the instructions from Washington, Mr. Foster sent the following dispatch to Baron Jomini, Acting Minister of Foreign Affairs, wherein it was made clear for the benefit of the Russian Foreign Office that the Government of the United States could not remain neutral when one of its citizens was subjected to discriminatory treatment solely because he was a professor of a particular religion; it was suggested also that Pinkos was entitled to demand reparation for the financial loss unjustly suffered.[12]

[*Mr. Foster to Baron Jomini*]

Legation of the United States
St. Petersburg, September 2/14, 1880

EXCELLENCY: The expulsion from this city of Henry Pinkos, a citizen of the United States, with the aggravating circumstances attending it, having been brought to the attention of my government, I have been instructed by the Secretary of State to make known to your excellency the views of my government thereon, and to protest against the treatment which said citizen has received.

Although the case has been heretofore brought to the attention of your excellency's department, it may be well to recall the facts

[12] Foreign Relations, 1880, page 881.

attending it. In the month of April last, before I assumed the charge of this legation, Henry Pinkos applied to the consul-general of the United States in this capital for relief from an order which he said he had received from the police authorities to leave St. Petersburg, the only reason for his expulsion, as he understood it, being that he was a Jew. He was provided with a passport fully authenticating his American citizenship. The consul-general, upon inquiry, was informed that he was an industrious and quiet trades-man, and with a wife and one child had been residing in this city for some months. In the frequent interviews of the consul-general with the police authorities no charges or intimations were ever made that Pinkos was other than a peaceable and law-abiding resident.

The only relief which the consul-general and the chargé d'affaires of this legation could obtain from the police authorities was a sus-pension for a few days of the order of expulsion, until Mr. Hoffman was able to communicate with the foreign office and obtained through Mr. de Giers permission for Pinkos to remain for three months, to enable him to close up his business. At the expiration of this period Pinkos, having sold his little property at a sacrifice, proceeded to obey the order, placed his baggage on board a vessel at Cronstadt, and when preparing to embark with his family he was asked by the police for his passport; whereupon he presented his American passport with which he had entered the country, with the police indorsement upon it ordering him to leave St. Petersburg, which he supposed was sufficient. The police informed him that this was not sufficient, and compelled him and his family to return to St. Petersburg. The captain of the vessel refused to refund him the passage-money paid, and sailed without him, carrying off his luggage. Having obtained from the authorities the permission required by the police, finding himself penniless, he was indebted to private charity for the means to leave the country, which he has done in compliance with the original order referred to above.

While the order was in its form merely an expulsion from St. Petersburg, Mr. Pinkos understood it to be virtually an order to leave the empire, in view of the fact that similar measures had been taken in Moscow and other cities, and of the announcement in the public press, that foreign Jews were to be excluded from the country.

The Secretary of State instructs me to state to your excellency that in the presence of the fact that an American citizen has been ordered to leave Russia on no other ground than that he is the professor of a particular creed or the holder of certain religious views, it becomes the duty of the Government of the United States, which impartially seeks to protect all of its citizens of whatever origin or faith, solemnly, but with all respect to the Government of His Imperial Majesty, to protest. As this order of expulsion is understood to apply to all foreign Jews, in certain cities or localities, at least, of Russia, it is, of course, apparent that the same is not directed specially against the government of which Mr. Pinkos is a citizen, and, indeed, the long standing amity which has united the interests of Russia with those of the Government of the United States would of itself forbid a remote supposition that such might be the case. Notwithstanding this aspect of the matter the United States could not fail to look upon the expulsion of one of its citizens from Russia, on the simple ground of his religious ideas or convictions, except as a grievance, akin to that which Russia would doubtless find in the expulsion of one of her own subjects from the United States, on the ground of his attachment to the faith of his fathers.

It having been intimated to the Secretary of State by this legation that the reason of this order may be found in the supposed implication of Jews in the plots formed against the life of His Imperial Majesty, the Emperor, the Secretary directs me to say that in so far as this may be true, the Government of Russia has the entire sympathy of the Government of the United States, in all just preventive efforts, and if there existed any good evidence that Mr. Pinkos has been connected with any of these attempts, the Government of the United States could not object to this expulsion on that ground. But neither the police authorities, in the several communications which the members of the consulate-general and this legation have had with them, in their efforts to obtain relief for Mr. Pinkos, nor your excellency's department, in the notes addressed to this legation on the subject, have ever intimated the existence of such a charge. Nor does the character of citizens of the United States of Jewish faith afford ground for the supposition that they would be likely to engage in conspiracies or plots against the established government of the country. From the foundation of the United States as a nation, they have been entitled to full and unrestricted privileges of citizens, and have shown themselves to be peaceable and law observing in their conduct, quiet and industrious in their habits and are esteemed a valuable portion of the community, so that in so far as the regulation for the expulsion of foreign Jews from Russia affects American citizens, whatever may be the conduct of their co-religionists of this or other countries, it is an unjust reflection upon American Jews as a class and a discrimination which cannot be acquiesced in by my government.

As, then, it does not appear that any criminal or improper conduct has been established against Mr. Pinkos, the Secretary confidently submits to His Imperial Majesty's Government, whether in view of the fact that Mr. Pinkos has been interrupted in his peaceful occupations and expelled from Russia on the sole ground that his religious views are of one kind rather than another, he is not justly entitled to make reclamation for the damage and loss to which he has been subjected.

In thus presenting, for consideration and appropriate action, the views of my government upon this important subject, I improve, etc.,

JOHN W. FOSTER

While the Pinkos case was still pending, there arose the new case of Marx Wilczynski. Though the facts in the latter case were somewhat different, they appeared together in the ensuing correspondence. Both cases, however, involved the right of American Jews to reside in the capital of Russia. The facts in this new case are given in the following dispatch which the American Minister sent to the Russian Acting Minister of Foreign Affairs:[13]

[*Mr. Foster to Russian Acting Minister of Foreign Affairs*]

Legation of the United States
St. Petersburg, October 7, 1880

EXCELLENCY: I beg to bring to your excellency's attention the following facts, as they have been reported to me by the legation of the United States at Berlin.

Mr. Marx Wilczynski, a citizen of the United States, is the agent of an American mercantile firm, and as such has much business in Russia. On his last visit to this country he was granted a passport by the American legation at Berlin, with which he entered Russian territory, observing the proper requirements in regard to passports, and encountered no difficulty until he reached St. Petersburg, where he was not permitted by the police authorities to remain, for the reason that he was a Jew; and an indorsement to that effect was placed upon his passport. He states that when this order was served upon him he did not have time to apply to this legation for advice or assistance, and he has taken the first opportunity after his expulsion to resort to the nearest diplomatic representative for interposition in his behalf. The interests of the American mercantile firm which he represents require him to return to this country and this city. I enclose herewith the passport with which Mr. Wilczynski came to Russia, in order that your excellency may see the prohibitory order placed upon it by the police of this city.

---

[13] Foreign Relations, 1881, page 992.

After due examination, I have to request that the passport may be returned to me.

It became my duty, in the note which I had the honor to address to your excellency on the 2d (14th) ultimo, in a case similar to the present one, to make known the views of my government in regard to the expulsion of one of its citizens simply for the reason that he was a Jew rather than a believer in any other creed; and I must again respectfully but solemnly protest against this new infringement upon the rights of American citizens, and of the comity which should exist between friendly nations.

Your excellency will not fail to notice that the action of the police authorities in the present case, as well as that of Mr. Pinkos, bears the grave aspect of an interference with the reciprocal liberty of commerce, which is guaranteed by solemn treaty stipulations, and the development of which is so ardently desired by both countries.

On account of this new instance, it is regarded as important that it should be made clear to your excellency's government that, in the view of the Government of the United States, the religion professed by one of its citizens has no relation whatever to that citizen's right to the protection of the United States; and that in the eye of my government an injury officially dealt to Mr. Wilczynski or Mr. Pinkos, in St. Petersburg, on the sole ground that they are Jews, presents the same aspect that an injury officially done to a subject of Russia in New York for the reason that he attends any particular church there would to the view of His Imperial Majesty's government.

I have, therefore, respectfully to request that Mr. Wilczynski may be freely permitted to return to Russia to prosecute his business engagements, and that the police authorities of St. Petersburg be instructed not to molest him in his lawful pursuits. In view of the exigencies which may require his early return, I venture to express the hope that it may be found convenient to favor me with an early reply to this request.

It is very gratifying to me to have this opportunity to reassure your excellency of my highest esteem and profound consideration.

JOHN W. FOSTER

Mr. Wilczynski, now in Berlin, approached Mr. Andrew D. White, then United States Minister there, whom we shall meet later as American Minister at St. Petersburg, and asked him to try and have the order of his expulsion rescinded as his business required him to stay in Russia a while longer, or at any rate, to inform him what rights, if any, American citizens of the Jewish faith had in Russia. To an inquiry on this point addressed to Mr. Foster, Minister White received a dispatch informing him of Mr. Foster's recent protests to the Russian Government in a similar case and stating that, though he was doubtful of his success, he would send a note to the Foreign Office on this new case. Meanwhile, he had advised Mr. Wilczynski to stay in Berlin and not try to re-enter Russia without specific permission from the authorities.[14]

[*Mr. Foster to Mr. White*]

Legation of the United States
St. Petersburg, October 18, 1880

MY DEAR COLLEAGUE: I am in receipt of your letter of the 15th instant, with which you inclose the passport of the American citizen Marx Wilczynski, with the indorsement of the police of St. Petersburg, forbidding him to reside here, and you inquire whether such order can be rescinded and what rights American citizens of the Israelitish faith have in Russia.

The laws of Russia impose certain disabilities upon all Jews, among which is the prohibition against residence in St. Petersburg and certain other localities. In the past few years this prohibition has been repeatedly enforced against American citizens of the Jewish faith, and acquiesced in by my predecessors. I was thoroughly convinced of the injustice of the prohibition, but did not feel warranted in reversing the precedent set by my predecessors, without first referring the question to the Department. Secretary Evarts has instructed me in a recent case to protest against the expulsion of Jewish American citizens, and I have accordingly done so. I will repeat the protest whenever occasion requires, and endeavor to obtain relief for citizens of the United States; but whether the Russian Government will be influenced by my protest and endeavors remains to be seen.

In Mr. Wilczynski's case I will send the minister of foreign affairs a note protesting against the action of the police authorities, and will ask that instructions be given to said authorities not to disturb him in his lawful pursuits in case he should return to this city.

It will not be safe, however, for Mr. Wilczynski to come to Russia until I shall have obtained an assurance from the minister that he can do so without interference on the part of the authorities. It may be some time before I can receive an answer from the minister,

[14] Foreign Relations, 1881, page 991.

as the Emperor is now in the Crimea, and General Melikoff, to whose department the subject pertains, is also temporarily absent from this city. In case Mr. W.'s business affairs should make it urgent that he have an early reply, you will please to inform me, and I will then consider the propriety of calling in person at the foreign office and pressing an early solution of the matter.

The prohibition against Jewish residence in St. Petersburg was not strictly enforced until the late Nihilistic movement caused an order to be issued expelling all foreign Jews. I am satisfied that sooner or later the Russian Government must modify or repeal its illiberal laws respecting the Jews, and I will lose no proper opportunity to do what I can to hasten that event; but it is very doubtful whether it will consider the present an opportune time.

I am, etc.,

JOHN W. FOSTER

Before the cases of Pinkos and Wilczynski were concluded, Mr. John Hay, Acting Secretary of State, sent the following note to Mr. Foster, commending him upon the manner in which he was conducting the Pinkos case.[15]

[*Mr. Hay to Mr. Foster*]

Department of State
Washington, October 22, 1880

SIR: I have to acknowledge the receipt of your Nos. 37 and 41, of the respective dates of the 16th and 21st ultimo, reporting your action upon the recent instructions of the Department in the special case of Henry Pinkos, and upon the general subject of the expulsion of American citizens from Russian cities on no other ground than profession of the Hebrew faith.

Your course appears to have been discreet, and it is hoped that you will press your representations to the successful establishment of the principle of religious toleration for our citizens peacefully residing or traveling abroad, which we as a nation have such a deep interest in maintaining.

I am, etc.,

JOHN HAY
Acting Secretary

[15] Foreign Relations, 1881, page 993.

Further stimulus to press the case of Mr. Wilczynski came from Secretary Evarts who, on December 29th, sent the following cablegram to Mr. Foster:

Urge treaty obligations in the Wilczynski case. Further information awaited.

This case soon came to a favorable conclusion. From a dispatch from Mr. H. Sidney Everett, Chargé d'Affaires during the absence of Mr. White from Berlin, to Mr. Foster, it would appear that Mr. Wilczynski was already in St. Petersburg with the full knowledge of the Russian authorities.[16]

[*Mr. Everett to Mr. Foster*]

Legation of the United States
Berlin, December 18, 1880

Sir: In Mr. White's absence I have the honor to acknowledge your letter of the 14th instant, returning Mr. Wilczynski's passport and stating that he would be allowed to stay six months if he returned there. At the time his old passport was sent to you Mr. Wilczynski took out a new one, and said that he should not have any difficulty in returning to St. Petersburg, and staying as long as he wished for business purposes, as he was personally known to high officials in some of the departments, with which he had transacted business for some years. But his grievance was that he was expelled, as he understood, for being a Jew, and he wished to ascertain whether there was such a law against Jews, and whether the American legation could not protect our citizens against it.

I have been informed by one of the Russian secretaries of legation here that there is no law in St. Petersburg expelling Jews merely because they are Jews; but that probably this gentleman had failed to comply with some regulation in his business transactions, or had perhaps associated with some of the suspected characters in the city, or was one of the Polish refugees, who it appears are an obnoxious class there.

Mr. Wilczynski has not called at this legation again, and it is probable that he is now in Russia, as he expressed his intention of returning there very shortly.

With many thanks for the trouble you have taken in the matter, I am, etc.,

H. Sidney Everett

[16] Foreign Relations, 1881, page 1005.

The Russian Government was not as accommodating in the Pinkos case. Both in writing and in a long conversation which he had with the American Minister, Mr. de Giers, Russian Minister for Foreign Affairs, insisted that the authorities in this case had acted in strict accordance with existing laws. What the existing laws on the Jews were at the time was not clear to anybody. Upon inquiring about the same, Mr. Foster was given a volume of 1200 pages written in the Russian language, containing all laws and regulations governing the Jews in Russia. These went into great detail but were of a conflicting nature, and it was almost impossible for anyone to learn what those laws were or what they should mean in a particular case.

On December 30, 1880, Mr. Foster reported to Mr. Evarts a long conversation with Mr. de Giers, from which the following extract is made:[16a]

In the course of the conversation, I stated that while the object of the interview was to obtain proper recognition of the rights of American Jews, my government took a deep interest in the amelioration of the condition of the Jewish race in other nations, and I was satisfied that it would be highly gratified at the statement of the minister that a commission was now considering the question of the modification in a liberal sense of the Russian laws regarding the Jews. The experience of the United States had amply shown the wisdom of removing all discriminations against them in the laws, and of placing this race upon an equal footing with all other citizens.

Against the American Jews, Mr. de Giers was ready to enforce the laws as leniently as possible. In "meritorious cases" he would be willing to give American Jews the right to reside in St. Petersburg even above the limit of the usual six months. But, at the same time, he insisted that Russia and the Russian Jews were "different" and had to be treated accordingly.

Mr. Foster also reported a conversation with General Loris Melikoff, Minister of the Interior, who explained to him that while Russia would be glad to give liberal treatment to bona fide American citizens, "not disguised German Jews,"

[16a] Foreign Relations, 1881, page 998.

he saw no way of changing their laws. This he would do as a favor and not as a recognition of a right, for it was the Russian view that the Treaty of 1832 did not concede to American citizens of the Jewish faith any privileges which Russian Jews did not enjoy. Mr. Foster replied that he was sorry to learn that these laws could not be repealed, adding that such a course would be much more in accordance with the views entertained by the Government of the United States and that it would be much more gratifying to it to see all the prohibitions against Jews, native as well as foreign, abolished.

On December 31, 1880, Mr. Foster sent another long dispatch from which it would seem that, in spite of the prohibition, with certain exceptions, against residing in St. Petersburg, thousands of Jews who did not belong to the privileged few had been living there for many years with the acquiescence of the police.[17]

[*Mr. Foster to Mr. Evarts*]

Legation of the United States
St. Petersburg, December 31, 1880

Sir: In my No. 73 of yesterday I have given the result of my efforts to obtain a modification of the laws of Russia in regard to foreign Jews, so as to exempt American Jews from the prohibition against residence in St. Petersburg and other cities of the Empire. As a supplement to that dispatch, it may be of interest to have some information as to the condition and treatment of the Russian subjects of the Jewish faith.

From early times there have existed laws prohibiting the entrance or residence of Jews in Russia, and while there were occasional exceptions to the laws the prohibition was generally enforced with rigor up to the incorporation of Poland with the Empire. From that date it was sought to confine the Jews to the Polish provinces. But the Jews in these provinces furnished their full contingent, and, it is alleged by them, more than their ratio, to the Russian army; and as it often happened that at the expiration of their term of service they were in distant or different parts of the Empire from their homes, upon their discharge they were permitted to live in the provinces where discharged, because they were old soldiers, and in spite of the laws prohibiting the residence there of Jews.

[17] Foreign Relations, 1881, page 1005.

The presence of the greater part of this race in other districts of Russia than Poland is accounted for in this way, they being either discharged soldiers or their children.

But in addition to these a considerable number of Jews are found in the large cities and commercial towns, many of whom are authorized to become permanent residents under exceptions which have been made to the prohibitory laws. For instance, Jews possessing a certain mercantile standing are admitted as members of the first or commercial guild, and, with the authorization of the law, engage in banking and mercantile pursuits. And these members of the guild are permitted to employ a certain number of Jewish clerks, servants, artisans, or other employés. So, also, exceptions are made in favor of members of the learned professions and graduates of the universities or other educational or scientific institutions. The latitude of construction placed upon these exceptions depends very much upon the will of the local authorities, as also the strictness with which the prohibitory laws are enforced; so that in all the cities of Russia the number of Jewish residents will be found more or less in excess of the police registry and greater than the strict interpretation of the law, authorizes. For instance, persons who have given the subject close attention, as I stated to the minister of foreign affairs, estimate the number of Jewish residents in St. Petersburg at 30,000, while it is stated the number registered by the police authorities is 1,500. From the same source I learn that, while the government does not recognize their legal existence, nine synagogues in this city are known to the authorities, and that there are other private places of worship; and that, while only one Hebrew school is registered by the police, there are between three and four thousand children in unauthorized Jewish schools of this capital. As another indication of the extent of Jewish influence, it it worthy of note that one or more Jewish editors or writers are said to be employed on the leading newspapers of St. Petersburg and Moscow almost without exception. It is claimed that Jews of wealth, of established professions or occupations, or of good social standing or influence, have little difficulty in securing express or tacit exemption from the laws.

These facts indicate that the laws proscribing the Jewish race are not enforced with great strictness; and intelligent Jewish residents of this city, native Russian subjects, who are laboring for the amelioration of the condition of their brethren, recognize the great advance which has been made during the present reign in the liberal construction which is placed upon the laws, in the exceptions which have been made tending to relax their rigor, and in the increased privileges which have been granted, such as admission to the universities, the practice of professions and avocations, and holding of government offices, denied to them a generation ago. At the same time the proscription laws remain, and the government reserves to itself the right to enforce them with strictness or relax them at its will.

It is to be noted that intelligent Russian Jews repel the charge that their race in this country have manifested a spirit of lawlessness or hostility to the established government, and they deny that a greater proportion of Jews than of other classes have been implicated in the conspiracies or attempts upon the life of the Emperor, and in confirmation of their denial they point to the fact that of the sixteen persons who were arraigned last month in the state trials of the nihilists only one was a Jew.

I am, etc.,

JOHN W. FOSTER

James G. Blaine, who succeeded William M. Evarts as Secretary of State, followed in the footsteps of his predecessor. One of the first letters which Mr. Foster received from his new superior was a letter of commendation for the way he had presented the cases of Pinkos and Wilczynski, and the general treatment of the Jews in Russia. Mr. Foster's reply, dated March 25, 1881, contains for the first time the suggestion that the Government of the United States base its demands for non-discrimination against its citizens of the Jewish faith on the first article of the Treaty of 1832. It is strange indeed, but so far the American representatives seemed to have accepted the Russian interpretation which sought to exclude American Jews from enjoying the rights extended to other Americans in Russia. Mr. Foster was eager to have the State Department support him in the more liberal interpretation.[18]

[*Mr. Foster to Mr. Blaine*]

Legation of the United States
St. Petersburg, March 25, 1881

SIR: In acknowledging the receipt of Department No. 55, of the 3d instant, I desire to express my thanks for the kindly commendation of my presentation of the cases of Pinkos and Wilczynski, and of the general question of the treatment of the Jews in Russia.

[18] Foreign Relations, 1881, page 1012.

I make careful note of the desire manifested by the late honorable Secretary of State to appeal strongly to the treaty guarantee of personal freedom to American citizens sojourning peaceably, for business or pleasure, in Russia, without regard to their religious belief. I have constantly made this appeal in my conversations with and communications to the Russian authorities. But it will be noted in my No. 73 of December 30, that I called attention to the fact that the Russian government denies that the treaty of 1832 secures to American citizens of the Jewish faith sojourning in Russia any other or greater privileges than those enjoyed in this empire by Russian subjects of the same faith. From the concluding sentence of Department No. 55, it would seem that the late Secretary's construction of the treaty was that American citizens in Russia were entitled to the same rights and personal freedom as are extended to Russian subjects sojourning in the United States. This interpretation has never as yet been presented to the Russian Government, nor has the treaty been so considered by my predecessors. If that view is to be insisted upon, I will thank you for specific instructions regarding this point. As stated in my No. 73, the laws imposing disabilities upon Jews, both foreign and native, antedate the treaty of 1832, and the minister of foreign affairs claims that said treaty does not exempt American Jews coming here from their operation.

I have strongly insisted that the passport of his government should protect every peaceable American citizen coming to Russia, and that it is not proper to institute inquiry as to the religious belief of such citizen. The Department is correct in the supposition indicated, that no American citizen has been convicted of Judaism by "judicial procedure." But it is to be borne in mind that in Russia it is not necessary that a judicial procedure should take place, or even the "military stage of siege" exist, before a person undergoes the sentence of the law. The laws and regulations in question are usually intrusted to the police authorities, and it is sufficient for them to be satisfied in their own minds that the individual comes within the prohibitions to have them enforced.

I shall not fail to continue to press the subject upon the Russian Government at every proper opportunity,

I am, etc.,

JOHN W. FOSTER

It will be seen that the greatest difficulty centered about the meaning of the qualifying clause, "on conditions of submitting to the laws and ordinances there prevailing" of Article I of the commercial treaty of 1832 between the United States and Russia. According to the Russian view, the phrase "laws and ordinances" included the many laws affecting Jews in Russia; while it was the American contention that it did not include them.

Secretary Blaine's answer to Mr. Foster's inquiry asking for specific instructions regarding the interpretation of the treaty of 1832 is one of the most brilliant and classic documents of its kind. Though Mr. Evarts had expressed himself against the narrow interpretations of the Russians, his view had not been officially presented to the Russian Government, nor had it been so interpreted by Mr. Foster's predecessors in office. Mr. Blaine treated this question in a very long dispatch, only an extract from which is given in the Foreign Relations. It is evident from this document that Secretary Blaine had made a historical and analytical study of the Jewish question in Russia, going as far back as 1784 when Empress Catherine issued a *ukase* promising commercial privileges and religious liberty to foreigners irrespective of race and creed. Mr. Blaine could discover no law specifically limiting the privileges of foreign Jews in Russia, though the existence of such laws had often been alleged by the Russian Government. Imperial *ukases* before 1784 concerning the admission of foreigners into Russia are silent on all questions of faith. The *ukase* on immigration of 1807, modified in 1817, mentions no restrictions by reason of race or faith. As to the interpretation of Article I, Mr. Blaine avers that while there may be some doubt as to its literal interpretation, yet there can be no doubt that its spirit would be violated if the Jews were made an exception to the enjoyment of the personal rights which it confers on American citizens in Russia. But even if there were no treaty at all, the United States Government would still protest against any discrimination by a foreign power against its citizens on the basis of their religion or race.[19]

[19] Foreign Relations, 1881, page 1030.

[*Mr. Blaine to Mr. Foster*]

Department of State
Washington, July 29, 1881

* * * * *

SIR:

From a careful examination of the cases of grievance heretofore reported by your legation, it appears that the action of the Russian authorities toward American citizens, alleged to be Israelites, and visiting Russia, has been of two kinds:

First. Absolute prohibition of residence in St. Petersburg and in other cities of the Empire, on the ground that the Russian law permits no native Jews to reside there, and that the treaty between Russia and the United States gives to our citizens in Russian jurisdiction no other rights or privileges than those accorded to native Russians. The case of Henry Pinkos may be taken as a type of this class.

Second. Permission of residence and commerce, conditionally on belonging to the first guild of Russian merchants and taking out a license. The case of Rosenstraus is in point.

The apparent contradiction between these two classes of actions becomes more and more evident as the question is traced backward. The Department has rarely had presented to it any subject of inquiry in which a connected understanding of the facts has proved more difficult. For every allegation, on the one hand, that native laws, in force at the time the treaty of 1832 was signed prohibited, or limited the sojourn of foreign Jews in the cities of Russia, I find, on the other hand, specific invitation to alien Hebrews of good repute to domicile themselves in Russia, to pursue their business calling under appropriate license, to establish factories there, and to purchase or lease real estate. Moreover, going back beyond 1832, the date of our treaty, I observe that the imperial ukases concerning the admission of foreigners into Russia are silent on all questions of faith; proper passports, duly viséd being the essential requisite. And, further back still, in the time of the Empress Catherine, I discover explicit tolerance of all foreign religions laid down as a fundamental policy of the empire.

Before examining the issues directly before us, it may not be out of place to give a brief review of these historical data.

The ukase of the Empress Catherine, of 22d February, 1784, although concerning only the establishment of commercial relations with the new possessions of Russia on the Black Sea, contains the following notable declaration:

That Sebastopol, Kherson, and Theodocia be opened to all
the nations friendly to our empire for the advantage of their
commerce with our faithful subjects, . . . that the said nations
may come to these cities in all safety and freedom. . . . Each
individual of such nation, whosoever he may be, as long as he
shall remain in the said cities by reason of his business, or of
his own pleasure, shall enjoy the free exercise of his religion,
according to the praiseworthy precepts handed down to us by
the sovereigns our predecessors, and which we have again received and confirmed, "that all the various nationalities
established in Russia shall praise God, the All Powerful, each
one after the worship and religion of his own ancestors, . . . and
we promise, upon our imperial word, to accord to all foreigners
in these three cities the same advantages which they already
enjoy in our capital and seaport, St. Petersburg, etc.

The full text of this ukase, which breathes a spirit of large
and enlightened tolerance in advance of the policy of those days,
is well worthy of perusal, and may be consulted in vol. 4 of
Martens' "Recueil des Traités," 1st edition, Göttingen, 1795, pages
455–57.

The imperial ordinance of the Czar Alexander I, of 13th August,
1807, decrees a rigid system of passports for foreigners entering
Russia, and is applicable to "all foreigners, of whatsoever nationality," but intimates no restriction on travel or sojourn in Russia
by reason of race or faith. This ordinance was modified and amplified by the ukase of 25th February, 1817, but still without any
manner of religious proscription or restriction.

From this time down to 1860 I can find no trace of the enforcement, especially against American citizens, of the restrictions against
Jewish travel and residence which are stated to have existed when
our treaty with Russia was signed. It is a significant circumstance
that the acknowledged authorities on private international law,
writing during this period upon the legislation of all Europe as
affecting the persons and rights of aliens, make no reference to such
disabilities. Even the painstaking Fœlix is silent on this point,
although devoting much space to the treatment and rights of aliens
in Russia. I do not desire to be here understood as arguing that
the asserted disabilities did not exist at that time. The domestic
history of the Russian Empire shows plainly the restrictions placed
upon native Hebrews, and especially those of Polish origin, the
efforts to confine them to certain parts of the empire, and the
penalties sought to be imposed to deter them from mingling with
the Christian subjects of the Czar. But the same history shows
the gradual relaxation of those measures, until, in the capital
itself, the native Israelite population is said to number some thirty

thousand souls, with their synagogues and sectarian schools; while a special ukase of the late Czar distinctly recognizes to foreign Hebrews every privilege of residence and trade, in a certain guild, which native Christian subjects possess.

The ukase of the Emperor Alexander II, of 7th of June, 1860, after premising that the need of commercial development and the principles of international reciprocity make it proper to concede "to foreigners dwelling in Russia the same rights as those which our subjects enjoy already in the principal countries of Europe," proceeds to permit all aliens to enter any of the trading guilds on the same footing as natives and to thereupon enjoy all the commercial privileges which these guilds confer upon native Russian traders, with the following qualification:

First Remark.— Foreign Hebrew subjects, known by reason of their social position and the wide extent of their commercial operations, who come from foreign lands, may, after the established formalities, that is to say, upon a special authorization, issued in each case by the ministers of finances, of the interior, and of foreign affairs, trade in the empire and establish banking houses therein, upon procuring the license of a merchant of the first guild. It is likewise permitted to these same Israelites to establish factories, to acquire and to lease real estate conformably to the prescriptions of the present ukase.

This provision, it will be observed, extends to the whole territory of the empire. If, as I understand the response of the Russian ministry in the case of Henry Pinkos, native Israelites are forbidden by law from residing or trading in the capital, then this ukase places all foreign Jews (whether belonging to treaty powers or not) on a more favored footing. But if native Hebrews, as a fact, are permitted to reside in St. Petersburg and engage in trade in other guilds than the so-called "first guild," there may then well be question whether such restriction to a particular guild in the case of an American Israelite is consonant with the express opinions of the treaty of 1832, Article I. This point was, in fact, raised in the case of Theodore Rosenstrauss at Kharkoff, which is narrated at length, with all the correspondence therein exchanged, in Mr. Jewell's dispatch No. 20, of December 15, 1873; but it does not seem to have been then exhaustively considered whether the complainant received, under the treaty, the like treatment with the native Hebrews of Kharkoff, or whether he was constrained to obey the ukase of 1860, which, as I have above remarked, is framed for general application to all aliens and irrespective of treaty rights. It is, however, not my present purpose to reargue this old case, but simply to call attention to the fact that the Russian law may, and possibly does, modify and restrict treaty rights. The Rosenstrauss case was special in its nature, and concerned commercial privileges, under a promulgated license law of the empire. It may be necessary, at some future time, to discuss the question it involves, but just now I am concerned with a different class of cases, namely, those of American citizens visiting Russia for private business or for pleasure and travel, and duly provided with the passports of this government authenticating their national character and their consequent right to all the specific guarantees of our treaty.

This brings me again to the cases of Pinkos and Wilczynski. It is unnecessary here to recapitulate the facts therein, as they are amply presented by the files of your legation, and by the correspondence had with the Russian foreign office. It is sufficient to characterize them as instances of the notified expulsion from St. Petersburg, by the police or military authorities, of American citizens, not because of any alleged failure to comply with the ukase of 1860, or with the Russian commercial code, but simply on the allegation, unsupported by proof, that they professed the Israelitish faith, and that the law forbade the sojourn of native Israelites in the imperial capital. On this brief formulation of the case, this government believes that, under its treaty with Russia, and in view of its treatment of Russian subjects resorting under like circumstances to the United States, it has just ground for complaint, and expectancy of better treatment from the government of Russia.

The provision of our treaty of 1832 with Russia, governing the commercial privileges of the citizens and subjects of the two countries, is as follows:

Article I. There shall be between the territories of the high contracting parties a *reciprocal liberty* of commerce and navigation.

The inhabitants of their respective states shall *mutually* have liberty to enter the ports, places and rivers of each party *wherever foreign commerce is permitted.* They shall be at liberty to sojourn and reside *in all parts whatsoever* of said territoties, in order to attend to their affairs; and they shall enjoy, to that effect, the same security and protection as natives of the country wherein they reside, on condition of their submitting to the laws and ordinances there prevailing, and particularly to the regulations in force concerning commerce.

Article X confers specific personal rights reciprocally. In respect of this article an infringement alike of the letter and the spirit of the treaty is not only possible, but probable, under the rigid interpretation of the Jewish laws upon which Russia seems disposed to insist. Its stipulations concern the right to dispose of personal property in Russia owned by or falling to American citizens, who may receive and dispose of inheritances and have recourse to the courts in settlement of questions arising thereunder. It certainly could not be seriously claimed or justly admitted that an American Hebrew, coming within the provisions of this article, is to be treated as a candidate for commercial privileges, and required to take out a license as a trader of the first guild, subject to the approval of his application by the ministries of finance, interior, and foreign affairs. A personal right, not a mercantile privilege, is conferred. To bar an American citizen whose rights might be so concerned from personal appearance in protection of those rights would be a distinct departure from the engagement of the treaty; while to suppose that his case might come under the discretional authority of the police or the military power, which might refuse his personal sojourn in any part of the empire, or allow it under conditions depending on their good will, is to suppose a submission of the guarantees of the treaty to a tribunal never contemplated by its framers.

Upon a case arising, this government would hold that the treaty conferred specific rights on all American citizens in the matter of the disposition of their personal property, irrespective of any conditions save those which the article itself expressly creates; that their actual presence when necessary to protect or assert their interests is absolutely guaranteed whenever and for whatever time it may be needful; and that this international engagement supersedes any municipal rule or regulation which might interfere with the free action of such individuals.

It would be, in the judgment of this government, absolutely inadmissible that a domestic law restraining native Hebrews from residence in certain parts of the empire might operate to hinder an American citizen, whether alleged or known to profess the Hebrew faith, from disposing of his property or taking possession thereof for himself (subject only to the laws of alien inheritance) or being heard in person by the courts which, under Russian law, may be called upon to decide matters to which he is necessarily a party. The case would clearly be one in which the obligation of a treaty is supreme, and where the local law must yield. These questions of the conflict of local law and international treaty stipulations are among the most common which have engaged the attention of publicists, and it is their concurrent judgment that where a treaty creates a privilege for aliens in express terms, it cannot be limited by the operation of domestic law without a serious breach of the good faith which governs the intercourse of nations. So long as such a conventional engagement in favor of the citizens of another state exists, the law governing natives in like cases is manifestly inapplicable.

I need hardly enlarge on the point that the Government of the United States concludes its treaties with foreign states for the equal protection of all classes of American citizens. It can make absolutely no discrimination between them, whatever be their origin or creed. So that they abide by the laws, at home or abroad, it must give them due protection and expect like protection for them. Any unfriendly or discriminatory act against them on the part of a foreign power with which we are at peace would call for our earnest remonstrance, whether a treaty existed or not. The friendliness of our relations with foreign nations is emphasized by the treaties we have concluded with them. We have been moved to enter into such international compacts by considerations of mutual benefit and reciprocity, by the same considerations, in short, which have animated the Russian Government from the time of the noble and tolerant declarations of the Empress Catherine in 1784 to those of the ukase of 1860. We have looked to the spirit rather than to the letter of those engagements, and believed that they should be interpreted in the broadest way; and it is, therefore, a source of unfeigned regret to us when a government, to which we are allied by so many historical ties as to that of Russia, shows a disposition in its dealings with us to take advantage of technicalities, to appeal to the rigid letter and not the reciprocal motive of its international engagements in justification of the expulsion from its territories of peaceable American citizens resorting thither under the good faith of treaties and accused of no wrong-doing or of no violation of the commercial code of the land, but of simple adherence to the faith of their fathers.

That the two American citizens whose unfortunate cases have brought about this discussion were not definitely expelled from St. Petersburg, but were allotted, by the military authorities, a brief time to arrange their private affairs, said to coincide with the usual time during which any foreigner may remain in the empire under his original passport, does not alter the matter as it appears to our eyes. The motive alleged remains the same, and the principle involved is one recognized neither by our fundamental laws nor by any of the conventions we have concluded with foreign states.

It must not be forgotten that this issue, of the banishment of our citizens from a friendly territory by reason of their alleged religion, is a new one in our international relations. From the time when the treaty of 1832 was signed down to within a very recent period, there had been nothing in our relations with Russia to lead to the supposition that our flag did not carry with it equal protection to every American within the dominions of the empire. Even in questions of citizenship affecting the interests of naturalized citizens of Russian origin, the good disposition of the imperial government has been on several occasions shown in a most exemplary manner; and I am sure the actual counselors of His Majesty cannot but contemplate with satisfaction the near approach made in 1874 to the arrangement of negotiations for a treaty of naturalization between the two countries. On that occasion, as will be seen by consulting Mr. Jewell's No. 62, of April 22, 1874, the only remaining obstacle lay in the statutes of the empire touching the conferment and loss of citizenship, of which the examining commission and the consultative council of state recommended the modification in a sense compatible with the modern usage of nations.

I can readily conceive that statutes bristling with difficulties remain unrepealed in the volumes of the law of Russia as well as of other nations. Even we ourselves have our obsolete "Blue Laws"; and their literal enforcement, if such a thing were possible, might to-day subject a Russian of free-thinking proclivities, in Maryland or Delaware, to the penalty of having his tongue bored through with a red-hot iron for blasphemy. Happily the spirit of progress is of higher authority than the letter of outworn laws; and statutory enactments are not so inelastic but that they relax and change with the general advancement of peoples in the path of tolerance.

The simple fact that thousands of Israelites to-day pursue their callings unmolested in St. Petersburg, under the shadow of ancient proscriptive laws, is in itself an eloquent testimony to the principle of progress. And so, too, in Spain, where the persecution and expulsion of the Jews is one of the most notable and deplorable facts in history, and where the edicts of the earlier sovereigns remain unrepealed, we see today an offer of protection and assured right of domicile made to the Israelites of every race.

I leave out of consideration in the present instruction the question whether the citizens or subjects of other nations are more or less favored than our own in this regard. I have not, however, failed to notice the statement made to you by Mr. de Giers, in one of your reported conversations with him, that German and Austrian Jews are subjected to the proscriptions in question, and the implication therefrom that if the Governments of Germany and Austria do not complain, there is no reason why we should.

It is not for me to examine or conjecture the reciprocal motives of policy or of international convention which may govern in these instances. Neither have I failed to remark the seeming uncertainty with which the British Government has approached the case of the English Israelite, Mr. Lewisohn, who was recently required to quit St. Petersburg, notwithstanding that the personal guarantees of the Anglo-Russian treaty of January 12, 1859, in its eleventh, twelfth, and thirteenth articles, are more particular than in our own treaty, and were, presumably, like our own stipulations, framed with the intent of securing impartial rights and protection in Russia. I am perfectly willing to rest my argument on the moral weight of our treaty of 1832, although of course not averse to availing myself of any support which may come from any other quarter to fortify what we conceive to have been our clear purpose in executing that instrument. And under no circumstances would I in the name of this government be willing to accept a less measure of impartial privilege for a citizen of the United States visiting or sojourning in Russian territory than is assured to aliens in the like case by any stipulation with or usage toward any other nation on the part of Russia.

I had the honor in my letter of the 20th ultimo to Mr. Bartholomei to acquaint him with the general views of the President in relation to this matter.

I cannot better bring this instruction to a close than by repeating and amplifying those views which the President so firmly holds, and which he so anxiously desires to have recognized and responded to by the Russian Government.

He conceives that the intention of the United States in negotiating and concluding the treaty of December 18, 1832, and the distinct and enlightened reciprocal engagements then entered into with the Government of Russia, give us a moral ground to expect careful attention to our opinions as to its rational interpretation in the broadest and most impartial sense; that he would deeply regret, in view of the gratifying friendliness of the relations of the two countries which he is so desirous to maintain, to find that this large national sentiment fails to control the present issue, or that a narrow and rigid limitation of the construction possible to the treaty stipulations between the two countries is likely to be adhered to; that if, after a frank comparison of the views of the two governments, in the most amicable spirit and with the most earnest desire to reach a mutually agreeable conclusion the treaty stipulations between the United States and Russia are found insufficient to determine questions of nationality and tolerance of individual faith, or to secure to American citizens in Russia the treatment which Russians receive in the United States, it is simply due to the good relations of the two countries that these stipulations should be made sufficient in these regards; and that we can look for no clearer evidence of the good will which Russia professes toward us than a frank declaration of her readiness to come to a distinct agreement with us on these points in an earnest and generous spirit.

I have observed that in your conferences on this subject heretofore with the minister for foreign affairs, as reported in your dispatches, you have on some occasions given discreet expression to the feelings of sympathy and gratification with which this government and people regard any steps taken in foreign countries in the direction of a liberal tolerance analogous to that which forms the fundamental principle of our national existence. Such expressions were natural on your part, and reflected a sentiment which we all feel. But in making the President's views known to the minister I desire that you will carefully subordinate such sentiments to the simple consideration of what is conscientiously believed to be due to our citizens in foreign lands. You will distinctly impress upon him that, regardful of the sovereignty of Russia, we do not submit any suggestions touching the laws and customs of the empire except where those laws and customs conflict with and destroy the rights of American citizens as secured by treaty obligations.

You can further advise him that we can make no new treaty with Russia, nor accept any construction of our existing treaty, which shall discriminate against any class of American citizens on account of their religious faith.

I cannot but feel assured that this earnest presentation of the views of this government will accord with the sense of justice and equity of that of Russia, and that the questions at issue will soon find their natural solution in harmony with the noble spirit of tolerance which pervaded the ukase of the Empress Catherine a century ago, and with the statesman-like declaration of the principle of reciprocity found in the later decree of the Czar Alexander II in 1860.

You may read this dispatch to the minister for foreign affairs, and should he desire a copy, you will give it to him.

I am, etc.,

JAMES G. BLAINE

Mr. Foster being absent from St. Petersburg, Mr. Hoffman undertook to read Mr. Blaine's dispatch to Mr. de Giers, but was asked instead to leave it for the latter's careful perusal. This he did, but Mr. de Giers was only moved to say that while personally, and from the moral side of the question, he would like to see modification in the laws governing American Jews in Russia, yet from the legal point of view he must insist that the words "on condition of their submitting to the laws and ordinances there prevailing" were controlling, and subjected American Jews to the same treatment accorded native Jews. A similar reply and on the same basis went to the British Government which had protested against the treatment of a Mr. Lewisohn, a British subject, the facts of whose case were the same as those of the American citizen, Marx Wilczynski.

It should be remarked here that in spite of protests heard in the British Parliament relating to the Lewisohn case, the British Government finally adopted the Russian view and, at least as far as a treaty right in Russia was concerned, British citizens of the Jewish faith were, with the consent of their own Government, put in an inferior class. The British Government, as will soon be seen, was unwilling to co-operate with the Government of the United States when the latter suggested an aggressive attitude on this important question. On the other hand, the American Government never accepted the literal interpretation of the first article of the Russo-American treaty, and was determined to fight for the rights of its Jewish citizens until the treaty was finally terminated in 1912.

At about the same time, May, 1881, Mr. Foster sent a dispatch, different in character and much more unpleasant in nature, informing Washington of a disgraceful series of massacres that had taken place in the southwestern districts of Russia. These outrages had been at their worst in the cities of Elizabethgrad and Kief, where many Jews had been killed, and Jewish property worth millions of rubles had been destroyed. The police authorities had not dared to interfere, and even the railroad officials had refused to run trains for the Jewish refugees for fear of attack by the infuriated mobs "debauched with liquor and plunder."

The general cause of these outbreaks had been, according to Mr. Foster, the prevailing bigotry and religious hatred of the lower classes for the Jews. The immediate cause had been the fact that the country was not prosperous, had to pay heavy taxes which were exacted with great severity, and, as usual in such cases, the Jew, who was the tradesman and the money-lender, had been made the scapegoat.

The American Minister still cherished the hope that Czarist Russia would soon remove all proscriptive laws and disabilities imposed upon the Russian Jews; he believed that these horrible massacres would hasten the coming of that happy day. "If these events," wrote Mr. Foster, "lead to a serious consideration of the wisdom of abolishing all the Jewish disabilities, and of placing Russian legislation on this subject alongside that of the other enlightened nations, the loss of life and property will not have been in vain."

Late in 1881, Secretary Blaine attempted to win England over to taking joint steps against the Russian practice of discriminating against American and British citizens. The dispatch in which this proposal was offered to the British Government does not appear in the "Foreign Relations." The quotation herein given is taken from a pamphlet published by Max J. Kohler, who possessed a photostatic copy of a dispatch which was sent by Secretary Blaine to James Russell Lowell, then United States Minister at London. From the dispatch which was dated Washington, November 22, 1881, the following paragraphs are given by Mr. Kohler:[20]

I am well aware that the domestic enactments of a state toward its own subjects is not generally regarded as a fit matter for the intervention of another independent power. But when such enactments directly affect the liberty and property of foreigners who resort to a country under the supposed guarantee of treaties framed for the most liberal ends, when the conscience of an alien owing no allegiance whatever to the local sovereignty, is brought under the harsh yoke of bigotry or prejudice which bows the necks of the natives, and when enlightened appeals made to humanity, to the principles of just reciprocity and to the advancing spirit of the age, in behalf of tolerance, are met with intimations of a purpose to still further burden the unhappy sufferers and so to necessarily increase the disability of foreigners of like creed resorting to Russia, it becomes in a high sense a moral duty to our citizens and to the doctrines of religious freedom we so strongly uphold, to seek proper protection for those citizens and tolerance for their creed, in foreign lands, even at the risk of criticism of the municipal laws of other states.

It cannot but be inexpressibly painful to the enlightened Statesmen of Great Britain, as well as of America, to see a discarded prejudice of the dark ages gravely revived at this day,— to witness an attempt to base the policy of a great and sovereign state on the mistaken theory that thrift is a crime of which the unthrifty are the innocent victims, and that discontent and disaffection are to

[20] "The United States and German-Jewish Persecutions. Precedents for Popular and Governmental Action," by Max J. Kohler, pages 40–41. The full text of this dispatch is, of course, given in "Instructions, Russia," Vol 16, No. 103, Nov. 23, 1881, The National Archives, Washington, D. C.

be diminished by increasing the causes from which they arise. No student of history need be reminded of the lessons taught by the persecutions of the Jews in Central Europe, and on the Spanish Peninsula. Then, as now in Russia, the Hebrew fared better in business than his neighbor; then, as now, his economy and patient industry bred capital, and capital bred envy, and envy persecution, and persecution disaffection and social separation. The old tradition moves in its unvarying circle,— the Jews are made a people apart from other peoples, not of their volition, but because they have been repressed and ostracised by the communities in which they mixed. The *ghetto* of mediaeval times still preaches its eloquent lesson, which the nations have done well to heed. In Great Britain and in the U. S., the Israelite is not segregated from his fellow men, a social Esau, alike repellent and repelled. His equal part in our social framework is unchallenged; his thrift and industry add to the wealth of the state; and his loyalty and patriotism are unquestionable. So, likewise, in the great states of Europe, until we reach the Russian frontier, the Carpathian chain on the strait of Gibraltar [*sic*]. The Empire of the Czar, in its treatment of native Hebrews, ranks strangely, with the Roumania of the past before the enlightened counsels of the Treaty of Berlin prevailed, and with the Morocco of the present!

It was perfectly clear to the mind of the late President that an amelioration of the treatment of American Israelites in Russia could only result from a very decided betterment of the condition of the native Hebrews — that any steps taken toward the relief of one would necessarily react in favor of the other — and that, under the peculiar and abnormal aspects of the case, it is competent and proper to urge upon Russia action in consonance with the spirit of the age. To his successor in the Chief Magistracy, these conclusions are no less evident. And I am charged by the President to bring the subject to the formal attention of Her Britannic Majesty's Government, in the firm belief that the community of interests between the U. S. and England in this great question of civil rights and equal tolerance of creed for their respective citizens in foreign parts, will lead to consideration of the matter with a view to common action thereon. Should the views of the two Governments be found to agree herein, it would seem, moreover, a propitious time to initiate a movement which might also embrace other Powers whose service in the work of progress is commensurate with our own, to the end that Russia may be beneficially influenced by their cumulative representations and that their several citizens and subjects visiting the territory of the Empire on law-observing missions of private interest, shall no longer find their subjection of conscience to military forms and procedure which obtains nowhere else in Europe.

You may read this dispatch to Lord Granville and, if he desires it, leave with him a copy. You will say to him at the same time that, while abating no part of his intention to press upon the Russian Government the just claim of American citizens to less harsh treatment in the Empire by reason of their faith, the President will await with pleasure an opportunity for a free interchange of views upon the subject with the Government of Her Majesty.

Though Lord Granville informed Mr. Lowell that "Her Majesty's Government would always be most happy to act in concert with that of the United States on any question regarding religious liberty," the plan proved abortive, as, for political reasons, England failed to co-operate.

After long and arduous efforts, Mr. Foster was able to compile and list laws and regulations affecting foreign Jews who wished to trade with, or establish their business and residence in, Russia. Generally speaking, foreign Jews were not allowed to immigrate to Russia, nor could they become Russian subjects. But as is true of all Russian laws on this subject, there were many exceptions. Manufacturers, bankers, and commercial agents were excepted in some specific cases, but even they were subjected to many limitations and great inconveniences. Mr. Foster summarizes these laws in the following paragraph:[21]

It will thus be seen that Jewish citizens of the United States are virtually excluded from Russia, as few, if any, of them would be willing to comply with the requirements necessary for their admission under Russian laws. This code of Jewish regulations . . . will appear somewhat curious and antiquated in our country of unrestricted commercial intercourse, and especially the limitations, not only of a business, but even of a domestic character, which are thrown around the Jewish bankers and merchants (to use the language of the law) "known for their high social position and large operations and commercial enterprises."

[21] Foreign Relations, 1881, page 1022.

VIII. RUSSIA

1882–1902

For some time no new cases appeared in the correspondence. But in January, 1882, Mr. Hoffmann reports the case of James G. Moses, a case that has an element of humor in it and throws further light on the curious views held by the Russian authorities on the various religious divisions within the Jewish faith. Mr. Moses was an American citizen who came to St. Petersburg with the Ceniselli circus, as stable director. His name, though not his trade, betrayed him to the Russian police, and he was ordered out of the city. Mr. Moses went directly to Mr. Hoffmann, asking his intervention and claiming at the time that he was not "one of those Talmud Jews." Actually, he claimed, he belonged to the "American Reformed Church" whose equivalent in Russia was, in the opinion of Mr. Moses, the Karaite Jews.

General Kosloff, prefect of police, was approached and, after an interview with Mr. Moses and his employer, granted the necessary permission. "It appears," says Mr. Hoffmann in his dispatch, "that the Karaim or Reformed Jews are of a superior class and have never given the Russian Government any trouble or been found enrolled among the Nihilists."

In the meantime, anti-Jewish riots had again been the unpleasant subject of our diplomatic correspondence with Russia. This time the massacres occurred in Warsaw, the capital of Russian Poland. Later on, more riots occurred in Balta, in the south of Russia.

At the request of Mr. Hoffmann, Mr. Joseph Rawicz, United States Consul at Warsaw, was asked to prepare a report on the anti-Jewish riots in Warsaw, and from his account we learn the following wretched details.

They started with the appearance of a printed proclamation instigating the Christian population to riot; according to

Mr. Rawicz, "it is certain they did not spring out on this soil, but were conveyed here from the main source." A number of times he uses the phrase, "main source" without identifying it. What he meant to say, however, was that anti-Jewish agitation was not a Polish product but was imported from Russia.

The Warsaw riots took place on Christmas day, 1881, when a false fire alarm caused a panic which resulted in the death of 30 persons, and serious injury to 26 others. Voices from the crowd put the blame on the Jews, and the riots started. The rabble moved towards the Jewish neighborhood and pillaged 1025 shops, thus damaging the livelihoods of 10,000 persons, of whom many lost all their worldly belongings.

In Balta, one Jew was killed and then a great and wanton destruction of Jewish property started, leaving men, women and children bereft of food and lodging. The police interfered only in cases where the Jews dared defend themselves.

Mr. Hoffmann's report concluded with the following statement:[1]

But the position of the Russian Government in this matter is an exceedingly difficult one. In a conversation with General Ignatieff a few days since, he told me that the government had received the reports of the numerous local boards appointed by it last year to suggest measures for the amelioration of the condition of the Jews; that they had not only by a majority, but unanimously, recommended their expulsion from the Empire. "We have then," he said, "on the one hand 5,000,000 Jews, Russian subjects, clamoring to be freed from all special restraints, and we have on the other, 85,000,000 Russian subjects clamoring to have the 5,000,000 expelled from the Empire. What is to be done in such a case?"

Mr. Hoffmann did not answer the question, nor did he add any comment on it in his dispatch. He was, however, urged by Secretary Frederick T. Frelinghuysen to lodge a vigorous protest with the Russian Government, if, in his opinion, it would help to prevent similar wrongs in the future. He was reminded that the Government of the United States dislikes to intervene in the affairs of other nations, no matter

[1] Foreign Relations, 1882, page 452.

how much it may disapprove of them. Still, Mr. Hoffmann
was asked to convey to the Russian Government in as discreet a manner as possible, that the feelings of friendship
for Russia prompts the American Government to express the
hope that the anti-Jewish riots would soon end.[2]

[*Mr. Frelinghuysen to Mr. Hoffmann*]

Department of State
Washington, April 15, 1882

Sir: The prejudice of race and creed having in our day given
away to the claims of our common humanity, the people of the United
States have heard, with great regret, the stories of the sufferings
of the Jews in Russia. It may be that the accounts in the newspapers are exaggerated, and the same may be true of some private
reports. Making, however, due allowance for misrepresentations,
it can scarcely be doubted that much has been done which a humane
and just person must condemn.

The President, of course, feels that the Government of the
Emperor should not be held morally responsible for acts which it
considers wrong, but which it may be powerless to prevent.

If that be true of this case, it would be worse than useless for me
to direct you, as the representative of the United States, to give
official expression to the feeling which this treatment of the Jews
calls forth in this country. Should, however, the attitude of the
Russian Government be different, and should you be of the opinion
that a more vigorous effort might be put forth for the prevention
of this great wrong, you will, if a favorable opportunity offers,
state, with all proper deference, that the feeling of friendship which
the United States entertains for Russia prompts this government
to express the hope that the Imperial Government will find means
to cause the persecution of these unfortunate fellow-beings to cease.

This instruction devolves a delicate duty upon you, and a wide
discretion is given you in its execution. However much this Republic
may disapprove of affairs in other nationalities, it does not conceive that it is its right or province officiously and offensively to
intermeddle. If, however, it should come to your knowledge that
any citizens of the United States are made victims of the persecution, you will feel it your duty to omit no effort to protect
them, and to report such cases to this Department.

I am, etc.,

Fred'k. T. Frelinghuysen

[2] Foreign Relations, 1882, page 451.

The right of American Jews to obtain permits of residence in Russia had come up a number of times. There were rumors heard in the United States that foreign Jews in Odessa and other localities had been ordered expelled from the country. On advice from Washington, Mr. George V. N. Lothrop, in charge of the American legation, questioned the ministry of foreign affairs regarding these rumors and received an official denial. But one of the most important reports ever sent to the State Department by an American minister on the Jewish problem and its relation to the general political and social structure of a country was written by Mr. William Henry Hunt, American Minister in St. Petersburg in the years 1882–84. His death in St. Petersburg robbed the United States of one of the most able and liberal men sent abroad to represent our nation.

Even before he left for Russia Mr. Hunt interviewed many people concerning the Jewish problem. He found the subject interesting and important. He continued his investigation in Russia and Russian Poland, and incorporated his findings as well as his personal analysis in a report sent to Secretary Frelinghuysen on November 6, 1883, under the title "Condition of Public Affairs and Opinion in Russia and of the Jews in the Empire." Because of his frank criticism of the public affairs in that country and of officials who conduct them, the report was marked "Confidential," and was not printed in the "Foreign Relations of the United States."[2a]

The investigation, the report stated, was beset with discouraging difficulties. When the government is spoken of "men look around over their shoulders, behind them, and give evasive answers in whispers to questions put to them." All are afraid to talk for fear of official displeasure, exile, or even more severe punishment. The press, of course, was of little help to him. He found the whole country steeped in ignorance, full of fanatical hatred and religious intolerance. The Jews are under the control of the local authorities of the provinces and cities of the Empire. There is no separate

[2a] The full text is, however, found in Dispatches, Russia, Vol. 37, No. 86, Nov. 6, 1883, The National Archives, Washington, D. C.

code to guide officials in their treatment of Jews, but there are many laws and regulations, all in the Russian language and never translated. He characterizes them in the following sentences: "They consist of a rude and an undigested mass of ukases, provincial regulations and ministerial orders and proclamations. They are vague, confusing and often contradict one another. They are arbitrarily interpreted and applied to meet the exigencies of each case."

The chronic attacks on Jews by the Russian peasants, from which they return home triumphantly and under the impression that they are carrying out the wishes of God and Emperor, have been explained as natural reactions against the Jews who are engaged in usury. Mr. Hunt does not agree with this statement. Very few Jews are engaged in usury, and the many Christians who practice it remain unmolested. "It is not the calling but the creed that provokes ill-treatment. The force of example is felt in the palace of the noble and the hovel of the peasant, and so long as the law fails to interpose its timely shield for his protection amidst dangers,— whilst he is considered by the head of the state and church as one justly odious, of wicked and dangerous faith, and, in short, as but little better than a wild beast,— it is not difficult to account for the outbursts of violence and cruelty among ignorant and prejudiced peasants."

Mr. Hunt also paid a visit to Warsaw whose Jewish quarter he found to be "a sorry spectacle of squalor, degradation and servility — more ragged and less cared for than the poorest who overcrowd the tenement houses of our great cities." The Poles he discovered to be old hands in the ill-treatment of Jews. Though they hate the Russian, they have no sympathy or pity for the Jew. In their own time they themselves subjected the Jews of Free Poland to even greater oppression. Even now "they do not seem to recognize the equity of that even-handed justice that today impresses on them the lessons they but yesterday taught others."

Having formed an opinion on the subject, Mr. Hunt then tried to persuade the Russian Government to change its attitude to and treatment of the Jews in the Russian Empire. During a talk with Mr. de Giers, he brought up the topic of the Jews in Russia. The American Minister then told his auditor about the Jews of the United States, "of the munificence of their wealthy men among us, of the benevolent institutions they have founded or aided liberally in supporting, their great private charities, their conspicuous patriotism, the great public enterprises with which they were connected, their habits of sobriety, their exemplary lives in all their domestic relations, their proficiency in the fine arts, their distinctions in the learned professions and in the field of exact sciences, the important part they played in the economic life of the country." Mr. Hunt then suggested that the same could happen in Russia if they were treated as equals, and given full opportunity to give of themselves to their country.

To these exhortations Mr. de Giers replied that the Russian Jews constituted a race separate and apart from the rest of the people, and that the Jews in Russia did not possess the same intelligence as members of their race in other countries, and that they are "altogether unfitted for more liberty than they now possess."

Mr. Hunt continued to argue the case of the Jews, saying that at least an attempt should be made to find out how the Jew would use his liberty if it once were given to him. You cannot teach a man to swim unless you put him into the water. The separateness of the Jews, Mr. Hunt turned into an argument in their favor. "The unyielding, patient and steadfast adherence of the race to their ancestral faith and traditions, amidst long-suffering insult, injustice and cruel persecutions, challenges respect, though it may not invite approval from all."

Mr. de Giers was not impressed, and Mr. Hunt became convinced that remonstrances by foreign powers would not help the Jew in Russia.

The report concluded with the following hopeful statement, "Time will in the end, even though it may be far away in the future, unlock the doors of education and, by the light of justice, charity and reason, confer the blessings of liberty upon the Jew as well as upon his Russian oppressor." Mr. Lothrop was unsuccessful in his attempt to obtain, as a matter of right, permits of residence for American Jews.

With the coming of a new administration in Washington, and the appointment of Mr. Thomas F. Bayard as Secretary of State, Mr. Lothrop found it necessary to recapitulate the laws affecting American citizens of the Jewish faith in Russia. Mr. Bayard was at a loss to understand these laws, saying that as an American "he cannot comprehend [them] without difficulty or view [them] without regret." Mr. Bayard knew that the Russian Government was aware that we did not admit the principle of discriminating against American citizens because of their religious tenets. Yet there was no ground on which the United States could remonstrate anew against the prevalent discriminations, for they were against all Jews and not specifically Jews from the United States. As a matter of fact, the Russians were much more lenient to American Jews, and were more likely to heed protest from the American legation than from any other. Thus, while two English Jews, one of them a member of Parliament, were expelled from Moscow, apparently without intervention in their behalf by the British diplomatic agents there, the protest of the American Minister against the expulsion of a "most respectable Hebrew merchant of New York" proved effective, and the order of expulsion was revoked.

Russian law books were full of regulations and ordinances limiting the freedom of movement and choice of activity of the Jew in Russia, whether native or foreign. Normally, however, these were not strictly enforced, being only partly adhered to and often totally ignored. This fact explains why there were large Jewish communities in the two capitals, St. Petersburg and Moscow, and in many other cities outside the Pale of Settlement.

During reasonably normal times, especially if they lasted for a few years in succession, thousands of Jewish families had established homes and businesses in new places of residence. It is not at all strange that during such periods both the Jews in Russia and their friends outside were led to believe that the anti-Jewish laws had been repealed. This explains why, when, as it happened in 1890, the restrictions against them, long dormant, were revived and put into effect, the cry was raised that the Czarist Government had issued new edicts against the Jews, bringing upon them great hardships, the effects of which were felt even in countries other than Russia.

This brings us to another factor which now enters into the diplomatic correspondence between the United States and Russia, and which, in addition to others already mentioned, further prompted our Government to show great concern in the miserable plight of the Jews in Russia.

In 1890, Jews were expelled from those places where during a period of toleration they had established homes. These Jews had two alternatives, either to return to those provinces where Jews could go about their businesses unmolested, or to migrate to some other country where they would be more welcome. As the "Jewish" provinces were already overcrowded, thousands of Jewish families chose the latter alternative, left their native land, many of them choosing the United States for their adopted home.

In the decade 1880–90, no less than 200,000 Russian Jews entered the United States. The fear was then expressed that even with the best of intentions the United States could not absorb such a continuous influx of an alien element. This fear was shared by Mr. Blaine who again headed the State Department. Not only would their assimilation become a difficult process, but, as most of the new immigrants were indigent and helpless, anxiety was felt that they would become a heavy charge upon the community.

The factor of mass migration of Russian Jews into the United States changed somewhat the nature of the approach employed by our Government in its efforts to secure the amelioration of the conditions of the Jews in Russia. Before this period, continued insistence on the humanitarian aspect of the question could have been interpreted by the Russian Government as an intervention in an affair which was strictly internal. But when the Russian policy had consequences which directly and intimately affected the welfare of the United States, our Government could point out that it was one of the mutual duties of nations to enforce their own laws with due regard for the consequences which their enforcement might produce on the rest of the world.

Administrations changed quickly in Washington. During the last quarter of the past century the turnover in our ministers at St. Petersburg was rapid. In 1890, our minister at the Russian capital was Mr. Charles Emory Smith who did not have any deep convictions on the Jewish problem in Russia, and appears to have taken his cue on this question from the official Russian attitude, especially as expressed by Mr. de Giers, the Russian Minister for Foreign Affairs. In a dispatch to Mr. Blaine, dated September 25, 1890, Mr. Smith hurried to deny rumors prevalent in the United States and Europe that new proscriptive measures and revival of old and obsolete ones were now applied against the Jewish subjects of Russia.[3]

[*Mr. Smith to Mr. Blaine*]

Legation of the United States
St. Petersburg, September 25, 1890

Sir: You have been advised by previous dispatches from this legation that the published rumors of new proscription measures, or the revival and oppressive application of old and obsolete edicts, against the Hebrew residents and subjects of the Russian Empire are declared by the Russian Government to be entirely groundless. Notwithstanding the authoritative denial of these reports, they still crop up from time to time, and are persistently repeated with a degree of circumstance well calculated to create the impression that they have some foundation of fact. This continued imputation of purpose and acts, to which, if really entertained or executed, we could not be indifferent, renders it proper that I should apprise you of some further evidence on the subject.

The statement recently appeared in the columns of the London Times that, despite the disavowal of the Russian Government, some five or six hundred Hebrew families residing at Odessa had

---

[3] Foreign Relations, 1890, page 701.

been summarily notified that they must immediately abandon their homes, and, in fact, that they had already been expelled from the country. It has come to my knowledge that, in view of this publication, the British embassy at this capital called on the British consul at Odessa to investigate the story and report upon its truth. His report has now been made, and I am able to communicate its substance. He directed his inquiries not only among the Government officials, but among the Hebrews themselves, and the latter were as emphatic as the former in declaring that no order of the character described had been issued and no movement of the kind attempted. He found no confirmation of the story in any quarter. A number of Hebrew families had emigrated or were preparing to do so, but this action was entirely voluntary on their part, and was not taken under compulsion. This emigration was explained by the rabbis and the highest authorities among the Hebrews as due to the fact that there were many youths in those families, and that, as the number admitted to the universities in Russia is limited, they removed to other countries to secure the opportunity of higher education; and thus it was made clear that there was no foundation for the particular charge which has been preferred against the Government.

These reports of new proscriptive designs against the Hebrews on the part of the Russian Government have naturally created more concern in other countries than here, because, so far as can be ascertained, they had their sole origin and obtained their sole credence remote from the scene. Had there been any good reason for supposing that measures so repugnant to every sentiment of justice and humanity were actually undertaken or seriously contemplated, it would have been a duty to report them for such consideration as they would have required. But it is a source of special gratification to be able to present not only the denials of the Government, but confirmatory testimony that these injurious allegations are baseless.

I have, etc.,

CHAS. EMORY SMITH

Meanwhile in Washington the House of Representatives had taken official notice of the rumors regarding the new persecutions of Jews in Russia, and on August 20, 1890, adopted a resolution requesting the President to communicate to the House any information on this question which he might possess. Though Mr. Blaine was able to reassure the House with Mr. Smith's dispatch given above, he himself was not fully satisfied with it. In his dispatch of February

18, 1891, Mr. Blaine discourses at length for the benefit of Mr. Smith on all the phases of the new proscription against the Jews and its effect on the internal situation in the United States.[4]

[*Mr. Blaine to Mr. Smith*]

Department of State
Washington, February 18, 1891

SIR: On the 20th of August last the House of Representatives adopted a resolution requesting the President to communicate to that body any information in his possession concerning the enforcement of proscriptive edicts against the Jews in Russia. To this resolution the President responded on the 1st of October, and accompanying his response there was a report in which, with reference to the rumors that new measures of repression were about to be put in force, I said:

Such a step, if in reality contemplated, would not only wound the universal and innate sentiment of humanity, but would suggest the difficult problem of affording an immediate asylum to a million or more of exiles without seriously deranging the conditions of labor and of social organization in other communities.

The correspondence communicated to the House of Representatives included your reassuring dispatch No. 44, of the 25th of September last; and this dispatch, together with assurances received in conversations with the diplomatic representative of Russia at this capital, tended to allay the apprehension necessarily aroused by the prospect either of the adoption of new measures or of the harsh enforcement of the old.

Up to the present time the Department has not been advised that any new edicts affecting the Jews have been promulgated. The cases of distress that have been brought to our notice are the result, in some instances, of the new interpretation, and, in others, of the strict enforcement of regulations which have for some years been in existence, but of which the severity was not generally understood because they were not rigorously applied.

The Department is informed that for many years the Jews in Russia have, as a race, been compelled to live within a certain area denominated the pale of settlement. Under the laws of May, 1882, it is understood that their places of residence within this area have been restricted by forbidding them to live in villages and to force them into the towns. The effect of the recent and summary enforce-

[4] Foreign Relations, 1891, page 737.

ment of this measure in certain districts has been to deprive many of their means of livelihood. It is also understood that under the laws for many years in existence Jewish artisans have been permitted to reside outside of the pale of settlement. The Department is informed that by a new interpretation of the law many classes of workers formerly regarded as artisans are now denied that privilege, and being suddenly forced to quit their homes and to swell the number of their race in the overcrowded towns within the pale of settlement, find themselves unable to gain a subsistence by the pursuit of their respective occupations.

Other measures, such as the withdrawal of the privilege of pursuing many occupations, the denial of admission to the schools, and the actual expulsion as "alien vagrants" of persons long domiciled in Russia, contribute to swell the emigration. I forbear to enumerate the edicts particularly applicable to the family, by which the ties of relationship are rent and a premium put upon their severance. I do not dwell on these things, not only because it is not my purpose to indulge in a general criticism of the anti-Jewish laws, but also because those that I have explicitly referred to in the main account for the cases that have been brought to my notice.

That numbers of Jews have been and are daily being compelled to quit their homes in Russia by the enforcement of these oppressive measures, is amply shown by the present immigration of destitute Russian Jews into the United States. Heretofore this immigration, although large, being mainly made up of persons who were in some measure prepared for the change, has not overtaxed the resources of the various benevolent associations which are so generously maintained and admirably administered by the Jews of the United States. I am told on excellent authority that within ten years some 200,000 Jews of Russian origin have been received into this country, have been furnished, when necessary, with occupation and homes, and have become speedily assimilated into the body politic, of which they form an orderly, thrifty, and law-abiding element.

The gravest fears are expressed lest this resource should fail if taxed with a great influx of Russian Jews, who, by reason of their sudden expulsion from their homes and their unfamiliarity with the language and ways of life in this country, would stand in need of immediate, and in many cases of long-continued, assistance and care.

You are aware that the problem of efficiently controlling immigration has been before the national legislature for some years. Measures have already been adopted for its regulation, and several schemes of further legislation are now pending before Congress.

These measures, however, have not been due to an inhospitable disposition. The policy of this Government in respect to the admission of aliens to its shores has been most liberal. It has afforded to many thousands a home and a ready entrance into its political and social life, and it still offers to spontaneous, self-helpful, and independent immigration a cordial welcome.

If measures of restriction have been adopted, it is only because it has been found necessary to avert the injection into the population of elements not assimilable and the bringing or sending hither of the indigent and helpless to become a charge upon the community. In no instance has any measure of expulsion or of oppression been adopted in respect to those who are already here, all of whom stand under the equal protection of the laws.

But the hospitality of a nation should not be turned into a burden. And, however much we may sympathize with wanderers forced by untoward circumstances to quit their homes, and however ready the disposition to relieve the deplorable condition into which they may be cast by the application of the laws of their native country, the Government and people of the United States cannot avoid a feeling of concern at the enforcement of measures which threaten to frustrate their efforts to minister to the wants and improve the condition of those who are driven to seek a livelihood within their borders.

We are not forgetful of the ties of good relationship that have long subsisted between the United States and Russia, and of the friendly acts of Russia towards our country in the past. The Government and people of the United States are fully animated with a desire to preserve this cordiality of feeling, and for this reason they the more strongly deprecate the enforcement in Russia, in respect to a portion of her people, of measures which not only arouse a general feeling of disappointment, but which also operate to impose a tax upon the charitable and humane in this country.

The Government of the United States does not assume to dictate the internal policy of other nations, or to make suggestions as to what their municipal laws should be or as to the manner in which they should be administered. Nevertheless, the mutual duties of nations require that each should use its power with a due regard for the other and for the results which its exercise produces on the rest of the world. It is in this respect that the condition of the Jews in Russia is now brought to the attention of the United States, upon whose shores are cast daily evidences of the suffering and destitution wrought by the enforcement of the edicts against this unhappy people. I am persuaded that His Imperial Majesty the Emperor of Russia and his councilors can feel no sympathy with measures which are forced upon other nations by such deplorable consequences.

You will read this instruction to the minister of foreign affairs and give him a copy if he desires it.

I am, etc.,

JAMES G. BLAINE

In a dispatch to Washington, dated February 10, 1891, Mr. Smith reports on a long and "suggestive conversation" which he had had with Mr. de Giers. But Mr. Blaine, having a longer acquaintance with the conditions of the Jews in Russia, had more set opinions than his minister in St. Petersburg. In a dispatch of February 27, 1891, Mr. Blaine informed Mr. Smith that he had received new evidence that various sections of the American people showed a grave concern about the new hardships experienced by the Jews in Russia, and that almost daily the State Department was receiving communications on this subject which the Government of the United States could not ignore.[5]

[*Mr. Blaine to Mr. Smith*]

Department of State
Washington, February 27, 1891

SIR: Your dispatch No. 75, of the 10th of February, reporting a conversation with Mr. de Giers in relation to the treatment of the Jews in Russia, was received by the Department on the 25th of the same month. On the 18th of February, just a week previously, I addressed to you a communication to be read to Mr. de Giers on the same subject.

While the statement in that communication touching the harsh treatment of the Jews are completely confirmed by Mr. de Giers, I have observed with not a little satisfaction, his readiness in suggesting this topic of discussion and his expression of willingness to consider any inquiries which you might make. It was believed that the Government of Russia would not disregard the evidences which have appeared in various countries of the general interest and solicitude which have been excited throughout the civilized world by the reports of the oppression of the Jewish race in the dominions of His Imperial Majesty. Nevertheless, the fact that the subject

[5] Foreign Relations, 1891, page 740.

has been brought forward by the imperial minister of foreign affairs himself increases our hope that the representations of this Government, based upon the deplorable aspects of the question which have been brought to its notice, will not only receive the consideration to which they are thought to be justly entitled, but will also more fully impress the Government of Russia with the fact that the effects of the repressive policy against the Jews are not confined to that country, but that they also excite the sympathy and appeal to the generous and charitable efforts of the people of other lands.

Ever since the transmission to you of the instructions of the 18th of February the Department has received fresh evidences of the immediate and material, as well as of the broad and general, interest which has been felt in this country in regard to the hardships of the Jewish subjects of His Imperial Majesty. Almost every day communications are received upon this subject, temperate and couched in language respectful to the Government of the Czar, but at the same time indicative and strongly expressive of the depth and prevalence of the sentiment of disapprobation and regret. No government can be insensible of a fact of so much significance, and I am happy to perceive the appreciation of the sentiments and interests of other people which the conversation of Mr. de Giers discloses.

I am, etc.,

JAMES G. BLAINE

Mr. Smith appears to have been slow in sizing up the situation as it then presented itself, and to have given too much credence to reports and promises of Russian officials. On February 28, 1891, he repeated that there was no evidence of the application and enforcement of the new measures against the Jews; that only in a few and unimportant cases had some Jews been induced to withdraw from their established homes.[6]

[*Mr. Smith to Mr. Blaine*]

Legation of the United States
St. Petersburg, February 28, 1891

SIR: In view of the numerous and varied reports during the last few months concerning the purpose and action of the Russian Government in regard to the Jewish people living within the Empire, I have deemed it useful to institute some inquiries on the

* Foreign Relations, 1891, page 740.

subject through the consuls of the United States. To this end I
sent out in January a circular letter. The design of this circular
was not to initiate a minute investigation into details which would
require much time, but to elicit trustworthy information upon the
spirit and tendencies which mark the present policy toward the
Jews. It was deemed necessary to communicate only with the
consuls located in the section where the Jews are found in considerable numbers, and the circular was therefore addressed only
to the consuls at Warsaw, Odessa and Riga.

They all agree in declaring that there is no evidence of the application and enforcement of new measures against the Hebrews. At
the same time, those on the western frontier of the Empire observe
signs of the more stringent execution of old laws which have heretofore been so loosely and lightly observed as practically to be inop-
erative.

As to St. Petersburg and Moscow, the best information I can
gather leads to the conclusion that the present policy of the Government is inducing some withdrawal of the Jews from these
centers. The long-established laws permit only Jewish merchants
of the first guild and Jews of certain other professional or artisan
classes to reside in these cities. But the prohibition against Jews
outside of these classes has not been enforced with any degree of
strictness, and under the influence of this laxity thousands who
are interdicted by the terms of the law have settled in St. Petersburg and Moscow. I do not understand that there is any harsh or
general movement to enforce the law now, but am informed that
such inquiries have been set on foot as to create the fear on the part
of those not embraced within the tolerated classes that trouble
may be experienced, and that under this apprehension some of
them are removing from the two chief cities of the Empire.

I have, etc.,

CHAS. EMORY SMITH

In a later dispatch, dated March 12, 1891, Mr. Smith
reports on the presentation of instructions which he had
received from Mr. Blaine.[7]

[*Mr. Smith to Mr. Blaine*]

Legation of the United States
St. Petersburg, March 12, 1891

SIR: I have the honor to report that I yesterday waited upon
the minister of foreign affairs, Mr. de Giers, with a copy of your

[7] Foreign Relations, 1891, page 741.

instruction No. 78, relating to the edicts and policy of Russia concerning the Jews. Upon hearing my statement of the object of my call Mr. de Giers requested me not to read the dispatch to him, but to leave a copy, which he could examine at leisure.

I then gave him a brief verbal outline of its contents, referring to the resolution of inquiry passed by the House of Representatives in August of last year touching rumored proscriptive edicts against the Jews and to your report in response. You had received assurances, so you stated in this dispatch, which tended to allay apprehensions that had been aroused by alarming publications, and the Department had no information that any new measures hostile to the Jews had been undertaken. The cases of distress which had been brought to its attention were explained by the more rigorous enforcement of old laws whose severity had not been understood so long as they had not been applied. That the Jews in Russia were subjected to coercive and oppressive measures which compelled them to quit their homes was shown by the number of unfortunate and indigent Russian Jews who were now arriving in the United States. You had been informed on excellent authority that within a period of ten years this immigration amounted to 200,000. Most of these immigrants had been well provided for, but a further influx of destitute persons entirely unprepared for the conditions and requirements of American life would be a very serious burden for the American people. It was in this aspect of the results forced upon our country that the condition of the Jews in Russia under existing measures presented itself to the attention of our Government and people, and, in view of the mutual duties of nations, constrained this expression of their sentiments.

On this statement of the general tenor of your dispatch, Mr. de Giers hastened to ask at the outset what was its conclusion — what demand it presented. I replied that it presented no demand, but was a declaraction of the views of the Government and people of the United States, which was submitted for the consideration of the Imperial Government of Russia under a sense of its own obligations. Mr. de Giers inquired particularly as to the statement that 200,000 Russian Jews had immigrated to the United States within ten years. I repeated your statement on this point. He rejoined that if such a number of people had gone to the United States as workers to aid in developing the country, he supposed they would be acceptable, but if they went to "exploit" the American people, as he expressed it, he could understand how objectionable it was. After some further observations of a general character Mr. de Giers concluded by saying that the dispatch would be received in the same friendly spirit in which it was sent; that he would submit it to the Emperor; and that, if it was determined to make reply either verbally or in writing, it would be duly communicated.

I have, etc.,

CHAS. EMORY SMITH

In a dispatch of April 6, 1891, not published in the Foreign Relations, Mr. Smith reported to Secretary Blaine a talk he had with Mr. de Giers. In this talk the American Minister suggested that an international conference should be called "to consider the conditions of the Israelites and the question of restoring Palestine to the hands of this people as the asylum and home of such of their race as might choose to go from other lands." Mr. Smith then referred to the petitions sent to President Harrison praying that he use his good offices to bring about such a conference. (See the chapter on Palestine.) Mr. de Giers replied in a personal and unofficial way that if the United States should propose such a conference, Russia would co-operate.[7a]

On April 20, 1891, Mr. Smith had to send a totally different dispatch to Washington from that of March 12. From Russian journals he finally learned about the expulsion of 200 Jewish families from Moscow. He added that "it is probable that these are only the forerunners of further expulsions," which he hoped would be "gently and gradually" executed.

When one remembers that even Mr. de Giers complained of the difficulty he and other ministers in St. Petersburg had had in controlling subordinate officials, one can imagine just how "gently and gradually" this new application of old laws, officially ordered from above, was effected by the same subordinate officials. Only a week later, Mr. Wurts, Chargé d'Affaires during the absence of Mr. Smith on leave, forwarded a translation of a typical imperial ukase concerning the domicile of Jews. It referred to the city of Moscow, where the Minister of the Interior, in concert with the Governor of Moscow, was ordered to take all the necessary measures to

[7a] Dispatches, Russia, Vol. 42, No. 87, The National Archives, Washington, D. C.

have all Jewish workmen and artisans sent away gradually from Moscow into the zone assigned for their settlement. Mr. Wurts regrets to say that there are rumors that the laws are being applied "with undue severity." The Chargé, it seems, did not rely entirely on Russian newspapers and official pronouncements for his information. He must have known, and it is evident from his dispatch that he wished to convey the impression, that rumors of this kind had enough of a foundation of fact for him to take official cognizance of them.

Meanwhile, Mr. Smith had become interested in the colonization scheme of Baron Maurice de Hirsch, hoping that through that project of mass settlement of Jews in South America, the problem of the Russian Jew would be at least partially solved and, at the same time, a portion of the Jewish emigration could be diverted to other countries than the United States. To that end Mr. Smith met Mr. Arnold White, who represented the Jewish Colonization Association in its negotiations with the Russian Government. He even touched on the subject in his conversations with Mr. de Giers. On closer study, however, Mr. Smith discovered that the Argentine project could not change fundamentally the pressing question of Jewish emigration from Russia, for, according to the most optimistic estimates, the project could not take care of more than 25,000 emigrants a year, while the natural increase of the Jews in Russia was between 150,000 and 180,000 a year.

The efforts of Mr. Arnold White resulted in the formation of a central committee in St. Petersburg, and many local committees elsewhere in Russia, with the purpose of assisting and controlling the emigration of Russian Jews by their transplantation to other countries. On June 16, 1892, Mr. Wurts sent a translation of an imperial law on this subject, which is printed in full in the Foreign Relations, 1892. It would seem, from a reading of this law, that the last word, both in making the policy of this Central Committee and in the execution of it, was retained by the Minister of the Interior.

American citizens of Russian nativity returning to Russia, for a visit or a prolonged stay, were frequently arrested on the ground that they had left their country of birth and had become citizens of their adopted country for the sole purpose of evading their military duties. All protests of American ministers and consuls against such arrests proved of no avail. The Russian authorities persisted in refusing to waive their right to punish a former subject for an offense committed prior to his naturalization as a citizen of a foreign state, though in no case was banishment to Siberia, the usual punishment for evasion of military service, ever meted out to a naturalized American citizen. In one particular case, that of a Mr. Kempinsky, the Emperor granted clemency, and released the prisoner, but no concession was thereby made to the American claims. Jacob Goldstein, whose case we are now going to take up, was arrested on the same ground, namely, for having evaded military service. Mr. Goldstein suffered much unpleasantness during the clarification of his identity and status. His case as a whole had a peculiar aspect.

Mr. John W. Foster, former United States Minister to Russia and now Secretary of State, received from Mrs. Jennie Goldstein, the wife of Jacob, the following letter:[8]

New York, August 17, 1892

HONORABLE SIR: On February 23, 1892, one Jacob Goldstein left this port by steamer *Spree* of the Bremen line. On the same day, the said Jacob Goldstein paid to Messrs. C. B. Richard, bankers, No. 61 Broadway, New York City, certain moneys to procure for the said Jacob Goldstein a passport, and at the same time delivered to them his citizenship papers, all of which will more fully appear by the certificate of the said Messrs. Richard & Co., herewith enclosed; that said passport was issued to the said Jacob Goldstein, and the same was, together with his citizenship papers, sent to the said Jacob Goldstein by the said Messrs. Richard & Co., and as I have been informed the same was received by the said Jacob Goldstein upon his arrival on the other side; that a few days after his arrival he, the said "Jacob Goldstein," an American

[8] Foreign Relations, 1893, page 526.

citizen, "was arrested by some government [officer] at Kharkov, Russia," and his passport and citizenship papers taken away from him, and still is detained at said place.

As I have been informed, the cause of the detention of the said Jacob Goldstein is that the Russian Government claims that the said Jacob Goldstein is amenable to militia duties.

Enclosed please find two photographs of the said Jacob Goldstein for the purpose of identification; also a letter from the Hon. Charles Smith, the present alderman of the Eighth assembly district, in which the said Jacob Goldstein has resided for over twelve years, also a letter from the lodge that the said Jacob Goldstein is a member of.

I am the wife of the said Jacob Goldstein and reside with the children, of which I am the mother and the said Jacob Goldstein the father, at No. 43 Delancy Street, New York City.

By giving this your earliest attention, I remain, etc.,

JENNIE GOLDSTEIN

N.B.— Please address all communications to Mr. Philip Gratz, Jr., No. 333 Grand street, New York City and oblige, etc.,

JENNIE GOLDSTEIN

In spite of the "said's" and the "same's" of Mrs. Goldstein's letter and the three affidavits enclosed in it, the Russian Government was not certain that the "said" Mr. Goldstein was the "same" Mr. Goldstein who had applied and received his passport from the State Department. In fact, it was their contention that "said" Mr. Goldstein was really a Mr. Yankel Zlotow, whom they accused of coming to Russia with a false passport.

New complications soon began to accumulate in quick succession. First, Mr. Goldstein himself changed his story while under arrest, thus aggravating his case by arousing the suspicion of Russian officials, and making it more difficult for the American consul to come to his assistance. According to his new version, Goldstein was really a native of Germany and not of Cszelecz, Russia, as stated under oath in his naturalization papers. Similarly, his present claim that he had arrived in the United States as a child and could not, therefore, remember the exact year of his arrival conflicted with the statement in his application for naturalization that he had arrived in the United States in July, 1879, at the age of 17 years.

The new claims of Mr. Goldstein, or "the person detained at Kharkov and claiming to be Goldstein," as he is now referred to in the correspondence, were belied by the fact that the "detained person" spoke Russian fluently, a very suspicious circumstance, for German immigrants who leave Germany early in their childhood for the United States do not as a rule command the Russian language. The prisoner's unsuccessful attempt to hide his knowledge of the Russian tongue heightened the suspicion, now shared also by the American Minister at St. Petersburg and the United States Consul, Thomas E. Heenan, at Odessa, that the man detained was impersonating Jacob Goldstein. However, the Russian claim that there was no doubt whatsoever that the person detained at Kharkov and claiming to be "Goldstein" was really Yankel Zlotow received a severe blow when Mrs. Zlotow, a resident of Kharkov, failed to identify the "detained person" as her son Yankel.

The Russian Government committed many more *faux pas* during the prosecution of this affair. One of these errors showed ignorance by responsible and highly placed Russian officials of the elementary principles of the Federal Government of the United States and its constitutional relation to the states of the Union; the other misstep unnecessarily and tactlessly offended our representative in the Russian capital, because the Russian Government went over his head and appealed to Washington in a minor case which could easily and much more speedily have been settled on the spot.

In a dispatch to Minister Andrew D. White, Secretary Foster noted that "by the admission of the Russian authorities themselves," they intended sending Mr. Goldstein's passport and certificate of naturalization to New York for investigation, and added:

This proceeding naturally occasions some surprise, and is only explicable on the conjecture that the Russian authorities are ignorant of the Federal character of these papers. The Government of the United States is the sole judge of the competence and validity of the passport which it issues and of the evidence of national citizenship on which it is granted. It does not pertain to the authorities of New York to examine the validity of a United States passport.

Somewhere and somehow, the Russian authorities learned the true nature of these documents, and it was Baron Schilling, Russian Chargé *ad interim* at Washington, who brought the passport to the Department of State to check its genuineness.

But even this procedure was not the correct one. The presentment by an individual of an American passport issued by the Secretary of State, with the seal of the Department on it, should alone serve as *prima facie* evidence of the truth of all statements made therein. Should the genuineness of the passport, for some reason or another, be doubted, the proper place to inquire about it would be the Legation of the United States in the country where the bearer of the passport chances to be. The detention of a suspected person until the United States Government in Washington could attest his identity subjects him to needless hardship. In the case under discussion, the procedure was not only dilatory but also useless, for the attestation to the genuineness of a passport could not prove or disprove the alleged identity of the detained person with Yankel Zlotow, nor could it establish whether the present holder of the passport and other papers acquired them lawfully as Jacob Goldstein, or was falsely impersonating the individual to whom they were issued.

Mr. Goldstein was arrested some time in March, 1892. On May 19, 1893, Minister White wrote the following short dispatch to Mr. W. Q. Gresham, the new Secretary of State in Washington:[9]

---

[9] Foreign Relations, 1893, page 541.

[*Mr. White to Mr. Gresham*]

Legation of the United States
St. Petersburg, May 19, 1893

Sir: Referring to my No. 22 and previous dispatches relating to Jacob Goldstein, I have the honor to state that a letter from Mr. Consul Heenan, at Odessa, informs me that the local court at Kharkoff has decided in Goldstein's favor, but that he "took French leave" last December, has not been since heard of, and that his present whereabouts are unknown.

I am, sir, etc.,

Andrew D. White

Mr. Goldstein's disappearance removed his case from further consideration, but left a number of questions unsolved.

Two minor cases which came up in the same year need only be mentioned very briefly. In the first, that of David Waldenberg and his son Jacob, the United States rightfully refused to extend its protection to them, and the renewal of their passport was denied. The father, a native of Russia, had become a naturalized American citizen, and, after only a few years' residence in the United States as a citizen, returned to his native country, where he lived for thirty years, during which he showed no intention of returning to the United States and resuming the rights and duties of an American citizen. On the advice of Secretary Gresham, however, the son of Mr. Waldenberg could receive a passport if he decided to leave for the United States and perform there all duties incumbent on a good citizen, but not otherwise.

The case of Joseph Glowacki is important for the fact that it proves to what extent the central Government of St. Petersburg would countenance a wrongful act committed by a local official if the victim of that act happened to be a Jew, and also because it gives an inkling of the Russian conception of the morale of its communities.

Joseph Glowacki, an American citizen, was summarily expelled from Russia on a charge made against him by a drunken Russian who had a personal grudge against him, that

Glowacki had spoken disrespectfully of the Czar. Mr. White's intercession gained for Glowacki the permission to return to the Empire, but not to the village from which he had been expelled, "it being hardly to be expected that the return in triumph of one of the proscribed class (Glowacki is a Hebrew) to the scene whence he had been summarily ejected would be permitted, in view of the bad effect it would have on the morale of the community."

While it is true that the work in behalf of Jews in Russia was done by the executive branch of our Government, the Department of State and its representatives at Moscow, the Congress of the United States too had a share in this activity. In many cases, it was the action of Congress which preceded and prompted the activity of the State Department.

The case of Theodore Rosenstraus caused the 46th Congress to pass the following joint resolution, on June 10, 1879:[10]

[*Joint Resolution in Relation to Treaty Negotiations with Russia as to American Citizens*]

Whereas, it is alleged that by the laws of the Russian government no Hebrew can hold real estate, which unjust discrimination is enforced against Hebrew citizens of the United States resident in Russia; and

Whereas the Russian government has discriminated against one T. Rosenstraus, a naturalized citizen of the United States, by prohibiting him from holding real estate, after his purchasing and paying for the same, because of his being an Israelite; and

Whereas such disabilities are antagonistic to the enlightened spirit of our institutions and age which demand free exercise of religious belief, and no disabilities therefor; and

Whereas the Secretary of State, under date of April 28, 1879, expresses doubt of his ability to grant the relief required, under existing treaty stipulations; Therefore,

Resolved by the Senate and House of Representatives of the United States of America in Congress assembled, That the rights of the citizens of the United States should not be impaired, at home or abroad, because of religious belief; and that, if existing treaties between the United States and Russia be found, as is alleged, to

[10] See above, page 177.

discriminate in this or any other particular, as to any other classes of our citizens the President be requested to take immediate action to have the treaties so amended as to remedy this grievance.

Representative S. S. Cox of New York introduced a resolution on January 26, 1882, requesting the President to communicate to the House all diplomatic correspondence with Russia "relative to the expulsion of American Israelites from Russia and the persecution of the Jews in the Russian Empire." This resolution was passed by the House and acted upon by President Arthur when, on May 2nd of the same year, he transmitted the diplomatic correspondence required by the House. Similar resolutions were introduced by Mr. Cox, in July, 1882, in 1884, and in 1886.

On February 29th, 1892, Mr. J. Logan Chipman of Michigan introduced a resolution requesting from the President of the United States information whether, under Russian laws of discrimination against Jews, American Jews were similarly subject to these restrictions, in spite of Article I of the Treaty of 1832, and secondly, whether in the eyes of the Russian Government these restrictions supersede the provisions of the treaty which permit an inhabitant of the United States to sojourn and reside in any part of Russia whatsoever.[11]

In reporting the resolution back to the House on April 6, 1892, the Committee on Foreign Affairs questioned further whether, according to the Russian interpretation of the treaty, it was to be expected that American Jews would receive the same "security and protection" which is accorded to the native Jews of Russia; also, should it be expected that American Jews traveling in Russia for business purposes be made subject to all the "laws and ordinances" which limit their brethren in Russia? Such a discrimination, the committee thought, would be a violation of the treaty and an unfriendly act toward the United States on the part of Russia.

A resolution to sever diplomatic relations with Russia was introduced June 10, 1892, by Representative Irvin Dungan

---

[11] House Resolution No. 94, *Congressional Record*, 52nd Congress, 1st Session, Vol. 23, Part 3, page 3003.

of Ohio. This resolution was based on a much broader view than previous ones. It reads:[12]

Resolved, by the Senate and the House of Representatives of the United States in Congress Assembled, That the President of the United States is hereby directed to sever our diplomatic relations with the Russian Government, till such time as that Government shall cease discrimination against the Hebrews because of their religious faith, and remove the arbitrary and brutal restrictions now imposed upon them, against the protest of the civilized world.

Further resolutions demanding that the President effect a change of attitude by the Russian Government were introduced in Congress almost annually, becoming stronger and stronger as year followed year. But the Russian Government made things worse by its total refusal to visé the passport of all American Jews who, for some reason or other, desired to visit the Russian Empire.

The judicial branch of our Government did not have an opportunity to pass upon the true meaning of Article I and its relation to Russian anti-Jewish legislation. But there is good reason to surmise what its decision would have been had a case involving the interpretation of the disputed article come before it. In the case of *Geofroy v. Riggs* the Supreme Court, speaking through Mr. Justice Field, laid down the general rule for interpretation of treaties:[13]

It is a general principle of construction with respect to treaties that they shall be liberally construed, so as to carry out the apparent intention of the parties to secure equality and reciprocity between them. As they are contracts between independent nations, in their construction words are to be taken in their ordinary meaning, as understood in the public law of nations, and not in any artificial or special sense impressed upon them by local law unless such restricted sense is clearly intended. And it has been held by this court that where a treaty admits of two constructions, one restrictive of rights that may be claimed under it and the other favorable to them, the latter is to be preferred.

In another case the Supreme Court said:[14]

[12] House Resolution No. 140, *Congressional Record*, 52nd Congress, 1st Session, Vol. 23, Part 6, page 5228.

[13] 133 U. S. 271.

[14] *Kennet* v. *Chambers* (14 Howard 38).

For, as the sovereignty resides in the people, every citizen is a portion of it . . . . and when that authority has plighted its faith to another nation that there shall be peace and friendship between the citizens of the two countries, every citizen of the United States is equally and personally pledged.

It may, therefore, rightfully be claimed that our Government, through all its branches, spoke out clearly in favor of such an interpretation of the Treaty of 1832 which would treat American Jews as equals in every respect with their compatriots. It was clearly the duty of American diplomacy to see that Russian agreement with this interpretation be obtained. Yet, until the time under discussion, the early eighteen nineties, all attempts in that direction had failed. The Russian Government had proved to be the stronger in the continued debate, and had actually achieved silent acquiescence on the part of the United States to its own view. In spite of strongly worded messages from the State Department and American representatives in Russia, all that American diplomacy could claim for its efforts was an occasional exception in favor of a particular individual. The Russian Government was careful not to surrender its principles, and it is unpleasant to report that our Government was satisfied with these meagre crumbs and allowed the other side to interpret our conciliatory attitude as a sign of weakness. It is no wonder therefore, that in 1892, partly because of American complacence, and partly because of the growth of Pan-Slavism in Russia, the Government advanced a step further and dared enforce the Russian discriminatory laws on American soil.

The case of Mrs. Mannie Lerin, was the first in which Russian discrimination against Jews within the jurisdiction of the United States was brought to light. Until then the Russian Government could argue, with legal if not moral justification, that it could not let the American principles of equality interfere with its domestic policy. But no such argument could be advanced now, when Russian discriminatory practices were carried out on American territory.

Mrs. Mannie Lerin, a naturalized citizen of the United States, applied early in 1893 to the Russian consul general

in New York City to visé her passport so that she might
visit her parents in Russia. This the Russian consul refused
to do on the ground that he had general instructions to
decline to visé a passport of a former subject of Russia who
had left that country without permission and with the intention of evading military service.

Advised of the facts, Secretary Foster addressed himself
to Prince Cantacuzène, Russian Minister at Washington, inquiring whether the general theory behind the consul's refusal
to visé the passport of Mrs. Lerin was correct, and, further,
why a visa was refused "in this particular instance," as Mrs.
Lerin, being a woman, was not subject to military service.
Prince Cantacuzène's affirmative reply follows:[15]

[*Prince Cantacuzène to Mr. Foster*]

Legation of Russia
Washington, February 20, 1893

DEAR SIR: In reply to your note of February 16, concerning the
refusal of our consul-general in New York to visé the passport of
Mrs. (not Miss) Mannie Lerin, a naturalized citizen of the United
States, I beg to say that it appears from the information I just
received from our consul-general that the said Mrs. Lerin declared
herself to be a Jewess.

In the present circumstances Mr. Olarovsky acted according to
the instructions of his Government, interdicting to visé passports
of foreign Jews, with the exception of certain cases, under which
Mrs. Lerin can not be placed.

Accept, etc.,

CANTACUZÈNE

In reply to this blunt note, Mr. William F. Wharton,
Acting Secretary of State, contented himself with a simple
acknowledgment of the Russian Minister's note "under the
reserve necessarily imposed upon the Government by its
Constitution and laws, and by its just expectation that its
certification of the character of American citizenship will be
respected."

---

[15] Foreign Relations, 1893, page 547.

Mr. Wharton was much more outspoken in his dispatch dated February 28, 1893 to Mr. Andrew D. White. Describing the whole question as embarrassing and painful, he continues:[16]

It is to be inferred from Prince Cantacuzène's note that the declaration of Mrs. Lerin's religious profession was elicited from her by some interrogative process on the part of the Imperial consul-general.

It is not constitutionally within the power of this Government, or of any of its authorities, to apply a religious test in qualification of the equal rights of all citizens of the United States; and it is therefore impossible to acquiesce in the application of such a test, within the jurisdiction of the United States, by the agents of a foreign power, to the impairment of the rights of any American citizen or in derogation of the certificate of this Government to the fact of such citizenship.

On several occasions in the past this Government has made temperate but earnest remonstrance against the examination into the religious faith of American citizens by the Russian authorities in Russia. The asserted right of territorial sovereignty over all sojourners in the Empire has, to our deep regret, outweighed our friendly protests.

His Majesty's Government, however, surely cannot expect the United States to acquiesce in the assumption of a religious inquisitorial function within our own borders, by a foreign agency, in a manner so repugnant to our national sense.

I cannot but surmise that some strange misapprehension exists in this regard in the mind of His Majesty's Government, which your accustomed ability and tact may explain and perhaps remove

Regarding the subject as too important to discuss with anyone but the minister for foreign affairs, (Mr. de Giers was absent from St. Petersburg) Mr. White decided to wait for a favorable opportunity to bring up the subject and attempt to win the Russian Government over to the acceptance of the American doctrine on this particular matter. There is no record that Mr. White ever discussed the subject during his service in St. Petersburg, for Mr. de Giers was some time later replaced by Prince Lobanow, and Mr. White was succeeded by Mr. Clifton R. Breckinridge.

[16]Foreign Relations, 1893, page 536.

Mr. White's stay as minister is noteworthy for the fact that it gave him an opportunity to be the author of one of the periodic reports on the condition of the Jews in that Empire, which our ministers to Russia used to send to the Department of State. Mr. White, one of the finest and ablest of our diplomats, had served when a young man as an attaché to the legation in St. Petersburg, and seemed to have given much thought to the Jewish question whenever and wherever it presented itself.

His report is a classical document and deserves to be read in full by every student of the Jewish question and by the student of the Jew in Russia in particular.[17] It reminds one of an earlier report on the same subject, that of Mr. Theodore Fay, on the Jewish situation in Switzerland, which is treated elsewhere in this study; both reports were expressions of the American attitude on religious liberty and political equality as contrasted with that of some other countries.

In this report, Mr. White analyzed with searching and scholarly mind all the phases of the unhappy question. All accusations and allegations against the Russian Jew are discussed and weighed and the conclusion reached that either these were baseless or that "results [were] mistaken for causes."

The attitudes and shortcomings complained of are, in Mr. White's opinion, a result of an age-long oppression and persecution, and not something native and typical of the Russian Jew. On the other hand, he points to the moral rectitude and sobriety of the Jew in a country where one would expect that alcoholism would be widespread among those in great misery, and that a great proportion of the criminal classes would grow up in such a wretched atmosphere. The most rabid anti-Semites in Russia have never made the charge of inebriety and criminality against the Jew.

Of the 5,000,000 Jews then in Russia, very few were wealthy or in comfortable circumstances; the vast majority were in poverty and misery, and had great difficulty in keep-

[17] For full text of Mr. White's report see appendix below, page 389.

ing body and soul together. What would be the effect of the expulsion of Jews from the prohibited provinces and their forced return to the Pale, may be learned from the following quotation from the report: "A case was a few days since mentioned to me in which a small town of 8,000 or 10,000 inhabitants had recently received into its population nearly 6,000 Israelites from the surrounding country."

Mr. White especially condemns the subjection of Jews to discrimination in the professions, particularly in medicine and surgery, "in spite of the fact that from the middle ages until now their race has been recognized as having a peculiar aptitude for medicine and surgery." Every attempt of the Jew to escape from the ghetto and its handicaps was put down by the Russian authorities, the most painful of these restrictions being the limit put on the number of Jewish children allowed an education in the school system of the country: "no matter how gifted a young Israelite may be, his chances of receiving an education are small."

The allegation that Jews were hated because, as money-lenders, they often charge their clients as much as 100% interest a year, is strikingly answered by the assertion that Christian moneylenders charge as high as 800% interest, and that the presence of the Jew in a particular town or village inevitably tends to reduce the rate of interest paid for loans in that place. In a similar manner does Mr. White refute the charges of fanaticism, socialism, nihilism, lack of patriotism, unproductivity, showing in rebuttal that whenever the Jew is only given a chance he proves of the greatest service to his country, and cites as evidence the names of Judah Touro, Sir Moses Montefiore, Nathan and James de Rothschild, Baron de Hirsch, Edward Lasker, Ludwig Bamberger, Martin Edward Simson, Mark Antokolsky and others.

After describing the humaneness and patriotism of the famous Jews just mentioned, Mr. White continues:

The same broad and humane characteristics have been shown among the vast majority of Israelites eminent in science, philosophy, literature, and the arts. Long before the Israelite Spinoza wrought his own ideal life into the history of philosophy, this was noted, and it has continued to be noted in Russia. During my former residence here there were two eminent representatives of the proscribed race in the highest scientific circles, and they were especially patriotic and broad in their sympathies; and to-day the greatest of Russian sculptors, Antokolski, an Israelite, has thrown into his work not only more genius, but also more of profoundly patriotic Russian feeling, than has any other sculptor in this period. He has revived more evidently than has any other sculptor the devotion of Russians to their greatest men in times past, and whenever the project of erecting at St. Petersburg a worthy monument to the late Emperor shall be carried out, there is no competent judge who will not acknowledge that he is the man in all Russia to embody in marble or bronze the gratitude of the nation.

As to the edict for expulsion of Jews from their new habitation, Mr. White remarks that new laws on this subject were unnecessary. There were at the time, according to Mr. White, more than 1,000 decrees and statutes relating to the Jews, besides secret or open circulars and all sorts of regulations and ordinances. And now, as had become the custom, Russian officials were engaged in a new spasmodic attempt to enforce them, at the expense this time of clerks, bank employees, bank directors, apothecaries, doctors and other professionals.

The question of Russian consular jurisdiction in the United States cropped out again in 1895. The Russian authorities duly noted American protestations against the practice of inquiring into the religion of an American citizen on American soil, but seemingly were not moved by them to the extent of stopping the practice. Indeed, apparently the Russian Government did not even find it necessary to reply to these protestations, for, as Mr. Breckinridge later informed Washington, the records of the legation at St. Petersburg, after a careful search, had not disclosed any statement of the Russian position on this subject.

On April 15, 1895, Mr. Gresham wrote to Mr. Breckinridge:[18]

[18] Foreign Relations, 1895, page 1056.

[Mr. Gresham to Mr. Breckinridge]

Department of State
Washington, April 15, 1895

SIR: Your attention is called to the Department's No. 60, of February 28, 1893, to your predecessor, Mr. White, and to his reply of April 11, 1893, No. 81 (see Foreign Relations, 1893).

The subject thereof, viz, the refusal of the Russian consul-general at New York, under instructions from his Government, to visé passports issued by this Department to persons of the Jewish faith, has again come up for consideration.

You are desired, unless good reason to the contrary occurs to you, to present to the Russian Government the views of this Government as contained in the dispatch of February 28, 1893, above referred to.

I am, etc.,

W. Q. GRESHAM

This time there started a long exchange of dispatches on the troubled passport question, with the American Government having the last word, which in this case meant failure to effect a change in the Russian policy. Mr. Breckinridge rightly argued that, as it was constitutionally impossible for an American official to apply a religious test in qualification of equal rights of all citizens of the United States, the application of such a test could not be acquiesced in when practiced by foreign agents within its own jurisdiction. The fact that this objectionable practice was now being resumed after it had been discontinued for some time, made it "impolitic and unjust to be silent, and useless to speak in any terms but the plainest."

Needless to say, this last remark was not in the dispatch to Prince Lobanow; it is found in the dispatch to Secretary Gresham. The spirit of courtesy was stronger in the other dispatches, but at the expense of plainness and directness.

During a short absence of Mr. Breckinridge from St. Petersburg, Mr. Herbert A. D. Peirce, serving as chargé d'affaires *ad interim*, had a very interesting interview with

Prince Lobanow, on which he reported to Mr. Edward F. Uhl, acting Secretary of State in Washington, in the dispatch of June 13, 1895. On this occasion the Chargé d'Affaires called the attention of the Prince to the importance of the Jews as a class in the United States and to their great and beneficial influence on the country, stressing, parenthetically, the fact that the United States is governed by "the will of the people."

A new personage now appeared on the scene, and he too was visited a number of times by Mr. Peirce. The new man was Baron Osten-Sacken. The Baron insisted that the treatment accorded to Jews, both in Russia and outside of it, was not a religious question, but a racial one, "in which the two questions are inseparable."[19]

Baron Osten-Sacken expressed himself as hopeful that it would be possible to revise the Russian practice as regards

[19] However, at the hearings before the Committee on Foreign Affairs, on a joint resolution providing for the termination of the treaty of 1832, Representative Henry M. Goldfogle is quoted as follows: "Russia dishonors the passport on religious grounds. If the holder of the passport was born a Jew and afterwards been converted to another faith, he can, because of that conversion, have his passport unqualifiedly viséed. There would be no objection to his going into Russia. Russia would not then recognize him as a Jew .... If, on the other hand, he happened to be born a Christian and then became a convert to Judaism, Russia would refuse to recognize his passport and would dishonor it upon the ground that he was a Jew." Additional proof that Russian discrimination was based on religious rather than on racial grounds could be deduced from the fact that similar treatment had been meted out to Christian clergymen other than those of the Greek Orthodox religion. Bishop M. J. Hoban of Scranton, Pa., was refused admission to Russia for a two-day visit. Bishop Hoban was a Catholic. Professor Hyvernat of the Catholic University at Washington, an authority on Persian inscriptions, was expelled from Russia when it was discovered that he was also a Catholic priest. Protestant missionaries, too, were excluded from Russia. As we shall see later, the other Russian argument, that discrimination against the Jew was based on economic rather than religious causes, also falls to the ground, which only goes to prove that even here Russian authorities were consistently inconsistent and inefficient, and could not rationalize rationally.

See "Hearing Before the Committee on Foreign Relations on Termination of the Treaty of 1832 Between the United States and Russia," published by the Government Printing Office, 1911, by the authority of a Resolution by the House of Representatives, Dec. 21, 1911.

admission of American Jews into the Empire, though were he to be asked for an official note on this subject, it would have to be unfavorable. Under the circumstances, fearing that pressing for the principles seemed to engender complications, Mr. Peirce actually asked the Baron to postpone sending a reply to an earlier note by Mr. Breckinridge.

Mr. Peirce's dispatch follows:[20]

[*Mr. Peirce to Mr. Uhl*]

Legation of the United States
St. Petersburg, June 13, 1895

SIR: Referring to your No. 46, of April 26, and to Mr. Breckinridge's reply thereto, No. 71, of May 17, in which he enclosed a copy of his note to Prince Lobanow on the subject of the refusal of the Russian consul at New York to visé the passports of Israelites, I have the honor to say that in a recent conversation which I have had with the Prince, the subject being referred to, I took occasion to call his excellency's attention to the importance of the Hebrews as a class in the United States, referring to their numbers, condition and influence in the community as potential factors in a country governed, as is ours, by the will of the people. Prince Lobanow expressed himself as impressed with its importance, and making a note of the matter said he would consult with the minister of the interior on the subject at an early day.

Since then I have had occasion to call several times on Baron Osten-Sacken, to whom all questions in the foreign office relating to Israelites have been intrusted. In the course of inquiries as to whether the two gentlemen of Hebrew faith referred to in Mr. Breckinridge's dispatch above mentioned would be permitted to enter Russia, the matter of the visé of passports has come up, and Baron Osten-Sacken has informed me that he received Mr. Breckinridge's note from Prince Lobanow, accompanied by a memorandum calling special attention to the subject. Regarding the entry of Jews into Russia, Baron Osten-Sacken states the position of Russia to be, that she looks upon their presence in the Empire as prejudicial to the Russian people. That certain numbers of them being here she must take care of them, and that this she proposes to do in her own way and according to her own views as to the best interests of all Russian subjects. That viewing the Jewish question as she does, as one of race and not of religion, but

[20] Foreign Relations, 1895, page 1058.

in which the two questions are inseparable, so far as her purposes are concerned, she refuses to permit foreign Jews of any nationality to enter her borders and swell the number already here. For this reason the Government has instructed all Russian consuls in all countries, to refuse to visé the passports of foreign Jews. On the other hand, and speaking of his own opinion, as the real purpose of the laws forbidding the entry of foreign Jews into Russia is to prevent their settlement here and their engaging in trade within Russian territory, and not to prevent the entrance of tourists, temporary sojourners, or Jews whose purpose in coming is not of an objectionable nature to the Government, Baron Osten-Sacken said that, in his opinion, there should be a change in the present practice regarding the admission of foreign Jews.

I expressed the hope that the Imperial Government would find it compatible with its policy to admit American citizens into Russia, without inquiry as to their religious opinions or race, upon presentation of their passports. That with us the Hebrews had proved themselves to be good and law-abiding citizens, who prospered without preying upon others, but that whatever might be the opinion of the Imperial Government on this question, the interpretation and application of the Federal laws discourage citizens of the United States, of all creeds, taking up permanent residence in a foreign country and continuing to claim the protection of our Government as such citizens; that such citizenship involves certain obligations which require a residence in our country, and that therefore it is unlikely that Hebrews bearing American passports would become permanently settled in Russia. This Baron Osten-Sacken admitted was a forcible argument, and he expressed himself as hopeful that it would be possible to bring about a satisfactory revision of Russian practice as regards the admission of American Jews into the Empire.

At the same time, he said that were an answer to Mr. Breckinridge's note demanded the reply could not be favorable. That the laws of Russia are framed with regard to her own views of her own good. I took occasion to point out to the Baron that the purport of Mr. Breckinridge's note was to protest against the extraterritorial act of an agent of a foreign Government, upon our soil, applying a religious test to citizens of the United States, an act not constitutionally within the power of any officer of our own Government to perform, and not to criticise the Russian laws.

Under these circumstances, presenting a hopeful prospect of securing a more satisfactory condition of affairs in this vexed question, and as pressing for the principle seemed to endanger complications, I felt that the discretionary clause in your No. 46 should deter me from taking the responsibility of insisting on a reply to the note in question at the present juncture. I therefore requested Baron Osten-Sacken to hold the note in abeyance for the present. To this he assented, and agreed to hold it as a memorandum of the case.

I have, etc.,

H. D. PEIRCE

Chargé d'Affaires *ad interim*

An implied rebuke to Mr. Peirce may be inferred from the reply he received from Mr. Alvey A. Adee, Acting Secretary of State:[21]

[*Mr. Adee to Mr. Peirce*]

Department of State

Washington, July 5, 1895

SIR: I have received your No. 91, of the 13th ultimo, reporting your interviews at the Russian foreign office in the matter of the refusal of Russian consular officers in the United States to visé the passports issued by this Government to its citizens of Jewish faith.

Your conclusion that it is inexpedient to press the complaint to a formal answer at present appears to be discreet, but the Department must express its deep regret that you have encountered in the foreign office a reluctance to consider the matter in the light in which this Government has presented it. The Russian Government can not expect that its course in asserting inquisitorial authority in the United States over citizens of the United States as to their religious or civil status can ever be acceptable or even tolerable to such a Government as ours, and continuance in such a course after our views have been clearly but considerately made known may trench upon the just limits of consideration.

I must, however, caution you against any suggestion of retaliatory or resentful action on our part. A due sense of national dignity constrains this Government to avoid all appearance of a minatory policy in its dealings with other powers. In this matter, especially, it is to be borne in mind that each Government is the judge for itself, of the extent to which foreign consuls may be permitted to act under their own laws within its territories, and that such permission is determined by the corresponding exequatur.

The United States conspicuously illustrate their convictions on this subject in respect to their own consuls. The customs laws of the United States require the administration of a consular oath to exporters presenting manifests of goods for certification; but upon the representation of certain European Governments, among

21 Foreign Relations, 1895, page 1059.

them Great Britain and Germany, that the administration of such an oath by a foreign consul to a subject of the country is an invasion of the judicial independence thereof, our consuls have been enjoined to refrain from the act complained of in all cases affecting a subject of a sovereign of the country where they reside. It might, however, have been deemed entirely competent for the Governments of Great Britain and Germany to insert in the consular exequatur an express inhibition of the obnoxious act.

I am, etc.,

> ALVEY A. ADEE
> Acting Secretary

The apparent lack of decision on the part of American officials to see this thing through encouraged the Russian consuls in the United States to continue their practice of inquiring into an applicant's religion before his passport was viséed and refusing to visé it if the applicant happened to be a Jew.

This vexed question was raised again when Mr. Richard Olney, Secretary of State, received the following single-sentenced letter from a Mr. Waix:[22]

Boston, July 15, 1895

As I am a citizen of the United States of America and would like to go for a short while on some business to Russia, and as I have sent my passport, signed by your honor the 18th of last June, No. 654, to the consul-general of Russia, A. E. Olarowsky, in New York, to visé it, and as you will please see from the answers of the consul, certified copies enclosed, he refused to visé it (my passport) on account that I am a Jew by religion, therefore I have the honor to ask you to advise me how shall I do, as without the visé of the consul they won't let me pass the frontier of Russia.

> Your obedient servant,
> MAIOR WAIX

Mr. Waix enclosed the following two letters from the Russian consulate in New York City:

---

[22] Foreign Relations, 1895, page 1060.

[*Mr. Peterson to Mr. Waix*][23]

Imperial Russian Consulate-General
New York, June 27, 1895

DEAR SIR: In reply to your letter of June 26, inclosing passport
and $1.20, I would inform you that before your passport can be
viséed you must inform me where you were born, and what your
religion is — if Christian or Jew.

I shall retain your passport and fee until receipt of your answer.

Respectfully,
C. G. PETERSON, Vice-Consul
(For the Consul-General)

[*Mr. Olarowsky to Mr. Waix*][24]

Imperial Russian Consulate-General
New York, July 1, 1895

DEAR SIR: I have the honor to acknowledge receipt of your
letter of 28th ultimo, and desire to inform you that I cannot visé
your passport. You must get permission from the ministry of the
interior at St. Petersburg to visit Russia before I can visé your
passport.

Herewith passport and postal note.

Respectfully,
A. E. OLAROWSKY
Consul-General

More conferences were held between Mr. Breckinridge and
Prince Lobanow and Baron Osten-Sacken. Prince Lobanow
reiterated the Russian claim that discrimination against the
Jew was not because of his religious faith, but he failed to
declare on what other grounds it was based. Incidentally,
these conversations proved to Mr. Breckinridge to what extent even the most enlightened among Russian officials were
ignorant of American institutions and how great was their
difficulty in separating a question of extraterritoriality from
questions internal to themselves. To the Russians, the whole
controversy was nothing more than a question whether an

[23] Foreign Relations, 1895, page 1061.
[24] *Ibid.*

American administrative regulation should prevail over one of their own, which usually was changeable at the will or caprice of some high official. Baron Osten-Sacken asked, therefore, for the specific language of the American law in regard to religious liberty.

The American Minister had therefore to turn teacher in the constitutional law of the United States and instruct the Russian Foreign Office in the history of this country, of the existence of the Federal Government and of State Governments, and of the relation between the two, of the distinction between "granted" or "delegated" power given to the General Government, and the powers which the States retained for themselves. This first lecture on the Constitution of the United States was given in the following letter to Baron Osten-Sacken:[25]

[Mr. Breckinridge to Baron Osten-Sacken]

Legation of the United States
St. Petersburg, June 25, 1895

YOUR EXCELLENCY: Referring to our recent conversation upon the subject of the exercise of consular or foreign jurisdiction within the limits of the United States upon matters respecting a religious establishment or belief, I now comply with your request for a statement of the language of our Constitution with reference to the power of the United States Government itself to there exercise such jurisdiction.

I will just call your attention to the peculiar character of our constitutional requirements.

The States existed separately and independently before the General Government existed. They created the General Government. It is true that many new States have been admitted into the Union since the original States created the Government, but this has been out of territory originally ceded to the General Government by the States — land which, at the time, lay beyond the settled zone — or out of land since acquired by the General Government by purchase or conquest, and in a way originally provided for.

[25] Foreign Relations, 1895, page 1063.

So when the States created the General Government they "granted" and "delegated" certain powers to it, as enumerated in the Constitution, and they retained all the other powers themselves. Our Government has very great powers. It is supreme within the limits of those powers; but the point is, that it can lawfully do nothing unless the power to do so has been granted to it.

It is a very serious matter to us, then, when our Government is desired to conform to a policy, if the power to do so has not been "delegated" to it. It cannot assume the power, or get it in any way except by a change of the Constitution, granting the Government that power.

The very great difficulty of effecting a change in the Constitution will be readily seen when it is stated that it takes two-thirds of both branches of Congress, or two-thirds of the States, to propose an amendment; and after it is proposed, it requires a majority vote in three-fourths of the States to adopt it. Such is the difficulty that no changes have been made except at two periods of our history. The first was the period, just after the formation of our Government, ending in 1804. Then there was no change until 1865, at the close of the civil war, when certain changes were made as the result of that great war.

Although Article IX of the amendments of 1790 says, "The enumeration in the Constitution, of certain rights, shall not be construed to deny or disparage others retained by the people," and Article X of the same group of amendments says, "The powers not delegated to the United States by the Constitution nor prohibited by it to the States, are reserved to the States, respectively, or to the people," yet in the face of all this, although Congress has not been granted any power in regard to religious matters, so great was the fear of the States and the people that Congress might upon pretext attempt such legislation that the first of all the amendments, Article I, says, "Congress shall make no law respecting an establishment of religion, or prohibiting the free exercise thereof."

Thus, you see, my Government is prohibited in the most positive manner possible by the very law of its existence from even attempting to put any form of limitation upon any of its citizens by reason of his religious belief. How, then, can we permit this to be done by others? To say that they can thereby be discriminated against by foreign Governments, and are only safeguarded against their own, would be a remarkable position for us to occupy.

Fortunately we approach this matter in that spirit of friendship and reciprocal consideration and respect which has always marked the intercourse of our countries, and I am happy to say that it grows with time. I need not say that it will afford me the greatest pleasure to respond to any further requests with which I may be honored; and I do not doubt for a moment that upon full consideration an adjustment will be found alike consistent, honorable, and fully satisfactory to both of our Governments.

I am, etc.,

CLIFTON R. BRECKINRIDGE

It was in response to this lecture by the American Minister that Prince Lobanow made the interesting declaration that the refusal to visé passports of foreign Jews was not founded on religious objection, for certain categories of Jews (tourists, manufacturers and bankers) were allowed to enter Russia and reside there for a while. The refusal to visé could even be said to be a philanthropic act, for, by warning them while still in the United States, the Russian Government saved applicants from "difficulties and dangers which they would encounter later if they had not been advised."

As to the American Constitution, there really is no conflict between it and the Russian practice, for "the refusal of the visé is not at all an attack upon any established religion; it is a consequence of a foreign law . . . , which only has its effect outside of the territory of the Union."

A similar reply was received by Mr. Breckinridge from Baron Osten-Sacken who declared: "As to the American Constitution, I must confess that it seems to me to be here beside the question."

Mr. Breckinridge found it necessary further to elucidate this particular point in the Constitution. From a note to Prince Lobanow of July 8, 1895, we quote the following paragraph:[26]

Our Constitution does not say that Congress shall not make a law simply "prohibiting" or "authorizing" a religious exercise or belief, as your excellency seems to understand.

It says that "Congress shall make no law respecting an establishment of religion, nor prohibiting the free exercise thereof." Certainly if a law deprives any people or person of a certain faith, because of that faith, of all or of any part of the rights, privileges, and immunities enjoyed by any other citizen, or class of citizens, it is made "respecting" that religion, and it militates against "the free exercise thereof" as much so as if the sect had been mentioned in the title of the act and the consequences had been named as pains

[26] Foreign Relations, 1895, page 1066.

and penalties for the conscientious belief and observances entertained and practiced.

This explanation, however, fell upon deaf ears. The Russian officials simply refused to learn the American Constitution.

In a dispatch of August 22, 1895, Mr. Adee observed that Russian discrimination against foreign Jews was just an extension of the policy toward its native Jews. The same policy of persecution and hatred which, in its economic aspects, was depriving the Jew of the elementary right of security of his property, was being applied to both native and foreign Jews, and thereby violating another provision, Article X, of the Treaty of 1832.[27]

[*Mr. Adee to Mr. Breckinridge*]

Department of State
Washington, August 22, 1895

SIR: I have received your No. 116, of the 24th ultimo, giving the correspondence between yourself and the Russian foreign office on the subject of the viséing by Russian consuls in this country of passports issued to American citizens of Jewish faith. Your presentation of this Government's views of that question meets with the approval of this department.

Apart from the constitutional objections to the discrimination made by Russian consular officers against American Jews, this Government can never consent that a class embracing many of its most honored and valuable citizens shall within its own territory be subjected to invidious and disparaging distinctions of the character implied in refusing to visé their passports. For, notwithstanding Prince Lobanow's suggestion that his Government's consular regulation upon the subject under consideration does not apply to all Israelites and therefore cannot be regarded as a discrimination against them on religious grounds, the fact remains that the interrogatories propounded to applicants for the consular visé relate to religious faith, and upon the response depends the consul's actions.

Viewed in the light of an invidious discrimination tending to discredit and humiliate American Jews in the eyes of their fellow-citizens, it is plain that the action of Russian consular officers does produce its effect within American territory, and not exclusively in Russian jurisdiction.

[27] Foreign Relations, 1895, page 1067.

But the Russian discrimination against American Jews is not confined simply to the matter of viséing passports. This department was informed a few years since by the Russian minister here that Russian consuls in this country would refuse authentication to legal documents for use in Russia when Jews are ascertained to be interested. This is not merely an unjust and invidious discrimination against Jews, but would seem to be plainly a violation of the spirit of Article X of the treaty of 1832 between this country and Russia in respect of the property rights of American citizens in that country.

Since you have received my instruction No. 92 of July 5, you may incorporate the substance of that, together with the views herein expressed, in your next note to the Russian Government upon this subject. The text of the Russian law, of which you have very properly requested a copy, is awaited with interest here, but it is not deemed probable that the question, viewed in the light in which I have just considered it, will be affected by any municipal legislation of the Empire.

I am, etc.,

ALVEY A. ADEE
Acting Secretary

One wonders why the Department of State had been silent all these years on this important issue which, legally, was stronger than the one under discussion.

Mr. Breckinridge soon received a copy of the Russian laws relating to the entry of foreign Jews. The policy underlying them is condensed in the following quotation from a dispatch of Prince Lobanow to Mr. Breckinridge, of August 12/24, 1895:[28]

The Imperial Government, having already many millions of Jewish subjects, only admit their congeners of foreign allegiance when they seem to present a guaranty that they will not be a charge and a parasitic element in the State, but will be able, on the contrary, to be useful to the internal development of the country. It is because he had it in view to protect himself from an influx of a proletariat of this nature that the Russian legislator has established clearly the categories of Israelites of whom the entrance on our territory can be admitted.

These laws failed to settle the issue between the State Department and Prince Lobanow, for the right of Russian

[28] Foreign Relations, 1895, page 1068.

agents in foreign territory to inquire into the business standing of the principal of a commercial house employing a Jewish agent was herein defended. Thus, before the question of
viséing his passport was settled favorably or not, a Jewish
commercial agent or banker had to satisfy the consul of the
importance of his establishment, and then let the consul
decide whether he met the requirements or not. Another
note of protest was sent to Prince Lobanow, but the latter
did not find it expedient to answer, and discussion of the
principle which evoked the extended correspondence was left
pending.

Before we leave the question of Russian consular refusal
to visé passports of American Jews, we have to dispose of
another argument in justification of that practice put forward
by the Russians, especially Baron Osten-Sacken. It was the
Baron's contention that consuls were usually granted latitude
in the matter of viséing passports, thereby acquiring some of
the exterritorial rights and diplomatic immunities given by
international law to representatives of foreign states.

As a matter of fact, consular agents enjoy exterritorial
rights of some sort only in the so-called backward countries.
In other countries, they can enjoy special rights only with the
sanction, explicit or tacit, of the Government of such countries. Every sovereign state is the judge for itself of the extent to which foreign consuls may be permitted to act, and
such permission is determined by the corresponding exequatur. In the matter under discussion, the State Department
could point to the fact that United States consuls in Great
Britain and Germany were enjoined from administering a
consular oath to exporters presenting manifests of goods for
certification, after the British and German Governments protested that the administration of such an oath by a foreign
consul to a subject of the country was an invasion of their
judicial independence. In the United States, Russian consulates were not on Russian territory and any policeman
could seize the goods of a consul if he did not pay his debts.

The records of the diplomatic correspondence during the
remaining years of the nineteenth century show that Russian

consuls in this period receded somewhat from their inquisitorial practice, though they did not stop it altogether. From time to time the Department of State received reports of the refusal by Russian consuls to visé passports of Jews even of the "privileged categories" on the sole ground that they were Jews. Most probably, reference to the practice was so infrequent because very few Jews applied for visas. Thus, while the issue remained unsettled as between the United States and Russia, there were no immediate stimuli to bring it to a final decision.

In 1897, the Russian consul refused to visé the passport of Mr. Adolph Kutner, who wished to visit his family in Russia, on the ground that he was a Jew. Mr. G. C. Perkins, Senator from California, on May 27, 1897, introduced a resolution requesting that the Government intercede with the Government of Russia and try to prevail upon it to permit Americans of whatever religion to visit Russia, "if they are not liable to become a charge upon the Empire by reason of poverty or an inability to support themselves by honest labor." Mr. Kutner was described in the resolution as being "one of the wealthiest and most progressive and most public-spirited of the residents of California, and in no way liable to become a charge upon the Russian Government, but able, if a resident, to be useful to the internal development of that country." A similar resolution was introduced in the House by Representative Curtis H. Castle, also of California.

The refusal to visé Mr. Kutner's passport, one of a number of similar cases, showed the insincerity of Russia's contention that its exclusion of foreign Jews was not because of their religious affiliations, but because of a desire on the part of the Russian Government to protect itself from an influx of a proletariat. Our government had apparently grown so weary that all that American representatives in Russia now asked for was adherence by the Russians to the "generous" exception they made in favor of a few categories of Jews, surrendering, for diplomatic reasons or because of pure inertia, the larger principle involved. Perhaps, too, they foresaw the futility of further struggle and gave it up in utter disgust.

A number of interesting cases involving Jews who were in one difficulty or another with the Russian Government occurred in the years 1895–1903, but into these it is not necessary to go in great detail. There was the case of John Ginzberg, or, as the Russian Government insisted on calling him, Shimon Ginzberg, who, having been refused a visa to enter Russia, his native country, had dared enter it without official permission. He was held in prison for almost two years, and his case moved from one ministry to another, the ministries of Foreign Affairs, the Interior, and Justice, all being in charge of him at one time or another, before he was finally allowed to leave the country. There was no doubt of his innocence, and his simplicity and honesty gained for him the sympathy of the American ministers with whom he corresponded frequently. Mr. Herbert A. D. Peirce, the American Chargé d'Affaires, was quite surprised to learn at the Russian Foreign Office that, measured by Russian standards, Mr. Ginzberg, even after having been imprisoned for two years and finally left destitute in a foreign country, was dealt with very leniently. Rightfully could John ("Shimon") Ginzberg complain in one of his charming letters to Mr. Breckinridge: "Good Master and Gentlemen: Upon my soul I can not understand the Russian ways how they do justice."

A disposition among some of the statesmen in Russia to mitigate the severity of treatment of foreign Jews, especially of American citizenship, may be discovered here and there. But the question of the right of expatriation, on which issue the respective Governments of the United States and Russia held opposite views, still remained unsettled. The American Government strenuously objected to a regulation requiring all native Russians who had acquired American citizenship, without consent from the Imperial Government, to perform five years of military service as a condition for permission to reenter Russia. The Secretary of State, Mr. John Sherman, learned of this law from the development in the case of Harry Marks, a naturalized citizen, who had left Russia at the age of 17. Sherman's impression that this regulation affected Jews only was corrected by a note from Count Lamsdorff to

Mr. Ethan A. Hitchcock, United States Minister at St. Petersburg; this note, dated December 8/20, 1897, stated that "all the subjects of the Empire without distinction of religion are held to serve during that time under the flag."

The policy of the American Government at that time, with regard to Jews in Russia, consisted in essaying to help individual cases while not insisting on a modification of the principle upon which these individual cases came into difficulties. It is best characterized by the following dispatch sent by Secretary Sherman to Mr. Breckinridge, in which Mr. Sherman concluded that it was unnecessary to argue henceforth about principles with the Government of Russia, as the views of the respective Governments on the treatment of Jews in Russia were irreconcilable. In the futu reit would be the policy of American representatives in Russia to deal with this class of questions according to the elastic formulas of unwritten diplomacy, hoping that the future would bring a more formal agreement upon the essential principles involved.[29]

[*Mr. Sherman to Mr. Breckinridge*]

Department of State
Washington, June 18, 1897
Sir:

I have to acknowledge the receipt of your No. 561, of the 24th ultimo, in further relation to the interesting case of Frederick G. Grenz, a naturalized American citizen, who has been acquitted of the charge of having expatriated himself without Imperial permission.

This gratifying result, and the remarks of Baron von Osten Sacken, appear to justify your inference that there is a growing disposition among the more advanced statesmen of Russia to regard the old policy and treatment in this class of cases as being "too drastic to meet the requirements of today." It would afford this Government much satisfaction to witness a change in the direction of recognizing the larger policy of most of the modern States by which the right of the citizen or subject to peaceably change his allegiance by orderly process of law is admitted by statute or confirmed by the conclusion of naturalization treaties. The spirit of accommodation which, after many failures through a long series of years, at length enabled the Russian Government to negotiate

[29] Foreign Relations, 1897, page 443.

with the United States a convention of extradition on the most advanced modern lines may, it is hoped, yet permit of an agreement upon the terms of a treaty whereby the irritating questions affecting our naturalized citizens of Russian origin may be removed from the field of discussion and given that practical settlement which may not hopefully be devised so long as the two Governments approach the matter from diametrically opposed standpoints.

The Department is disposed to commend the course pursued by you and by Consul Heenan in so dealing with the case of Mr. Grenz as to avoid academic discussion of the abstract merits of the controversy. This Government has no desire to force that of Russia to any abrupt acquiescence in the doctrines we profess as to the liberty of the subject, which tenets we may frankly admit are derived from sources very distinct from the historical traditions of imperialism. It is willing to recognize the good disposition which Russia has shown in her own way and through her own municipal and judicial workings toward personally deserving American citizens who have incurred statutory or technical disabilities in Russia. It would deplore on the part of Russia, as much as it would avoid for its own part, any attempt to narrow the controversy to rigid limits and to bring about a deadlock from which neither party may recede with self-respect. It is prepared now, for many years past, to give to its representatives in Russia the widest latitude to deal with this class of questions according to the more amiable and elastic formulas of unwritten diplomacy, in the confidence that by pursuing this mutually deferential course a more formal agreement upon the essential principles involved may eventually be found within reach.

It would be gratifying to discern a similar disposition on the part of Russian agents in this country. The Russian Government has lately been made acquainted with the indisposition of the United States to acquiesce in any inquisitorial office on the part of the Russian agents toward American citizens within the jurisdiction of the United States, whereby a religious test and consequent disability as respects civil rights in Russia may be imposed. The response has been elicited that the test complained of is not essentially religious, but rather racial and political; and in proof of this, the laws of Russia providing for the favorable treatment of foreign Jews of certain categories seeking to enter Russia have been officially communicated. By the judicial order of March 14, 1891, the power of legations and consulates to visé passports for Russia extends — without previous authorization of the ministry of the interior — to Jewish bankers, chiefs of important commercial houses, and the brokers, representatives, clerks, and agents of such houses. Nevertheless, this Department from time to time learns of the refusal of Russian agents in this country to authenticate the passports of Jews unquestionably belonging to the privileged categories, no other reason for refusal being assigned them than that the applicants are Jews. The recent case of Mr. Adolph Kutner, a wealthy and highly esteemed merchant of California, to whom a visé was refused by the chargé d'affaires because he "was not a Christian," has created a painful impression in the Senate, to members of which high body Mr. Kutner is well and favorably known. A resolution introduced by Senator Perkins, on the 25th ultimo, seeks to emphasize the contrast between the professions of the Russian Government in regard to the favorable treatment of alien Jews resorting to the Empire, and the prohibitory practice of the Russian agents in this country. That resolution having been referred by the Committee on Foreign Relations to this Department for an expression of its views on the subject, a letter, of which copy is inclosed, was addressed to the chairman of that committee on the 5th instant, in which the position of the Russian Government is truthfully but temperately stated.

This matter is not now presented by way of argument and protest, but in order that you may in such friendly and discreet manner as may be practicable suggest to the minister for foreign affairs that one annoying feature of the case may be justly eliminated if the discretion conceded by the Russian law to the Imperial legations and consulates in the matter of authenticating passports of Jews resorting to Russia were made effective and practical as to Jews of the privileged classes; or, in the language of Prince Lobanof's note of August 12/24, 1895, were in fact operative to admit Jews "of foreign allegiance when they seem to present a guarantee that they will not be a charge and a parasitic element in the State, but will be able, on the contrary, to be useful to the internal development of the country."

This suggestion is made in the same amicable spirit which appears to have prompted the disposal of the Grenz case, and which characterizes your dispatch on the subject and this reply. It can not now be foreseen whether the resolution will be adopted as introduced, but should the Senate approve it, the course of the Department thereunder would be greatly facilitated were it ascertained in advance that the action of the Russian agencies in the United States will be in full harmony with the liberal features of the Russian law.

Respectfully yours,

JOHN SHERMAN

The readiness of Mr. Sherman to deal with the Russian Government in a friendly way, without arguments on the principles involved, was not reciprocated by that Government. In a dispatch to the Secretary of State, announcing the final disposition of the case of John Ginzberg, mentioned above, Mr. Breckinridge wrote, on March 8, 1897:[30]

I may remark that an apparent result of the continuous and earnest efforts of the past two or more years is some amelioration of the unbending severity that previously marked the policy of the Russian Government in cases of this kind. Until, however, the still ineffectual efforts to effect a conventional arrangement with Russia, upon the subject of expatriation, are more successful, our citizens of Russian origin, unless with previous Russian consent, expose themselves to the gravest hardship by returning to the Empire.

It was this conviction that forced the Department of State to publish the following notice regarding liability of naturalized citizens of the United States under military and expatriation laws of their native country:[31]

Department of State
Washington, August 1, 1901

Notice to American Citizens Formerly Subjects of Russia who Contemplate Returning to that Country.

The information given below is believed to be correct, yet is not to be considered as official, as it relates to the laws and regulations of a foreign country.

* * * * * *

Naturalized Americans of Russian birth, of the Jewish race, are not allowed to enter Russia except by special permission. For this they must apply to the minister of the interior, but the Department can not act as intermediary in making the application.

There is no treaty between the United States and Russia defining the status of American citizens of Russian birth upon their return to Russia.

[30] Foreign Relations, 1897, page 435.
[31] *Ibid.*, 1901, page 453.

No one is admitted to Russia without a passport. It must be visaed by a Russian diplomatic or consular representative. Upon entering Russia it should be shown at the first Government house, and the holder will be given another passport or permit of sojourn. At least twenty-four hours before departure from Russia this permit should be presented and a passport of departure will be granted and the original passport returned. A fresh permit to remain in Russia must be obtained every six months.

IX. RUSSIA

1903-1933

In April, 1903, occurred the horrible pogrom at Kishineff. It started as pogroms usually did in old and benighted Russia. A young Russian boy was found murdered on February 16, 1903. Later it was discovered that he had been killed deliberately by a relative who was to benefit financially by the boy's death. However, the Jews of the neighborhood were immediately accused of having murdered him for religious purposes; thus the ritual murder libel of the middle ages was revived in twentieth-century Russia. *Bessarabetz*, a local newspaper, agitated against the Jews and instigated the pogrom, which lasted three days, April 19-21. The pogrom was all pre-arranged and carefully planned; even outside help was hired for the purpose of murdering and plundering the innocent Jews.

The Jewish leaders of Kishineff had appealed, early in April, to the Governor for help and had forewarned him of what could be expected during the Easter holidays when the mob, already urged on by the *Bessarabetz*, might break loose under the religious frenzy of the Easter celebration. Their appeal was to no avail. During the riot, the police remained inactive, and it was not till the end of the second day, when the greatest damage had already been done, that the military was summoned.

According to the official report made by the Central Relief Committee at Kishineff, 2,750 Jewish families suffered from the pogrom; 47 persons were killed, and over 400 injured, damage in property amounting to 2,500,000 rubles.

On April 20, 1903, Secretary John Hay inquired by telegraph from Robert S. McCormick, American Ambassador
at St. Petersburg, whether the Jews of Kishineff were in
great want and suffering, as was then persistently reported
in the press; Jews of the United States would like to extend
to them financial aid and other supplies if such help would
be permitted to reach the sufferers. Mr. McCormick was instructed to obtain the desired information "without discussing the political phase involved."

On May 9, almost three weeks after the pogrom of Kishineff, Mr. McCormick surprisingly replied that it was "authoritatively" denied that the Jews of Southwestern Russia
were in any need of help; the offer of help was appreciated,
but as aid of any kind was unnecessary, it was gratefully
declined.

But only four days later, Mr. McCormick had an alto-
gether different story to tell. Although by that time even
St. Petersburg must have learned of what had happened in
Kishineff on April 19–21, yet the information of the American
minister was obtained not from official sources but from the
London *Standard* of May 1.

Mr. McCormick's dispatch of May 13 is very short and
reads as follows:[1]

[*Mr. McCormick to Mr. Hay*]

American Embassy
St. Petersburg, May 13, 1903

Sir: Referring to your cablegraphic instructions in the matter
of alleged famine conditions among the Jews in Kishenev, I have
the honor to enclose herewith a cutting from the London Standard of
May 1, . . . which will throw some light on the subject of that
instruction.

I have, etc.

Robert S. McCormick

The enclosure is a long and detailed report made by an
English correspondent who had arrived at Kishineff only two
days after the massacre. According to his report, the cruelty

[1] Foreign Relations, 1903, page 712.

of the mob and the loss in Jewish lives and property was much greater than had been stated in the report of the Jewish Committee referred to above. "The Russian rioter," reports the correspondent, "seldom or never employs the knife. Small hatchets and stout wooden clubs, the latter frequently held by a wrist strap, and stones clutched in the hands and used as battering weapons are the chief features of the ruffian's armory." No wonder the bodies of the dead and injured were badly mutilated.

There was sufficient reason to believe that higher officials in St. Petersburg were personally involved in the massacre. They not only knew that a pogrom was contemplated in Kishineff but even hinted that official support was to be expected. Notwithstanding the fact that Viatcheslav K. von Plehve, Minister for Internal Affairs, dismissed Lieutenant-General von Raaben as well as other military and police officials from their posts in Bessarabia, von Plehve's real part in the Kishineff affair may be learned from the following statement made by Andrew D. White, after the assassination of von Plehve by a revolutionist: "His part in the horrible massacre and plunder of the Jews — men, women, and children — at Kishineff, caused him to be regarded with abhorrence by the whole world."

Meanwhile, in the United States, 77 public meetings were held in 50 towns situated in 27 states, in protest against the pogroms of Kishineff and to express American abhorrence of the maltreatment of the Jews by the Russian Government. Speaking at a protest meeting held in Carnegie Hall, New York City, at which Mayor Seth Low presided, ex-President Grover Cleveland said:[2]

Every American humane sentiment has been shocked by a late attack on the Jews in Russia — an attack murderous, atrocious and in every way revolting. As members of the family of mankind, and as citizens of a free nation, we are here to give voice to the feeling that should stir every true man, and every American worthy of the name. There is something intensely horrible in the wholesale murder of unoffending, defenseless men, women and

[2] "The Voice of America on Kishineff," by Cyrus Adler, page 123.

children, who have been tacitly, if not expressly, assured of safety under the protection of a professedly civilized government. Such things give rise to a distressing fear that even the enlightenment of the twentieth century has neither destroyed nor subdued the barbarity of human nature, nor wholly redeemed the civilized world from "man's inhumanity to man."

A representative committee of Jews which presented itself to the Secretary of State on June 15, 1903, heard from Mr. John Hay the following statement:[2a]

No person of ordinary humanity can have heard without deep emotion the story of the cruel outrages inflicted upon the Jews of Kishineff. These lamentable events have caused the profoundest impression throughout the world, but most especially in this country, where there are so many of your co-religionists who form such a desirable element of our population in industry, thrift, public spirit and commercial morality. Nobody can ever make the Americans think ill of the Jews as a class or a race — we know them too well. In the painful crisis through which we are now passing the Jews of the United States have given evidence of the highest qualities — generosity, love of justice, and power of self-restraint.

Secretary Hay then went with the committee to the White House and presented them to President Theodore Roosevelt, who said:[2b]

I have never in my experience in this country known of a more immediate or a deeper expression of sympathy for the victims and of horror over the appalling calamity that has occurred.

It is natural that while the whole civilized world should express such a feeling, it should yet be most intense and most widespread in the United States; for of all the great Powers I think I may say that the United States is that country in which from the beginning of its national career most has been done in the way of acknowledging the debt due to the Jewish race and of endeavoring to do justice to those American citizens who are of Jewish ancestry and faith.

The President concluded that he would not be worthy of his position if he failed to express his deep sympathy, sorrow and horror over an outrage like this done to the Jewish people anywhere in the world.

In 1905, during the stay of Count Witte in the United States as the chief representative of Russia in the peace nego-

---

[2a] "The Voice of America on Kishineff," page 471.   [2b] *Ibid.*, page 472.

tiations with Japan following the Russo-Japanese War, President Roosevelt sent him the following letter, asking Russia to respect American passports, irrespective of the religion of their holders, and thereby remove the last cause of irritation between Russia and the United States.[3]

[President Roosevelt to Count Witte]

Oyster Bay, New York
September 10, 1905

MY DEAR MR. WITTE:

I beg you to accept the accompanying photograph with my hearty regards.

I thank you heartily for the message you gave me from His Majesty announcing his generous purpose of interpreting the most favored nation clause hereafter so that America shall stand on an equality with other powers in this regard.

Will you, I pray, present to His Majesty my warm acknowledgments for this act?

In furtherance of our conversation of last evening, I beg you to consider the question of granting passports to reputable American citizens of Jewish faith. I feel that if this could be done it would remove the last cause of irritation between the two nations whose historic friendship for one another I wish to do my best to maintain. You could always refuse to give a passport to any American citizen, Jew or Gentile, unless you were thoroughly satisfied that no detriment would come to Russia in granting it. But if your Government could only see its way clear to allow reputable American citizens of Jewish faith, as to whose intentions they are satisfied, to come to Russia just as you do reputable American Christians, I feel that it would be from every standpoint most fortunate.

Again assuring you of my high regard, and renewing my congratulations to you and to your country upon the peace that has been obtained, believe me,

Sincerely yours,
THEODORE ROOSEVELT

Count Witte received also the following memorial from a number of leading American Jews:[4]

---

[3] *American Jewish Year Book*, 1909–1910, page 39.
[4] "Jacob H. Schiff, His Life and Letters," by Cyrus Adler, Vol. II, pages 129–32.

[Memorial to Count Witte]

September 5, 1905

His Excellency, Sergius de Witte,
Envoy Plenipotentiary, etc.,
of His Imperial Majesty, The Emperor of Russia.

ESTEEMED SIR:

Mindful of our privilege in meeting you during your recent stay at Portsmouth, N. H., we deem it well, before you leave the United States and return to your own country, to submit in writing, if only for a thorough understanding or for further reference, some of the statements to which we gave expression when we had the privilege of visiting you and of listening to your valuable views.

We believe ourselves to be justified in insisting that the claim of the Russian Government that the question of the condition of the Jews in Russia is a purely domestic one with which the people and governments of other countries have no concern, can no longer be maintained. When a government, either through the application of exceptional laws or by other means, forces great masses of its subjects to seek to improve their condition through emigration to other countries, the people of these countries which give an asylum to such refugees from persecution and oppression may, with entire propriety, criticize the conditions which have caused such an influx into their country, and may properly insist that these conditions shall be improved in such manner and to such extent that the causes of the forced emigration shall cease to exist, and this without justifying the charge that they are meddling with affairs that should not concern them.

This we believe to be the attitude of the American people in general. We, as Jews, have the added interest in the condition of the Jews in Russia which ties of race and faith always and properly call forth, and we deem it, therefore, nothing less than our plain duty to do all in our power to procure an amelioration in their status. As we stated to you at our conference, it is our very decided conviction that nothing but the granting of full civil rights to the Jewish subjects of the Czar will entirely remove the conditions which have been the cause of so much disturbance in Russia and adverse criticism abroad. You have answered us that the Russian Jew in general is not sufficiently prepared for the exercise of full civil rights, and that the feeling of the Russian people is such that the Jew cannot be placed on an equal footing with them without causing serious internal disorders, and you suggested that it might be advisable and practicable gradually to remove the existing disabilities and thus to prepare the way for an eventual total granting of civic equality.

As to this, we aver that the million or more of Russian Jews who have come to the United States have become good citizens, notwithstanding their sudden emergence from the greatest darkness into the most intense daylight of political and civil liberty, and that they have shown themselves entirely equal to the responsibilities which have been placed upon them as citizens of this great Republic. Nor has it ever been different in modern history and experience. Napoleon in 1806, Germany at a somewhat later period, and England in Cromwell's time granted, without injury to the State, full civil rights to the Jews living then under conditions much darker than those under which they now live in Russia.

While it may be true that a state of envy against the Jews exists among part of the Russian people, for which the Russian Government is to some extent responsible, still, in our opinion, placing the Jew at once on a footing of civic equality with the rest of the population would cause no more friction than each one of the steps leading to the same ultimate end. This very objection urged by you seems to us good reason why this should be settled once and for all, instead of allowing it to drag on painfully, creating new disturbances at every stage.

The claim that among the ranks of those who in Russia are seeking to undermine governmental authority there are a considerable number of Jews may perhaps be true. In fact, it would be rather surprising if some of those so terribly afflicted by persecution and exceptional laws should not at least have turned against their merciless oppressors. But it is safe to assert that, as a whole, the Jewish population of Russia is law-abiding, and there is little doubt that once given civil rights, with all the opportunities that this will carry with it, the Jew in Russia will become as valuable a member of the commonwealth and prove to be as ardent a lover of his country as have been the Jews of every country which has accorded them the rights of citizens. The fact will not be disputed that in the United States the Jew has become an ardent American; in England a loyal Englishman; in France a patriotic Frenchman, and in Germany a thorough German.

The people of the United States, as must be known to you, are close observers of all that is taking place in Russia during this momentous period of her existence. Their sympathies are, for the time being, alienated from Russia because, liberty- and justice-loving, they have recoiled from the horrors of Kishineff and from the terrible conditions which, though long existing, have only now been fully disclosed. Jewish influence in the United States, especially political, already carries great weight, and is steadily increasing, being constantly recruited from the large immigration of Russian Jews. Can it be expected that the influence of the American Jew upon public opinion will be exerted to the advantage of the country which systematically degrades his brethren-in-race, making their fate almost unendurable?

No matter how many Jews may emigrate, there will always remain a minimum of six or seven million Jews in Russia, and thus it appears quite evident that the Russo-Jewish question must be settled in Russia. Settled promptly and thoroughly in the enlightened spirit which your Imperial Master has shown in so many other instances, this vexatious question will remove at once and forever a factor so damaging to Russia at home and abroad.

We therefore earnestly hope that the exchange of views which has taken place between us may lead to that solution which we are convinced you and the other best minds of your country actually desire.

With sincere assurances of high respect, with our best wishes for your safe return home and for your future welfare, we remain

Your Excellency's
Most truly,

JACOB H. SCHIFF
ISAAC N. SELIGMAN
OSCAR S. STRAUS
ADOLPH LEWISOHN
ADOLPH KRAUS

A petition signed by thousands of Americans, of all races and religions, leaders in public and private life, was sent to the Czar of Russia through the Department of State. The Emperor, however, refused to receive it. The text of the petition and of the accompanying letters follows:[5]

[*Mr. Hay to Mr. Riddle*]

Department of State
Washington, D. C., July 15, 1903

RIDDLE, St. Petersburg:

You are instructed to ask an audience of the Minister of Foreign Affairs and to make him the following communication:

EXCELLENCY: The Secretary of State instructs me to inform you that the President has received from a large number of citizens of the United States, of all religious affiliations and occupying the

---

[5] "The Voice of America on Kishineff," by Cyrus Adler, pages 478–81.

highest positions in both public and private life, a respectful Petition relating to the Jews and running as follows:

To His Imperial Majesty the Emperor of Russia

The cruel outrages perpetrated at Kishineff during Easter of 1903, have excited horror and reprobation throughout the world. Until your Majesty gave special and personal directions, the local authorities failed to maintain order or suppress the rioting. The victims were Jews and the assault was the result of race and religious prejudice. The rioters violated the laws of Russia.

The local officials were derelict in the performance of their duty.

The Jews were the victims of indefensible lawlessness.

These facts are made plain by the official reports of, and by the official acts following, the riot.

Under ordinary conditions the awful calamity would be deplored without undue fear of a recurrence, but such is not the case in the present instance. Your petitioners are advised that millions of Jews, Russian subjects, dwelling in South-western Russia, are in constant dread of fresh outbreaks.

They feel that ignorance, superstition and bigotry, as exemplified by the rioters, are ever ready to persecute them; that the local officials, unless thereunto specially admonished, cannot be relied on as strenuous protectors of their peace and security; that a public sentiment of hostility has been engendered against them and hangs over them as a continuing menace.

Even if it be conceded that these fears are to some extent exaggerated, it is unquestionably true that they exist, that they are not groundless, and that they produce effects of great importance.

The westward migration of Russian Jews, which has proceeded for over twenty years, is being stimulated by these fears, and already that movement has become so great as to overshadow in magnitude the expulsion of the Jews from Spain and to rank with the exodus from Egypt.

No estimate is possible of the misery suffered by the hapless Jews who feel driven to forsake their native land, to sever the most sacred ties, and to wander forth to strange countries.

Neither is it possible to estimate the misery suffered by those who are unwilling or unable to leave the land of their birth; who must part from friends and relatives, who emigrate; who remain in never-ending terror.

Religious persecution is more sinful and more fatuous than war. War is sometimes necessary, honorable and just; religious persecution is never defensible.

The sinfulness and folly which give impulse to unnecessary war received their greatest check when your Majesty's initiative resulted in an International Court of Peace.

With such an example before it, the civilized world cherishes the hope that upon the same initiative there shall be fixed in the early days of the twentieth century, the enduring principle of religious liberty; that by a gracious and convincing expression your Majesty will proclaim, not only for the government of your own subjects, but also for the guidance of all civilized men, that none shall suffer in person, property, liberty, honor or life, because of his religious belief; that the humblest subject or citizen may worship according to the dictates of his own conscience, and that government, whatever its form or agencies, must safeguard these rights and immunities by the exercise of all its powers.

Far removed from your Majesty's dominions, living under different conditions, and owing allegiance to another Government, your petitioners yet venture, in the name of civilization, to plead for religious liberty and tolerance; to plead that he who led his own people and all others to the shrine of peace, will add new luster to his reign and fame by leading a new movement that shall commit the whole world in opposition to religious persecution.

I am instructed to ask whether the Petition will be received by your Excellency to be submitted to the gracious consideration of his Majesty. In that case the Petition will be at once forwarded to St. Petersburg.

I avail myself, etc.,

You will report at the earliest possible moment your execution of this instruction.

Hay

Mr. Leo N. Levi, President of the Independent Order of B'nai B'rith, received the following letter from Mr. Hay:[5a]

[Mr. Hay to Mr. Levi]

Department of State
Washington, October 31, 1903

Leo N. Levi, Esq., President of the Executive
Committee of the Independent Order of
B'nai B'rith, New York

[5a] "The Voice of America on Kishineff," by Cyrus Adler, page 481.

My dear Sir:

I have received at the hands of the Honorable Simon Wolf your letter of October 5. He has also delivered to me the bound copy of the Kishineff petition. It gives me pleasure to accept the charge of this important and significant document and to assign it a place in the archives of the Department of State.

Although this copy of your petition did not reach the high destination for which it was intended, its words have attained worldwide publicity, and have found a lodgment in many thousands of minds. This petition will be always memorable, not only for what it contains, but also for the number and weight of the signatures attached to it, embracing some of the most prominent names of our generation, of our men renowned for intelligence, philanthropy and public spirit. In the future, when the students of history come to peruse this document, they will wonder how the petitioners moved to profound indignation by intolerable wrongs perpetrated on the innocent and helpless should have expressed themselves in language so earnest and eloquent and yet so dignified, so moderate and so decorous. It is a valuable addition to public literature, and will be sacredly cherished among the treasures of the department.

I am, etc.,

Very respectfully yours,
JOHN HAY

The subject of discrimination against American citizens of the Jewish faith in the Empire of Russia was brought up again in 1904, following continuous agitation on this question in the press, at public forums and in both Houses of Congress. In July of that year, Secretary Hay sent to Ambassador McCormick a dispatch wherein it was pointed out that to bring an end to the discriminatory treatment of American Jews in Russia would result in great benefits to Russia.[6]

[*Mr. Hay to Mr. McCormick*]

Department of State
Washington, July 1, 1904

Sir: On the 21st of April last the House of Representatives of the United States adopted a resolution in the following words:

RESOLVED, That the President be requested to renew negotiations with the governments of countries where dis-

[6] Foreign Relations, 1904, page 790.

crimination is made between American citizens on the ground of religious faith or belief to secure by treaty or otherwise uniformity of treatment and protection to American citizens holding passports duly issued by the authorities of the United States, in order that all American citizens shall have equal freedom of travel and sojourn in those countries, without regard to race, creed or religious faith.

The subject to which this resolution relates has heretofore been the occasion of friendly but sincerely earnest representations to the Russian Government on the part of that of the United States. The instructions on file in your office, and the correspondence had by your predecessors with the Imperial foreign office leave no doubt as to the feeling of the Government of the United States in regard to what it has constantly believed to be a needlessly repressive treatment of many of the most reputable and honored citizens of the United States. Similar views have been expressed, by my predecessors as well as by myself, in conferences with the representatives of Russia at this capital. That these friendly representations have not hitherto produced the results so befitting the close intimacy of the relations of the two countries for more than a century and so much in harmony with their traditional amity and mutual regard is not, in the President's judgment, ground for relaxing endeavors to bring about a better understanding, if only on the score of expediency and reciprocal convenience.

I have therefore to instruct you to inform Count Lamsdorff that the text of the foregoing resolution has been sent to you for your information and for your guidance in interpreting this expression of the feeling of the people of this country, through their direct representatives, as to the treatment of the citizens in question. You will make known to his excellency the views of this Government as to the expediency of putting an end to such discriminations between different classes of American citizens on account of their religious faith when seeking to avail themselves of the common privilege of civilized peoples to visit other friendly countries for business or travel.

That such discriminatory treatment is naturally a matter of much concern to this Government is a proposition which his excellency will readily comprehend without dissent. In no other country in the world is a class discrimination applied to our visiting citizens. That the benefits accruing to Russia are sufficient to counterbalance the inconveniences involved is open to question from the practical standpoint. In the view of the President it is not easy to discern the compensating advantage to the Russian Government in the exclusion of a class of tourists and men of business, whose character and position in life are such as to afford in most cases a guarantee against any abuse of the hospitality of Russia and whose intelligence and sterling moral qualities fit them to be typical representatives of our people and entitle them to win for themselves abroad no less degree of esteem than they enjoy in their own land.

I have, etc.,

JOHN HAY

Writing to Count Lamsdorff, Ambassador McCormick repeated and enlarged upon this argument of expediency and reciprocal convenience, although, he admitted, there were higher grounds on which to appeal. The Russian Minister replied that a special commission had been instituted by the Minister of the Interior with a view to revise the passport regulations then in force; through his representative on this commission, he would acquaint the other members of the commission with the views and desires of the Federal Government of the United States.

In 1905, during the Russo-Japanese War, the Russian Emperor made a liberal gesture to his people. The nature of this was reported to the United States Government by Mr. George von L. Meyer, who succeeded Mr. McCormick as ambassador at the Russian capital, in the following dispatch to Mr. Elihu Root, the Secretary of State:[7]

[Mr. Meyer to Mr. Root]

American Embassy
St. Petersburg, May 5, 1905

SIR: I beg leave to report that the ukase issued by the Tsar on the Russian Easter Sunday (April 30) makes religious freedom to all Russian sects, except the Jews, an accomplished fact. . . .

If the ukase is carried out in all its completeness, it will be the greatest concession of individual liberty since the liberation of the serfs, and may be the first step toward a separation of church and state.

I have, etc.,

G. v. L. MEYER

[7] Foreign Relations, 1905, page 767.

The calling of a Russian parliament, the Duma, was another move in the same direction. Though the Jews were left out in the Easter ukase, a number of Russian liberal statesmen, then filling important posts in the Russian cabinet, were endeavoring to liberalize the Russian laws affecting the Jews.

On November 1, 1906, Ambassador Meyer reported that the Council of State had decided not to deal with the Jewish problem separately, but to regard it as forming part of the general question of granting equal political rights to all nationalities in the Russian Empire. Exactly a month later, the Ambassador reported that Premier Stolypin had introduced a bill removing restrictive police regulations in 25 government provinces within the Pale of Jewish Settlement; promulgating similar arrangements for Jews outside the Pale; and removing the restrictions regarding trade to which Jews were subjected. This bill, however, never became law, for Czar Nicholas II refused to affix his signature to it.

In 1905–06 there occurred in Russia a series of pogroms which in the extent of loss of life and property exceeded all previous outbreaks of this kind. In Rostoff, Warsaw, Odessa, and many other towns and villages, Jews were attacked, murdered, their bodies mutilated and their property plundered or destroyed. The worst of all pogroms took place in Siedletz and Bialystok. In a number of cases American consuls asked for military protection.

Spencer Eddy, Chargé d'Affaires during the absence of Ambassador Meyer, received telegraphic communications from American consuls in various parts of Russia affected by the anti-Jewish riots, and he in turn cabled the information to the State Department in Washington.

Here are some few facts extracted from the many telegrams which reached Washington from St. Petersburg:

In Odessa, thousands of Jews were killed, suffering and destitution were great; in Warsaw, 100 Jews were killed and wounded; 15 Jews were killed in Rostoff and 11,000 ruined financially; in Marinopol, Chenitchesk, Leyansk, Babmut, Ekaterinoslaw, and many other towns the losses were severe.

On April 7, 1906, Acting Secretary of State Bacon cabled Mr. Meyer that American Jews feared renewal of pogroms during the ensuing Easter, and asked Mr. Meyer whether the Russian Government had taken any precautionary measures against such repetition. In reply, Ambassador Meyer wired that he had received assurances from Count Witte, Russian Minister of Foreign Affairs, that there would not be any disturbances. The Minister of the Interior had given a similar assurance to the chairman of a Jewish committee. The police were now to be held responsible for any future disturbances. Mr. Meyer concluded the telegram with a skeptical note. Unfortunately, his skepticism of Russian assurances, even when given by a reputedly liberal minister, Count Witte, proved to be too well founded. For the pogrom of Bialystok and Siedletz occurred later in the same year.

In the official reports on the pogroms of Bialystok and Siedletz the blame was in both cases put on the "machination of the revolutionary parties," the Government absolving itself of any guilt or act of connivance. We have, however, the statement made by Prince Urussov in the Duma that he had documentary evidence to prove that the Government itself had instigated the anti-Jewish riots.[8] Similarly, Mr. Witold Fuchs, United States vice consul at Warsaw, supplementing his short telegram of September 10, 1906, to Mr. Spencer Eddy, reading, "Siedletz exact repetition of Bialystok," sent the following dispatch:[9]

[*Vice-Consul Fuchs to Chargé Eddy*]

American Consular Service
Warsaw, September 14th, 1906

Sir:

I have the honor to confirm my wire of the 10th instant, reading:
"Siedletz exact repetition of Bialystok."

In supplement to this and to the general report of the "pogrom," as given by the press, I wish to add the following particulars:

[8] See "Memoirs of a Russian Governor," by Prince Serge Dmitrivevich Urussov.

[9] Foreign Relations, 1906, page 1311.

There can not be the least doubt but that the "pogrom" was premeditated and prepared by the troops, soldiers having been seen on the eve of the massacre enter lodgings and instruct the Christian population to hang out devotional objects as preservatives against what was going to happen. There was no khooligans [sic] on the premises, it appears, to provoke or to take part in the massacre.

I am informed from reliable quarter that the number of Jews killed amounts to 137 (corpses identified), the number of wounded about thrice as many. The Jewish shops and houses along the principal streets and the central market pillaged.

Characteristic feature is that in opposition to the wholesale massacre of Jews and devastation of their homes was killed one (1) Christian civilian and one (1) soldier, another soldier being wounded. As to property one Christian shop and one hotel plundered.

On the other hand, however, it cannot be denied that attempts upon the lives of gendarmes, higher police officials, and military men had lately been particularly numerous in Siedletz.

I have, etc.,

WITOLD FUCHS
Vice-Consul

Altogether, more than 300 pogroms took place in Russia in the years 1903–06, in most cases with the implicit or explicit sanction of Russian officials. On June 22, 1906, the United States Congress passed a joint resolution, introduced in the Senate by Anselm J. McLaurin of Mississippi, and in the House of Representatives by Robert G. Cousins of Iowa, which read:[10]

Resolved by the Senate and House of Representatives of the United States of America in Congress assembled, that the people of the United States are horrified by the report of the massacre of Hebrews in Russia on account of their race and religion, and that those bereaved thereby have the hearty sympathy of the people of this country.

On July 31, 1906, the State Department cabled to Mr. Eddy to furnish it with a report on the condition of the Jews throughout Russia, as it had been the custom of American representatives in that country to do from time to time.

[10] Senate Joint Resolution No. 68, *Congressional Record*, 59th Congress, 1st Session, Vol. 40, Part 9, page 8919.

After consulting Russian law on the subject of the Jews and various Russian government documents, and conversing with men who were in a position to know the situation, Mr. Eddy wrote a very long report which he dispatched to Washington on September 15 of that year. The student of the history of the Jews of Russia will gain much from reading this report which is both thorough and fair. Two details are worthy of mention here. Speaking of the privileges enjoyed by special classes of Jews who were allowed to travel about or reside temporarily in different parts of the country, Eddy noted the significant fact that these privileges were personal and did not apply to the wife or children of the possessor. Discussing the life of the Jewish artisans and workmen, Eddy pointed out that the Jewish artisan who was not independent earned about $120 a year and worked anywhere from 15 to 18 hours a day. These observations moved him to say that "the fact that they are none the less a fairly healthy and long-lived class speaks highly for the stamina of the race." Mr. Eddy concludes with what in the light of subsequent events was an optimistic note, that "it is possible to believe that the condition of the Jewish population, bad as it is, is also no worse than it has been, and it seems just to hope that the near future will bring the same betterment of conditions to them as it bids fair to bring to the Russian people generally."

In the United States, meanwhile, opinion was gradually crystallizing in favor of the termination of the Treaty of 1832 under which Russia claimed that its domestic law could be applied to American citizens. Already in 1904, the platforms of both leading parties had promised equal protection to all American citizens abroad. The platforms of national conventions of the same parties in 1908 contained a more specific demand for equal treatment to American Jews in Russia. Thus the Democratic platform contained the following plank:

We pledge ourselves to insist upon the just and lawful protection of our citizens at home and abroad, and to use all proper methods to secure for them, whether native born or naturalized, and without distinction of race or creed, the equal protection of law and the enjoyment of all rights and privileges open to them under our treaty; and if, under existing treaties, the right of travel and sojourn is denied to American citizens or recognition is withheld from American passports by any countries on the ground of race and creed, we favor prompt negotiations with the Governments of such countries to secure the removal of these unjust discriminations. We demand that all over the world a duly authorized passport issued by the Government of the United States to an American citizen shall be proof of the fact that he is an American citizen and shall entitle him to the treatment due him as such.

Similar sentiments were expressed in the platforms of the Republican and the Independent Parties. But it was mainly due to the efforts of the American Jewish Committee, through Judge Mayer Sulzberger, its president and Louis Marshall, member of its executive committee, that the Treaty of 1832 was finally consigned to the fate it had long deserved. In this connection, the name of the famous financier Jacob H. Schiff and the venerable statesman Oscar S. Straus should also be mentioned.

On May 28, 1907, Elihu Root, who succeeded John Hay as Secretary of State, issued a circular which he sent through the Bureau of Citizenship to all applicants for a passport who were natives of Russia. The circular read:

Notice to American Citizens Formerly Subjects of Russia who Contemplate Returning to that Country

A Russian subject who becomes a citizen of another country without the consent of the Russian Government commits an offense against Russian law, for which he is liable to arrest and punishment, if he returns without previously obtaining the permission of the Russian Government.

This Government dissents from this provision of Russian law but an American citizen formerly a subject of Russia who returns to that country places himself within the jurisdiction of Russian law and cannot expect immunity from its operations.

Jews, whether they were formerly Russian subjects or not, are not admitted to Russia unless they obtain special permission in advance from the Russian Government, and this Department will not issue passports to former Russian subjects or to Jews who intend going to Russian territory, unless it has assurance that the Russian Government will consent to their admission.

No one is admitted to Russia without a passport, which must be viséed or indorsed by a Russian diplomatic or consular representative.[11]

It will be remembered that on April 1, 1901, the State Department issued a circular covering the same question. But while the earlier circular merely informed naturalized Americans of Russian birth who intended to return to their native country that they must first apply to the Russian Minister of Interior for a special permission, this new circular of Mr. Root actually meant that he, too, recognized two classes of American citizens, non-Jewish and Jewish, and that the Department of State was going to act on that principle. For the first time in American history, a Jew had to submit himself to an inquisition into his religion by a representative of his own Government.

In due time, the circular became known and voices of protest were heard everywhere.

In a letter to Secretary Root, Messrs. Louis Marshall and Edward Lauterbach complained that the issuance of this circular meant a reversal of the old American policy, and that instead of opposing with all its powers the discrimination by the Russian Government against American Jews, the American Government itself was segregating from the mass of American citizens those who were of the Jewish faith and withholding from them one of the privileges of citizenship, the giving of a passport and the protection of his country while traveling. Similar criticism was voiced on the floor of the House of Representatives by Mr. Henry M. Goldfogle.

Mr. Root thereupon withdrew the circular and substituted another from which all reference to Jews was omitted. Messrs. Marshall and Lauterbach still objected, however, to the phrase "and cannot expect immunity from its operations"; for, in declaring that an American citizen could not expect immunity in such a case, our Government was

[11] "Termination of the Treaty of 1832 between the United States and Russia." Hearing before Committee on Foreign Affairs of the House of Representatives, December 11, 1911, page 240.

adopting the Russian view of expatriation, in contravention of the law of the United States on this subject.

Three sections of the United States Revised Statutes deal with the right of expatriation and the duty of the President to protect American citizens, when abroad, in the enjoyment of this right. It is quite relevant to quote them here in full:

Section 1999. Whereas the right of expatriation is a natural and inherent right of all people, indispensable to the enjoyment of the rights of life, liberty, and the pursuit of happiness; and whereas in the recognition of this principle this Government has freely received emigrants from all nations, and invested them with the rights of citizenship; and whereas it is claimed that such American citizens, with their descendants, are subjects of foreign States, owing all allegiance to the governments thereof; and whereas it is necessary to the maintainance of public peace that this claim of foreign allegiance should be promptly and finally disavowed: Therefore, any declaration, instruction, opinion, order, or decision of any officer of the United States which denies, restricts, impairs, or questions the right of expatriation, is declared inconsistent with the fundamental principles of the Republic.

Section 2000. All naturalized citizens of the United States, while in foreign countries, are entitled to and shall receive from this Government the same protection of persons and property which is accorded to native-born citizens.

Section 2001. Whenever it is made known to the President that any citizen of the United States has been unjustly deprived of his liberty by or under the authority of any foreign government, it shall be the duty of the President forthwith to demand of that government the reasons of such imprisonment; and if it appears to be wrongful and in violation of the right of American citizenship, the President shall forthwith demand the release of such citizen, and if the release so demanded is unreasonably delayed or refused, the President shall use such means, not amounting to acts of war, as he may think necessary and proper to obtain or effectuate the release; and all the facts and proceedings relative thereto shall as soon as practicable be communicated by the President to Congress.

Though the objectionable circular was soon recalled[12] it became clear that the passport question would not be solved

---

[12] Mr. Philander C. Knox, who followed Mr. Root as the Secretary of State, reinstated the phrase to which Messrs. Marshall and Lauterbach objected.

through diplomatic channels. The whole Treaty of 1832 had
to be denounced and another one, which would not discriminate as between American citizens, substituted. This could
be achieved by presidential notice to the Russian Government that the Government of the United States desired to
terminate the treaty. Article XII of that instrument specifically provided such a method of termination which would
take effect a year after notice. The alternative would be
for Congress to pass a joint resolution requesting the President to give such notice.

Presidential notice was suggested by Judge Mayer Sulzberger, president of the American Jewish Committee, in a
letter to President Theodore Roosevelt on May 18, 1908,
in which the history of the passport question is briefly
reviewed and wherein it is further pointed out that American
ideals and self-respect as well as the very principles of the
American Constitution were being endangered by continuing the status quo. President Roosevelt directed that the
letter be referred to the consideration of Secretary Root,
who promised to give it his attention.

From this exchange of letters, we learn the interesting
fact that the Russian Government was willing to give a
passport to any Jew who would be willing to engage passage
on a Russian steamer. Mr. Herman Bernstein, author and
business representative, going to Russia on business and also
to study the emigration question, was given a visa without
any delays or difficulties after the consul learned that Bernstein had purchased a ticket for Libau on the steamship
St. Petersburg. The Russian consular authorities, who knew
that Mr. Bernstein was a Jew, did not insist that he answer
the question as to his religion. Had Bernstein attempted
to enter Russia by any other steamship company or by any
foreign boundary, he would have been excluded.

In his speech of acceptance of the Republican nomination
for the presidency of the United States, Mr. William H.
Taft made a special reference to the fact that "in some
countries . . . distinctions are made in respect to the treatment of our citizens traveling abroad and having passports

of our executive, based on considerations which are repugnant to the principles of our Government and civilization." He then committed his party and administration "to continue to make every endeavor to secure the solution of such distinctions which in our eyes are both needless and opprobrious."

Some hope was entertained that the new American ambassador to Russia, Mr. W. W. Rockhill, would start negotiations with Russia for a new treaty or a reinterpretation of the old one. In the summer of 1909, a conference was held at the White House at which were present, besides President Taft, Mr. Philander Knox, the Secretary of State, Mr. W. W. Rockhill, the newly appointed ambassador, and Judge Mayer Sulzberger, Mr. Jacob H. Schiff and Doctor Cyrus Adler, representing the American Jewish Committee. The whole passport situation was discussed and various means suggested for the solution of this vexatious question, but nothing of a definite character was decided upon. On February 10, 1910, the American Jewish Committee was compelled once more to address a letter to President Taft calling his attention to the fact that while the Government of the United States had not yet succeeded in gaining from the Russian Government equal treatment for its Jewish citizens, other Governments had done so. The Governments of France, Austria, and Germany, in recent treaties concluded with Russia, had insisted on a clause exempting their Jewish nationals from the anti-Jewish laws of the Empire.

On May 25, 1910, another conference was held between the President and the same persons who took part in the earlier conference. A memorandum of this interview was later sent to the President and signed by Judge Sulzberger, Dr. Adler and Mr. Schiff. The text of the letter itself follows:[13]

New York, June 3, 1910

THE PRESIDENT:

The undersigned beg leave to submit herewith a memorandum of the remarks concerning the American Passport in Russia made by the parties to the interview of Wednesday, May 25, 1910,

[13] "The Passport Question," in *American Jewish Year Book*, 1911-1912, page 51.

which the President was good enough to grant. Since this interview, there has been held a meeting of the Executive Committee of the American Jewish Committee [here follows a list of the names]. As in duty bound, we presented a report of the interview and the Executive Committee unanimously approved the recommendation we had the honor to make, namely, that as a preliminary step our Government should insist upon the transfer of the negotiations from St. Petersburg to Washington and that failure either in accomplishing this or in achieving desired results therefrom should be followed by denunciation of treaties. The Committee strongly recommends that all this should be done promptly as a vindication of earnestness on a subject which found a place not only in the platform of the Republican party, but of all other parties that presented candidates to the American people at the last election. This fact indicates that the subject is one not only of interest to the particular class of citizens involved, but that all the citizens of the United States of every party affiliation are concerned as a matter of national honor in the full recognition of the American passport and resent the assumption of a right on the part of the embassy or consuls of any foreign power to make inquisition into the religious affiliations of American citizens and practice discriminations as a result of such inquisition.

It is the view of the Committee, as indeed it has been maintained for many years by our Department of State, that this action is in violation of our treaties with Russia and of our own national policy, and that the reasons given by the Russian Government of "economic necessity" or "internal policy" are mere pretexts on the part of Russia for violating a treaty that it suits her better not to observe. We hold that our Government owes it to itself as a vindication of its reputation for intelligence to insist that as treaties are international agreements entered into by responsible parties all considerations of economic values and internal policies are presumed to have been weighed by each party before the promulgation of the treaties, and that so soon as the treaties are promulgated unilateral action is barred and no change can be made either in the wording or meaning save by the consent of both parties. We believe that the time has arrived to demonstrate the position of the United States, not by war nor by threats or hints of war, but by the most solemn national protest — denunciation of treaties — should our righteous demands not be granted.

We also urge that a measure so vital to the United States should not be delayed or rejected because European nations may — possibly for reasons which affect their political relations with Russia — not wish to join us for the present. We believe, moreover, that it would be more in accordance with American policy that our Government should proceed upon its own initiative and upon the basis of its own treaties without seeking either the concurrence or assistance of European powers. If our Government after pursuing a proper policy should still fail to induce Russia to take the right and just course, it would have the glorious record of high moral endeavor. There are reasons, however, which warrant the conclusion that so soon as Russia realizes that our Government is in earnest not only in registering its views, but in following them up by successive steps, and that its efforts are not merely for popular consumption, Russia's attitude will change. We believe that the removal of the negotiations to Washington would be the most important factor in hastening such a realization. That such removal is not without precedent we are well advised. But even if it were, the attempt to create the precedent would be all the more important and all the more likely to produce a favorable issue to the negotiation. In the modern world, wherein there is a growing international conscience, the demonstration of national injustice or national bad faith is a powerful lever. Even Russia needs the support of a world-opinion and in some measure realizes the fact.

We stand prepared, should the President wish it, to demonstrate that we are presenting to the President views which have been held by our Government and from time to time presented to the Russian Government, without avail, for a period of forty years; that we are making no new proposal, but pointing out as we believe the way which may prove effective for our Government to secure a successful result to negotiations which have hitherto failed. Deeply as we deplore the inhuman conduct of the Russian Government toward the Jews living in that Empire, and believing fully as we do that in view of the enforced migration to America resulting from this policy our Government would be justified in protesting to Russia in its own behalf and in behalf of humanity, we nevertheless and with great effort suppress our natural sentiments upon this point and confine ourselves solely to urging upon the President the securing of rights accorded us under our constitution and laws and by the treaties which our own country has entered into. We urge that in the negotiations, which we hope will shortly be transferred to Washington, our Government confine itself to securing all rights accorded to its citizens under its treaties with Russia, and that it hold the Russian Government to the same points of discussion, thus avoiding any claim that the internal policy of another Government is involved.

We have the honor to be, Mr. President,

Your most obedient servants,

MAYER SULZBERGER
JACOB H. SCHIFF
CYRUS ADLER

As it soon became evident that the evils of the 1832 treaty would not be rectified by the action of the Executive branch of the American Government, the American Jewish Committee decided to launch a public agitation for the termination of the treaty with Russia. This agitation was opened by Louis Marshall in a public address on "Russia and the American Passport" delivered before the Union of American Hebrew Congregations, January 11, 1911. A month later, on February 10, Representative Herbert Parsons of New York introduced a resolution providing for the termination of the treaty between the United States of America and Russia concluded at St. Petersburg December 18, 1832. A similar resolution was introduced by Senator Charles A. Culberson on February 28, 1911. Two hearings were held by the House Committee on Foreign Affairs, in February and December, 1911. Mr. William G. McAdoo, Judge Sulzberger, Mr. Louis Marshall, Col. Harry Cutler, Mr. Jacob H. Schiff, Hon. Oscar S. Straus and others appeared before the Committee.

The burden of all the testimony was the same: that the passport question was not a Jewish but an American question, and while the cause seemed to be a Jewish one, it was Americanism in its purest and highest form that was really on trial.

The following Joint Resolution was introduced on December 4, 1911, in the House by Representative, later Governor, William Sulzer, of New York:[14]

Joint Resolution Providing for the Termination
of the Treaty of 1832 between the U. S. and Russia

Resolved by the Senate and House of Representatives of the United States of America in Congress assembled, that the people of the United States assert as a fundamental principle that the rights of its citizens shall not be impaired at home or abroad because of race or religion; that the Government of the United States concluded its treaties for the equal protection of all classes of its citizens, without regard to race or religion; that the Government of the

---

[14] House Joint Resolution No. 166, *Congressional Record* 62nd Congress, 2d Session, Vol. 20, Part I, page 311.

United States will not be a party to any treaty which discriminates, or which by one of the parties thereto is so construed as to discriminate between American citizens on the ground of race or religion; that the Government of Russia has violated the treaty between the United States and Russia, concluded at St. Petersburg December eighteenth, 1832, refusing to honor American passports duly issued to American citizens, on account of race and religion; that in the judgment of the Congress the said treaty, for the reasons aforesaid, ought to be terminated at the earliest possible time; that for the aforesaid reasons the said treaty is hereby declared to be terminated and of no further force and effect from the expiration of one year after the date of notification to the Government of Russia of the terms of this resolution, and that to this end the President is hereby charged with the duty of communicating such notice to the Government of Russia.

This resolution passed the House by 300 to 1, on December 13, 1911, the only dissenting vote being that of Representative George R. Malby, who declared that the only reason he voted against it was that he did not think that the resolution would remedy the evil involved.

Secretary of State Knox sent the following cablegram to Ambassador Curtis Guild, December 15, 1911:[15]

[*Mr. Knox to Mr. Guild*]

Department of State
Washington, December 15, 1911

The President's message on foreign relations, communicated on the 7th to Congress, contains the following paragraph:

By direction of the State Department our ambassador to Russia has recently been having a series of conferences with the minister of foreign affairs of Russia with a view to securing a clearer understanding and construction of the treaty of 1832 between Russia and the United States and the modification of any existing Russian regulations which may be found to interfere in any way with the full recognition of the rights of American citizens under this treaty. I believe that the Government of Russia is addressing itself seriously to the needs of changing the present practice under the treaty and that sufficient progress has been made to warrant the continuance of these conferences in the hope that there may soon be removed any justification

[15] Foreign Relations, 1911, page 695.

of the complaints of treaty violation now prevalent in this country. I expect that immediately after Christmas recess I shall be able to make a further communication to Congress on this subject.

The above reference by the President to the passport question was decided upon under circumstances which will be made evident to you by the following quotation from a personal and confidential letter which I addressed to the Russian ambassador on the 6th instant:

> I have the honor to hand you for your confidential infor-mation a copy of what the President proposes to say in his message upon the passport question. You will find it in prac-tically the same form as when I read it to you yesterday morning. Further consideration of the subject more and more convinces me that the easiest way to avoid the embarrass-ments likely to be produced by a discussion of the pending resolution in Congress would be to do as we were talking of yesterday, namely, solve the difficulties connected with the old treaty by terminating it and negotiating a new one in which there could be set down clearly the matters upon which both Governments would agree. The President's message will probably carry the matter over until after the holidays, and the interval might be availed of to work out some such solu-tion as I suggest. I would be happy to have some further suggestion from you.

Accordingly you will seek an immediate interview with the minister for foreign affairs and hand him a note in the following terms:

> Under instructions from my Government and in pursuance of conversations held by the Secretary of State with the Russian ambassador at Washington, I have now the honor to give to the Imperial Russian Government on behalf of the United States the official notification contemplated by Article XII of the treaty of 1832, whereby the operation of the said treaty will terminate in accordance with its terms on January 1, 1913.
>
> Your excellency will recall that pourparlers between the two Governments during the last three years have fully recog-nized the fact that this ancient treaty, as is quite natural, is no longer fully responsive in various respects to the needs of the political and material relations of the two countries, which grew constantly more important. The treaty has also given rise from time to time to certain controversies equally regretted by both Governments.

In conveying the present formal notification to your excellency I am instructed to express the desire of my Government, meanwhile, to renew the effort to negotiate a modern treaty of friendship, commerce, and navigation, upon bases more perfectly responsive to the interests of both Governments. I am directed by the President at the same time to emphasize the great value attached by the Government of the United States to the historic relations between the two countries, and the desire of my Government to spare no effort to make the outcome of the proposed negotiations contribute still further to the strength and cordiality of these relations.

I avail myself on this occasion to offer to your excellency the renewed assurance of my highest consideration.

A copy of this telegram has been handed to the Russian ambassador here for his information.

KNOX

An hour later Secretary Knox sent another telegram to Ambassador Guild suggesting that, in order to forestall passage by the Senate of the resolution abrogating the treaty, already passed by the House, both Governments announce simultaneously the termination of the treaty, and the willingness to negotiate a new one "more responsive to the interests of both Governments and more adequate to the needs of their important relations."

M. Sazanoff, the Russian Minister for Foreign Affairs, refused to agree to a newspaper announcement by both countries, and threatened that Russia would not reconsider signing another treaty except on the lines of the old one. He was then officially notified that, in accordance with Article XII of the treaty, the United States had decided to abrogate it, the abrogation to take effect January 1, 1913.

On December 18, 1911, Ambassador Guild cabled the translation of a note which he had received from M. Sazanoff, which read:[16]

[Mr. Sazanoff to Mr. Guild]

In note No. 72 of December 4/17, your excellency has transmitted to me official notification of the United States Government, provided by Article XII of the treaty of 1832, in accordance

---

[16] Foreign Relations, 1911, page 699.

with which said treaty will cease to be in force on December 19–
January 1, 1913.

At the same time you stated that in the meanwhile your Government is desirous of entering into negotiations for the conclusion of
a new treaty of friendship, commerce, and navigation on a basis
which would better answer the requirements of both countries.

Taking due notice of the aforesaid, I take advantage of this
occasion, sir, to express my distinguished consideration.

SAZANOFF

The termination of the Treaty of 1832 with Russia was
approved by the three leading parties, each of which adopted
a plank in its platform commending the action taken by our
Government on this issue.

The Democratic Convention of 1912, held in Baltimore,
adopted the following plank:[17]

We commend the patriotism of the Democratic members of
the House of Representatives, which compelled the termination of
the Treaty of 1832 and we pledge ourselves anew to preserve the
sacred rights of American citizenship at home and abroad. No
treaty should receive the sanction of our Government which does
not recognize the right of expatriation.

The Republican National Convention adopted a similar
plank in its platform which read as follows:[17]

We approve the action taken by the President and Congress
to secure with Russia, as with other countries, a treaty that will
recognize the absolute right of expatriation, and that will prevent
all discrimination of whatever kind between American citizens,
whether native born or alien, and regardless of race, religion, or
previous political allegiance. The right of asylum is a precious
possession of the people of the United States, and it is to be neither
surrendered nor restricted.

The Progressive Party, with former President Theodore
Roosevelt as its presidential candidate, also had a plank on
this question in its platform.

When, late in 1912, there appeared in a number of newspapers a series of articles which indicated that conversations

[17] *American Jewish Year Book*, 1913–1914, page 442.

were being held between the Russian Ambassador and Mr. Knox, the Secretary of State, with a view, it was reported, to continuing existing commercial relations, leaving for some future date a formal agreement on the passport question, Mr. Louis Marshall, for the American Jewish Committee, addressed a letter to President Taft, dated November 15, 1912. In this letter Mr. Marshall declares that if the reports were true "it will be at a loss to our moral sense." On November 23 Mr. Marshall wrote a second letter, in which he pointed out that there had been additional articles in the press stating or hinting that negotiations for a modus vivendi with Russia were in progress.

To this letter the President replied as follows:[18]

[*President Taft to Mr. Marshall*]

The White House, Washington
November 26, 1912

MY DEAR MR. MARSHALL:

I have your letter of November 23d, in which you refer to the reports that we are engaged in making a temporary agreement with Russia to take the place of the agreement which we have abrogated. I beg to assure you that we expect to make no agreement of this kind, or of any kind. What we have been doing is examining the existing treaties and statutes and international law applicable to a situation like that which will occur after our treaty with Russia of 1832 shall cease to be. We do not expect to change by any agreement, or so-called modus vivendi, the status quo, which the abrogation of the treaty will leave on the first of January next by its ceasing to have effect.

WM. H. TAFT

In August, 1913, the United States Treasury Department announced that Russian wood pulp and paper would not be admitted under the minimum tariff accorded under the favored nation clause, owing to the abrogation of the Treaty of 1832. No new treaty was concluded between the United

---

[18] *American Jewish Year Book*, 1914–1915, page 392.

States, nor had one been negotiated up to the outbreak of the World War.[19]

No reference concerning Jews is found in the diplomatic correspondence with Russia until late in 1917, that is after

[19] The famous trial of Mendel Beilis of Kiev, who, in 1911, was accused of having murdered a Russian lad for ritual purposes, aroused intense indignation all over the world, and formed the subject of correspondence between the Russian Ambassador at Washington and the Ministry for Foreign Affairs in St. Petersburg. (For this correspondence and the story of the whole trial see "The Decay of Czarism" by Alexander B. Tager, a study based on unpublished materials in the Russian archives.) In the Senate of the United States, Senator J. Hamilton Lewis introduced the following resolution on October 22, 1913: (*Congressional Record*, 63rd Congress, 1st Session, Vol. 50, Part 6, page 5735).

Whereas the public press reports that the Government of the Empire of Russia is now engaged in the prosecution of a Jewish laborer, Mendel Beilis, upon the charge of having murdered a Christian boy for the purpose of using Christian blood for religous purposes; whereas there appears absolutely nothing in the Jewish religion or doctrines requiring such a practice, but on the contrary the use of blood in any manner is absolutely prohibited by the Mosaic law, Leviticus XVI, 10;

Whereas eminent divines and scholars of all religions and denominations have testified to the falsity of this accusation that the Jewish religion requires the use or the sacrifice of human blood;

Whereas the constant and relentless persecution of the Jews in Russia is bringing to our shores thousands of Russian Jewish refugees, who must be taken care of, and the United States Government is therefore directly interested in this matter; and

Whereas the Beilis trial is calculated to incite the ignorant people in Russia to commit outrages against Jewish people, and as a result of such fear the Jewish immigration to the United States since the commencement of the Beilis trial has already increased: Therefore be it

Resolved by the Senate of the United States: That the Senate of the United States looks with disfavor upon the prosecution of the Beilis case, and that the proper officers of the Government be directed to use the good offices of the Government of the United States with the Government of Russia to the end that the unjust ritual charge against the Jewish people at large, and Mendel Beilis in particular, be withdrawn, and the Jewish people receive the vindication justice requires.

A similar resolution was introduced in the House by Representative Adolph J. Sabath of Illinois.

The American protest also took the form of an appeal to the Czar, signed by the leading representatives of the various Christian denomina-

the Czarist regime had fallen, the Czar himself had abdicated, and a liberal Provisional Government had been established.

On March 26, 1917, a few days after the Provisional Government was organized, Ambassador David R. Francis wired to Secretary Lansing that the new government was in great need of funds, and that American financial aid would be a master stroke, adding that it was "immeasurably important to the Jews that the revolution should succeed. If the Jews make such advances, great discretion should be exercised lest the revolution assume a phase which would arouse opposition of anti-Semites who are numerous here."

The same spirit of precaution and hesitancy on the part of the new Russian government may be discovered in a dispatch from Ambassador Francis a few weeks later, April 4, 1917. The prejudice against the Jews, he said, had not yet been eradicated; it was especially prevalent among the peasants; this prejudice would become a dangerous weapon in the hands of the opponents of the present regime if it proved too friendly to the Jews.

On April 16, Secretary Lansing sent the following telegram to Mr. Francis:[20]

[*Mr. Lansing to Mr. Francis*]

Washington, April 16, 1917

Please deliver following telegram:

Miliukov, Petrograd (or Baron Gunzburg): American Jewry is alarmed by reports that certain elements are urging separate peace between Russia and Central powers. A separate peace may, in our opinion, lead to the ultimate restoration of an autocratic government and the degradation of the Russian Jews below even their former deplorable condition. We are confident Russian Jewry are

---

tions, in which they pointed out the historical falsity of the ritual murder charge against Jews, this falsity having been attested by four Popes, many monarchs, and even by Prince Obolensky, a former head of the Holy Synod of the Russian Empire. (See *American Jewish Year Book*, 1914–1915, page 79.)

[20] Foreign Relations, 1917, Supplement II, Vol. I, page 25.

ready for the greatest sacrifices in support of the present democratic government as the only hope for the future of Russia and all its people. American Jewry holds itself ready to cooperate with their Russian brethren in this great movement. Marshall, Morgenthau, Schiff, Strauss, Rosenwald.

(If sent to Baron Gunzburg, add: May we ask you to submit this to your Government.)

LANSING

It was also suggested in a confidential cable to Ambassador Francis that an American mission, including a prominent Jew, might leave for Russia, and Mr. Francis was to have this matter discussed with Paul N. Miliukov, Russian Minister for Foreign Affairs, and other members of the ministry.

The reply, also by cable, to the above message was as follows:[21]

[Mr. Francis to Mr. Lansing]

Petrograd, April 25, 1917

Your 1321, 16th. Minister for Foreign Affairs today requested following response be transmitted to signatories of message therein:

The Russian Provisional Government is very appreciative of the sympathy which the authorized representatives of American Jewish citizens are so good as to accord to its efforts to assure the triumph of the great principles of democracy, of liberty, and of equality of all Russian citizens without distinction of nationality or religion.

As regards the uncertainty shown by the American Jewry on account of the rumors of agitation of certain elements for a separate peace I can assure them that these rumors are wholly without foundation; no Russian party, whatever its political programme, has contemplated nor could contemplate the eventuality of a separate peace with the foreign aggressor.

The great danger which menaces new Russia and the entire world if heed should be paid to the efforts which have for their end the maintenance of the fearful German militarism are only too well known here.

FRANCIS

[21] Foreign Relations, 1917, Supplement II, Vol. I, page 39.

That the sentiments and hopes expressed in the cable, which is the last published correspondence with the old Russia, were not borne out by subsequent events is all too well known. The Provisional Government was soon replaced by the Bolshevik regime which, after a long and severe civil war, won the upper hand in Russia and has held it ever since. For a number of years, during the civil war, thousands of Jews were massacred in those territories which were for a time under the rule of one or another of the Czarist generals.

Under the Soviet regime all legal discrimination against Jews, as Jews, disappeared. In common with the other inhabitants of Russia the Jews were treated not as confessors of one or another religion, but as members of the economic class to which they belonged. If they were persecuted, imprisoned, or even executed, it was because they were employers or capitalists, and as such they were considered "exploiters" and "enemies of the state." "Proletarian" Jews, on the other hand, were given the same treatment as the Soviet Government gave to all its subjects of the same class.

As a religious minority, the Jews enjoy fewer rights than they did even under the Czarist regime. Because it is the policy of the Bolsheviks to combat all religion, the religious Jews suffer equally with the adherents of the other religions. With the coming of the Bolsheviks, too, all attempts at Russification of the racial minorities in the Russian Empire were abandoned, and the Jews were given the opportunity to form an autonomous state in Biro-Bidjan, Siberia.

For almost twenty-two years the Government of Soviet Russia was not recognized by the United States. The Administration of President Franklin D. Roosevelt, however, has resumed political relations with the Government of Russia. In the exchange of letters between President Roosevelt and Maxim Litvinov, Russian Commissar for Foreign Affairs, which effected the recognition of the Union of Soviet Socialist Republics, the President insisted that Russia assure religious liberty and freedom of worship to all American citizens in Russia, irrespective of their faith or creed. In reply Mr. Litvinov assured the President that the Government of the Union of Soviet Socialist Republics guarantees to the nationals of the United States the right to "free exercise of liberty of conscience and religious worship" and protection "from all disability or persecution on account of their religious faith or worship."[22]

[22] For full text of these letters see "Establishment of Diplomatic Relations with the Union of Soviet Socialist Republics," *Department of State, Eastern European Series, No.* 1, Washington, 1933.

PART FOUR

CENTRAL EUROPE

X. SWITZERLAND[1]

Some of the most insistent and long drawn out correspondence between the Government of the United States and a foreign country in behalf of American citizens of the Jewish faith was with the Government of Switzerland, always counted among the more liberal governments in Europe. Up to as recently as 1874, the Jews in Switzerland were still suffering from political and civil disabilities.

The United States and France protested against such discrimination against their citizens, but their protests were of no avail, chiefly because of traditional prejudices and of the peculiarities of the Swiss cantonal system of government. The power of the central government was limited, and even had it been willing to recognize the residential and commercial rights of foreign Jews, such recognition would not have been constitutionally valid, as such matters were within the province of the respective cantons.

In 1850, the United States negotiated a commercial treaty with Switzerland. In his message, transmitting the treaty to the Senate, President Fillmore objected to it, saying:[2]

There is . . . a decisive objection arising from the last clause in the first article. That clause is in these words:

On account of the tenor of the federal constitution of Switzerland, Christians alone are entitled to the enjoyment of the privileges guaranteed by the present article in the Swiss Cantons. But said Cantons are not prohibited from extending the same privileges to citizens of the United States of other religious persuasions.

[1] For a fuller discussion of the subject matter of this chapter see the article "Switzerland and American Jews," by S. M. Stroock, in *Publications of the American Jewish Historical Society*, No. 11.

[2] "A Compilation of Messages and Papers of the Presidents," by James D. Richardson, Vol. 5, page 98.

This distinction the United States could not countenance and it was clearly the duty of the President to object to it from the beginning. The clause allowing such cantons as desired it to extend equality to Jews could not be considered as satisfactory.

President Fillmore continued:

It is indispensable not only that every privilege granted to any of the citizens of the United States should be granted to all, but also that the grant of such privilege should stand upon the same stipulation and assurance by the whole Swiss Confederation as those of other articles of the convention.

Daniel Webster, then Secretary of State, and Senator Henry Clay, who said that "the treaty was not fit to be made," objected to the above clause, and as a result, the Senate refused to ratify the convention.

Mr. A. Dudley Mann, who represented the United States Government in these negotiations, subsequently negotiated another treaty, which was ratified. The wording of the objectionable clause was changed to read as follows:

The citizens of the United States of America and the citizens of Switzerland shall be admitted and treated upon a footing of reciprocal equality in the two countries, where such admission and treatment shall not conflict with the constitutional or legal provisions, as well Federal as State and Cantonal of the contracting parties.

It will be seen that the right of domicile of non-Christians was still left to the jurisdiction of each canton to decide. Protests against the clause were raised all over the country, by Jews and Christians alike.

While the treaty was still before the Senate a large number of American Jews signed a petition which they sent to that body hoping that the treaty would be modified before ratification. The text of the petition read:[3]

To the honorable the Senate of the United States:

The petition of the undersigned respectfully shows: that they are citizens of the United States professing the Jewish religion, and that their brethren in faith and fellow-citizens are often necessarily

[3] Stroock, *op. cit.*, page 20.

absent in foreign lands. That when so absent they are in very many instances deprived of most of their civil and religious rights, while the citizens and subjects of the lands thus intolerant enjoy, under our laws, equal privileges with our citizens.

Your petitioners therefore pray, that the attention of these Governments may be directed to this want of reciprocity in the rights accorded to foreigners among us, and those extended to our citizens in other countries, and that in its wisdom it will endeavor to obtain for every American citizen abroad, of every creed, a just degree of civil and religious freedom.

At that time, too, a number of Catholic countries in Europe were discriminating against American citizens of the Protestant faith. There was therefore a general demand in the country to secure by treaty for all American citizens under foreign flags the same liberty which is guaranteed "to all citizens of every nation of the whole world who reside under the flag of our union."

There was agitation in both Houses of Congress to the same effect. Resolutions were introduced, special studies were made, and there was ground to believe that the American Government would make a serious effort to obtain equality for its citizens, both Jews and Protestants, while abroad.

In presenting the Jewish petition to the Senate, Senator Lewis Cass of Michigan, said:[4]

MR. PRESIDENT: It affords me much pleasure to present a petition from a number of American citizens of the Hebrew faith, who desire to unite with their Christian fellow-citizens in asking the interposition of the Government to secure to all our countrymen abroad the rights of religious worship. This union, in order to promote the accomplishment of this great object, is a happy illustration of the spirit of equality and toleration which marks our institutions. Persecuted for centuries with bitter hostility, subjected to a tyranny, civil and religious, more oppressive than that endured by any other people, driven from the promised land granted to their forefathers, the separate existence to this day of the children of Israel is a perpetual miracle, establishing the truth of their history as well as of our religion, foretold, as it was, in the earliest period, and seen, as it still is, in the latest. In their migrations they have at length reached a continent, unknown to the patriarchs, by whose rivers they may sit down without weeping, to

[4] *Congressional Globe*, 33d Congress, 1st Session, Vol. 28, Part 2, page 929.

change the language of their Psalmist, even when remembering Zion, and where the law secures equal rights to all, be they Jew or Gentile. Exposed as the members of this persuasion yet are, in portions of Europe and America, both Protestant and Catholic, to the most illiberal prejudices, and to religious disabilities, the position of our citizens abroad who belong to it has peculiar claims to the consideration and interposition of the Government. Beside their legal right to equal protection, there is no portion of our population whose peaceable and law-abiding conduct better proves than theirs does, that they are well entitled to all the privileges secured to every American by our system of Government. I repeat, sir, I am gratified that they are taking part in this great movement, and I trust that ere long, they as well as all our other citizens, sent by the accidents of life to foreign countries, may receive the benefits of it. I present this petition and another of similar import; and, I move that they be referred to the Committee on Foreign Relations.

The petitions were so referred, but they did not prevent the final ratification of the treaty.

On October 31st, 1857, President Buchanan received a Jewish delegation which presented to him a memorial adopted by a national convention of Israelites which had met in Baltimore on October 28 of the same year. The delegation, reporting on the visit to the President, declared that "after listening to the views and objects expressed, and receiving the memorial, the President viewed at some length the principles involved in that treaty; expressed his conviction, that the treaty would never have received the approval of his predecessor, had it been understood in its present effect, and unequivocally promised a speedy and energetic course of action with a view to a remedy, not inconsistent with international faith."[5]

The President, however, was not very successful.

John Appleton, Assistant Secretary of State, though regretting the discrimination against the Jews, yet accepted it as a fact and refused to do anything about it. In a letter to a committee of Jews of Baltimore, he made the following statement:[6]

[5] *The Israelite*, Vol. 4, November 6, 1857.
[6] Stroock, *op. cit.*, page 23.

Undoubtedly in some portions of the [Swiss] Confederation the local laws are less liberal to Israelites than to others, and this is deeply to be regretted; but the Government of the United States has no control over the legislation of a foreign state and can only employ its influence and good offices to relieve the difficulties which such legislation may impose in any given case.

Here it must be noted that the same relations that existed between the Federal Government in Switzerland and the various cantons, which composed it, also existed between the cantons and the respective communes of which they were composed. Thus it was constitutionally possible for a commune to pass and enforce laws which were contrary to the liberal doctrines professed by the mother canton.

After the first treaty with Switzerland failed of ratification in the United States Senate, and during the period when the second was under consideration, Mr. Theodore S. Fay, United States Minister to Switzerland, author of the famous Israelite note, referred to later in this chapter, acquainted the State Department with the treatment American Jews might expect in Switzerland. Also, for the first time, Mr. Gootmann, whose case caused some agitation in the United States, appeared in the diplomatic correspondence between Fay, his Government, and the Swiss Confederation.

Mr. A. H. Gootmann, an American Jewish merchant, was for a time a resident in the municipality of Chaux de Fonds in the canton of Neuchâtel. In August, 1853, in a letter to Mr. Fay, he asked the latter to take such measures as would assure him of the rights of American citizens abroad, which, being "a believer in the Mosaic disposition" were then being denied him. He had been warned twice by the secretary of the municipal council of Chaux de Fonds to leave the commune.

Mr. Fay thereupon wrote the following note to the Federal Council:[7]

[7] House of Representatives, 36th Congress, 1st Session, Executive Document no. 76, page 3. (In following footnotes referred to as "Executive Document.")

[Mr. Fay to the President and Federal Council]

Legation of the United States
Berne, August 31, 1853

The undersigned, minister resident of the United States of America, has the honor to lay before their excellencies, the president and other members of the high federal council, copy of communication from Mr. A. H. Gootmann, who has been by the municipal council of la Chaux de Fonds refused permission to reside in the canton, for the reason that he is an Israelite merchant.

Although the right of a government to deny to strangers the privileges of residing on its territory cannot be disputed, and an article of the federal constitution of Switzerland guarantees the free exercise only of Christian forms of worship, yet the undersigned trusts that the liberal policy of the United States government in permitting every citizen of Switzerland freely to reside on its territory, and pursue under the protection of its laws every field of industry, may be borne in mind and reciprocated.

The undersigned, in soliciting the obliging intervention of the high federal council in favor of the application of his countryman, has the honor to reiterate the assurances of his most distinguished consideration.

THEO. S. FAY

The Federal Council sent a note on the same subject to the canton of Neuchâtel. In their reply, the cantonal authorities pointed to the very liberal principles the canton had adopted in the matter of according permission to foreigners to sojourn and the right of establishment "without giving itself any trouble about the religious creed the applicant may hold." It was pointed out, however, that the municipality of Chaux de Fonds was an exception to the general rule; for reasons peculiar to its geographical position, its industry and population, the municipality refused to allow Jews to settle within its boundaries. What the citizens of Chaux de Fonds feared most was the immigration of Jews from the neighboring Alsace, "said to be of a low description." The position of the commune, it was stated, was supported both by the Federal Council and by international law.

Owing undoubtedly to the intervention of Mr. Fay, Mr. Gootmann was for a time unhampered, and Mr. Fay was able to inform Mr. Marcy, Secretary of State, of the closing of the first phase of the Gootmann case:[8]

[*Mr. Fay to Mr. Marcy*]

Legation of the United States
Berne, February 14, 1854

Sir: I had the honor to communicate in my No. 25, under date Berne, October 17, 1853, a correspondence with the federal council upon the subject of a Mr. Gootmann, an American citizen, who had been expelled by the authorities of Chaux de Fonds, canton of Neufchatel, on the grounds of his being an Israelite merchant.

Subjoined is a letter from Mr. Gootmann, who, it appears, has been permitted to remain at Chaux de Fonds, as I conclude, in consequence of my interposition. I did not reply to him definitively, because I had not received any definite communication from the federal council. I have now advised him (the note annexed) to accept as a favor, without demanding as a right, the permission to remain where he is until the point may be decided by the pending treaty.

I have the honor, sir, to be, with the highest consideration, your obedient servant,

Theo. S. Fay

In other words, the rule as to the rights of foreign Jews in Chaux de Fonds was not changed, but an exception was made in favor of Mr. Gootmann.

Meanwhile, the second treaty was ratified. Mr. Gootmann made another attempt to validate his domicile in Chaux de Fonds. The treaty, however, contained no basis on which such validation could be given. Having made the personal acquaintance of Mr. Gootmann, Mr. Fay again brought his case before the Federal Council in the following letter:[9]

[*Mr. Fay to Swiss Federal Council*]

United States Legation
Berne, March 27, 1856

The undersigned, minister resident of the United States of America, has the honor to ask from their excellencies, the president and other members of the high federal council, their obliging

[8] Executive Document, page 6. (See footnote [7] above.)
[9] *Ibid.*, page 8.

intervention with the government of the canton of Neufchatel in order to obtain for Mr. A. H. Gootmann a *permis de séjour* in that canton. Mr. Gootmann is an American citizen, against whom, except that he is an Israelite, there is not the least objection.

By the annexed certificate it will be seen that he has already transacted his affairs at Chaux de Fonds during five years, and that he enjoys the entire confidence of very respectable persons. He disposes also of sufficient capital for the business in which he is engaged.

It is true that the treaty of 1850 does not grant to Israelites the right of domicil in Switzerland; but considering the character of Mr. Gootmann, and the recommendations which he possesses, the undersigned ventures to hope for a favorable result; and he profits by the occasion to renew to their excellencies, etc.,

THEO. S. FAY

Correspondence about this case continued until 1856, when it seems to have been satisfactorily settled, but the agitation which it occasioned brought up the question of the revision of the existing treaty with Switzerland.

Through the American press Mr. Fay became aware of this agitation and was prompted to write on the subject to the State Department, pointing out that the obnoxious and objectionable clause in the treaty could not be removed without a revision of the federal constitution of Switzerland.

[*Mr. Fay to Mr. Cass*][10]

United States Legation
Berne, October 13, 1857

SIR: * * * * *

I perceive by an American newspaper that there has been a meeting of Jews in the United States upon the subject of our treaty with Switzerland. It may be superfluous to repeat that the obnoxious clause in the treaty was unavoidable without a revision of the federal constitution of Switzerland.

The exclusion of the American Israelites is not even required by the interest of Switzerland. It is true the admission of American Jews would necessitate that of Jews of other nations, and par-

---

[10] Executive Document, page 11. (See footnote [7] above.)

Switzerland.

[*Mr. Fay to the President and Federal Council*]

United States Legation
Berne, December 3, 1857

The undersigned minister resident of the United States has received instructions from his government to call the attention of the high federal council to the treatment occasionally applied to that portion of American citizens professing the Hebrew faith.

The undersigned is aware that certain reasons are supposed to exist for the treatment alluded to, but he believes they will disappear upon examination, and that, while the true material interests of Switzerland would not be impaired by a compliance with the solicitation of his government, it will be found that such compliance is not irreconcilable with existing constitutions and laws.

Before presenting his views, the undersigned has the honor respectfully to request:

1st. The names of the cantons in which restrictions against Israelites have not been abolished.

2nd. What the exact nature of that legislation is, as far as it can be applied to American Israelites.

3rd. If any satisfactory reason exists for refusing to thousands of highly respectable American citizens the reciprocal equality required by the spirit of our treaty, and accorded to all Swiss upon every part of the territory of the United States.

The undersigned profits by the occasion, etc.,

THEO. S. FAY

At that time, early December, 1857, Mr. Fay was already engaged in research on his famous note. He seemed to lay much stress on the possible results to be gained from his researches. Both to Mr. Cass in Washington, and to President Fornerod of Switzerland, he imparted the information that he was working on a note, which was bound to change public opinion in Switzerland, especially in the backward cantons, on the question of the Jews. The warning of Fornerod, that the constitution would still be there, and the knowledge that an earlier attempt along the same lines by the French Government had met with failure, did not dissuade Mr. Fay from continuing his work. Even before the completion of his note, its subject excited great interest among the diplomatic representatives in Berne, and the general populace. Public lecturers chose oppression of Jews as the topic for their lectures. In Berne, Professor Schmid, of the Berne University, expressed regret that Switzerland was among the nations which still preserved anti-Jewish laws, and hoped to see their abolition.

Stimulated by Mr. Fay's action the British Secretary of State for Foreign Affairs, Lord Clarendon, sent the following dispatch to Mr. J. G. R. Gordon, British representative in Switzerland:[14]

[*Lord Clarendon to Mr. Gordon*]

Foreign Office, Dec. 17, 1857

SIR: Her Majesty's government approve the language held by you to the United States Minister at Berne, as reported in your dispatch of the 9th instant, on the subject of the present position of the Jews in Switzerland, and I have to instruct you to take such opportunities as you may think expedient of informing the federal government of the sincere satisfaction with which Her Majesty's government would learn that the disabilities under which the Jews labor in Switzerland, had been modified, if not entirely removed.

I am, etc.,

CLARENDON

The answer to Mr. Fay's request for specific information was late in coming, partly because both the new President, Dr. Furrer, and the Chief of the Department of the Interior were ill.

Although Mr. Staempfli, the Vice-President, was eager to assist, Mr. Fay could not have felt very optimistic. Attempts of England and France in the same direction had failed. A treaty between Switzerland and Persia had not been executed solely because the latter insisted that her Mohammedan subjects be granted equality. These points are cited and Mr. Fay's pessimism are reflected in the following dispatch to Secretary Cass:[15]

[14] Executive Document, page 15. (See footnote [7] above.)
[15] *Ibid.*, page 16.

[*Mr. Fay to Mr. Cass*]

United States Legation
Berne, January 19, 1858

SIR: As I am yet without answer to my note on the Israelites, I called yesterday on the vice president, Mr. Staempfli. The severe illness of the president, Dr. Furrer, and also of Mr. Pioda, chief of the department of the interior, is probably one of the causes of the delay. Mr. Staempfli promised to expedite the matter as far as possible, and represented himself as anxious to promote our design.

I have not much expectation of being able to obtain at this moment all we wish. The subject ought not to be pressed without regard to real difficulties. Persia has recently asked equality for her Mohammedan subjects, and a proposed treaty has consequently fallen through. The same demand in favor of Israelites has been already at different times presented by other governments. Both England and France have been refused, and this fact somewhat complicates the question. It is not one to be solved by too great pressure, which would rather delay than promote the desired purpose. What would the United States government reply should France and England require a change in our Constitution, and what would France and England say if a concession, refused to them, should be instantly accorded to the United States? Supposing Switzerland inclined to yield to our demand, could she do so without danger to herself? Should we be willing to force upon her a precedent which, once recorded, might subject her to similar requirements from other quarters directed against other clauses of her Constitution? In short, sir, you will expect me to conduct the correspondence in view of these considerations without losing sight of our object. Switzerland is justly sensitive as to the interference of foreign powers, and can and will concede more to forbearance than to threats. I have little doubt that the restrictions complained of, if not prevented by imprudent foreign interposition, will disappear in the course of ten years.

After receiving the report of the different cantonal legislatures, I shall endeavor to present the question in so clear a light as to demonstrate that a more liberal course is required by the dignity and even by the material interest of Switzerland herself. I hope also to procure a larger interpretation of the law in favor of our fellow-citizens, that some practical benefit may immediately result.

* * * * *

THEO. S. FAY

Months passed and Mr. Fay was still not in possession of the information he had requested, although he was again assured by the Vice-President that public opinion in Switzerland was changing upon the subject of the restrictions against the Jews, and that there was a certain movement in a more liberal direction. Knowing the existence of considerable sensitiveness to all foreign interference, Mr. Fay had to treat the question with great delicacy. A little more persistence would have surely caused embarrassment in official circles, and this he discreetly chose to avoid. His procedure in this case is well illustrated in the following note to Mr. Cass:[16]

[*Mr. Fay to Mr. Cass*]

United States Legation
Berne, March 9, 1858

Sir: President Furrer being ill, I called this morning upon Vice-President Staempfli to inquire the cause of the delay in answering my note upon the subject of the Israelites, communicated December 3, 1857. He said application had been made to the cantonal governments for the desired information, which had not yet arrived, and which he would place in my possession as soon as possible. He added that public opinion in Switzerland was changing upon the subject of the restrictions complained of. I replied I was sure my government had no intention to make any imperative demand of a nature to embarrass. I should be glad to communicate to it the state of legislation as soon as convenient, and in my note to the federal council I should endeavor to treat the question with all true delicacy, but presenting such suggestions as it seemed to me must promote a speedy general movement in a more liberal direction. There is, as before stated, considerable sensibility upon all foreign interference. I must respect this natural sentiment.

Theo. S. Fay

The more study Mr. Fay gave to the Jewish problem and its implications, the more conscious he became of the great wrong perpetrated against the Jews. He must have felt that all his attempts to ameliorate the condition of American Jews in this small "corner of this earth" were altogether inadequate, and apologizes for what may seem to be his lukewarmness in pressing the matter before the Council.

[16] Executive Document, page 16. (See footnote [7] above.)

[*Mr. Fay to Mr. Cass*][17]

United States Legation
Berne, April 13, 1858

SIR: I have the honor to communicate a note which I have just addressed to the federal council, April 9, on the subject of a new act of intolerance, by Basle-Ville, against an Israelite American citizen, Mr. Sigmund Muhlhauser, whose passport was signed by yourself September 17, 1857. Of his standing and character I have had no proof, but not the least reason to suppose anything derogatory. He applied for permission to reside and carry on his business as optician in Basle, and received for answer copy of a decree of the executive council to the effect that his application could not even be considered from the fact of his being an Israelite. I have the honor to annex copy of this decree, and also of his complaint to me.

The half canton of Basle-Ville occupies a surface of about a German square mile, possesses several communes, and touches on either side France and the Grand Duchy of Baden. One hundred and seven Israelites, by the statistical table, reside there. I have simply presented his case, reserving remarks for a future note.

I have availed myself of the occasion to remind the federal council that I am patiently waiting a reply to my note of December 3, 1857.

I beg your indulgence, sir, for what may seem lukewarmness in my manner of conducting this correspondence. I feel, on the contrary, a particular desire to call the serious attention of Switzerland, her governments and people, to the disgraceful state of this question. In order to do so successfully, I must proceed with great delicacy, avoid any national susceptibility, and anticipate in my note the principal points which can be alleged in reply. It would be useless to deny that they have the law on their side. I must, therefore, only endeavor to show that the law is as much in conflict with the real material interests as it is with the reputation of a free and civilized country.

* * * * *

THEO. S. FAY

Another reason for this "apology" may have been the fact that Mr. Fay learned through the American press, and was later notified, that President Buchanan was personally interested in his attempts before the Federal Council, and,

---

[17] Executive Document, page 18. (See footnote [7] above.)

that he, the President, "indulges the hope that the measures taken by you to secure that result may be successful." This was conveyed to him in the following dispatch from Mr. Cass:

[*Mr. Cass to Mr. Fay*][18]

Department of State
Washington, April 17, 1858

SIR: Your dispatches to No. 282 inclusive have been received. The President learns with pleasure that your efforts in behalf of the American Israelites in Switzerland have not been relaxed. The removal of the restrictions contained in the cantonal laws so oppressive to Jewish citizens of the United States is, as you are aware, a matter which the President has much at heart; and he indulges the hope that the measures taken by you to secure that result may be successful.

I am, etc.,

LEWIS CASS

It must also be noted that Mr. Fay did not and could not demand anything in this matter from the Swiss Government as a right, for the treaty between the United States and Switzerland was very clear on this question. He had to use a much softer tone, because what he asked was a favor, and had to base his arguments on general principles of equity and comity and not upon strictly legal and contractual grounds.

The interest of President Buchanan in the Jewish question was later used as an argument in an interview which Mr. Fay had with President Furrer of the Swiss Confederation. Incidentally, this interview greatly encouraged Mr. Fay in the hope that his efforts would meet with success. Dr. Furrer seemed to recognize the justice and fairness of Mr. Fay's arguments, and even suggested that the American Minister become personally acquainted with the political leaders in the Cantons. He offered personally to introduce him to influential political persons in Basle.

Finally, in May, 1858, after a delay of over six months, Mr. Fay was in possession of the information which he sought.

[18] Executive Document, page 22. (See footnote [7] above.)

From this he learned that, although in most of the cantons, Jews were admitted to carry on business, yet, in a number, restrictions against Jews were still in force, and, to all appearances, ineradicable. Altogether, it was not encouraging to Mr. Fay, after all his efforts on behalf of the Jewish people, to read that in St. Gall, for example, as in a number of other cantons, neither Swiss nor foreign Jews could legally obtain the right of establishment, and that, because of an unreasonable fear of Alsatian Jews, a number of Swiss cantons, especially those bordering on France, still persisted in refusing all Jews the right of establishment. In Basle, there were special laws against the harboring of Jews, and a third of the fine imposed for harboring a Jew went by law to the informer.

The tone and substance of the answers from some of the cantons must have grieved Mr. Fay very deeply, for, in a letter to the President and the Federal Council of May 29, 1858, acknowledging the receipt of all the answers and the accompanying letter of the Council itself, we find what amounts to a threat to the Swiss Government. Mr. Fay wrote:[19]

It is true the United States has no right to interfere in the internal legislation of Switzerland, but it has, undoubtedly, a right to inquire into the value of the treaty, and if it appears that this grievance might, without any comparative inconvenience, be, in a considerable degree, remedied by a simple readiness to examine both sides of the subject, and if Switzerland refuse to show that friendly readiness, it would be proper for the undersigned to lay the case before his government for its consideration, with his opinion that the complaint of the American Israelites is equitable, and grows out of a wrong inflicted upon them without sufficient motive, in defense of which no argument can be used which cannot be shown to be without foundation. . . .

Special objection was taken to the following sentence in the accompanying letter, which read:

Finally, the Swiss federal council permits itself the further observation, that its consul general at Washington has been instructed to inform the government of the North American free

[19] Executive Document, page 29. (See footnote [7] above.)

States, that in future it would be useless to attempt to procure the right of establishment for any Jew in the Swiss cantons, for that any reclamation on that point would thenceforward be rejected.

Through Secretary of State Cass, Mr. Fay asked Captain Jonas P. Levy of Washington, D. C., for the following information:

How many Jews are there in the United States; what wealth do they represent; to what classes of society do they belong; are they in possession of offices of public trust; how many and what kinds of Jews could avail themselves of the opportunity to settle in Switzerland should this country secure them the equality which they enjoy in the United States; in what other countries are the Israelites received as in the United States; and finally, what countries have abandoned, or are in the course of abandoning an illiberal policy with regards to the Jews?

In his reply to Mr. Cass, dated July 12, 1858,[20] Captain Levy informed the Secretary of State that there were at that time about 400,000 Jews in the United States, half of them natural-born; that all professions and trades were open to them; that many of them held the highest offices of trust under the Government; and that similar treatment was accorded them in nearly every part of the world where freedom and religious liberty exist.

The writing of the Israelite note consumed more time than Mr. Fay had originally expected. In addition to research, study and reflection, he had consultations with many persons. Especially interested in the condition of the Jews in Alsace, since the Jews of this French province served as an excuse for anti-Jewish laws, Mr. Fay paid a visit to Alsace with Rabbi Nordman of Basle, "a learned Israelite rabbi." Mr. Fay hoped with the information given to him by the rabbi to be able to destroy all prejudices against Alsatian Jews, so that "no Swiss authority will ever dare to advance that objection again to an argument." Mr. Fay went to all sorts of sources for information. A Christian missionary for the conversion of Jews supplied him with the information that, in a number of cantons,

[20] Executive Document, page 57. (See footnote [7] above.)

Jews were not permitted to bury their dead in the territory under the jurisdiction of the canton, and must transfer them across the Swiss frontier. When informed of this cruel law by the American Minister, President Furrer was quite shocked.

Mr. Fay's enthusiasm and tireless work on behalf of the rights of American Jews in Switzerland, and of the Jewish people as a whole, may be observed from a reading of the following two notes to Mr. Cass:

[*Mr. Fay to Mr. Cass*][21]

United States Legation
Berne, October 28, 1858

SIR: The "*Berner Zeitung*" of 26th instant mentions with disapprobation and even contempt the illiberality of the government of Thurgau in having recently refused the right of establishment to another Israelite, said to be an American citizen. As this person has not addressed a complaint to the legation, I have thought it best to take no official notice of it, for I wish to avoid making violent demands which we have not legal right to make, and which would only irritate and diminish the probability of a satisfactory termination of my correspondence.

The printed paragraph reads as follows:

"*The Council of State of the canton of Thurgau has just refused the right of domicile to an Israelite pleading his American citizenship. The Thurgovian Christianity must be in a very tottering state to be frightened by a son of Abraham.*"

Some time ago I received a copy of the "*Israelite*," an American newspaper, containing an article upon the Swiss restrictions against the Israelites, with an account of the visit of the editors of the "*Israelite*" and the "*Deborah*," and of other Jewish gentlemen, to the State Department in August last, and an extract from my dispatches, with the *résumé* forwarded by me of the legislation of the cantons with regard to the Jews.

I thought it proper to show this to President Furrer, who had it translated and placed upon the table of the federal council. The article contained some biting remarks in language the most unreserved; but I thought it better to show it myself rather than

---

[21] Executive Document, page 57. (See footnote [7] above.)

it should be sent by any one else. I have no doubt copies of it will be communicated to the cantonal government, and that a good effect will be produced, although not so good as if the language had been less strong than the arguments.

I had an interview with President Furrer this morning. I told him I was deeply interested in bringing this matter to a fair conclusion. There was much to be said on the Swiss side, I knew; but there was much also on the American side. I was busily preparing my note. He had seen my solicitude to avoid indiscretion in asking of Switzerland anything more than was just, wise, consistent with her independence, and required by her material interests. He said there was a very strong spirit in some of the cantons, particularly in Basle-Campagne, and began telling how many Israelites there were in Switzerland. I told him I believed I knew and had counted nearly every one; that the question might be easily settled to the satisfaction of the American government and of all the respectable Israelites of the United States. He said there was the constitution, and there was the absolute sovereignty, on that point, of the cantonal governments. I replied I could not feel satisfied that the question would be properly examined, when my remarks to the federal council were always met by the plea of incompetency; and I inquired whether it would be agreeable for me to negotiate directly with the cantonal governments. He said, no, not officially, not in writing; but there could be no objection to personal intercourse. I replied — supposing the cantonal magistrates to be reasonable men — I thought they would not even desire to refuse the just demands of the American government, when they plainly understood what it was and what it was not. He said it was very probable I could do much by endeavors of that kind.

I shall present my note to the federal council, and then, if not, sir, instructed to the contrary, undertake to press my views personally upon the leading magistrates of the most illiberal cantons. Our friends on the other side of the Atlantic must have patience, and understand that nothing can be done by precipitation, and still less by bullying. Switzerland in the matter stands upon her constitution and laws, and the United States government would be the last to use intimidation. We must influence by reason. This, I believe, can be done in the way I propose. One paragraph, like that above cited from a popular Swiss newspaper, pointing the finger of ridicule, helps our cause more than any threatening note I could write.

I have, etc.,

THEO. S. FAY

[*Mr. Fay to Mr. Cass*]²²

United States Legation
Berne, November 9, 1858

Sir: * * * * *

The Israelite question unfolds itself with continually increasing interest. I am earnestly engaged on my note, in which I propose to hold up the entire question so that its true character cannot be denied. The mouth of all foreign governments and preceding treaty-makers has been till now closed by a plea of the Alsacian Jews. I think, after the *renseignements* which I am now collecting, no Swiss authority will ever dare to advance that objection again as an argument; and I am more and more of the opinion that it may become expedient to denounce our treaty, until the expunction of the offensive clause.

I propose a visit to Alsacia, (but six or eight hours' distant by railroad,) partly that I may examine with my own eyes, and partly that I may consult Mr. Nordman, a learned Israelite rabbi, by whose assistance, I understand, I may complete my table of Jewish statistics.

I have, etc.,

THEO. S. FAY

The note was finally completed in May, and presented to the Swiss Government. This document, which is written in a strong and convincing manner, started with a review of the whole correspondence on this question so far, and an analysis of the restrictive laws against Jews in the cantons. Of the twenty-four cantons, he found ten to be illiberally disposed, seven absolutely restrictive, and an equal number absolutely free. It is interesting to note that, although the federal constitution speaks of the Christian religion as against all other religions, the restrictive laws of the cantons generally refer only to the Hebrew religion. Turkish, Persian and Chinese evidently were not exposed to the same disability as were Jews. Then he enumerated all the arguments and reasons presented as an explanation or justification of the anti-Jewish policy. Of these, he cited seven, namely:

---

²² Executive Document, page 60. (See footnote ⁷ above.)

the federal constitution; the treaty; the incompetency of
the Federal Council; the impropriety of a foreign government
interfering with the legislative power; the existence of an
institution in the United States (slavery) which appears
as strange to Switzerland as her Israelite legislation can
appear to people of the United States; Christianity; and
finally special local circumstances, such as general prejudice
against the Israelites, and the danger of an Israelite inunda-
tion from the neighboring countries, especially Alsace.

Mr. Fay discussed each point individually, showing its
falseness or inapplicability. Thus, the constitution guarantees to the governments, federal and cantonal, a right to
refuse establishment to all except Christians, but it does
not impose an obligation to that effect; therefore, the
cantons could not plead the constitution as a reason for
their inability to do a thing, which the constitution does
not forbid them to do. The same is true of the argument
based on the treaty concluded between the United States
and Switzerland, which requires a mutually liberal interpretation of the constitutional and legal obstacles to reciprocal equality; here he points out that in a number of cantons,
the laws against the Jews are contrary to their own constitutions, which guarantee liberty of conscience, liberty of
commerce and industry, liberty of opinion.

Never, said Mr. Fay, did he demand that the Federal
Council should force the cantons to change their laws.
All he asked was that it be the medium through which he
could present to the cantons the request of the American
Government on the question of Jewish disabilities. He felt
sure that he had committed no impropriety in presenting
his case to the Swiss people, though he insisted that "no
nation is so independent with regard to other nations as to
have a right to object when a friendly government, not
with arrogance, but with respect, points out injuries inflicted and solicits, if possible, redress."

He then directed attention to the fallacy of the argument
based upon the institution of slavery to which many Swiss
nationals were opposed by saying that, first, it had no con-

nection with the subject under discussion, and then, also, no Swiss coming to the United States was injured by that institution.

The sixth argument, the one based on Christianity, caused Mr. Fay to express himself as follows:

Of all the errors of the last eighteen centuries there is not a greater than the supposition that any wrong or insult to the Hebrew nation is commanded or justified by the Bible.

On the contrary, he said the Jews are to be regarded as the chosen people and wrongs inflicted upon them are sins in the eyes of God.

The principal objection to the free entry of Jews was the fear of a large immigration of Alsatian Jews. This fear, Mr. Fay said, was not based on fact, and he went on to demonstrate his point by statistics and unanswerable arguments. Whenever Jews in Switzerland, or around it, have resorted to immoral modes of gaining their bread, it was because they were driven to it by the policy of the authorities, on whose shoulders the blame should fall. Swiss practice was, indeed, contrary to the general experience of other civilized nations, where petty jealousy (*concurrence de botique*) and old hatreds did not stand in the way of enlightened policy and international comity.

A corrected copy of this note was sent to Washington in June, 1859,[23] and, with the permission of the State Department, Mr. Fay had this note printed in the French and German languages. Very favorable comments were showered upon it and its author, and the first edition was soon exhausted.

Favorable results in a number of cantons followed. His old friend, Dr. Furrer, informed Mr. Fay in October 1859, that "an immense majority of the Council (of Zurich) is disposed to change the legislation respecting the Israelites in the interest of humanity and progress." Many other cantons followed, and gradually, one after another removed all

[23] For full text of the note see Executive Document, page 67.

restrictions against the Jews. The following dispatch from
President Furrer to Mr. Fay relates to the Zurich canton:[24]

[*Dr. Furrer to Mr. Fay*]

Berne, October 25, 1859

Honorable Sir: With the present, I have the satisfaction of
transmitting a debate in the general council of Zurich, by which
you will see that an immense majority of the Council is disposed
to change the legislation respecting the Israelites, in the interest
of humanity and progress. Let us hope that this example will not
be without consequences.

Be as good as to accept, honorable sir, the assurance of my distinguished consideration.

D. Furrer

In 1861, as a result of a change in administration in
Washington, Mr. Fay was succeeded by Mr. George G.
Fogg, who was asked by Mr. Seward, the new Secretary of
State, to continue the efforts to remove restrictions against
Jews begun by Mr. Fay, and to "take such steps as you may
deem judicious and legal to advance the benevolent object
in question."[25]

In a dispatch of April 16, 1864, Mr. Fogg informed Mr.
Seward that the Federal Council was now disposed to modify
their treaty with the United States so as to concede equal
rights and protection to all citizens of the United States,
irrespective of their race or religion.[26]

It was not, however, until 1874 that the new Swiss Constitution finally established religious liberty, and made the
question of the treatment of aliens a federal matter. There
is no doubt that the efforts of the United States, as exercised
through Mr. Fay, were a strong contributing factor to the
modernization and liberalization of the Swiss federal system
of government.

[24] Executive Document, page 99. (See footnote [7] above.)
[25] *Occident*, Vol. 19, page 322.
[26] Diplomatic Correspondence, Vol. 4, page 392.

XI. AUSTRIA

Like most other European governments, the Government of the Austro-Hungarian Empire had extended, in the year 1848, civil and religious equality to its Jewish subjects. This equality, however, was never complete. The question of a Jew's *Hoffähigkeit* (fitness for attendance at court), admittedly a local one and not subject to international intercession, became an international problem causing serious friction between the Governments of the United States of America and Austria-Hungary.

Early in May, 1885, President Cleveland appointed Mr. Anthony M. Keiley of Virginia Envoy Extraordinary and Minister Plenipotentiary of the United States at Vienna. Baron Schaeffer, Minister of the Austro-Hungarian Empire at Washington, was notified of this appointment by Secretary of State Bayard in the following note:[1]

[*Mr. Bayard to Baron Schaeffer*]

Department of State
Washington, May 4, 1885

BARON:

I have the honor to inform you that the President has appointed Anthony M. Keiley, of Virginia, one of our distinguished citizens, to succeed Mr. Francis as the envoy extraordinary and minister plenipotentiary of the United States at Vienna.

In communicating this intelligence, I desire to bespeak for Mr. Keiley, through your kind offices, that favorable reception at Vienna which is due to his merits as an American citizen of great ability and character.

I improve, etc.,

T. F. BAYARD

[1] Foreign Relations, 1885, page 48.

Without awaiting the expected word from Vienna informing Washington that Mr. Keiley was persona grata, the appointed minister left the United States.

Mr. Keiley was on the high seas on his way to Paris where
he was to entrain for Vienna, when, on May 9, Baron
Schaeffer delivered to Secretary Bayard a telegram from
Vienna, intimating that there prevailed at Vienna "scruples
against his choice." The text of the telegram follows:[2]

[*Count Kalnoky to Baron Schaeffer*]

Vienna, May 8, 1885

We regret the nomination of Mr. Keiley as minister plenipotentiary and envoy extraordinary to the imperial court and his sudden
departure from America, as here, too, like in Rome, *prevail scruples
against this choice.*

Please direct *in the most friendly way* the attention of the American
Government to the generally existing diplomatic practice to ask
previously to any nomination of a foreign minister the *agréement*
(consent) of the Government to which he is accredited.

You are therefore requested to *earnestly entreat* them that the
newly-nominated minister may not reach Vienna before our confidential consent to his nomination has taken place.

The position of a foreign envoy wedded to a Jewess by civil marriage would be untenable and even impossible in Vienna.

COUNT KALNOKY

When Count Kalnoky was informed from Washington that
Mr. Keiley would not be stopped en route to Vienna, he informed Mr. Bayard that "this nomination will doubtless be
attended with great difficulties, and the new minister will
find himself in a most painful situation upon his arrival in
Vienna."

In a lengthy letter to Baron Schaeffer, dated May 18,
Secretary Bayard, after reviewing the events up to that date,
protested as follows:[3]

[2] Foreign Relations, 1885, page 48.
[3] *Ibid.*

The reason, and the only reason, given for the indisposition of the Government of Austria-Hungary to receive Mr. Keiley, stated in the telegram and repeated by you verbally to me, consists in the allegation that his wife was "a Jewess," and that his marriage to one of that faith would render his position, in the words of the telegram, "untenable and even impossible in Vienna."

On Saturday, the 16th day of May, at 4 p.m., I received your communication of that date as follows:

> I have the honor to inform you that, in reply to the communication addressed by me to His Majesty's Government that Mr. Keiley would not be stopped *en route* to Vienna, Count Kalnoky has instructed me to let you know that this nomination will doubtless be attended with great difficulties, and the new minister will find himself placed in a most painful situation upon his arrival in Vienna.

The question thus raised by your government involves principles of the greatest importance, and has no precedent as yet discoverable to me in modern times and in intercourse between friendly nations; and having submitted the matter to the consideration of the President, I am instructed by him to inform your Government, through you, that the ground upon which it is announced, that the usual ceremonial courtesy and formal respect are to be withheld from this envoy of the United States to your Government, that is to say, because his wife is alleged or supposed by your Government to entertain a certain religious faith, and to be a member of a certain religious sect, cannot be assented to by the Executive of the Government of the American people, but is and must be emphatically and promptly denied.

The supreme law of this land expressly declares that "no religious test shall ever be required as a qualification to any office or public trust under the United States," and by the same authority it is declared that "Congress shall make no law respecting an establishment of religion or prohibiting the free exercise thereof."

This is a government of laws, and all authority exercised must find its measure and warrant thereunder.

It is not within the power of the President nor of the Congress, nor of any judicial tribunal in the United States, to take or even hear testimony, or in any mode to inquire into or decide upon the religious belief of any official, and the proposition to allow this to be done by any foreign Government is necessarily and *a fortiori* inadmissable.

To suffer an infraction of this essential principle would lead to a disfranchisement of our citizens because of their religious belief, and thus impair or destroy the most important end which our constitution of Government was intended to secure. Religious liberty is the chief cornerstone of the American system of government, and provisions for its security are imbedded in the written charter and interwoven in the moral fabric of its laws.

Anything that tends to invade a right so essential and sacred must be carefully guarded against, and I am satisfied that my countrymen, ever mindful of the suffering and sacrifices necessary to obtain it, will never consent to its impairment for any reason or under any pretext whatsoever.

In harmony with this essential law is the almost equally potential unwritten law of American society that awards respect and delicate consideration to the women of the United States and exacts deference in the treatment at home and abroad of the mothers, wives, and daughters of the Republic.

The case we are now considering is that of an envoy of the United States, unquestionably fitted, morally and intellectually, and who has been duly accredited to a friendly Government, towards which he is thoroughly well affected; who in accordance with the laws of this country, has long since contracted and has maintained an honorable marriage, and whose presence near the foreign Government in question is objected to by its agents on the sole ground that his wedded wife is alleged to entertain a religious faith which is held by very many of the most honored and valued citizens of the United States.

It is not believed by the President that a doctrine and practice so destructive of religious liberty and freedom of conscience, so devoid of catholicity, and so opposed to the spirit of the age in which we live can for a moment be accepted by the great family of civilized nations or be allowed to control their diplomatic intercourse.

Certain it is, it will never, in my belief, be accepted by the people of the United States, nor by any administration which represents their sentiments.

Permit me, therefore, being animated only by the sincerest desire to strengthen the ties of friendship and mutual respect between the Governments we respectively represent, most earnestly and respectfully to crave careful consideration of this note, and to request your Government to reconsider the views you have communicated to me in respect of the possible reception of Mr. Keiley on the mission of amity and mutual advantage which, in the amplest good faith, he was selected by this Government to perform.

Into the religious belief of its envoy, or that of any member of his family, neither this Government nor any officer thereof, as I have shown you, has any right or power to inquire, or to apply any test whatever, or to decide such question, and to do so would constitute an infraction of the express letter and an invasion of the pervading spirit of the supreme law of this land.

To the contention that there was a breach of diplomatic practice by the United States in that it did not follow in this case the usual custom of waiting for the consent of the accredited government before announcing the nomination, Mr. Bayard devoted the following note:[4]

[*Mr. Bayard to Baron Schaeffer*]

Department of State
Washington, May 20, 1885

BARON:

With reference to the note which I had the honor to address to you on the 18th instant concerning the appointment of the Hon. A. M. Keiley as the envoy extraordinary and minister plenipotentiary of the United States near the Government of Austria-Hungary, I have now the honor to present to you the view of this Government with respect to a point which had been advanced by your Government, and which I had, in preparing that note, set aside for more convenient examination.

In the telegram sent to you by Count Kalnoky, on the 8th instant, in relation to Mr. Keiley, a translation of which you kindly handed to me, I note that he desires the attention of this Government to be directed to what he designates at the generally existing diplomatic practice to ask, previously to any nomination of a minister abroad, the consent of the Government to which he is to be accredited.

In the conversation we held at the time you delivered that translation to me I stated to you that such practice did not prevail with this Government, nor was such consent sought in advance of its nominations of envoys to foreign states.

Upon reflection the importance of the question becomes apparent. Consequently, I have made careful search for the precedents and practice in this Department for the last ninety years. The result enables me to inform you that no case can be found in the annals of this Government in which the acceptability of an envoy from the United States was inquired about or ascertained in advance of his appointment to the mission for which he was chosen.

[4] Foreign Relations, 1885, page 51.

Whilst the practice to which Count Kalnoky refers may, in a limited degree, prevail among European states, yet in this respect the exceptions are very numerous, and there are important reasons why, in this country, the practice should never have been adopted, and why its adoption would not be practical or wise.

Our system of frequently recurring elections at regular and stated periods provides, and was intended to provide, an opportunity for the influence of public opinion upon those to whom the administration of public affairs has been intrusted by the people temporarily, and for a fixed time only, on the expiration of which an opportunity for a change in its agents and policies is thus afforded.

The affiliation in sentiment between a political administration thus defeated at the polls and a foreign nation closely interested in maintaining certain international policies and lines of political conduct, might render it difficult for an administration, elected for the very purpose of producing a change of policy, to procure the consent of the foreign Government to the appointment of agents whose views were in harmony with the latest and prevailing expression of public opinion as the result of popular election.

As this Government has never adopted the policy of employing professional diplomatists specially dedicated to the duties of the service, and as it has no titled or privileged class to select from for the performance of such duties, it is constrained to choose its representatives abroad from those who have been bred to other pursuits. In following this course, care is taken to secure persons of intelligence and standing, believed to be worthy of the confidence of their own Government and who would not be likely to offend the susceptibilities of society or of the authorities of the foreign country. The choice of such representatives may not invariably have been wise, but I will venture to say that it has been in the main as nearly so as human fallibility will allow.

If, however, upon the announcement of a mission, the Government to which the chosen envoy is to be sent objects to him, and declines to receive him on the ground of some vague report to his discredit — probably originating in the disappointment of personal rivalry or in envy — it may result in creating an issue founded upon retaliation, and thus permit petty personal objections to seriously embarrass important public affairs, and, perhaps, in the end, prevent the accrediting of a representative of either Government. This to us would be especially undesirable in respect to Austria-Hungary, one of the most ancient and respected Governments in Europe, to which the United States are bound by many lasting ties of amity.

Permit me to observe, here, that, whilst the wise and time-honored custom of this Republic precluded the prior submission of the President's choice of his agent to the approval of the Government you represent, yet I availed myself of the earliest opportunity to courteously acquaint you, by my note of the 4th instant, and your Government directly by means of an instruction sent the same day to the United States legation at Vienna, of the choice and appointment of Mr. Keiley to that mission, and to bespeak for him, through your kind offices, that favorable reception at Vienna due to his merits as an American citizen of great ability and character. In so doing, I followed with pleasure the common usage of this Government on such occasions, and one which in many instances — although I find numerous exceptions — has been observed by other Governments towards this.

It is hoped, in view of the foregoing considerations, that His Majesty the Emperor of Austria and King of Hungary will find in the appointment of Mr. Keiley as envoy extraordinary and minister plenipotentiary of the United States no sufficient ground to reject him in that character because of His Majesty's sanction not having previously been asked.

Accept, etc.,

T. F. BAYARD

Obviously the Austrian Government could not base its refusal to receive Mr. Keiley on the pretext of a diplomatic breach of doubtful value. Also, it was not willing to let it rest on the sole fact that Mrs. Keiley was of Jewish extraction. To take such a stand openly would expose the Austrian Government to attack from liberals at home and abroad, and, what is more important, would prove altogether insufficient and even obnoxious to the Government of the United States. In consequence of these considerations, the Austrian Government was forced to change its line of defense. Instead of insisting solely upon the breach of diplomatic practice or the alleged religion of the appointee's wife, a new flaw was discovered in the political past of Mr. Keiley, and this became the subject of prolonged diplomatic discussions and correspondence.

This new argument against Mr. Keiley is brought out in the following note to Mr. Bayard:[5]

[5] Foreign Relations, 1885, page 55.

[Baron Schaeffer to Mr. Bayard]

Washington, June 11, 1885

Sir: Referring to your notes of the 18th and 20th of May last, I have the honor to inform you that these papers have been laid before Count Kalnoky, and that I have been instructed by his excellency to inform you, confidentially, that His Majesty's Government must absolutely decline to make your deductions the basis of a discussion with the Government of the United States, upon religious liberty and diplomatic law.

In Austria-Hungary, as well as in the United States, the constitution grants entire liberty to all forms of religious worship. *Our objections to Mr. Keiley's appointment as minister of the United States to the Imperial Court are founded upon want of political tact evinced on his part on a former occasion, in consequence of which a friendly power declined to receive him; and upon the certainty that his domestic relations preclude that reception of him by Vienna society, which we judge desirable for the representative of the United States with which power we wish to continue the friendly relations existing between the two Governments.*

Count Kalnoky adds that Keiley's rather sudden appointment and abrupt departure cannot be regarded very considerate proceedings, that his objections to said nomination remain in full force, and that he feels bound to express the repeated wish that Mr. Keiley may not arrive in Vienna just now.

Accept, etc.,

Schaeffer

The reference in Baron Schaeffer's letter to Mr. Keiley's "want of political tact" was to the fact that, at a meeting of Catholics in Virginia, in 1871, Mr. Keiley spoke in support of a resolution protesting against the invasion of the Papal States by King Victor Emanuel, which, the resolution declared was "a crime against solemn treaties and against the independence of the head of the Church on earth."

Here it must be added that Mr. Keiley was first appointed to represent the United States at Rome. But when Rome refused to receive him, as personally unacceptable to the King of Italy, the prerogative of Italy to deny consent was recognized by the United States, and Mr. Keiley thereupon resigned his commission.

The phrase "just now," at the end of Baron Schaeffer's letter caused Mr. Bayard to inquire whether only a temporary delay was intended or whether the Austrian Government's refusal to receive him was to be taken as final. And, in reply to the new objection against Mr. Keiley, the Secretary said: "I do not feel called upon to discuss [it], because it seems difficult to imagine the basis for such an objection to a gentleman who has as yet never been in Europe nor held official relations to any foreign state."

Meanwhile, the American Ambassador in Paris, Mr. McLane, was asked from Washington to inform Mr. Keiley of the complications that had ensued subsequent to his departure, and to ask him to remain in Paris until the matter would be settled. This information was given in a letter delivered to Mr. Keiley at the railroad station in Paris, where he was about to board a train for Vienna. Mr. John M. Francis, who was to be replaced by Mr. Keiley, continued serving as the United States Minister; he now enters this famous case in a rather curious role. Still another fault was now discovered in the diplomatic qualification of Mr. Keiley, as will be seen from the following note of Mr. Francis:[6]

[*Mr. Francis to Mr. Bayard*]
(Extract)

Legation of the United States
Vienna, June 17, 1885

MY DEAR MR. SECRETARY:

Calling at the foreign office yesterday, it was intimated to me by Mr. Szögyényi, chief of section, minister (*sic*) of foreign affairs, that serious objections had been made by the Austrian Government to Mr. Keiley, which would render his recognition here as my successor extremely inconvenient. He said a friendly Government, a near neighbor, had objected to him as the United States representative at its court, and its views had found earnest expression here since the President had named him as United States minister to Austria-Hungary. The alleged fact that his wife was a Jewess did not influence the judgment of His Majesty's Government in the premises, for Austria is tolerant and liberal in respect

[6] Foreign Relations, 1885, page 28.

of religious matters; but it cannot prescribe society usage, which might be unpleasant in that regard.

I said in response to these observations that I deeply regretted the existence of this feeling entertained on this subject, but of course it could not be expected that I would enter into discussion concerning it. . . .

I am, etc.,

JOHN M. FRANCIS

Through all the discussion of this case, one can discover the Austrian Government's attempt to keep underground its real objections to Mr. Keiley, namely, that his wife was of Jewish blood and therefore *unhoffähig*. With any other power a mere hint that Mr. Keiley was not wanted would have been sufficient. It was unfortunate for the Austrian Government to come up against a government which was not willing to sacrifice the sanctity of its constitution to a diplomatic nicety. In a conversation with Mr. Francis, Count Kalnoky declared that if the case were reversed and it were the government of the United States which had raised objections to the appointment of a minister proposed by the Government of Austria-Hungary, the latter would not have failed to accept the objections and would have taken appropriate action without entering into a discussion before the world. "We would say the Government of the United States is a judge of this matter for itself; it is not for us to make up that judgment." He asked that the Government of Austria-Hungary be given the same consideration. This pleading could not help but fall upon deaf ears. The difference between the points of view of the respective governments on the meaning of religious equality was too great to be bridged by an appeal to "good feelings" and "kind relations."

The Vienna press took up the subject and treated its development at great length. Needless to say, the position of the Austrian Government was defended. Even the *Neue Freie Presse* justified the refusal on the ground that the acceptance of Keiley would affect the susceptibilities of King Humbert of Italy. Mr. Francis rightly suspected that the tone of these articles was given at the Foreign Office. None of the newspapers even suggested that the alleged

Jewish descent of Mrs. Keiley was ever considered a factor in the rejection of her husband as envoy. The *Neue Freie Presse* raised the case to a place in the high politics of the time. It commented thus: "This Keiley case is a barometer which shows that the desire and inclination exists between Vienna and Rome to leave nothing undone to strengthen the friendship between the two courts."

Incidentally, there is reason to believe that Mr. Francis was not as strong in his protest as he might have been; though one must come to this conclusion only by reading between the lines, for at no time did he directly recommend the withdrawal of Mr. Keiley; yet one wonders what was the nature of the few paragraphs deleted from the official publication, but to which he calls attention in a letter to Mr. Bayard, of June 24th, 1885, of which the concluding paragraph reads: "I have only to add that a sense of duty impels me to call your attention again to my confidential communication of the 17th instant, and, especially to the three last paragraphs of that letter." As a matter of fact, the whole brunt of defending the attitude of the United States in this matter fell on the able shoulders of the Secretary of State, who bore it both courageously and with dignity.

In a letter to Mr. Francis of July 1, 1885, Mr. Bayard found it necessary again to go over the whole series of events up to that date. In the recital one may discover a veiled admonition by the Secretary of State to the envoy at Vienna, that the facts warrant stronger representation at the court of the Emperor than they had received so far. From this letter, the following quotations are extracted:[7]

[*Mr. Bayard to Mr. Francis*]

Department of State
Washington, July 1, 1885

Sir: I received yesterday your personal letter of the 17th ultimo. As the matter of Mr. Keiley's recognition, to which it partly relates, has been the occasion of prolonged correspondence here with the

[7] Foreign Relations, 1885, page 32.

Austro-Hungarian minister, I treat the two opening paragraphs of your letter as officially on file, and give it answer in this form for your guidance in dealing with the subject with the representatives of the Austro-Hungarian Government.

The action of that Government in respect of the estimable gentleman appointed to be your successor has been marked by unusual features, some of them of an unpleasing character.

Early in March last Mr. Keiley had been nominated by the President and confirmed by the Senate as minister to Italy; and some weeks thereafter expressions of objection by the Italian Government were conveyed to me by Baron Fava, its minister to the United States. The objection alleged was based upon a speech made by Mr. Keiley in 1871 on the occasion of a public meeting held at Richmond, Va., to give expression to the sentiments of certain Roman Catholic citizens of that place in relation to the then pending conflict between Victor Emanuel and the Vatican. Because of those utterances the present Italian Government discovered and averred that Mr. Keiley was to them *persona non grata.*

Upon learning their objection Mr. Keiley returned his commission to the President, who forthwith appointed him to the mission to Austria-Hungary.

Mr. Keiley had then already made all his preparations to go to Rome, and his family and personal effects were in New York ready for embarkation, so that he left at once for his new post at Vienna

The diplomatic intercourse of this Government is intended to be conducted towards foreign powers in directness and simple good faith. Having no corps of professionally educated diplomatists, we select, as has been done in the instance of Mr. Keiley, an intelligent and upright citizen of high personal character to represent the honor and interests of our country near a foreign Government. This envoy is believed to be thoroughly worthy and entirely friendly to the Government and people to whom he is accredited. We have had no traditional causes of misunderstanding or wounded susceptibilities with the Government of Austria-Hungary, and Mr. Keiley having never before been accredited to any foreign power, the suggestion of Count Kalnoky that he shows "want of political tact" is therefore wholly without color of reason or basis of fact.

* * * * *

The Government of Italy has exercised its own discretion in respect of receiving an envoy from the Government of the United States, and there the matter should be concluded so far as that Government is concerned. . . .

It would appear intolerable were the good relations and diplomatic intercourse of the United States with Austria-Hungary to be thus embarrassed and obstructed by the special prejudices of any third Government or of those who may represent such Government in foreign courts.

* * * * *

Desiring earnestly that the amicable relations which have so long existed between these two Governments and their peoples should be strengthened and not strained, I hope you will frankly convey the purport of this instruction to the Government of Austria-Hungary, in order that all objection to the friendly reception of Mr. Keiley may be withdrawn and a condition of feeling which I shall deplore but which I believe is likely to follow persistence in his rejection for the causes, or rather want of causes, stated, may be averted.

Mr. Keiley is now in Paris. Should you have occasion to address him you can do so in care of Minister McLane.

I will ask you to present your letter of recall after you have had your interview with the minister for foreign affairs in relation to Mr. Keiley. You will thereupon turn over the legation to the secretary, Mr. Strong, as chargé d'affaires *ad interim,* and he can act in that capacity until he is relieved, either by Mr. Keiley, or by the arrival of a new secretary of legation, to whom he will relinquish both his regular office and his temporary charge.

You will advise me, briefly by telegraph, the result.

I am, etc.,

T. F. BAYARD

Eventually, Mr. James Fenner Lee replaced Mr. Francis in the negotiations, which continued and were to be concluded one way or another with the arrival of Baron Schaeffer from Washington. Baron Schaeffer, incidentally, was not to return to his post at Washington, for he had been so indiscreet as to deliver his instructions in writing when better diplomacy demanded that he deliver them orally. Hence, on his return to Vienna for consultation on the pending issue, his superiors suddenly discovered that he was too ill to go back to his mission in the United States.

On August 4, 1885, Mr. Lee wired Washington that Count Kalnoky had finally decided that he could not receive Mr. Keiley, and asked that the United States appoint another minister. In a conversation with Mr. Lee, duly reported to Mr. Bayard in a communication of August 6, Count

Kalnoky reiterated that the objections to Mr. Keiley did not involve in any manner the question of liberty of conscience, for in this respect Austria is as liberal as the United States. But there was no doubt that anti-Semitism in Vienna was a fact and "a person of proximate Semitic descent would be excluded both by the social and diplomatic circles of Vienna," and furthermore, that the fact was beyond the control of the Government.

It is worthy of note that Count Kalnoky conceded that he had not been approached on this subject by the Italian Ambassador, and the alleged insult to King Humbert of Italy was purely a product of the imagination of the Austro-Hungarian Minister of Foreign Affairs. It should also be added, parenthetically, that the Emperor, Francis Joseph, though kept informed of developments in the Keiley case by his Minister, had not expressed any individual opinion concerning it, leaving the final decision to him.

Lest the case of the United States be misunderstood, and the argument be advanced that the Washington Government went out of its way to impose Mr. Keiley upon an unwilling friendly government, Mr. Bayard informed the new Chargé d'Affaires that such an interpretation would be wrong and contrary to the facts. He again reviewed the facts and arguments of the whole case, in a letter which, because of its relevance and forcefulness, is here given in full:[8]

[*Mr. Bayard to Mr. Lee*]

Department of State
Washington, August 31, 1885

SIR: Your telegram, dated the 4th instant, and your dispatch, No. 127, of the 6th instant, have duly informed me of the final and deliberate decision of the Government of Austria-Hungary, communicated to you by Count Kalnoky in your interview with him on the 4th instant, not to receive the Hon. Anthony M. Keiley as the envoy extraordinary and minister plenipotentiary of this Government.

The reasons or causes which are avowed to have led the Government of Austria-Hungary to this conclusion may be found in the

[8] Foreign Relations, 1885, page 38.

correspondence heretofore exchanged, and it is not my design to restate the straight-forward efforts of the United States to send a competent and worthy representative of American interests and feelings near the Government of Austria-Hungary.

It may, however, be proper here to note that the United States never pressed Mr. Keiley upon Austria-Hungary nor have they insisted upon his acceptance. His Imperial and Royal Majesty's Government, on learning of Mr. Keiley's appointment, stated certain objections and invited the Government of the United States to admit their sufficiency by withdrawing its envoy.

This course would have raised no difficulty had the objections presented been such that the President could have recognized their pertinency and force, and, of his own executive action, annulled the appointment.

But the disinclination to accept Mr. Keiley was placed by Austria-Hungary on grounds which could not be admitted by the President, with due regard to the provisions of the Constitution, nor be held by him to constitute any disability under our law or custom. The President's freedom of action being thus barred by the Austrian presentment of the case, no alternative remained, the status having been duly made known by us, but to await from the Imperial and Royal Government a positive announcement of its purposes with regard to the acceptance or rejection of Mr. Keiley, and this announcement has at last been definitely communicated to you.

Nations, like individuals, are the proper guardians of their own self-respect and honor, and the people of the United States must decide upon their acceptance of the novel conditions of diplomatic intercourse which have been set up and insisted upon by Austria-Hungary in the case of Mr. Keiley.

By no act of mine nor with my consent can the Government of the United States be placed in an attitude of supplication for favor, or become a petitioner for recognition on terms prescribed by any foreign power, and this expression meets the full approval of the Executive.

There is, therefore, and can be, no suggestion of expostulation or protest by us against the unprecedented action of the Government of Austria-Hungary.

All that has been said and written by us has been designed to make it clear that, as between the revocation of Mr. Keiley's appointment by this Government and his rejection as an envoy by that of His Imperial and Royal Majesty, the responsibility of the final decision must rest with the latter, which, having now signified its determination and accomplished its object, must abide the result.

International comity, as understood and practiced by the United States, is substantial and sincere, and applies to the public interests of the Governments and to the vast concerns embraced and controlled by governmental action. It is not the intention of the Government of the United States, as it cannot be the wish of the people of this country, from which the power of administration is derived, to allow the important and dignified objects which diplomatic intercourse was designed to promote to be lost sight of or subordinated to the prejudices and caprices of a limited social circle.

We recognize the necessity of high personal character and intelligence in the envoys of the United States, and their possession o-perfect amity and good faith toward the Government and the people to whom they are sent. No breach of social conventions on their part is contemplated, neither is personal immorality to be condoned. Individual worth and competency are tests by which their fitness is to be measured. Judged by this indispensably high standard, no breath of imputation against Mr. Keiley's good fame is discoverable.

Whilst this Government concedes as freely as it exercises the right to refuse to receive an envoy, yet when that right is so exaggerated and expanded as to become a virtual claim of the function of selection as well as of rejection, we must demur.

On the face of Count Kalnoky's telegram to the Austro-Hungarian minister at this capital, in the communications, both written and verbal, made to me by Baron von Schaeffer, and in the reports by Mr. Francis of his interview with Mr. Szögyényi at the foreign office and your own report in full of Count Kalnoky's statements to you in your final interview with him on this subject, two facts appear: First, that the alleged race and religious faith of the wedded wife of an envoy of the United States is held a cause of his rejection; and further, that objections by a third party —"a friendly power"— are necessary to be removed in order to allow a proper reception to be extended.

These conditions are simply intolerable, and are, in the case of the United States, not only inhibited by the plain letter and undying spirit of our constitution of government, but are inconsistent with that decent self-respect which forbids a nation of sixty millions of freemen to accept the position of a diplomatic dependency of the "friendly power" whose behests appear to have been acquiesced in and carried out by Austria-Hungary in the present instance.

The issues thus raised are grave, and I will now pursue their discussion, as they will in all probability be submitted to the representatives of the American people upon the meeting of the two Houses of Congress in December next.

While consideration of the merits is thus laid aside, two matters of detail and fact, which were stated by Count Kalnoky in his last interview with you on the 4th instant, require my attention in this instruction.

First. His excellency avers that his intention was to have had his views stated verbally to me by Baron von Schaeffer. I can only say, as to this, that whatever may have been his private intentions, the full copy of his telegram to Baron von Schaeffer, of May 8, was by the latter carefully translated and handed to me in writing, and that the objection to the religious faith of Mr. Keiley's wife, which appeared in that telegram, was the main point of discussion between Baron von Schaeffer and myself, and was insisted upon by him against my earnest remonstrance and objection that the President could not withdraw Mr. Keiley on such grounds. A month later, on the 11th of June, Baron von Schaeffer, in writing, communicated to me Count Kalnoky's declaration "that his objections to said nomination remain in full force."

Secondly. His excellency remarked to you that "he thought it undiplomatic to have intimated, without adducing some confirmatory proof, that Italy was influencing the decision of his Government."

My desire to attain absolute truth in my relation of facts has certainly been greater than to excel in the periphrases of diplomacy, but his excellency must have been either unmindful of uninformed of the statements of his associate Mr. Szögyényi, chier of section in the ministry for foreign affairs, made to Mr. J. M. Francis, then the United States minister, on June 16, at the foreign office, or he certainly would not have averred that my comment was undiplomatic.

On that occasion, Mr. Szögyényi distinctly informed Mr. Francis that "a friendly Government, a near neighbor, had objected to him" (Mr. Keiley) "as the United States representative at its court, and its views had found earnest expression here" (in Vienna) "since the President had named him as United States minister to Austria-Hungary."

Mr. Keiley's mission was the only object of that interview, and statements emanating from a source so authoritative can scarcely be held to need "confirmatory proof."

It may not be superfluous in this connection to refer to the language of Count Kalnoky in his letter to Baron von Schaeffer, as communicated to me by the latter under date of May 19, as exhibiting the influence upon his intentions of the "friendly power" referred to, wherein he states his objections to the reception of Mr. Keiley as being "based upon want of political tact evinced on his part on a former occasion, in consequence of which a friendly power declined to receive him, and upon the certainty that his domestic relations preclude that reception of him by Vienna which we judge desirable for the representative of the United States."

You are instructed to make known to Count Kalnoky the facts in regard to the communication of his telegraphic dispatch in writing, and its subsequent confirmation in Baron von Schaeffer's letter to me, and also the statement of Mr. Szögyényi to Mr. Francis in relation to the "earnest expression" at Vienna, of the wishes of a third party concerning the diplomatic relations of Austria-Hungary and the United States.

The personal and individual opinions of His Majesty, the Emperor, to which Count Kalnoky made reference in your interview, we must of course hold to have been expressed by his distinguished minister.

I cannot close this instruction without referring to the remark addressed to you by Count Kalnoky, that "the antisemitic social feeling here [in Vienna] was a fact; that a person of proximate semitic descent would be excluded both by the social and diplomatic circles of Vienna, and that fact was beyond the control of his Government." This fact, if beyond the control of the Imperial and Royal Government, is equally beyond the cognizance of the executive power of this Republic, which could not admit a principle which, through the exclusion of "persons of proximate semitic descent" and others married to "persons of proximate semitic descent" would establish a religious test, and disfranchise from holding public office a very large and important body of our citizens.

It is a cause of astonishment that in an era of advanced civilization in which musty prejudice and illiberal discrimination among religious sects and races of mankind are giving such gratifying proofs of their rapid extinction, when throughout the wide world the death of the venerable and philanthropic Montefiore is so genuinely mourned, when the council of highest rank and most exclusive privilege of the British Empire is glad to enroll in its peerage a member of the noted house of Rothschild, that from so enlightened a Government as that of Austria-Hungary should proceed the declaration that "proximate Semitic descent" will be sufficient to proscribe individuals of admittedly blameless and virtuous personality from appearing at that court clothed in the representative character of a friendly power.

I am, etc.,

T. F. BAYARD

Soon after learning the final decision taken by the Austrian Government, Mr. Bayard wired the American Minister, Mr. McLane, at Paris to inform Mr. Keiley of the Austrian refusal to receive him and to advise him to return to the

United States forthwith. Thereupon Mr. Keiley left France on August 15, arriving in New York City on the 26th. He immediately proceeded to Washington to acquaint himself with the correspondence between the foreign offices of the respective governments as well as to learn the attitude of the Administration on the final outcome of his case. While there, he learned that the Government of the United States had no intention to recall him and thereby countenance the extraordinary objections raised by Vienna, but decided to leave the conclusion of the matter to his own judgment. Mr. Keiley found his course to a decision clear for he felt that duty called him to remove his person from this controversy as soon as possible. He therefore resigned his commission to President Cleveland, refusing at the same time to accept any compensation for expenses incurred during the four months his case was in suspense.

In the letter to Mr. Bayard, dated September 1, 1885,[9] in which he returned his commission as envoy at Vienna, Mr. Keiley reviewed the whole case in a lengthy summary, of which the following excerpts are especially worthy of notice. Commenting on the only real objection to his appointment, namely, the fact that his wife was a Jewess, Mr. Keiley indignantly remarks:

This objection, thus announced with a certain bluntness, disdaining even the affectation of respect for modern ideas of freedom, is, as we shall see, repeated at every step of this correspondence with a persistence which discloses either the purpose of a deliberate and gross insult to the American people or a desire to mask under a false reason avowed though disreputable, a true reason too disreputable to be avowed. I say an insult to the American people, because in this, its first form of statement, as ever throughout this correspondence, it is proclaimed that in the official regard of Austria, Hebrew blood brands as with a leprosy, not only excluding all tainted with it from high honor at Austria's hands, but disqualifying beyond remedy even the agents of other Governments who may have business with Austria, so fatal indeed, that even a marriage connection with it by a citizen of whatever blood or belief, unfits him for the representation of a foreign and friendly power at this imperial and royal court.

[9] Foreign Relations, 1885, page 41.

He then refers to the other objection, which was that if the Government of Austria should accept him, the Italian Government, which had previously refused to receive him, might interpret such an acceptance as a rebuke to its own stand. He rightfully states that Count Kalnoky was not frank on the question whether the Italian Government made any presentation to the Austrian Government on this matter, and that Kalnoky's answer to a direct reference had been evasive and ambiguous. In summarizing his case, Mr. Keiley says the following:

If Count Kalnoky, in affirming that the Italian Government had not approached him on this subject, merely meant to say that Italy's objection, though made, was not presented through a particular channel, he simply illustrated the proverbial insincerity of diplomatic intercourse. If, however, he meant to deny that Italy's objection was presented in any way, he accentuates the insult to the United States, since he confesses, that, in order to propitiate that power, he shut the door of the Austrian court in the face of an American minister for a cause which Italy herself did not deem of sufficient gravity to suggest.

Mr. Keiley concludes with the observation that the acts of Austria and her ministers in this case, if rightly interpreted, would mean that Austria reserves for herself the right to prescribe a religious test for office in the United States; and he expressed the view that these acts and their obvious interpretation would arouse the resentment of all proud and patriotic Americans. He ends his letter with the following paragraph:

Nor is that resentment to be less decided from the circumstance that the race and religion thus proscribed have won their place with the foremost of the earth by an eminence in statesmanship and finance, in arts and letters, which has conquered the inherited intolerance of centuries, and the further circumstance that the blow which wounded them pierced also the most ennobling relation of human society.

Mr. Keiley was offered another position which he refused to accept because he did not desire to be taken for an indiscriminate seeker of public office.

In reply to Mr. Keiley's letter of resignation, Secretary Bayard wrote:[10]

[*Mr. Bayard to Mr. Keiley*]

Department of State
Washington, September 15, 1885

Sir: I have the honor to acknowledge the receipt of your letter of the 7th instant, which contains your resignation of the position of envoy extraordinary and minister plenipotentiary to Austria-Hungary.

The statement of the facts attending your appointment in May last, and your voyage to and from Europe in pursuance of your mission, which accompanies your letter, is entirely accurate, and the reasons you assign for no longer retaining the commission intrusted to you are consonant with your own dignity and personal character as an upright citizen and honest public servant.

The President and those who are associated in his counsel are completely satisfied with your attitude and action throughout this remarkable episode in our diplomatic history, and all deeply regret that the country has been prevented by the unprecedented and intolerable action of the Austro-Hungarian Government from having the advantage of your personal presence at Vienna and of your services there as a competent and worthy representative of the interests and honor of the American people and their Government.

I am thoroughly aware of, and exceedingly deplore, the serious personal inconvenience and pecuniary loss which have been entailed upon you by the wholly unexpected course of the Government to which you were accredited. And whilst I might, for some reasons, have deprecated your refusal to accept the other official positions of honor and emolument of which the option was tendered to you, yet your action in declining to place yourself in the attitude of an indiscriminating seeker or recipient of public salary and position is so in keeping with the estimate formed of your character that I am sure it will receive the hearty and enviable acclaim and approbation of your fellow countrymen.

The proprieties attaching in diplomatic communications have necessarily caused the correspondence in this case between the Governments of the United States and Austria-Hungary to be withheld from publication, and much honest misunderstanding, and, I regret to say, no little malevolent misstatement, have been allowed to pass uncorrected, but the incident of the declination by

[10] Foreign Relations, 1885, page 45.

the Government of Austria-Hungary to receive you as envoy of the United States, upon the grounds alleged, is destined, I believe, to have important consequences.

I will not believe that the people of the United States will ever consent to the creation or enforcement of such tests as have been insisted upon by the Government of Austria-Hungary as conditions precedent and qualifications for the selection of their representatives in foreign courts by the United States. Such action must naturally cause widespread amazement, coupled with indignation and resentment, when the history of the case is made public, nor do I believe that these sentiments will be confined to our own country, but that, wherever religious liberty is valued and respected, a common judgment will be formed.

In closing this communication, I reiterate my expression of disappointment that you have disconnected yourself temporarily from the public service. Whilst the immediate cause for this voluntary act of severance is to be regretted, yet I congratulate you that your name is honorably associated with the maintenance and vindication of principles which constitute the very soul of personal liberty, and which lie at the foundation of our Government. To be allied with such principles is honor at all times, with success as a certain finality.

I am, etc.,

T. F. BAYARD

In his annual message to Congress, December 8, 1885, President Cleveland had the following to say about the Keiley case:[11]

Question has arisen with the Government of Austria-Hungary touching the representation of the United States at Vienna. Having, under my constitutional prerogative, appointed an estimable citizen of unimpeachable probity and competence as minister at that court, the Government of Austria-Hungary invited this Government to take cognizance of certain exceptions, based upon allegations against the personal acceptability of Mr. Keiley, the appointed envoy, asking that in view thereof, the appointment should be withdrawn. The reasons advanced were such as could not be acquiesced in, without violation of my oath of office and the precepts of the Constitution, since they necessarily involved a limitation in favor of a foreign government upon the right of selection by the Executive, and required such an application of a religious test as a qualification for office under the United States as would have

[11] Foreign Relations, 1885, page iv.

resulted in the practical disfranchisement of a large class of our citizens and the abandonment of a vital principle in our Government. The Austro-Hungarian Government finally decided not to receive Mr. Keiley as the envoy of the United States, and that gentleman has since resigned his commission, leaving the post vacant. I have made no new nomination, and the interests of this Government in Vienna are now in the care of the secretary of legation, acting as chargé d'affaires *ad interim*.

For two years the affairs of the United States Government in Vienna were transacted through the Secretary of the Legation. It was not until 1887 that the two Governments exchanged ministers, thus returning to normal diplomatic relations.

Some years later, Mr. Anthony M. Keiley became a member of the International Tribunal of Egypt, afterwards rising to the Court of Appeals in Alexandria.

A reference to the Keiley case appeared three years later, which showed that, whether as a direct result of this episode or not, the Government of Austria-Hungary saw fit to change somewhat its opinion and official relations to certain members of the Jewish race. In the "Foreign Relations of the United States, 1888," we find the following communication from Alexander R. Lawton, then United States Minister to Austria.[12]

[*Mr. Lawton to Mr. Bayard*]

Legation of the United States
Vienna, January 6, 1888

SIR: In view of the anti-Semitic imbroglio which somewhat excited the Governments of Austria-Hungary and the United States, not long since, it is interesting to note that during the recent "holidays" Baron and Baroness Albert Rothschild were declared by imperial decree *hoffähig*, that is to say, they will for the future be admitted to court balls. This is the first time that such a privilege has ever been conceded to persons of Jewish origin or faith, and it is causing a great sensation in the highest society of Vienna. Very many quarterings of nobility (sixteen, I believe) are the usual requisites of *Hoffähigkeit*; and it was not until last year that the wives of cabinet ministers, not being mem-

[12] Foreign Relations, 1888, page 22.

bers of noble families, were admitted to court by reason of their husbands' offices.

This exclusion from court circles has been sorely felt by the Rothschild family, and it has been rumored during the last year that Baron Albert intended to dispose of his palace residence and other property in Vienna, and retire altogether from Austria with his colossal fortune.

I have, etc., *

A. R. LAWTON

Though a number of Jewish names have appeared in our correspondence with Austria since the Keiley Case, the fact of their being of Jewish race and religion was of no importance in the outcome of their cases.

In common with other countries in central and eastern Europe, Austria too bound herself to accord full protection and equality of the law to all its inhabitants, irrespective of birth, nationality, language, race or religion. Section V (Articles 62–69) of the Treaty of St. Germain deals with the protection of minorities in Austria. Also, as in other countries, these provisions have not proven effective, and the spirit of intolerance which has been spreading over continental Europe has found a welcome in Austria too.

In November, 1933, while on a tour through Austria, Mr. George H. Earle, then United States Minister at Vienna, warned every provincial governor that if their country ceased to be "a haven of religious and racial freedom," trade relations with the United States would certainly suffer heavily. In an interview with newspapermen after his return from seeing the country, he was quoted as follows:[13]

As an American, I am interested in this question [anti-Semitism]. It is well known [that] 90 per cent of Americans either came or are descended from persons who came to escape racial or religious persecution. Americans therefore would have no sympathy for a country where such persecution is carried on.

It is the right of any country to frame its own racial policy. It is equally America's right to refuse its sympathy to a country with whose policy towards the Jews or other races it should disagree.

[13] *The New York Times*, November 15, 1933, page 4.

On Friday, March 11, 1938, German troops crossed the
Austrian border and occupied the country, thus ending the
independence of Austria. The conquest of Austria was
recognized by the nations of the world including the United
States which gave it de facto recognition. The occurrences in
Austria since March 11, 1938, are treated in the chapter on
Germany.

XII. GERMANY

In pre-war Germany Jews enjoyed civil, religious and political equality, though, as we shall see later, they were even then objects of attack by agitators encouraged, more or less openly, by official sanction from the court at Berlin. Note, for example, the acquiescence of both Kaiser William I and Prince von Bismarck in the anti-Semitic activities of Adolf Stöcker, the court preacher. In a number of cases, however, the Government of Germany was of great assistance in the struggle of Jews for civil and religious equality in some backward countries of Europe, notably Rumania.

The correspondence with Germany deals with such instances and also with disputes regarding military service of former German subjects who had become naturalized citizens of the United States.

In 1872, the Government of the United States requested its representatives abroad to transmit a note to the leading European powers suggesting that they jointly intervene with the Government of Rumania with a view to improving the condition of the oppressed Jews in that country.[1] From Mr. George Bancroft, United States Minister in Germany, Secretary Fish received the following reply:[2]

[Mr. Bancroft to Mr. Fish]

American Legation
Berlin, August 26, 1872

SIR: The note which, in conformity with your instruction, No. 495, I addressed to this Government respecting the protection of the Israelites in Roumania, met with the most friendly reception at the foreign office, and has been submitted to the Emperor.

In a conversation with the acting secretary of state for foreign affairs, on Saturday, I was assured that this government received

[1] See chapter on Rumania, page 107.
[2] Foreign Relations, 1872, page 194.

the communication with great satisfaction, as an evidence of the confidence reposed in it by the Government of the United States, and has the best disposition to give effect to the humane desires expressed by the President.

I remain, etc.,

GEORGE BANCROFT

At the Berlin Conference of 1878, Prince von Bismarck was very helpful to the Jewish cause in Rumania; and from a dispatch from Mr. John A. Kasson, our minister at Vienna at that time, to Secretary Evarts, we learn that Germany broke off negotiations for a treaty of commerce with the Government of Rumania because the latter was unwilling to treat German-Jewish subjects on the same basis as other German subjects.[3]

It is also quite apropos to remark here that in the Treaty of Bucharest, which incorporated the abortive separate peace signed between the Central Powers and Rumania at Bucharest, April 24, 1918, Article VII of that treaty, imposed by a victorious Germany on a vanquished Rumania, provided as follows: "All worships shall be recognized: Roman-Catholic, Uniate, Protestant, Mohammedan and Jewish; they shall all have the same freedom and protection as the Orthodox. All residents of Rumania shall become citizens without special measures, including the Jews."

The question of military duty of naturalized American citizens in Germany formed an important subject in the diplomatic correspondence between the United States and the Government of Imperial Germany and with the Government of Prussia before the establishment of the German Empire in 1871. German immigrants who became naturalized in the United States were, when they returned for a visit to their native country, arrested and impressed into military service. Many of these citizens were Jews, and there is no doubt that this fact aggravated their case in the eyes of the German officials.

[3] Foreign Relations, 1878, page 42.

In 1866 there was the case of Simon Israel. Mr. Israel left Prussia in 1853, at the age of 17, for the United States where he remained for 10 years, meanwhile acquiring American citizenship. While on a visit to Prussia in 1863 he was forced into the military service of the Prussian Army where he contracted diseases impairing his eyesight and general health. His almost constant illness came about as a direct result of his having been forced to exercise beyond his physical endurance. Baron Thile, speaking for the Prussian Foreign Office, refused to act on the case, claiming that Mr. Israel had not lost his Prussian nationality and "his conduct in the regiment has not been, up to this time, sufficiently irreproachable to justify his release." Mr. Israel, however, was later released by a special pardon from the King of Prussia, a procedure which Prussia usually resorted to as final solution of a diplomatic impasse. The legal question involving the citizenship of naturalized American citizens of German origin was left pending.[4]

The question of regulating the nationality of Americans who had left the United States and settled in Prussia, and of Prussians who had left their native country and settled in the United States, and who after they had become naturalized in their respective new homes, returned for a longer or shorter visit to their native country, was settled by a special treaty concluded in 1868 between Prussia and the United States. This naturalization treaty was the first of a series of treaties concluded by the United States with a number of states in Europe, a series popularly known as the Bancroft Treaties, after George Bancroft, who had been the American Minister to Prussia.

Article IV of the naturalization treaty with Prussia reads as follows:

[4] A scholarly paper on the question of the American views on the right of expatriation was written by Mr. George H. Yeaman, United States Minister to Copenhagen. See his "Allegiance and Citizenship, an enquiry into the claim of the European Governments to exact military service of naturalized citizens of the United States," in Diplomatic Correspondence, 1867, pages 663–678.

The intention to take up permanent residence shall be regarded as existing when the person naturalized resides for more than two years within the territory of the other part.

In a dispatch of February 22, 1868, Mr. Bancroft, commenting on this article, said that "a German naturalized in America and returning to Germany for two years, does not necessarily renounce his American citizenship; only he may be called upon to declare his purpose explicitly."[5]

Bismarck gave the most liberal interpretation to the treaty when it was discussed in the North German Diet, saying that "we will treat the five years' absence in America, when connected with naturalization, as a fulfillment of the military duty in the North German Confederation."[6]

To a question of Mr. Eduard Lasker, who asked clarification of Article IV of the proposed treaty, Bismarck gave the following reply, as paraphrased by Mr. Bancroft.[7]

The German-American citizen on resuming his relations as a citizen of North Germany would, under the treaty, stand in the light of a foreigner emigrating into North Germany; that he could not be held to the discharge of any *old* military duty, but only to such *new* military duty as would attach to every foreigner emigrating into North Germany and becoming naturalized there.[8]

Though the conclusion of the naturalization treaty did not at once terminate cases of conflict over the nationality of certain individuals, their solution no doubt became much easier as a result of it. Among the many cases which were the subject of diplomatic correspondence between the respective governments there were many involving Jews, but in almost all cases the ancestry of the persons was not an

[5] Diplomatic Correspondence, 1868, Part 2, page 48.

[6] *Ibid.*, page 51.

[7] *Ibid.*, page 52.

[8] It should be noted that the military duties of a German subject extended even in peace time to over 20 years. It began with three years military service at the commencement of his twentieth year, then four years more as a reserve, five years more of membership in the *Landwehr* came next, this again being followed by service in the *Landsturm* until the expiration of his 42nd year.

element either in the discussion or in the final solution reached with the agreement of both parties to the treaty.

However, there was at least one exception to the above rule, the case of Aaron Weill, where the fact that Mr. Weill was a Jew undoubtedly complicated his case.[9]

Aaron Weill was born in Alsace in 1855, migrated to the United States in 1872 and was naturalized in 1879. In 1880, on a visit to Reichshofen, his native town, in Alsace, a fine was imposed on him because he had not presented himself for military service in 1877. Weill refused to pay, claiming exemption under the Bancroft treaty, and when told that he must either pay or leave the country he appealed to Mr. Andrew D. White, then serving as United States Minister to Germany. Meanwhile Weill was imprisoned. His case occasioned a prolonged correspondence between the American Minister and the German Foreign Office. Mr. White also made a number of visits to the German Foreign Ministry, but was unsuccessful in obtaining the release of Mr. Weill.

It should be noted here that the Bancroft treaty was not considered by either Germany or the United States to apply to Alsace and Lorraine, provinces newly acquired from France as a result of the Franco-Prussian War of 1870–71. As an act of comity, however, Germany did not press the point and treated naturalized citizens from these two provinces in the same manner as if they had gone to the United States from any other part of Germany. In this case, however, the German Foreign Office insisted that Weill either pay the fine imposed or leave the country, and that he be kept imprisoned pending his decision.

Mr. White finally won Bismarck and the German Foreign Office over by a diplomatic ruse, the details of which are to be found in White's autobiography. After having thought

---

[9] From the report on this case as given in the autobiography of Mr. Andrew D. White, we learn that, in his interview with Prince von Bismarck, the fact that Mr. Weill was a Jew was mentioned, Mr. White saying that it was evidently hateful to the Chancellor to have "this young Alsatian Israelite" escape military service. (Andrew D. White, "Autobiography," page 593).

out his plan, Mr. White informed Mr. Weill merely that the legation was doing its best to secure his freedom, and here we shall let Mr. White tell the story in his own words:[10]

To say more than this involved danger that the affair might fall into the hands of sensation-mongers, and result in howls and threats against the German Government and Bismarck; and I knew well that, if such howls and threats were made, Bismarck would never let this young Israelite out of prison as long as he lived.

It seemed hardly the proper thing, serious as the case was, to ask for my passports. It was certain that, if this were done, there would come a chorus of blame from both sides of the Atlantic. Deciding, therefore, to imitate the example of the old man in the school-book, who, before throwing stones at the boy in his fruit-tree threw turf and grass, I secured from Washington by cable a leave of absence, but, before starting, saw some of my diplomatic colleagues, who were wont to circulate freely and talk much, stated the main features of the case to them, and said that I was "going off to enjoy myself"; that there seemed little use for an American minister in a country where precedents and agreements were so easily disregarded. Next day I started for the French Riviera. The journey was taken leisurely, with interesting halts at Cologne and Aix-la-Chapelle; and, as I reached the hotel in Paris, a telegram was handed me — "Your man in Alsace-Lorraine is free." It was evident that the chancellor had felt better and had thought more leniently of the matter, and I had never another difficulty of the sort during the remainder of my stay.

Mr. Weill was very thankful to Mr. White for his efforts in his behalf, first telegraphing him the fact of his release, and then expressing his gratitude in the following letter:[11]

Reichshofen, Alsace
November 5, 1880

DEAR SIR: Through your energy and powerful help I am happy to tell you that I gained my liberty Wednesday evening, half-past six, immediately telegraphing you to that effect.

I assure you that I am so glad that I cannot find words enough to express my sincere thanks for the noble work you have done

[10] Andrew D. White, "Autobiography," Vol. 1, page 594.
[11] Foreign Relations, 1881, page 447.

for me. The few American residents in this place are jubilant
over your success.

In the meantime receive my high esteem and everlasting thanks.

I remain, etc.,
Aaron Weill

During Mr. White's stay in Berlin he wrote a dispatch
analyzing the situation of Jews in Germany. This document
depicts vividly the civil and social disabilities to which Jews
in Germany were being subjected in spite of the fact that
ten years earlier the constitution of the newly formed German
Reich had abrogated all distinctions as between citizens
because of religion or ancestry. Mr. White's comments on
these conditions are illuminating and are an index to the
broad-mindedness and great-heartedness of the man. The
dispatch follows in full.[12]

[*Mr. White to Mr. Blaine*]

Legation of the United States
Berlin, April 29, 1881

Sir: As you have doubtless heard much of the "Anti-Jewish
movement" in Germany and may be interested in the facts regarding it, I have drawn up an account of its general history, which I
have now the honor to forward.

The force of active opposition to the Jews in Germany, known
as the anti-Semitic agitation, had its origin in the "Christian
Socialists," a party formed in 1878 to oppose Social Democracy, its
founder being one of the Berlin court preachers, the Rev. Dr.
Stöcker. Social Democracy was then at its height. The Emperor's
life was in continual danger, and two daring attempts to assassinate
him had been made in the public streets. Socialistic opinions were
gaining victories at the polls, and the conservative and moderate
part of the community was becoming greatly alarmed. This was
the state of affairs when Prince Bismarck passed the socialistic law
of October, 1878, which declared Berlin in a state of siege, and
when Dr. Stöcker set forth the social and religious means of regen-
erating the working classes of the country. As a main factor in the
origin of the discontent which filled those classes, Stöcker pointed
to the Jews, who had, he said, alienated the community from

[12] Foreign Relations, 1881, page 465.

Christianity, continually reviled the Christian religion in their press, were, as in the case of Lassalle, the founders of impracticable socialistic schemes, and had been in 1873 and 1874 the originators of hundreds of bubble companies, to the break-up of which was due, in no small degree, the industrial depression and the prevalent want of "commercial morality." Dr. Stöcker therefore called upon the working class to become "Christian Socialists," especially were they to remain loyal to the Emperor; to resist the attack on the Christian religion made by Jewish skeptics, and to seek relief from social evils by legislation rather than by revolution and outrage. To this end he proposed laws regulating factory labor, compulsory insurance against accidents, the formation of trades guilds, and the extension of paternal government generally.

This programme was advocated at public meetings of the Christian Socialist party, which often ended in great uproar. All of it attracted much attention; but its most popular feature was undoubtedly that attacking the Jews. Not much eloquence was needed to inflame the anti-Semitic feeling of many patriotic Germans. Envy at the wealth of the Jews, especially those of Berlin, had probably more influence in arousing hostility than the religious, ethnological, and aesthetic reasons advanced by Dr. Stöcker.

The 600,000 Jews in Prussia are possessed of great wealth. They are exclusive socially; and do not encourage intermarriage.[13] The finest places of worship and of business, and the most prosperous newspapers are theirs. Since 1848 their influence as lawyers, professors, and legislators has become extraordinary, so that at present the chief orators of the Prussian Diet and the Imperial Parliament, several of the foremost members of the Berlin faculty, and many of the most vigorous men of letters and writers for the press are Jews. The restrictions upon their liberty were removed by the exertions of the Liberal and Progressive parties, and to these accordingly they have always attached themselves, hoping, doubtless, to wring from the Conservative and Court parties yet greater concessions — concessions which shall, for example, place them on a footing of social equality with Christians in court and military circles.

Among the first supporters of the Stöcker agitation were, therefore, many of the naturally conservative — the landed proprietors, the *junkers* or petty nobility, the great nobility and the court.

---

[13] Unfortunately, Mr. White errs in this paragraph. The Jews of Prussia never reached the number of 600,000 nor were they all possessed of great wealth. It is a matter of record that there was much intermarriage between German Jews and German Christians. See "The Jews of Germany," by Marvin Lowenthal, page 270.

Jews, they said, had identified themselves with the Liberal and Progressive parties, with social Democratic agitations and all that is usually supposed to be inimical in Germany to political and social safety; and Jews had as a necessary consequence fallen into discredit among those who were interested in the existing order of things.

The meetings of the Christian Socialists grew more and more frequent during 1879, and more devoted to expressions of anti-Semitic feeling. Towards the close of that year Dr. Stöcker issued his views regarding the Jews in a pamphlet. His gravest charge against them was their attitude towards the Christian religion, which he declared they were undermining in their newspapers and books. He pointed to the education of German children by Semitic schoolmasters as a great evil, attacked the "overbearing" conduct of the Jews in Berlin, where they number 45,000; remarked upon the fact that 30 per cent. of the scholars in German high schools were Jews; that out of 100 Jews 71.3 were employers, while out of 100 Protestants only 38.7 had reached that position; that 55 per cent of the Jewish and only 12 per cent of the Protestant population was engaged in trade; and was especially severe upon Jewish disinclination to physical labor, and upon their "anti-Germanic" character.[14]

Up to this point Dr. Stöcker had carried on his agitation in comparative obscurity; but now he and his party suddenly became notorious. His pamphlet ran through five or six editions, and soon there engaged in the controversy a man of far more ability and influence — Dr. Treitschke, professor of history at the Berlin University — a member of the Imperial Parliament, and one of the most admired of German historians. In a political journal, edited by him, he wrote several articles dealing with the question and republished them in pamphlet form.[15]

In these he took ground against the Jews on the ground that they are "non-German;" that they have produced no national German literature, no great works of art; that they conduct a press which discredits all purely German tendencies; that they are not assimilated with the German nation, remaining a nationality within a state whose people they regard as antagonists; and that they continue to swarm over the German borders from Poland as "trouser-selling youths" in order to become rich by preying on the easy-going Germans. On this coming in of the Jews from the

[14] Adolf Stöcker, "Das Moderne Judenthum in Deutschland, besonders in Berlin," Berlin, 1880.

[15] Heinrich von Treitschke, "Ein Wort über unser Judenthum," Berlin, 1880.

eastern provinces he laid especial stress. He declared Prussian Poland a kind of vast hive, sending constantly new swarms of barbarians to pervert the ideas and eat out the substance of the German people. He asserted that in this lies the fundamental difference between the state of the question in Germany and in other countries; that in England, France, and Spain, the Jews are comparatively few, subjected from childhood to the influence of Christian civilization and that they are rapidly assimilated by society; whereas in Germany they come in hordes, greedy for prey, too many and too far gone in their ideas to be assimilated.

These articles aroused a storm. The spring and summer of 1880 produced a great crop of Jew literature; the booksellers' shop-windows were darkened by it; Professor Treitschke's position was vehemently attacked by writers of the Liberal and Progressive press, and as vehemently defended by the Conservative press. Several Jewish university professors replied to his argument, but when a Christian minister put in a word for peace the Crown Prince strongly and publicly recommended the pamphlet to the latter.

Among the replies the most effectual was one by Dr. Harry Breslau, a personal friend of Treitschke, and, like him, a professor of history in the University of Berlin.[16]

Breslau pointed out the numerous sins of Germans against Jews at present, and especially in times past, showing particularly, too, how the Roman Catholic press of Germany had, in 1875, begun a crusade against them; that the restrictions imposed upon them until 1812 and 1848 had rendered their assimilation with Germans impossible; that many had become entirely German in sentiment, and that thousands had made sacrifices for the fatherland; that the German press was not so entirely under the influence of the Jewish editors and correspondents as was supposed; and he called attention to the enormous debt modern civilization owes to the ancient literature of the Jews, and all this in an admirable spirit and temper.

Despite the efforts of the Crown Prince and the sober reasoning of Professor Breslau, the agitation grew in intensity. Dr. Stöcker continued to hold his meetings and new pamphleteers appeared every day in various parts of the empire with new developments of the arguments of Stöcker, Treitschke, and other opponents. The Jew was no longer to be hated as a usurer; but he was to be combated for reasons of "race," for his "non-Germanism." An anti-Semitic league was formed, which drew up a petition to the chancellor, and which was circulated throughout Germany for signature.

[16] Harry Breslau, "Zur Judenfrage, Sendschreiben an Prof. H. v. Treitschke," Berlin, 1880.

It implored Prince Bismarck (1) to limit, at least, if not wholly hinder, the immigration into Germany of foreign Jews; (2) to exclude Jews from all offices of authority, and to restrict their activity in the legal career, particularly on the bench; (3) to prevent their becoming teachers in the Christian schools, and to admit them only in very exceptional cases into others; and (4) to cause statistics to be collected as to the Hebrew population of the empire.

Throughout the summer of 1880, this petition formed the text for thousands of anti-Semitic addresses, and in the autumn the agitation reached its highest point. It had spread among the students at the universities of Berlin, Leipsic, and Göttingen, who formed anti-Jew societies; even schoolmasters and professors in gymnasiums were affected by it. In Berlin two of the last-named class provoked a Jewish trader into an assault upon them in a public conveyance, and in Leipsic a Jew was led to assault a "baiter," as the anti-Semitic agitators are called.

Public indignation was at length aroused. In Berlin it resulted in the offending gymnasium professor being expelled from his position, and in a public declaration against the anti-Jew agitators by Professors Deoysen,* Virchow, Hoffmann, (now rector of the university), Mommsen, and others distinguished for scholarly and political activity. But large meetings, at which from 4,000 to 6,000 persons were present, continued to be held, and the disorderly proceedings at some of these gave rise to much comment in the foreign press. The strictly Germanic idea was studiously maintained. Public announcements calling the meetings asked none but men of German origin to be present, and if Jews were detected in the audience they were somewhat unceremoniously expelled to the accompaniment of groans and hisses. Yet it does not appear that any Jew received bodily injury at these meetings, and the reports published in foreign journals to the effect that Jews were the objects of general assault and insult throughout Germany were undoubtedly exaggerated.

The most serious phase of the agitation was that finding expression in the universities. In Berlin the anti-Semitic students refused to hear the lectures of certain Jewish professors, entitled though these are by ability, age, and past services to the greatest respect. All friends of the Jews among the professors, even the rector and Professor Mommsen, were made to feel the antagonism of the anti-Semitic league by the shouts which drowned their lectures.

On the 20th of November the petition was discussed in the Prussian Diet in connection with a question put by a member of the Progressionist party as to the attitude of the government

---

*Misspelling for "Droysen."

towards such a petition. Count Stolberg-Wernigerode, vice-president of the ministry, replied that a petition of the kind referred to had not been presented to the government, and could not therefore be officially taken into consideration; but that at the same time the government would not hesitate to say that the existing laws insured the equality of all religious creeds in political respects, and that the ministry had no intention of altering the state of the law. The standing orders of the Diet allow a debate to follow a question, but they exclude the possibility of the House passing a resolution upon the subject of an interrogation.

The result of the animated two days' debate which followed this answer of the minister could not, therefore, be revealed by a division and vote; but it was clear to those present that a majority of the members did not have much fault to find with the agitation. The chief speakers in the first day's debate were Professor Hänel, the leader of the Progressionists, who had asked the question, and who strongly opposed the whole agitation; a leading member of the Central or Roman Catholic party, who complained that "the Jews contribute the main contingent to the non-productive, speculative part of society," and who "did not think they had justified the hopes attending their emancipation," a Conservative, who stated on behalf of his party "that a feeling of deep displeasure prevailed against the Jews among nearly all classes of the people, because the Jews, especially in their press, did not show that respect for the institutions of the state which the Christians had a right to demand"; Professor Virchow, the well-known scientist, who complained that the answer of the government, though quite correct, was very cool, and cited statistics to show that there was no cause for alarm as to the immigration or overgrowth of the Jews, and traced the present popular antipathy to them to the baser passions, especially envy at their possessions.

In the course of the second day's debate, which was longer and more tumultuous than the first, Mr. Richter, a leader of a section of the Liberals, said there were more Christian than Jewish usurers; that a Jew, Dr. Lasker, had been the first to expose the swindling joint stock companies, and that the founder of the largest popular savings bank was a Jew. He stated further that the movement was much more dangerous than that of the Social Democracy, and asked that its leaders be deprived of their offices and dignities.

The next speaker was the Rev. Dr. Stöcker, who had done so much to stimulate public feeling on the question. He described the movement as social and economical, resulting from the fact that "half a million Jews take a position in Germany out of harmony with their numbers." He then denounced the Jewish press, which is nearly synonymous with the Liberal press, for its attack on the Christian religion, and pointed to the Israelite Alliance as a powerful political combination, which must be wrestled with.

Several other speakers took part in the debate, which ended in great uproar, the question being really left where the House had found it. The public journals eagerly discussed the debate, those of Progressive views claiming that it had forever silenced the Stöcker party, and those of Conservative and semi-official character declaring that the question should never have been asked, and that the debate had injured the Jewish position.

But it was soon shown that the current of popular feeling had not diminished. Crowded and stormy meetings continued to be held, at which the attacks on the Jews were revived; and a new series of pamphlets on the question was issued. The most noticeable of these was one by Professor Mommsen, whose object was to prove that, in the formation of the modern German Empire, the Jews had co-operated in proportion not less materially than the other races. He also made an attack on Professor Treitschke for his part in the agitation, which ended in personal recriminations between the two historians.

The example thus set by the professors was followed by the university students, great numbers of whom refused to hear their Jewish instructors, and attended anti-Semitic meetings, which in some instances had to be dispersed by the police.

At this latter series of discussions the political character of the movement became more apparent, resolutions being passed to the effect that "the citizens of Berlin are convinced that the Liberal party should not identify itself with Judaism if not wishing to drive the electors into the Conservative camp."

Notwithstanding the answer of the vice minister president in the Prussian Diet and the tone of the semi-official press, the attitude of the government, or at the least, the personal inclinations of its leading members and of the court, became more and more a matter of public interest, and it was doubtless with a desire to satisfy this curiosity that a writer in the Grenz Boten, which has often been privileged to reveal the policy of the chancellor, energetically protested against the belief that Prince Bismarck favors the anti-Semitic movement, and commented very severely upon Court Chaplain Stöcker's connection with it. The chancellor's semi-official organ also, the "Norddeutsche Allgemeine Zeitung," especially denied that the government secretly favored the agitation, but the meetings were allowed to continue, and the place of Dr. Stöcker, who had gone on a lecturing tour in the provinces, was supplied by Dr. Henrici, a quondam schoolmaster and a successful mob orator. His efforts kept up the agitation throughout January, breeding much hatred; and aided in the establishment of an additional anti-Semitic newspaper, for which, it was reported, the sum of 50,000 marks had been subscribed. The petition was briskly advertised and on April 13, when the number of signatures had reached 255,000, was presented to the chancellor. Of these one-fifth came from Silesia; the province of Brandenburg supplied about 38,000, including 12,000 from Berlin; Westphalia, 27,000; the Rhine province, 20,000; Bavaria, 9,000; and Baden and Hohenzollern, 7,000.

Of the views of the Emperor very little, if any, indication has been given. He has acknowledged certain loyal resolutions, transmitted to him by an anti-Semitic meeting, but has spoken with much severity of some riotous proceedings of over-zealous Jew haters. As to the crown prince, when the agitation had been rekindled by the parliamentary debate, he publicly attended the worship at the Jewish synagogue, doubtless to express his sympathy with the attacked; and in January, he again took occasion openly to express his entire disapproval of the agitation.

At present the movement shows signs of becoming more and more political in character, losing its distinctive social features by an alliance with the Conservative parties. As offshoots from the Christian Socialists, there have come into existence the *Anti-Semitic League* and the *Volks Verein* (People's Union). The first has the avowed object of simply attacking the Jews, and the latter aims at expressing national conservative opinions in opposition to Jewish, Liberal, and Progressionist views. These societies continue to hold meetings, which are now, however, extremely orderly, in consequence of a new city police regulation forbidding all direct attacks, or incentives to attacks upon any section of the community. That the anti-Semitic feeling is still the mainstay of these societies is beyond question; it manifests itself as bitterly as ever in their public journals, and becomes embodied in new conservative associations.

That this is shrewd policy is hardly to be doubted, and its result will doubtless be seen at the next elections. There are, especially in Berlin, strong prejudices against Jews even among "Liberals" and "Progressionists." Around those who claim to have personal grievances against the Jews, the tradesmen who have been driven from better business quarters into worse by "rings" of Hebrew dealers; the people whose rents have been raised when the houses they occupied came into the possession of Jews; the smaller speculators whose occupation has been taken from them by Jewish millionaires; the borrowers sold out by Jewish usurers; and the bankrupts who attribute their failure to unscrupulous Jewish trading and to combined and systematic competition on the part of Jews until the Christian trader is driven out of the field; around these men there are gathered those who oppose Judaism from less material motives; those who regard with alarm the ascendency of Jewish power in politics, literature, and art, where, it is declared, purely Germanic ideas are scarcely permitted to come to light, and where the idealism of the German character, which has again and again been the well-spring of German vigor, is being gradually weakened by the materialistic and skeptical tendencies of Jewish thought.

But larger and more hopeful ideas are also at work. Thinking men can hardly fail eventually to see that the services of Jews to Germany have been very great; that harsh dealings are attributable to Christians as well as Jews; that the characteristics complained of are mainly due to ages of wrong; that time will steadily work an amalgamation of races; and that the result of such a union will be to increase German vigor. The present anti-Semitic movement is to be regretted as a temporary hindrance to the process, but that it will result in any new constitutional or legislative barriers, I see no reason to believe.

I have, etc.,

AND. D. WHITE

There is no further reference to Jews in our diplomatic correspondence with Germany published since 1881.

In the Weimar Constitution of 1919, the German Jews were accorded full equality in all the aspects of the national life of Germany, and many Germans of Jewish extraction held responsible positions in the short existence of the republic. Unfortunately, the German people and leaders were unwilling or unable to face the unpleasant reality of the Versailles Treaty and its consequences, and in 1933, the republic came to an end with the accession to power of the National Socialist Democratic Labor Party, under the leadership of Adolf Hitler, who was appointed Chancellor of the Reich by President Paul von Hindenburg. Upon the latter's death, Hitler became Reichsfuehrer, i. e., *Leader* of the Reich.

In 1920, the Nazi, or National Socialist, Party formulated its doctrine in a 25 point program. Of the 25 points, the following refer to Jews:[17]

[17] Gottfried Feder, "The Program of the N.S.D.A.P.," authorized translation by Edgar T. S. Dugdale, Munich, 1932.

4. None but members of the nation may be citizens of the State. None but those of German blood, whatever their creed, may be members of the nation. No Jew, therefore, may be a member of the nation.

5. Anyone who is not a citizen of the State may live in Germany only as a guest and must be regarded as being subject to foreign laws.

6. The right of voting on the State's government and legislation is to be enjoyed by the citizen of the State alone. We demand therefore that all official appointments, of whatever kind, whether in the Reich, in the country,* or in the smaller localities, shall be granted to citizens of the State alone.

7. We demand that the State shall make it its first duty to promote the industry and livelihood of citizens of the State. If it is not possible to nourish the entire population of the State, foreign nationals (non-citizens of the State) must be excluded from the Reich.

8. All non-German immigration must be prevented. We demand that all non-Germans, who entered Germany subsequent to August 2nd, 1914, shall be required forthwith to depart from the Reich.

After a long list of demands which represent the "Socialist" side of the movements, and the enforcement of which, after three years in office was not even attempted, the platform returns to the Jewish question in the following points:

23. We demand legal warfare against conscious political lying and its dissemination in the Press. In order to facilitate the creation of a German national press we demand:

    a. that all editors of newspapers and their assistants, employing the German language, must be members of the nation.

    b. the special permission from the State shall be necessary before non-German newspapers may appear. These are not necessarily printed in the German language.

    c. That non-Germans shall be prohibited by law from participating financially in or influencing German newspapers and that the penalty for contravention of the law shall be the suppression of any such newspaper, and immediate deportation of the non-German concerned in it . . .

*Mistranslation for "Laender" meaning "states."

24. We demand liberty for all religious denominations in the State, so far as they are not a danger to it and do not militate against the moral feelings of the German race.

The party, as such, stands for positive Christianity, but does not bind itself in the matter of creed to any particular confession. It combats the Jewish-Materialist spirit within us and without us, and is convinced that our nation can only achieve permanent health from within on the principle "the good of the State before the good of the individual."

Though the Nazis went into office on January 30, 1933, it was not until after the election of March 5, 1933, that their stay was "ratified" by the German people. The Nazis did not obtain a majority vote, and even with the help of the Stahlhelm delegates, they composed only 52% of all German votes.

While there had been numerous attacks on Jews during the five weeks between January 20 and March 5, these attacks were sporadic and were aimed at those few Jews who also happened to be socialists or communists. But there was reason to fear that anti-Jewish riots, directed against Jews as such and of a much more serious nature, were contemplated to take place soon after the election.

On March 2, 1933, there appeared in American newspapers the following Associated Press dispatch from London:

The London Daily Herald said today that plans were complete for an anti-Jewish pogrom in Germany on a scale as terrible as any instance of Jewish persecution in 2000 years. The paper ascribes its information to a 'highest' source.

The whole Jewish population of Germany, totaling 600,000, is living under the shadow of a campaign of murder which may be initiated within a few hours and cannot at the most be postponed more than a few days, the Herald said.

A member of the American Jewish Committee who happened to be in Washington at the time, called the report to the attention of President Hoover. The President, on his last full day in the White House, directed the Secretary of State to cable the American Ambassador at Berlin, instructing him to make appropriate representation to the German authorities. A few days later, similar instructions were sent out by Cordell Hull, the Secretary of State of the incoming administration, in the name of President Roosevelt.[18]

In answer to many protests to the State Department against the anti-Jewish riots which took place immediately after the German election of March 5, 1933, Secretary Hull addressed the following telegram to Cyrus Adler, President of the American Jewish Committee, and Alfred M. Cohen, President of the B'nai B'rith, whom he had met in conference a few days before.[19]

Washington, D. C.
March 26, 1933

You will remember that at the time of your recent call at the Department I informed you that in view of numerous press-statements indicating wide-spread mistreatment of the Jews in Germany, I would request the American Embassy at Berlin consultation with the principal consulates in Germany to investigate the situation and submit a report. A reply has now been received indicating that whereas there was for a short time considerable physical mistreatment of Jews this phase may be considered virtually terminated. There was also some picketing of Jewish merchandizing stores and instances of professional discrimination. These manifestations were viewed with serious concern by the German Government. Hitler in his capacity as leader of the Nazi party issued an order calling upon his followers to maintain law and order, to avoid molesting foreigners, disrupting trade and to avoid the creation of possible embarrassing international incidents. Later Von Papen delivered a speech at Breslau in which he not only reiterated Hitler's appeals for discipline but adjured the victors of the last election not to spoil their triumph by unworthy acts of revenge and violence which could only bring discredit upon the new régime in foreign countries. As a result the Embassy reports that the authority of the regular police has been reenforced. The feeling has been wide-spread in Germany that following so far reaching a political readjustment as has recently taken place, some time must elapse before a state of equilibrium could be reestablished. In the opinion of the Embassy, such a stabilization appears to have been reached in the field of personal mistreatment and

[18] *American Jewish Year Book*, 1934–1935, pages 434–5.
[19] *Ibid.*, page 435.

there are indications that in other phases the situation is improving. I feel hopeful in view of the reported attitude of high German officials and the evidence of amelioration already indicated that the situation which has caused such wide-spread concern through-out this country, will soon revert to normal. Meanwhile I shall continue to watch the situation closely with a sympathetic interest and with a desire to be helpful in whatever way possible.

Cordell Hull

On April 9, 1933, Dr. Adler and Mr. Cohen sent Secretary Hull a memorandum written by Mr. Max J. Kohler, in which the author cited many instances in the past in which the Government of the United States had interceded in behalf of persecuted religious and racial minorities on the grounds of humanitarianism. Two more meetings were held with the Secretary of State, and on the date of the second meeting, April 28, 1933, the Department of State issued the following statement:[20]

Secretary Hull announced today that he had recently assured representatives of American Jewish organizations that he was con-tinuing to watch the situation confronting the Jews in Germany with careful and sympathetic interest. He would continue, he asserted, to do everything within diplomatic usage to be of assis-tance.

He gave the assurances to Dr. Cyrus Adler of Philadelphia, President of the American Jewish Committee, and I. M. Rubinow, of Cincinnati, Secretary of the Independent Order of B'nai B'rith, who called on him at the State Department. Their call followed one made by them late in March to inquire about the attitude of the United States Government. They received similar assurances at that time.

On June 28, 1933, Mr. William Phillips, then Under-Secretary of State, assured the American Jewish Committee that "every reasonable effort is being made to insure sym-pathetic and considerate treatment of aliens applying for visas in Germany."[21]

[20] *American Jewish Year Book*, 1934–1935, pages 436–7.
[21] *Ibid.*, page 438.

In a letter of August 5, 1933, addressed to the recently formed Joint Consultative Council,[22] Mr. Phillips gave out the information that the State Department had sent special instructions to consular offices inside and outside of Germany that wherever German Jews apply for visas to the United States the utmost consideration be shown to them. As a result of these instructions many thousands of Jews have found haven in the United States.

In July, 1935, a delegation consisting of representatives of the American Jewish Committee, the B'nai B'rith, and the Jewish Labor Committee, called upon Acting Secretary of State William Phillips and presented a remonstrance requesting that the American Government protest against racial and religious persecutions that prevail in Germany, and to take every step consistent with international practice to inform the German Government of the outraged sentiments of the American people. The remonstrance of the Jewish organizations read in part as follows:[23]

It is inconceivable that the American Government should stand passively by and neglect to lift its voice against these assaults upon humanity, or to utter its condemnation of the violation of the fundamental principles of human rights. Our country has traditionally recognized its moral and legal right, as well as its duty to speak in behalf of those persecuted for their religious beliefs and for minority groups or races deprived of their just rights.

Acting Secretary Phillips, in his reply, said:[24]

I fully understand your solicitude regarding the experiences which these groups are reported to be suffering in Germany. The concepts of religious freedom and liberty of conscience for all constitute the most fundamental principles of our own civilization and political faith. This being so, the American people are always sympathetic to the maintenance of their concepts in the United States as well as in other nations.

[22] The Joint Consultative Council was composed of representatives of the following three organizations: The American Jewish Committee, the American Jewish Congress and the B'nai B'rith.

[23] *American Jewish Year Book*, 1936–1937, page 619.

[24] *Ibid.*, page 621.

American public opinion clamored for an official condemnation of German anti-Jewish policy by the Administration in Washington. The voice of the people was expressed in many protest meetings held in every corner of the country, including one at Madison Square Garden, New York City, on March 27, 1933. The speech made by Senator Joseph T. Robinson of Arkansas, leader of the Democratic majority in the Senate, may be considered the administration's answer to this clamor, and as an official expression of the administration's views.[25]

Speeches in similar vein were made by Senators Jesse H. Metcalf, of Rhode Island; Royal S. Copeland, of New York; Henry D. Hatfield, of West Virginia; Millard E. Tydings of Maryland; David I. Walsh of Massachusetts; J. Hamilton Lewis, of Illinois; and Robert F. Wagner, of New York, a native of Germany.

Similar expressions were made on numerous occasions by many members in the House of Representatives. On May 24, 1933, Mr. Hamilton Fish, Jr., Representative from New York, introduced in the House the following concurrent resolution:[26]

Whereas the German Government is pursuing a relentless and ruthless policy of economic persecution and repression of Jews in Germany; and

Whereas it is the avowed intention of the German Government to deprive the Jews of their civic, political, and economic rights; and

Whereas the comparatively small number of Jews in Germany, not exceeding 600,000, or 1 percent of the German population, constitute a peaceful, law-abiding, industrious, and defenseless element of the population: Therefore be it

Resolved by the House of Representatives (the Senate concurring), That the Congress of the United States regrets the continued persecution of the Jews in Germany and expresses its sympathy for them in their hour of trial, humiliation, and economic discrimination, and requests the President of the United States to use his good offices and make friendly representation to the German

[25] *Congressional Record,* 73d Congress, 1st Session, Vol. 77, Part 6, page 5538.

[26] *Ibid.,* Part 4, page 4117.

Government in the interest of humanity, justice, and world peace, to respect the civic and economic rights of its citizens of Jewish origin, and to put an end to racial and religious persecution.

A number of similar resolutions were later introduced in both houses of Congress, including one by Senator William H. King of Utah, suggesting that the United States sever diplomatic relations with the Government of Germany. Senator Tydings of Maryland introduced the following resolution on January 4, 1934:[27]

Resolved, that the President is requested to communicate to the Government of the German Reich an unequivocal statement of the profound feelings of surprise and pain experienced by the people of the United States upon learning of the discriminations and oppressions imposed by the Reich upon its Jewish citizens; and be it further

Resolved, that the President is requested in such communication to express the earnest hope of the people of the United States that the German Reich will speedily alter its policy, restore to its Jewish nationals the civil and political rights of which they have been deprived, and undo so far as may be the wrongs that have been done them.

In the fall of 1933 the Assembly of the League of Nations took official cognizance of the problem of the refugees from Germany. It decided to create the office of High Commissioner for Refugees Coming from Germany for the purpose of co-ordinating all work on behalf of the refugees. At the same time it was also decided to set up a governing body composed of representatives from states and private organizations to assist the High Commissioner in his work.

Mr. James G. McDonald, of New York City, formerly President of the Foreign Policy Association, was named first High Commissioner. The Government of the United States appointed Dr. Joseph P. Chamberlain, Professor of Public Law at Columbia University, to be American representative on the Governing Board.

An indirect rebuke to Germany and a reminder to it that the American Government as well as its people were very

[27] *Congressional Record*, 73d Congress, 2d Session, Vol. 78, Part 1, page 176.

much interested in the condition of the German Jews was given in a note, dated June 28, 1934, which Secretary Hull sent to Rudolf Leitner, German Chargé d'Affaires in Washington. The following quotation, dealing with the suspension by Germany of service on her foreign debts, is relevant to our present discussion:[28]

The creation of any particular transfer situation and the possibilities of transferring funds needed to meet external obligations are by no means solely dependent on the policies pursued by creditor governments .... In any particular transfer situation, such as that which now faces Germany, the policies pursued by the debtor government are no less crucial elements. The German Government is no doubt aware that its policies have created opposition in many parts of the world, which has expressed itself in various trade conflicts and the probable reduction of Germany's capacity to transfer.

President Roosevelt himself has on a number of occasions expressed, directly and indirectly, his sympathy with the suffering German Jews.

In a speech at San Diego, California, on October 2, 1935, the President referred to Germany in the following manner:[29]

Our national determination to keep free of foreign wars and foreign entanglements cannot prevent us from feeling deep concern when ideals and principles that we have cherished are challenged.

In the United States we regard as axiomatic that every person shall enjoy the free exercise of his religion according to the dictates of his conscience. Our flag for a century and a half has been the symbol of the principles of liberty of conscience, of religious freedom and equality before the law, and these concepts are deeply ingrained in our national character.

It is true that other nations may, as they do, enforce contrary rules of conscience and conduct. It is true that policies that may be pursued under flags other than our own are beyond our jurisdiction. Yet in our inner individual lives we can never be indifferent, and we assert for ourselves complete freedom to embrace, to profess and to observe the principles for which our flag has so long been the lofty symbol.

On the occasion of the celebration of the second anniversary of the University-in-Exile, the faculty of which is com-

---

[28] *The New York Times*, June 29, 1934, page 1.
[29] *Ibid.*, October 3, 1935, page 1.

posed mainly of expatriated, or self-exiled, German professors, President Roosevelt sent the following letter to Dr.
Alvin Johnson, president of the University-in-Exile:[30]

[*President Roosevelt to Dr. Johnson*]

The White House
Washington, Jan. 14, 1936

MY DEAR DOCTOR JOHNSON:

Public duties unfortunately prevent my attendance at the dinner
to which you have kindly asked me. But I should like to congratulate you and the Graduate Faculty of Political and Social
Science upon the successful completion of your first two-year
period and to tender my best wishes for a brilliant future.

The principle which is symbolized by your Graduate Faculty,
namely, freedom of scientific inquiry, untrammelled by religious
or racial restrictions, is deeply rooted in the American tradition.
Ever since the beginning of our Republic, we have welcomed many
men and women of ability and character from other countries, who
had found their usefulness cut off by conditions which are alien to
the American system. Some of our most famous patriots, scholars
and scientists came to this country in 1848. The whole nation has
been enriched, morally and materially, through the abilities which
they placed at our service.

I am particularly gratified to learn that in your Graduate Faculty
there are representatives of the three great religions, Protestant,
Catholic and Jewish. It is one of the fundamental principles of
true Americanism that all religions are entitled to equal respect.
Freedom for every man to worship God according to the mandates
of his conscience implies the political, social and intellectual freedom which is the very foundation of our national life.

Your Graduate Faculty represents American adherence to the
principle of intellectual freedom. I wish it every success in carrying, as it does, the torch of truth-seeking for the good of mankind.

Very sincerely yours,
FRANKLIN D. ROOSEVELT

Another reference to Germany and its treatment of the
German Jews was made by Secretary Ickes at a dinner
given in his honor by the United Palestine Appeal, on May

[30] *The New York Times,* January 16, 1936, page 23.

24, 1936. In his speech on that occasion, Mr. Ickes made the following statement:[31]

It is my privilege to bring to you tonight a greeting from the President of the United States, expressing his interest in what you are trying to do. He has charged me to say to you who are an integral and valued element in the nation that he is distressed and disturbed by the reversion in certain parts of the world to days and deeds of an era which all enlightened people had long hoped would never return.

It is his conviction that so long as minorities of the nations of the world are deprived of liberty of thought and religion and the right to lead a normal, civilized life, there can be no true and permanent understanding between nations.

The President expresses through me to you, the representatives of a great and virile race, the hope that calmer and more dispassionate judgments will prevail and asserts the belief that the Government of the United States, in carrying out the will of the people, will ever give watchful care to the minorities within its borders, and will maintain inviolate those vital rights that are guaranteed by the Constitution even to the most humble of our citizens.

On a few occasions the words used by local officials to express their feeling against the persecution of the German Jews were so strong as to call forth protests from Berlin and subsequently an apology from our Government in Washington. The most notable of these cases are the Bremen flag case, and what may be called the second La Guardia incident.

On July 26, 1935, a group of American radicals gathered in front of the pier in New York City where the German steamer Bremen was preparing to leave for Europe and protested against the forcible holding without trial of an American sailor for allegedly spreading Communist propaganda in Germany. A few of the demonstrators rushed on to the boat and attempted to remove the swastika flag which was then flying at the bow. In the altercation that ensued many of the protestants were wounded and later arrested on the charge of unlawful assembly.

Magistrate Louis B. Brodsky later acquitted the defendants. He accompanied this action with the reading of a

[31] *The New York Times*, May 25, 1936, page 12.

written statement in which he expressed the opinion that to the defendants as well as to many others the swastika flag was regarded as "the black flag of piracy." The magistrate went on to say:[32]

In a large sense, indeed, it might seem as though whatever disturbances attended the sailing of the Bremen were provoked by this flaunting of an emblem to those who regarded it as a defiant challenge to society.

In answer to an indignant protest from Germany, Secretary Hull expressed the regret of the United States in a statement, part of which read as follows:[33]

The complaint of the German Government is specifically directed at the statements made by the magistrate in rendering his decision which that government interprets as an unwarranted reflection against it.

The Department is constrained to feel that the Magistrate, in restating contentions of the defendants in the case and in commenting upon the incident, unfortunately so worded his opinion as to give the reasonable and definite impression that he was going out of his way adversely to criticize the government, which criticism was not a relevant or legitimate part of his judicial decision.

I may explain that state and municipal officials are not instrumentalities of the Federal Government. Although in this country the right of freedom of speech is well recognized by our fundamental law, it is to be regretted that an official having no responsibility for maintaining relations between the United States and other countries should, regardless of what he may personally think of the laws and policies of other governments, thus indulge in expressions offensive to another government with which we have official relations.

At the second annual luncheon of the Women's Division of the American Jewish Congress, on March 3, 1937, Mayor La Guardia, while discussing the proposal to erect a building dedicated to the "Freedom of Faith" at the then coming World Fair in New York City, made the suggestion that there be added a chamber of horrors in which he would have

[32] *The New York Times*, September 7, 1935, page 1.
[33] *Ibid.*, September 15, 1935, page 1.

as a climax "a figure of that brown-shirted fanatic who is now menacing the peace of the world."

In response to official protest from the German Government, the State Department, through James Clement Dunn, head of the Division of the Western European Affairs, made, on March 5, the following oral statements to Dr. Hans Thomsen, counsellor of the German Embassy:[34]

The German Government through its embassy here makes complaint against certain utterances of Honorable Fiorello La Guardia in a public address at the Hotel Astor in New York on March the third, stating that such utterances seriously and severely reflect upon the head of the German State and the German Government.

In this country the right of freedom of speech is guaranteed by the Constitution to every citizen and is cherished as a part of the national heritage. This, however, does not lessen the regret of the government when utterances either by private citizens or by public officials speaking in an individual capacity give offense to a government with which we have official relations.

I very earnestly deprecate the utterances which have thus given offense to the German Government. They do not represent the attitude of this government toward the German Government. It is our policy to conduct the official relations with other nations upon a basis of complete and mutual respect for the rights and sensibilities of each other.

This apology too contained an indirect rebuke to the Government of Germany.

As an aftermath of this incident, the State Department had occasion to protest against a campaign of abuse begun by the Nazi press against America and Americans in general and the Jewish community of New York in particular. Especially obnoxious in this campaign were uncomplimentary remarks about the Women's Division of the American Jewish Congress in *Der Angriff*, the personal organ of Dr. Paul Joseph Goebbels, Minister for Propaganda and Enlightenment.

Mrs. Stephen S. Wise, president of the Women's Division of the American Jewish Congress, asked Secretary Hull to

[34] *The New York Times*, March 6, 1937, page 1.

"insist upon a public disavowal of this deliberately insulting and false utterance." Mrs. Wise pointed out that there being no free press in Nazi Germany, the German Government should be held responsible for everything that appeared in Nazi publications, and should therefore express publicly its regret in an official apology. Secretary Hull in a note to the German Government, and Ambassador William E. Dodd protested vigorously against attacks on Americans in the Nazi press. The German Government did not issue a public apology, but Foreign Minister Konstantin von Neurath gave an explanation to Ambassador Dodd in which he declared that no insult to the American nation was intended.

Only a few days later, Mayor La Guardia again became the cause of another protest from the German Government. At a mass meeting at the Madison Square Garden, held under the auspices of the American Jewish Congress and the Jewish Labor Committee, on March 15, 1937, Mayor La Guardia made a brief unscheduled address in which he declared that "public opinion of the world has decreed that Adolf Hitler is not personally or diplomatically 'satisfaktions-fähig'."[35] The German Ambassador Hans Luther thereupon called on Secretary Hull and voiced another protest against the Mayor of New York City.

In an official statement after the interview, Mr. Hull expressed the hope "that all who are participating in the present controversy, which is marked by bitter and vituperative utterances in this country and in Germany, may soon reach the conclusion that it would be to the best interests of both countries for them to find other subjects which can be discussed more temperately."[36]

On April 19, 1937, the Nazi Government promulgated a decree prohibiting all Jewish meetings for a period of sixty days. Many leaders of the German Branch of the Independent Order of B'nai B'rith were arrested, and all the lodges were dissolved and their property confiscated. Secre-

[35] *The New York Times*, March 16, 1937, page 1.
[36] *Ibid.*, March 18, 1937, page 1.

tary Hull, informed of the situation by Alfred M. Cohen, President of B'nai B'rith, expressed his deep concern at this act and promised to give the matter his earnest consideration.

Following the Nazi invasion of Austria, on March 12, 1938, anti-Jewish excesses began immediately and were perpetrated in a brutal and revolting manner.

On April 28, 1938, the Reich issued a decree ordering all Jews to declare their property holdings in Germany in excess of 5,000 marks. The manner in which this decree was worded seemed to indicate that it was intended to apply to all Jews owning property in Austria, regardless of their residence or their citizenship. The Government of the United States made emphatic protest against the application of the decree to American citizens. On May 11, 1938, the State Department made public the text of a note which our Ambassador to Germany, Hugh R. Wilson, presented to the German Government.[37] The note declared that the Government of the United States "considers that the application of measures of the nature indicated to the property of American citizens of the Jewish race would violate rights accorded American citizens under the Treaty of Friendship, Commerce and Consular Rights between the United States and Germany, signed December 8, 1923." All rights conferred by Article I of the treaty were made applicable to all nationals "without exceptions based on race or creed."

The note concluded with the demand that the German Government "give early assurances that the measures will not be applied to American citizens."

On June 25, the State Department made public the following summary of the German reply:[38]

The note from the German Government states that the competent internal administration authorities will waive application of the registration procedure to Jewish property in the hands of American nationals permanently domiciled abroad, unless they were former German nationals who have emigrated. The German

---

[37] *The New York Times*, May 12, 1938, page 4.
[38] *Ibid.*, June 26, 1938, page 20.

Foreign Office orally explained that this limitation referred to those who had emigrated for political reasons since 1933.

The plight of the Jews of Germany, grown much worse after the occupation of Austria, as well as the continued persecution of "non-Aryan" liberals who could not adapt themselves to the prevailing Nazi doctrines, moved the President of the United States to such an extent that he decided to call an international conference to discuss ways and means to help find new homes for these unwanted minorities.

On March 24, 1938, it was announced in Washington that the Government of the United States had sent a note to twenty-nine countries which proposed the creation of a special international committee to facilitate emigration of political refugees from Germany and Austria. The official summary of the note reads as follows:[39]

This government has become so impressed with the urgency of the problem of political refugees that it has inquired of a number of governments in Europe and in this hemisphere whether they would be willing to cooperate in setting up a special committee for the purpose of facilitating the emigration from Austria and presumably from Germany of political refugees.

Our idea is that, whereas such representatives would be designated by the governments concerned, any financing of the emergency emigration referred to would be undertaken by private organizations within the respective countries. Furthermore, it should be understood that no country would be expected or asked to receive a greater number of immigrants than is permitted by its existing legislation.

In making this proposal the Government of the United States has emphasized that it in no sense intends to discourage or interfere with such work as is already being done on the refugee problem by any existing international agency.

It has been prompted to make its proposal because of the urgency of the problem with which the world is faced and the necessity of speedy cooperative effort under governmental supervision if widespread human suffering is to be averted.

At a press conference on the following day, President Roosevelt observed that this effort to co-operate with

---

[39] *The New York Times,* March 25, 1938, page 1.

other nations in an attempt to rescue persecuted minorities, marked no change in the foreign policies of the United States, as since its establishment in 1789 it has always been the traditional attitude of our country to offer itself as a haven for political refugees. He pointed out that the Government's proposal was intended to help Jews, Protestants and Catholics, from Germany, as well as the persecuted minorities of Russia, Italy and Spain.[40]

On April 13, the President conferred at the White House with a number of representative persons from many walks of life and with them laid the groundwork for American participation in the international conference. This conference met at Evian, France, on July 6. Thirty-two nations were represented. Of those invited, Italy alone refused to attend.[41] Myron C. Taylor, former chairman of the United States Steel Corporation, was chosen by the President to head the American delegation to the Conference. Later Mr. Taylor was elected to preside at the conference which referred to itself as the Intergovernmental Committee on Refugees.

The conference provided an international forum for the exchange of opinion and information on the subject of refugees, and for discussion of the possibilities of finding havens for them. Deep sympathy was expressed by all representatives with the miserable situation of hundreds of thousands of emigrants or would-be emigrants. But most of the work done was of a preliminary nature. As was said by Mr. Taylor in his first address before the Intergovernmental Committee:[42]

We must admit frankly, indeed, that this problem of political refugees is so vast and so complex that we probably can do no more at the initial intergovernmental meeting than put in motion the machinery, and correlate it with existing machinery, that will, in the long run, contribute to a practicable amelioration of the unfortunate human beings with whom we are concerned.

[40] *The New York Times*, March 26, 1938, page 1.

[41] Since the conclusion of the Evian Conference, Italy has adopted as its own the racial theories of Nazi Germany and has started an active campaign of anti-Semitism.

[42] *The New York Times*, July 7, 1938, page 9.

Characterizing discrimination and pressure against minority groups as "contrary to the principles of what we have come to regard as the accepted standards of civilization," Mr. Taylor expressed the hope of the American Government that the meeting would be the initial step in the collaboration of the receiving governments in their assistance to the political refugees.

The conference lasted nine days. At its last meeting it decided to reconvene in London on the 3rd of August, 1938, when a permanent organization would be formed to be headed by an executive director with the power to negotiate with Germany for the purpose of gaining some privileges for refugees from Germany, especially in the matter of easing capital export restrictions.

Mr. Taylor closed the meeting with an optimistic observation, saying:[43]

We have heard from the governments of refuge and settlement confidential statements which hold out prospects for an increased reception of refugees within the framework of existing immigration law and practices. We have had from the private organizations estimates of the extent of the problem with which we are faced, together with proposals for solution which we shall take into account in formulating concrete plans for the continuation of our work.

Our work must, and it will, continue tirelessly, without interruption, in order that the hopes of the men, women and children who have placed their faith in our efforts may not be dispelled and their suffering embittered.

At the London meeting of August 3, Mr. George Rublee of New York City, a friend of President Roosevelt, was named director of the Refugee Bureau, Lord Winterton was elected chairman, and Myron C. Taylor vice-chairman. Unfortunately the efforts of the Intergovernmental Committee did not bear the fruits hoped for, as the German Government gave it only an informal recognition, and the terms on which it proposed to co-operate with it were unacceptable.

[43] *The New York Times*, July 16, 1938, page 4.

The problem of the involuntary migrants from Central Europe became more acute as a result of the Munich Pact between Germany, Italy, Great Britain and France, which incorporated the Sudetenland into Germany. Many Jews found themselves suddenly homeless and stateless, expelled from one country and not allowed to enter another. Many "no-man's-lands" were created on the frontiers between such countries, where Jews lived in utter misery and starvation during the winter months of 1938–39. Other Jews were wandering on the seas, going from one country to another in search of a haven — and not finding any.

This bad situation was further aggravated by the infamous attacks on the Jews of Germany on November 10, 1938. In their ferocity and cruelty the assaults on a defenceless minority which took place on that day far surpassed anything that had happened earlier in Germany under Hitler. Allegedly perpetrated as a reaction to the murder of Ernst vom Rath, a German Embassy official in Paris, by a crazed Jewish youth, these outrages actually bore all the signs of a premeditated and carefully planned pogrom. Tens of thousands of German Jews were sent to concentration camps on that "Black Thursday"; Jewish homes and business places in almost every corner in Germany were broken into, valuables stolen, and the furniture and other household goods smashed. Many of the Jews arrested were reported to have met their death in concentration camps as a result of cruel torture practiced upon them by their jailers. Hundreds of Jews, in fear of such a fate, preferred death at their own hands. Over 600 synagogues were burned, and many invaluable and irreplaceable religious manuscripts and ritual objects were destroyed.

The events of that day were followed by the imposition of a fine of one billion marks ($400,000,000) which the German Jews had to pay, to atone for the murder of vom Rath. Besides this fine, decrees were promulgated with the obvious intent of depriving Jews of all means of livelihood, thus forcing them to find a home elsewhere.

Public opinion in this country and all the world over

was outraged at the happenings in Germany of November 10, and voices of sympathy and protest were heard from government officials and from organizations of all kinds.

In the United States, President Roosevelt on November 15 called Ambassador Hugh R. Wilson back from Berlin. At the same time the President made public his personal reactions in the following statement:[44]

The news of the past few days from Germany has deeply shocked public opinion in the United States. Such news from any part of the world would inevitably produce a similar profound reaction among American people in every part of the nation.

I myself could scarcely believe that such things could occur in a twentieth century civilization.

With a view to gaining a first-hand picture of the situation in Germany I asked the Secretary of State to order our Ambassador in Berlin to return at once for report and consultation.

The American Government took, in addition, various steps to facilitate the coming into this country of as many refugees as were allowed under then existing immigration laws. Meanwhile, the protection of American citizens of Jewish faith who resided or had property in Germany was discussed in an exchange of notes between our Government and the Government of Germany.

On December 14, 1938, Mr. Prentiss B. Gilbert, then Chargé d'Affaires *ad interim* at Berlin, presented a note to the German Minister of Foreign Affairs, in which assurances were asked that the German Government would not subject American citizens to differential treatment due to their race or creed. The note went on to declare that the application of the provisions of the decree laws to American citizens of the Jewish faith would be contrary to a fundamental American principle, that of not permitting any distinction between citizens on the basis of race or creed; and that, in its relations with other nations, the Government of the United States had always declined the right to other nations to apply on their part such discrimination as between American citizens.

[44] *The New York Times*, November 16, 1938, page 1.

Baron Ernst Weiszäcker, Under Secretary, replied for the German Government in a note dated December 30, 1938. The German note contended that the American principle of non-discrimination on the basis of race or creed could not be made to apply to American citizens staying in a foreign country where such discrimination is practiced; that such discrimination was not contrary to international law; that the German Government would protect all American citizens in those rights to which they are entitled by virtue of treaties between the two countries, and that should the American Embassy show cases where such rights were violated the German Government for its part was prepared "to examine and settle them on the basis of prevailing treaty provisions."

On January 11, 1939, Mr. Gilbert addressed another note in which the American Government insisted that American views of equality of all American citizens irrespective of their faith or creed be respected by the German Government. Taking advantage of the German promise of its note of December 30, 1938, Mr. Gilbert presented a few cases of discrimination against American citizens.

The full text of the note follows:[45]

I have the honor to acknowledge the receipt of the note signed by Mr. Weiszäcker of December 30, 1938, concerning the treatment in Germany of American citizens, and under instructions of my Government to reply as follows:

My Government, maintaining the position set forth in the note of December 14, 1938 reiterates its fundamental position that it declines to recognize the right of other nations to apply on their part to American citizens measures which would have the effect of arbitrarily dividing them into special classes and subjecting them to differential treatment on the basis of such classification, irrespective of measures applied by other nations to their own citizens on the basis of differential classification of their own citizens.

The treatment accorded in Germany to American citizens, however, is governed not only by the principles of international law but by the prevailing treaties between Germany and the United States, and in this respect my Government has been gratified to note in Your Excellency's declaration that the rights to which

[45] Documents on American Foreign Relations, January 1938–June 1939. pages 330–1. (World Peace Foundation, Boston, 1939.)

American citizens are entitled by virtue of treaties between the two countries would be respected, and that the German Government for its part is prepared to examine and settle on the basis of prevailing treaty provisions cases which in the opinion of my Government are violations of such treaty rights and of which the German Foreign Office is informed by this Embassy.

My Government has accordingly instructed me to present to Your Excellency as they arise such cases of American citizens which heretofore it has been the practice to take up with the competent local authorities and with regard to which formal assurances in general form have repeatedly been sought from Your Excellency's Government that the measures in question would not be applied to American citizens.

I am therefore presenting for examination and settlement certain specific cases of the nature referred to which have already been brought to my attention and I shall pursue this practice should similar cases be brought to my attention in the future.

On December 22, 1938, Mr. Sumner Welles, Acting Secretary of State, published an official summary of conversations held by him with Dr. Hans Thomsen, German Chargé d'Affaires at Washington. On behalf of his government, Dr. Thomsen had protested against the attitude toward Germany of the American press and also against public statements by Secretary of the Interior Harold Ickes, who in a speech at Cleveland on Sunday, December 18, had criticized Henry Ford and Colonel Charles A. Lindbergh for having accepted decorations from the German Government, and in general had administered a severe lashing to that Government for its abusive and barbarous treatment of Jews.

The full text of the summary follows:[46]

Dr. Thomsen began the interview by informing Mr. Welles that his government desired to make a formal protest with regard to the address of Secretary Ickes. The chargé d'affaires then said that he was instructed to say that Germany trusted that the United States Government would make public an official expression of regret.

In reply Mr. Welles informed Dr. Thomsen that he was unwilling to accept the protest. While he had not read the full text of the speech delivered by Secretary Ickes, he had read detailed summaries which appeared in the press and which he assumed were accurate.

[46] *The New York Times*, December 23, 1938, page 1.

There were two phases of the speech as he understood it: one phase dealing with criticism on the part of Secretary Ickes of two American citizens because of their acceptance of decorations of the German Government. With regard to a purely domestic question such as the action of the two Americans and the criticism of such action by an American official, the Acting Secretary of State said he would not agree to discuss this matter with the representative of any foreign government.

With regard to remarks contained in Secretary Ickes's speech which might have been regarded as criticism of policies pursued by the German Government, Mr. Welles said the German Government must surely be familiar with the fact that the recent policies pursued in Germany had shocked and confounded public opinion in the United States more profoundly than anything that had taken place in many decades, and such references to this state of public indignation as may have been made certainly represented the feeling of the overwhelming majority of the people of the United States.

Mr. Welles said it seemed to him the desire of the German Government to make a protest of this character came with singular ill-grace. For the past few months he had followed carefully the German press, which he was sure the German chargé d'affaires could hardly dispute was completely under the influence and dictation of the authorities of the German Government, and he had rarely read more unjustifiable criticism or open attacks on members of another government than had been made in that press in their recent attacks against the President of the United States and the members of his Cabinet.

Mr. Welles continued by saying that so long as attacks of this kind persisted, unquestionably authorized by the German authorities, he reiterated, he could not conceive of there being any propriety in a protest on the part of the German Government regarding the speech made by the Secretary of the Interior.

At this point Dr. Thomsen interjected that he did not consider the criticisms made in the German press were on a par with the criticisms made by a member of the Cabinet of the United States.

As to that, Mr. Welles said that within the past few months he had read remarks made by officials of the German Government derogatory to the late President Woodrow Wilson and remarked that the chargé d'affaires must realize that, while Woodrow Wilson was dead, his memory was revered by the people of the United States and such attacks on the late President had been deeply resented in this country.

The Acting Secretary of State concluded the interview by saying that he personally believed public recriminations in any country against another country were not conducive to good relations between the peoples of the world, but nevertheless so long as the attacks against officials of the United States Government, which had been continuing for so long, persisted in Germany, the German Government could hardly suppose that attacks of the same character would not continue in the United States.

The year 1939 would normally have brought the problem of the Jews in Germany nearer to "solution." Leaving most of their possessions in Germany, many German Jews were glad to escape from their native land and start a new life elsewhere. Gradually their number in Greater Germany became smaller and it was expected that within a few years there would be no Jews left in Germany. As a result, however, of the conquests by Nazi Germany since the outbreak of the Hitler World War, additional millions of Jews in the invaded countries have come under Nazi tyranny. A recital of the barbarities to which they are being subjected would form one of the most shameful chapters in the history of civilization.

XIII. NOTE ON ITALY

The diplomatic correspondence of the United States which has been published contains no reference to any interchange of communications with the government of Italy with regard to Jews of either country or concerning Jews elsewhere. It was not until the fascist regime of Premier Benito Mussolini entered into an alliance with Germany that there was any occasion for such correspondence.

Although Premier Mussolini had declared on several occasions that fascism and anti-Semitism are incompatible, yet an anti-Jewish campaign in the press, beginning about the fall of 1936, was permitted to go on. Even during the progress of this campaign, assurances were given to Italian Americans visiting Italy that the government had no intention of taking any action detrimental to the Jews of Italy. In mid-July, 1938, however, following a visit to Italy of a group of so-called "racial experts" from Germany, a committee of Italian scientists issued a report of an alleged study which had led them to conclude that the Jews of Italy were of a different stock from the non-Jews, and that the latter were of pure "Aryan" lineage. Publication of this report aroused considerable amazed interest in many countries. Apparently the government of the United States was eager to learn the significance of the publication of this report, for we find that on July 28, 1938 our Ambassador in Italy, Mr. William Phillips, visited Foreign Minister, Count Galeazzo Ciano and inquired about the anti-Jewish campaign. Count Ciano was reminded of previous assurances that there was no room for anti-Semitism in Italy. According to report, Count Ciano replied that the racial problems were then in the process of study.

As was widely feared, the report of the scientists was actually the forerunner of a series of anti-Jewish decree laws.

The decree law of November 15, 1938, deals with the exclusion of Jews from schools; the one of November 17, 1938, defines the status of Jews.[1]

These decree laws made no distinctions between native Jews and Jews of foreign citizenship. On September 12, however, the Official Gazette published a decree law affecting specifically Jews of foreign citizenship temporarily residing in Italy or those Jews who had entered the kingdom after January 1, 1919. This decree provided that all such Jews must evacuate the Kingdom of Italy, Libya and the Aegean possessions not later than March 12, 1939.

On October 5, Ambassador Phillips presented the following note to Count Ciano, protesting the application of the decree to American Jews resident in Italy:[2]

I have the honor to inform Your Excellency that I have been instructed by my government to bring the following matter to your attention:

The Official Gazette of September 12, 1938, published the text of Decree-law No. 1,381, which provides among other things that from the date of publication foreigners both of whose parents are of the Jewish race are forbidden to fix their permanent residence in the Kingdom, in Libya and in the Aegean possessions; and that foreigners both of whose parents are of the Jewish race who at the date of publication are residing within the Kingdom, Libya and the Aegean possessions and who began their sojourn there in subsequent to January 1, 1919, must leave Italian territory within six months from the date of publication. Expulsion, after application of penalties, from Italian territory is provided for non-compliance with the above obligation. It is further provided that controversies which may arise in the application of the decree-law shall be settled case by case by decree of the Minister of the Interior.

The Official Gazette of September 13, 1938, published Decree-law No. 1,390, whereby all persons both of whose parents are of Jewish race are barred from the teaching profession in general and

---

[1] For text of these laws see *Contemporary Jewish Record*, Vol. II, No. 1, pages 10–12. It should be noted that Ethiopia, Eritrea and Italian Somaliland were excluded from the decree-law of September 12, 1938.

[2] *Ibid.*, Vol. I, No. 2, page 14.

from admission to all schools and institutions of learning recognized by the State.

While the treaty of commerce and navigation between the United States and Italy of 1871, which contained provisions for establishment and residence, has been abrogated, nevertheless, Italians who have been properly admitted into the United States may reside wherever they like therein and are accorded the full protection of our law with respect to their persons and property. In general they may freely engage in private business, trade, or occupation; they also enjoy religious freedom and there is no discrimination either on the ground of race or creed.

My government believes, therefore, that upon further consideration the Italian Government will decide that American citizens lawfully residing in Italy will not be discriminated against on account of race or creed and that they will not be subjected to provisions of the nature of those embodied in the decree-laws in question.

From the reply of the Italian Government in a note given to Mr. Phillips on October 17, 1938, it would seem that American Jews would be favored in the application of the law. The State Department did not publish the full text of the Italian reply but gave out the following synopsis of it:[3]

The Italian Foreign Office on October 17, 1938, handed the American Ambassador, Mr. William Phillips, a note in reply to this government's note on October 4, 1938, in regard to the status of American Jews in Italy.

The Italian Government points out in its reply that Royal Decree Law No. 136 of September 7, 1938, relates to foreign Jews in general and not only to Jews of American citizenship, and it gives assurances that in the application of the measures under discussion American Jews will not be treated less favorably than other foreign Jews.

The note furthermore draws attention to the fact that among the provisions adopted by the Fascist Grand Council on October 7, 1938, important exceptions for foreign Jews were decided upon.

Finally, the note points out that a special commission has been set up at the Ministry of the Interior for the examination of individual cases involving Jews of foreign as well as Italian citizenship.

The anti-Jewish measures were later codified and promulgated as laws by the cabinet.

[3] *The New York Times*, October 21, 1938, page 7.

PART FIVE

THE WAR YEARS,
1939—1945

XIV. HUMANITARIAN MEASURES AND POLITICAL QUESTIONS

Interpositions in behalf of Jews by the Government of the United States during World War II, acting on its own initiative and as one of the United Nations, have been of two categories, political and humanitarian. In the first category fall such subjects as the status of Palestine, the legal status of the Jews in French North Africa, the provisions of the Armistice agreements, the question of war crimes and war criminals, the Argentine suppression of the Yiddish press, and the Inter-American Conference in Mexico City. In the second category will be discussed problems in which questions of status and policy were overriden by the higher considerations of humanity. It includes chiefly activities in relation to refugees. Perhaps one should add that were it not for the fact that the United Nations were involved in a death struggle with the Axis Powers, an effort which demanded the total mobilization of their energies, the humanitarian impulses would have received a freer and fuller expression.

Palestine

The rise of the Nazis to power in Germany in 1933 swelled the stream of Jews seeking a haven in Palestine. As Jewish immigration figures mounted during the next three years, Arab opposition grew more violent. In 1936, Arab extremists initiated a reign of terror. There followed in the same year a "general strike" of the Arabs. The "strike" was abandoned only after British army contingents moved into Palestine.

In 1937 the Peel Commission, appointed by the British Government to investigate the causes of the unrest, recommended partition of the country. Rejected by both the Jews and the Arabs, this plan was abandoned. The Government then returned to its policy of seeking a compromise between

Jewish and Arab demands, and called a conference of the
leaders of both communities to meet in London in February,
1939. With the failure of this attempt, the British Government adopted a new policy which was announced in the
White Paper of May 17, 1939. According to the new plan,
immigration of Jews into Palestine would be allowed at a
rate which would bring their number up to approximately
one-third of the total population of the country. It set the
number of immigrants necessary for the achievement of
this goal at 75,000, to be admitted in the five following
years, after which immigration would be completely stopped.
In addition, the transfer of lands from Arabs to Jews was
to be completely prohibited in certain areas of the country
and restricted in others.

Following the publication of the White Paper, a flood of
requests reached the Department of State and the President
calling for American intercession in the Palestine question.
These requests for intercession were supported by various
arguments.

First, it was argued, the White Paper of 1939 was a violation of the Anglo-American Convention of 1924. This
Convention, which made the United States a signatory to
the Palestine Mandate and the Balfour Declaration, provided
that American citizens were to be given rights and privileges
equal to those of citizens of the member-states of the League
of Nations. It also prohibited the Mandatory Power from
effecting any change in the terms of the mandate without
first having obtained the consent of the United States.[1]
Accordingly, the White Paper, by acting to prevent American Jews from entering Palestine and from purchasing land
in the country, was in effect a violation of this Convention.
It set apart one class of American citizens — those of Jewish
origin — from all the rest and subjected them to discriminatory treatment.

[1] For text of Anglo-American Convention of 1924, see "Jewish National
Home in Palestine," hearings before Committee on Foreign Affairs, House
of Representatives, 78th Congress, 2nd Session, on House Resolution 418
and House Resolution 419, pages 402–411.

It was apparent, from the replies of the State Department to objections of this nature, that it did not accept this reasoning. The policy of the United States Government was to object only to such actions of the Mandatory, and to require its consent only for such changes in the Mandate, as would subject American citizens to discriminatory treatment in the narrow sense. It might object, for example, to evidences of discrimination in matters of commerce, to impairment of vested property rights, to interference with the establishment and maintenance of educational, philanthropic and religious institutions, and, in general, to evidence of inequality of treatment with other foreign nationals. However, the State Department asserted that it could find no indication of any such discrimination.

The United States was urged to assume a more active role in Palestine also on the ground of the substantial economic interests of Americans in Palestine. Above all, however, the appeals for American intercession were based on the unprecedented tragedy and need of the Jewish victims of Nazism for a place of refuge. The United States was asked to fulfil its historic role of defender of the oppressed and to exercise its influence in accordance with its great humanitarian tradition.

The protests against the British White Paper policy and the appeals for American intercession came, as noted, from many directions. Jewish organizations representing almost every shade of opinion in Jewish life repeatedly appealed to the State Department and to the President. Especially active in opposing the White Paper policy was the American Zionist Emergency Council, organized in August 1939, and comprising representatives from all Zionist groups. This body conferred on numerous occasions with leading officials of the State Department, as well as with British representatives in this country.[2] On May 1–2, 1943, the National Conference for Palestine of the United Palestine Appeal, held in Philadelphia, condemned the White Paper of 1939

---

[2] *American Jewish Year Book*, 1941–1942, page 101.

as illegal, unjust and inhuman, and called upon the Government of the United States to ask Great Britain for assurances "that Jewish immigration in Palestine shall not be abridged nor shall the purchase of land by Jews be restricted."[3]

On January 7, 1944, the American Jewish Committee submitted to Viscount Halifax, British Ambassador to the United States, a memorandum urging the repeal of the White Paper. This memorandum argued that the restrictions against the Jews contained in it were in violation of both the letter and spirit of the Balfour Declaration and the Palestine Mandate, and not consonant with the liberal tradition of the British Government and people. The memorandum was subsequently submitted to the United States Department of State.[4] Non-Jewish organizations, including the American Palestine Committee, comprising hundreds of leading Americans from all walks of life, and the Christian Council on Palestine, composed of approximately 1,500 Christian clergymen, called for the immediate opening of Palestine to the persecuted Jews of Europe. The two major labor organizations of the United States, the American Federation of Labor and the Congress of Industrial Organizations, on November 5, 1943, demanded the abolition of the White Paper. Many State legislatures during 1943 and 1944 adopted resolutions favoring the continued development of a Jewish homeland in Palestine and calling for the repeal of the White Paper.[5]

The policy of the United States Government not to intercede in the Palestine question was explained on many occasions during the war years. An official statement to this effect was made by the State Department in reply to a

[3] *American Jewish Year Book*, 1943–1944, page 208.

[4] *Ibid.*, 1944–1945, page 552.

[5] For details, see Carl J. Friedrich, "American Policy Toward Palestine," 1944, pages 40–43; Fink, "Jewish National Home in Palestine," supplemental statements to hearings submitted to Committee on Foreign Affairs, House of Representatives, 78th Congress, 2nd Session, on House Resolution No. 418 and House Resolution No. 419, pages 128–129; *American Jewish Year Book*, 1943–1944, pages 208–209.

protest from the American Jewish Committee. This protest argued that the exclusion of United States citizens of Jewish origin from immigration to Palestine "would obviously be an invidious discrimination against one class of American citizens" and "obnoxious to the fundamental ideals of our Republic and contrary to its traditional policy." To this objection, Gordon P. Merriam, Chief of the Division of Near Eastern Affairs of the United States Department of State, replied that the "status of American citizens under the White Paper is the same as that of nationals of countries which are members of the League of Nations. Any question, moreover, of the immigration of American citizens to Palestine does not appear to be a pressing one, since, in view of present travel conditions, it is not believed possible for American citizens to secure transport for this purpose."[6]

On other occasions, the State Department explained that the United States considered Palestine to be a British responsibility and therefore could not intercede. Such, for example, was the viewpoint expressed by Secretary Hull in a letter, dated January 18, 1944, addressed to Senator Burnet R. Maybank of South Carolina. The text of this letter follows:

I refer to your conversation with Mr. Brandt of the Department and to your subsequent letter of January 13, 1944, with which you enclosed a letter dated January 4, 1944, which you have received from Mr. Solomon Blatt, Speaker of the House of Representatives of South Carolina, relative to the Jewish National Home in Palestine.

In compliance with your request for information as to the attitude of the American Government toward this matter, I may say that Palestine is a British responsibility. Nevertheless, the Department maintains a close interest in the Palestine problem and follows closely all developments having a bearing upon the tragic plight of the Jewish people in Europe. You are familiar with the sympathetic attitude which the Department harbors toward the Jews in their present terrible circumstances, and it is doing everything possible, through the Inter-governmental Committee and otherwise, to alleviate their plight. Every aspect of this general problem is

[6] *The Committee Reporter*, publication of the American Jewish Committee, Vol. II, No. 4, June 1944.

a matter of immediate interest to this Government. The Department is accordingly keeping in touch with the different phases of this situation, in Palestine as in other parts of the world, and is doing what it can to be helpful.[7]

Only on the occasion of the tragic *Struma* incident in 1942 did the Department of State, in reply to an appeal for intercession, note that it had taken action. The incident of the *S. S. Struma* shocked a world that had already become inured to reports of Nazi persecutions and exterminations. The *S. S. Struma*, carrying 769 refugees from Nazi-occupied Europe, had attempted to land at a Palestinian port, but had been turned back. It then attempted to dock at a Turkish port, but was ordered out, despite the insistence of its captain that it was unseaworthy. Once in the open sea, it foundered and sank with but one survivor.

A joint delegation, representing the American Emergency Committee for Zionist Affairs, the American Jewish Committee, the American Jewish Congress, and the B'nai B'rith, visited Under-Secretary of State Sumner Welles on March 19, 1942, to protest the action of the British Government in turning away the ship bearing the refugees. The delegation presented other instances of treatment of refugees seeking a haven in Palestine, which were incompatible with human rights and out of harmony with the spirit of the Mandate and of Britain's moral obligation under it. It appealed to the State Department to intercede with the British Government to the end that these policies and practices be modified, that several hundred refugees interned in Palestine for over a year under threat of deportation be released, and that the almost 2,000 refugees deported to the Island of Mauritius be allowed to return to Palestine.

Mr. Welles, while not indicating the exact character of the State Department intercession, asserted that it had taken action and would continue to do what it could to avoid the repetition of such an unhappy occurrence.[8]

[7] Fink, Reuben, "America and Palestine," page 55.
[8] *American Jewish Year Book,* 1943–1944, pages 648–649.

Although in most cases, the Government of the United States did not find that it had the legal right to protest against British policy, numerous declarations were made during the war years by high officials of the government, which endorsed the establishment of the Jewish National Home in Palestine.

One statement, for example, which was regarded in Zionist circles as unusually significant and as giving encouragement to the hope that the United States would actively support Zionist claims during the post-war international negotiations, was a message from the late President Roosevelt read at a dinner of the American Palestine Committee in Washington, D. C., on May 25, 1942.

"The great physical, economic and educational development which has taken place in Palestine in the last two decades has been a perfect example of what can be accomplished by a free people working in a democracy. We are all looking forward to the day when that type of development may be continued in peace and harmony in the general march of mankind toward the accomplishment of the Four Freedoms everywhere in the world."[9]

The sympathy of President Roosevelt for the Jewish National Home found expression subsequently in the political program of the Democratic Party, which included the following paragraph in its platform, adopted on July 20, 1944:

We favor the opening of Palestine to unrestricted Jewish immigration and colonization, and such a policy as to result in the establishment there of a free and democratic Jewish commonwealth.[10]

On October 15, 1944, President Roosevelt affirmed his sympathy with this plank of the Democratic platform in a letter to Senator Robert F. Wagner of New York. He promised that, if elected, he would help to bring about its realization. The text of this letter follows:

[9] *American Jewish Year Book*, 1942–1943, pages 133–134; *The New York Times*, May 26, 1942, page 13.

[10] "Jewish National Home in Palestine," supplemental statements to hearings submitted to Committee on Foreign Affairs, House of Representatives, 78th Congress, 2nd Session, on House Resolution No. 418 and House Resolution 419, page 1.

Knowing that you are to attend the forty-seventh Convention of the Zionist Organization of America, I ask you to convey to the Delegates assembled my cordial greetings.

Please express my satisfaction that, in accord with the traditional American policy and in keeping with the spirit of the Four Freedoms, the Democratic Party at its July Convention this year included the following plank in its platform:

'We favor the opening of Palestine to unrestricted Jewish immigration and colonization, and such a policy as to result in the establishment there of a free and democratic Jewish commonwealth.'

Efforts will be made to find appropriate ways and means of effectuating this policy as soon as practicable. I know how long and ardently the Jewish people have worked and prayed for the establishment of Palestine as a free and democratic Jewish commonwealth. I am convinced that the American people give their support to this aim and if re-elected I shall help to bring about its realization.

A plank similar to that of the Democratic platform was also included in the platform adopted by the Republican Party at its convention in Chicago, Ill., on June 27, 1944.

The Palestine paragraph in the Republican platform read:

In order to give refuge to millions of distressed Jewish men, women and children driven from their homes by tyranny, we call for the opening of Palestine to their unrestricted immigration and land ownership, so that in accordance with the full intent and purpose of the Balfour Declaration of 1917 and the resolution of a Republican Congress in 1922, Palestine may be constituted as a free and democratic commonwealth.[11]

On October 12, 1944, Governor Dewey, Republican candidate for president, reaffirmed the stand taken by the Republican convention, stating that he was for the "re-constitution of Palestine as a free and democratic Jewish Commonwealth."[12]

With these planks, both major political parties in the United States placed themselves on record as pledged to exert their efforts towards abolishing the policy of the British White Paper of May 1939 and establishing a Jewish Commonwealth in Palestine. This was the first time that

[11] *Ibid.*, page 1.
[12] *Ibid.*, page 2.

Palestine was the subject of planks in the political platforms of both major parties in the United States.

The pressure of American public opinion which was responsible for the Palestine planks in the platforms of the political parties, also motivated the introduction of the pro-Zionist commonwealth resolutions in both Houses of Congress.

On January 1944, the Wright-Compton resolution was introduced in the House of Representatives and, on February 1, 1944, Senators Wagner and Taft introduced an identical resolution in the Senate. The text of these resolutions reads as follows:

Whereas the Sixty-seventh Congress of the United States on June 20, 1922, unanimously resolved "that the United States of America favors the establishment in Palestine of a national home for the Jewish people, it being clearly understood that nothing shall be done which may prejudice the civil and religious rights of Christian and all other non-Jewish communities in Palestine shall be adequately protected"; and

Whereas the ruthless persecution of the Jewish people in Europe has clearly demonstrated the need for a Jewish homeland as a haven for the large numbers who have become homeless as a result of this persecution, Therefore be it

Resolved, That the United States shall use its good offices and take appropriate measures to the end that the doors of Palestine shall be opened for free entry of Jews into that country, and that there shall be full opportunity for colonization, so that the Jewish people may ultimately reconstitute Palestine as a free and democratic Jewish commonwealth.[13]

Public hearings on the Wright-Compton resolution were held between Feburary 8 and 14 before the House Foreign Affairs Committee. Passage of the Resolution was urged by representatives of the Zionist groups in the country. Spokesmen for the Arab viewpoint opposed the resolution.[14]

Jewish groups who did not favor that part of the resolution calling for the establishment of a Jewish Common-

[13] Friedrich, *op. cit.*, Appendix B, page 101.

[14] "Jewish National Home in Palestine." Hearings before Committee on Foreign Affairs, House of Representatives, 78th Congress, 2nd Session, on House Resolution No. 418 and House Resolution No. 419.

wealth, nevertheless urged passage of the section of the resolution which requested the free entry of Jews into Palestine. Such was the testimony of the American Jewish Committee which recommended deferment of the "controversial question of the Jewish Commonwealth" and suggested the amendment of the resolution to express approval of placing Palestine under an international trusteeship responsible to the United Nations for safeguarding the Jewish settlement in, and Jewish immigration into, Palestine, — and preparing "the country to become, within a reasonable number of years, a self-governing commonwealth under a constitution and bill of rights that will safeguard and protect these purposes and basic rights for all." The American Council for Judaism, in its testimony, opposed the establishment of a Jewish State as a matter of principle; it objected, however, to the White Paper on the ground that it discriminated against Jews as such. Many Congressmen of both parties, spokesmen for the American Federation of Labor and the Congress of Industrial Organizations, and numerous other non-Jewish and inter-denominational groups, publicly advocated passage of the resolution. It was estimated that by the end of 1944, the overwhelming majority of the members of both houses of Congress had expressed themselves in favor of the resolution.

However, the resolution was finally tabled at the request of the War Department, which informed the House Committee on Foreign Affairs that, in its opinion, "without reference to the merits of these resolutions, further action on them at this time would be prejudicial to the successful prosecution of the war."[15] Nevertheless, the hope for winning congressional approval of the commonwealth resolution remained alive. In fact, the disclosure, on March 4, that

[15] For texts of statements of members of Congress, see *American Jewish Year Book*, 1944–1945, pages 151–152, 172–177; Fink, "Jewish National Home in Palestine," supplemental statements to hearings submitted to Committee on Foreign Affairs, House of Representatives, 78th Congress, 2nd Session, on House Resolution No. 418 and House Resolution No. 419, pages 3–127.

General Marshall had asked only that the resolution be deferred but not rejected, was followed, on March 9, 1944, by a statement which President Roosevelt authorized Dr. Stephen S. Wise and Dr. Abba Hillel Silver to make public in his name. This statement appeared to have been made for the purpose of giving assurance that the United States Government had not dropped the matter altogether, but would take it up again as soon as conditions allowed. The following is the text of this statement:

The President authorized us to say that the American Government has never given its approval to the White Paper of 1939.

The President is happy the doors of Palestine are today open to Jewish refugees, and that when future decisions are reached, full justice will be done to those who seek a Jewish National Home, for which our Government and the American people have always had the deepest sympathy and today more than ever, in view of the tragic plight of hundreds of thousands of homeless Jewish refugees.[16]

On October 10, 1944, Secretary of War Stimson, in a letter to the Hon. Robert A. Taft indicated that the military reasons for the War Department's previous opposition to the resolution no longer prevailed.

The removal of the military considerations led to the approval, in amended form, of the Wright-Compton Resolution by the House Foreign Affairs Committee on November 28, 1944. The amended resolution eliminated the word "Jewish" preceding "democratic commonwealth" and the phrase "will take appropriate measures."

It was assumed that approval of a similar resolution by the Senate Foreign Relations Committee would follow. But, on December 11, 1944, upon the advice of the State Department, the Wagner-Taft resolution was shelved. In explanation of its advice, the State Department issued the following statement:

The department has the utmost sympathy for the persecuted people of Europe and has been assisting them through active support of the work of the War Refugee Board in every possible way. The

[16] *The Conference Record*, Bulletin of Activities of the American Jewish Conference, March 1944, pages 1–2. *The New York Times*, March 10, 1944.

department considers, however, that the passage of the resolution at the present time would be unwise from the standpoint of the general international situation and has so informed the Senate Committee on Foreign Relations.[17]

On December 15, 1944, following the shelving of the Senate resolution, 12 out of 18 members of the Senate Foreign Relations Committee, made public a joint statement recording their personal approval of the joint Palestine resolution:

Although the Senate Foreign Relations Committee, at the request of the State Department, postponed action for the time being on the Palestine Resolution, we wish to record our own personal approval of the resolution which calls for free entry of Jews into Palestine and full opportunity for colonization, so that the Jewish people may as soon as practicable reconstitute Palestine as a free and democratic commonwealth.[18]

With the close of the 78th Congress, on December 19, 1944, the Palestine resolution lapsed in both Houses. However, it was again introduced in the House of Representatives on January 11, 1945 (79th Congress), by Representative James P. Geelan, Democrat of Connecticut. This resolution was identical with the measure introduced in the previous Congress by Representative Ranulf Compton whom Geelan had succeeded. The Geelan resolution retained the original wording of the Compton resolution, without the amendments introduced into it before its approval by the House Foreign Affairs Committee during the 78th Congress. A similar resolution was introduced into the new House by Representative Emanual Celler, Democrat of New York, on January 15, 1945.[19] This resolution, too, retained the original form.

At the time of writing, no similar resolution has been reintroduced into the Senate and no further action has been taken by the House of Representatives.

However, on March 16, 1945, in a statement which he authorized Dr. Stephen S. Wise to issue in his name, Pres-

[17] *JTA* [Jewish Telegraphic Agency] *Daily News Bulletin*, December 12, 1944.

[18] *Ibid.*, December 16, 1944.

[19] *Ibid.*, January 16, 1945.

ident Roosevelt reaffirmed his pledge to exert his influence in favor of the opening of Palestine to unrestricted Jewish immigration and of the establishment of a Jewish commonwealth.

"I made my position clear in October. That position I have not changed and shall continue to seek to bring about its earliest realization."[20]

This authorization was given following the wave of disappointment among Zionist sympathizers when, on his return from the Crimean Conference with Messrs. Churchill and Stalin, President Roosevelt reported to Congress on March 1, 1945, that it had been decided to defer the solution of the Palestine question until after the conclusion of the war. The President's interpolated comment in the course of his report that "of the problems of Arabia, I learned more about that whole problem, the Moslem problem, the Jewish problem, by talking with Ibn Saud for five minutes, than I could have learned in an exchange of two or three dozen letters," especially aroused much consternation.[21]

At the San Francisco Conference, Palestine as such was not on the agenda, since according to the agreement reached at Yalta by the Big Three, no discussions of specific territories were to take place at the United Nations Conference. Nevertheless, the Palestine question was brought up indirectly when the system of trusteeship which was to apply also to the existing mandates of the League of Nations came up for discussion.[21a]

Four basic principles of far-reaching significance to the future of dependent territories and their peoples were embodied in the United Nations Charter: first, that administering nations should be accountable to the world community; second, that the advancement of dependent peoples is of primary concern; third, that dependent territories must be

[20] *Ibid*, March 18, 1945.

[21] *The New York Times*, March 2, 1945.

[21a] Report to the President on the Results of the San Francisco Conference (Department of State, pub. 2349, Conference series 71), page 128.

administered in such manner as to contribute to the maintenance of peace and security; and, fourth, that equal economic opportunity should be accorded to all Member States of the United Nations.[21b]

As far as Palestine is concerned, a number of measures envisaged in the provisions of the United Nations Charter are bound to influence the future development of the country. Machinery was established for trusteeship of territories now held under mandate; the administering authority may be one or more states or the Organization itself; it will be a matter for subsequent agreements to decide which territories will be brought under the trusteeship system and upon what terms.

Of particular interest with regard to Palestine is a clause contained in Article 80 of the Charter, which states that until specific trusteeship agreement for a given territory has been concluded,

"nothing in this chapter shall be considered in or of itself to alter in any manner the rights whatsoever of any states or any peoples or the terms of existing international instruments to which Members of the United Nations may respectively be parties.[21c]

This stipulation guarantees that no changes can be made affecting Jewish rights under the provision of the Palestine Mandate in the interim period. (A proposal by Iraq which would have restricted the "peoples" mentioned in the above-quoted clause to those now inhabiting the territories was defeated.[21d] The same Article 80 provides also that the above clause "shall not be interpreted as giving grounds for delay or postponement of the negotiation and conclusion of agreements for placing mandated and other territories under the trusteeship system . . ."

Shortly after the close of hostilities in Europe, at the time of the Potsdam Conference, the governors of thirty-seven States at a conference at Mackinac Island, Mich.,

---

[21b] Report to the President, *op. cit.*, pages 125, 133.
[21c] *Ibid.*, page 218.
[21d] *JTA. Daily News Bulletin*, June 11, 1945.

asked President Truman to take immediate steps to open Palestine "to Jewish mass immigration and colonization." The petition stressed the urgency of the Jewish problem and its solution in Palestine, and expressed "the earnest hope that it may be thought opportune to give attention to this question in the course of your (the President's) forthcoming conversations with the Prime Minister of Great Britain and Marshal Stalin."[21e]

Taking cognizance of the precarious plight of the Jews in Europe, President Truman sent Earl G. Harrison, U. S. representative on the Intergovernmental Committee on Refugees, to inquire into the situation. Harrison's report, published early in August 1945, described the shocking condition of the displaced Jews of Europe.

Mr. Harrison found that the majority of the displaced Jews expressed a desire to settle in Palestine. As the number of available certificates for immigration to Palestine would be exhausted in the near future, he suggested that the British Government be approached with a request that 100,000 additional visas be granted for the resettlement of Jews then in Austria or Germany who did not want to remain there, were non-repatriable or who did not desire to return to their countries of origin.

In a letter to Prime Minister Attlee, dated August 31, 1945, President Truman enclosed a copy of the Harrison report, and urged upon the British Government to act without delay upon Mr. Harrison's recommendations. Mr. Truman reminded the Prime Minister that already at the Potsdam conference he had told him that "the American people, as a whole, firmly believe that immigration into Palestine should not be closed and that a reasonable number of Europe's persecuted Jews should, in accordance with their wishes, be permitted to resettle there."[21f]

At the time of writing (Summer 1945) the Palestine question was still under consideration.

[21e] *The New York Times*, July 5, 1945.
[21f] *Ibid.*, November 13, 1945.

France

The Nazi occupation of a major part of France including its capital, Paris, in June 1940 opened a four-year period of terror for more than a quarter of a million French Jews. Sporadic expulsions of Jews from Occupied France occurred early in 1942, and in July of that year, the Nazis began a systematic manhunt of Jews. During the following three months, tens of thousands of Jewish residents of Paris were rounded up and shipped off to labor and death camps. Some Jews managed to escape to Switzerland or Spain, while others fled to "Unoccupied" France, hoping to find safety there.

The Nazis then informed the Vichy Government of their intention to expel all internees, mostly Jews, under their jurisdiction, in Occupied France. It was reported that, on receiving this information, the Vichy Government asked the Germans to exempt French citizens from deportation and to substitute for them alien Jews interned in Vichy France. The Germans ostensibly agreed to this callous deal in human lives and requested the surrender of 13,000 new victims. Later, they characteristically violated the agreement and deported native French Jews as well.

The first deportation order of Vichy stated that all alien Jews, with the exception of certain enumerated categories, whose residence in France had begun after January 1, 1936 were to be expelled. When this order did not yield enough Jews to meet Nazi demands, instructions were issued to meet the quotas from among the interned Jews who had been residents of France since January 1933 and by including previously exempted categories.[22]

During the months of terror under Nazi and Vichy rule, the aid and intercession of the United States Government were solicited on numerous occasions. Thus, on August 27, 1942, a joint appeal was made to the State Department by four major American Jewish organizations — the American

[22] This account follows the Review of the Year, *American Jewish Year Book*, 1943–1944, pages 239–242.

Jewish Committee, the American Jewish Congress, the B'nai B'rith and the Jewish Labor Committee — requesting intercession with Vichy to prevent the deportation of Jews from "Unoccupied" France.[23]

In a reply to this appeal, Under Secretary of State Sumner Welles asserted that the State Department "has made the most vigorous representations possible to the highest authorities at Vichy."

The complete text of Mr. Welles' letter follows:

I have received your communication of August 27, 1942, enclosing a letter, signed by the President of the American Jewish Committee, the American Jewish Congress, the B'nai B'rith and the Jewish Labor Committee, in regard to the mass deportation of Jewish refugees from unoccupied France.

I am in complete agreement with the statements made concerning this tragic situation, which provides a new shock to the public opinion of the civilized world. It is deeply regretted that these measures should be taken in a country traditionally noted for adherence to the principles of equality, freedom and tolerance.

The American Embassy at Vichy has reported fully to the Department concerning developments in regard to these deportations and, in compliance with instructions sent by the Department, has made the most vigorous representations possible to the highest authorities at Vichy. I assure you that the Department and the Embassy will take an active interest in this matter.[24]

Whether these "most vigorous representations" were effective in saving any Jewish lives is not known. The Nazi grip on France probably was too strong for the Vichy authorities to respond favorably.

The Vichy discriminatory laws against the Jews in France were paralleled by similar legislation against Jews in French North Africa. On October 18, 1940, a decree denying to Jews participation in public service, civil and military, and in all public enterprises, such as motion pictures and radio broadcasting, was promulgated. This decree was to apply

[23] *American Jewish Year Book*, 1943–1944, page 192.

[24] *The New York Times*, September 5, 1942, page 3; Documents on American Foreign Relations, Vol. V, edited by L. M. Goodrich and J. Carroll, 1944, page 538. *The New York Times* also gives the text of letter of protest of the Jewish organizations.

to "Algeria, the colonies, protectorates, and mandated territories." The application of this decree to Morocco with its Jewish population of 161,132 was protested by the American Jewish Committee in a letter dated March 31, 1941, to the Department of State.

In this letter the State Department was reminded that it was Mr. Henry White, the American representative at the Algeciras Conference of 1906, convened at the initiation of President Theodore Roosevelt for the purpose of clarifying the international status of Morocco, who sponsored the voeu or resolution concerning treatment of the Jews of Morocco. The resolution, which was supported by all the delegates of the conference, required the Sultan of Morocco to "see to it that his Government does not neglect any occasion to make known to its functionaries that the Sultan maintains that the Jews of his Empire and all his subjects, without distinction of faith, should be treated with justice and equality."[25]

On April 11, 1941, a reply was received from Wallace Murray, Chief of the Division of Near Eastern Affairs, informing the American Jewish Committee that the American Legation at Tangiers had been requested to report upon the situation of the Jews of Morocco.

On October 17, 1941, a fuller reply was received from Adolf A. Berle, Jr., Assistant Secretary of State, stating that the report of the American Legation at Tangiers had been received, and that a study had been made of the American role at the Algeciras Conference. In this letter Mr. Berle explained that the proposal of the American delegation at the Algeciras Conference "was in no sense a demand or requirement that the Sultan of Morocco should give a guarantee of equality of treatment of Jews and other subjects in Morocco, but was merely an expression of a wish or trust that the Sultan continue the good policy which he had carried on after the reign of his father with respect to such

[25] For a detailed discussion of the Jewish question at the Algeciras Conference, see above chapter on Morocco, pages 36-41.

persons in Morocco." It is true, Mr. Berle asserted, that Mr. White had been directed by the then Secretary of State, Elihu Root, to urge "the consideration of guarantees of religious and racial tolerance in Morocco." But a subsequent instruction had cancelled those previously given "apparently due to the express request of representative Jews in Morocco who expressed themselves as satisfied with their treatment by the Sultan." Thus, the proceedings of the Algeciras Conference "do not provide a satisfactory basis for action by this Government."

But, continued Mr. Berle, "so far as the general question of religious freedom is concerned, the attitude of this Government is well known to all the European powers through numerous authoritative statements which have been made. A further statement at this time, as you will readily understand, is not likely to accomplish any useful result, and it seems probable that any real progress in this direction must await a general solution of the European problem." For the present, "all that can be done is to protect the interests of any American citizen or protégé affected by the legislation in question, and such persons thus far have not been threatened."[26]

In November 1942, British and American troops invaded North Africa. Very soon thereafter the Nazis occupied all of France, thus obliterating the formal differences in administration between the occupied and "unoccupied" zones.

The invasion of North Africa, however, meant immediate liberation for the Jews of these territories. Jewish and liberal French groups in the United States urged the immediate revocation of the Vichy anti-Jewish laws. That this would soon be done appeared almost certain when, in a statement of November 17, 1942, President Roosevelt said:

I have requested the liberation of all persons in North Africa who had been imprisoned because they opposed the efforts of the Nazis to dominate the world and I have asked for the abrogation

---

[26] The correspondence with the Department of State is contained in the correspondence files of The American Jewish Committee.

of all laws and decrees inspired by the Nazi government and Nazi ideologists.[27]

However, there followed a period of uncertainty during which the attitude of the French officials in authority over French North Africa remained unclear. Much criticism was directed by liberal circles in the United States against General Eisenhower's political arrangements in North Africa and the slowness with which the Vichy laws and decrees were eliminated. It was necessary for President Roosevelt to explain that the existing political arrangements were temporary, though necessary, expedients.[28]

On December 16, 1942, the President again gave assurances that the discriminatory laws against Jews would be repealed, asserting that the people of North Africa "have definitely allied themselves on the side of liberalism against all for which the Axis stands in government." He included in his statement of that date, a declaration issued by Admiral Darlan, then French Chief of State, which proclaimed that:

The High Commissioner has begun the restoration of rights to those persons from whom these had previously been taken because of race. Measures have been taken to stop immediately whatever persecution of the Jews may have resulted from the laws passed in France under German pressure. His announced purpose is to give just treatment to all elements making up the complex North African population to the end that all can dwell and work together under laws insuring mutual tolerance and respect for rights.[29]

Included among the decrees abrogated by Darlan was that which barred Jews from service in the armed forces. However charges continued to be made that these promises were not being fulfilled and that other forms of discrimination against Jews were still practiced.

Under the regime of General Henri Honoré Giraud, who succeeded Darlan on December 24, 1942 — two days after

[27] Department of State *Bulletin*, November 21, 1942, page 935.
[28] *American Jewish Year Book*, 1943–1944, pages 251–252; Department of State *Bulletin*, November 21, 1942, page 935.
[29] Department of State *Bulletin*, December 19, 1942, page 1007.

the former's assassination — additional, though by no means all, rights were restored to the Jews.

On March 7, 1943, Giraud took a step which on the surface promised the complete restoration of Jewish rights. He formally severed all legal connections with Vichy and Marshal Pétain, declaring that decrees signed in Vichy were no longer valid in French North Africa. At the same time, he confiscated the March 2, 1943, issue of the *Journal Officiel* of Algeria, which had published two Vichy decrees of October 19, 1942, on the status of Algerian Jews, and dismissed M. Maurice Bouni, Director of the General-Government, who was responsible for the decrees.[30] These steps were widely applauded in the United States.[31]

Mr. Welles, on April 10, lauded the March 14 speech of General Giraud, in which the latter revealed the major points of his program. Giraud's speech, however, raised a furore of opposition. For, in it, he announced that "for the same purpose of eliminating all racial discrimination, the Crémieux Decree, which in 1870 had established a difference in the position of the Moslem and Jewish natives, had been abrogated."[32] By this announcement, Giraud continued in force Vichy's abrogation of the Crémieux Decree.[33]

The text of the Crémieux Decree which in 1870 had granted French citizenship to Algerian Jews, reads:

The native Jews of the Departments of Algeria are declared to be French citizens. Consequently, their real and personal status will be ruled, from the date of promulgation of the present Decree by French law, without prejudice to rights acquired heretofore.

[30] *The New York Times*, March 8, 1943, page 5.

[31] *New York Sun*, March 8, 1943; *Christian Science Monitor*, March 8, 1943; also other newspapers.

[32] "Abrogation of the Crémieux Decree," Memorandum presented by the French-Jewish Representative Committee, affiliated with the World Jewish Congress, New York, 1943, page 2.

[33] Decree of October 7, 1940, issued under the authority and responsibility of Marcel Peyrouton, then Minister of Interior under Marshal Pétain, and Decree of February 18, 1942.

All contrary legislative dispositions, all Senatus-Consultes, Decrees, Regulations or Ordinances shall be abolished.[34]

By this Decree, the Jews of Algeria were enfranchised en masse. Moslems had to seek French naturalization individually, after renouncing aspects of Koranic law incompatible with French law. In fact, the large majority of Algerian Moslems had not in the past sought naturalization on these terms.

Giraud defended his action as an attempt to offset Axis propaganda among millions of Arabs in Algeria. Relations of Moslems and Jews, he explained, had to be such as to place both on an equal footing.[35] He also justified it as a military measure "designed to forestall wide discontent among the Moslems who constituted eighty percent of the French North African army.[36]

However, the disappointment among the 40,000 to 50,000 Algerian Jews deprived of their French citizenship, was bitter. The action of Giraud was condemned by Jews in Algeria and in the United States and by the Fighting French of General de Gaulle, who insisted that it did nothing to improve the position of the Moslems while it aggravated the status of the Jews. They asserted that this action, like that of Vichy, was motivated by the anti-Semitism of the European population in Algeria, whose economic interest it was to exploit and repress the Moslem population. This element resented Jewish enfranchisement as a dangerous precedent likely to suggest to the Moslem population the desirability of their own political and economic improvement.[37]

On March 18th, a delegation headed by Rabbi Stephen S. Wise, representing the American Jewish Congress and the

---

[34] *Ibid.*, page 5.

[35] *The New York Times*, March 19, 1943, page 5.

[36] *Ibid.*, March 22, 1943, page 3.

[37] See newspaper criticism in *New York Post*, March 16 and 23, 1943; Waverly Root in *Philadelphia Record*, March 19, 1943; Edwin L. James in *The New York Times*, March 21, 1943; *PM*, March 21, 1943; letter by Jacques Maritain to editor of *The New York Times*, April 25, 1943.

World Jewish Congress, visited Under Secretary Welles to protest the Giraud action. On the same day, Baron Edouard de Rothschild, then in the United States, in his capacity as president of the Consistoire Centrale des Israélites de France et d'Algérie, issued a statement vigorously condemning the annulment of the Crémieux decree.[38] Mr. Welles, replying to Baron Edouard de Rothschild's public condemnation of the Giraud action, defended the latter. In a letter dated March 27, he enumerated the rights which had been restored to Jews, and denied that Giraud's decisions were obscure and insufficient.

The full text of Under Secretary Welles' letter to Baron de Rothschild released to the press March 27, follows:

You will recall that last week you were good enough to send me the text of a statement which you had prepared for publication regarding the general position of the Jewish community in North Africa and, more particularly, the abrogation of the Crémieux Decree of 1870 in relation to the speech made by General Giraud on March 14.

I felt so strongly that your statement gave a completely erroneous picture of the position of Jews in North Africa and of General Giraud's measures in their behalf that I immediately telegraphed a summary of it to our representatives there. The following comment, prepared in consultation with an unbiased specialist familiar with the various legal points involved, has just been received. I hasten to send it to you in the belief that you will not wish to allow an erroneous impression of the situation to prevail.

1. The laws relating to the Jews which were of Nazi inspiration were abolished by General Giraud by an ordinance of the fourteenth of the current month. The Jews are guaranteed the right to practice the liberal professions including the holding of public office, the right to own property and freely to manage their property, assets and all business enterprises, and the right to attend institutions of learning of all degrees. The Jew is no longer indicated as of a race apart in the civil registry records. By ordering the reinstatement of all public officials, agents and employees excluded because they were Jews, General Giraud effaced an odious past. The order that property sequestered under provisional administration would be restored to the Jews and that the sales of real property and other assets would be null and void was given with the same objective.

[38] *American Jewish Year Book*, 1943–1944, page 197.

Consequently, Baron de Rothschild's affirmation that the decisions of General Giraud are obscure and insufficient is untrue.

2. French citizenship is retained by Jews born in France or descendants of parents born in France. Baron de Rothschild's affirmation that they lose their citizenship is untrue.

3. Only native Algerian Jews are effected by the Crémieux Decree. The Decree is abrogated but in the near future a procedure will be established whereby native Algerian Jews who desire to become citizens may acquire citizenship. It may be remembered that, following the precedent of 1914–1918, elections are deferred until the end of the war, that is to say until Metropolitan France is liberated. Consequently, native Algerian Jews who desire to participate in those elections will have ample time to become citizens. The affirmation of Baron de Rothschild that Jews will be unlawfully deprived of voting power is likewise absolutely untrue.[39]

Welles' defense of Giraud did not succeed in reassuring the dissatisfied groups. Baron de Rothschild criticized the statements of the "unbiased specialist" quoted by Welles as "erroneous and inaccurate." He asserted that the "Crémieux decree is as much a part of the statutory fabric of France as any other law . . . and [its cancellation] constitutes a grave and permanent danger for the present and the future."[40] Protests continued to be levelled against the Giraud action and, on May 20, a delegation representing the French-Jewish Representative Committee of the World Jewish Congress again visited Welles at the State Department and presented a memorandum giving a history of the Crémieux Decree. The memorandum asserted that "only by outrageous sophistry is it possible to proclaim the intention of eliminating all racial discrimination between Jews and Arabs by depriving the former of their French citizenship."[41] A more proper procedure, the memorandum argued, would be to elevate the Arabs to French citizenship.

The American Jewish Committee and the Jewish Labor Committee also were active in the movement to restore the

[39] Department of State *Bulletin*, March 27, 1943, page 255; *The New York Times*, March 28, 1943.

[40] *The New York Times*, April 4, 1943.

[41] "Abrogation of Crémieux Decree," *op. cit.*, page 15.

Crémieux Decree. In addition to carrying on correspondence and discussions with members of the French Committee of National Liberation, both in this country and abroad, the former organization on several occasions protested to the State Department. A letter of protest was sent to Mr. Welles on March 17, 1943, and another on May 17, 1943. The latter was accompanied by a documented memorandum on the historical and legal aspects of the problem. To the latter communication, Mr. Welles replied that the French, and not the American authorities, were responsible for the revocation of the decree.

Again, on July 7, 1943, the American Jewish Committee addressed a letter to Mr. Welles asking for the restoration of the Crémieux Decree. The reply, which was received on July 21, 1943, from James C. Dunn, then Adviser on Political Relations of the Department of State, was encouraging:

" . . . it is our hope and desire that means may be found at an early date whereby Algerian Jews may resume their status as French citizens . . . You may be sure that our hopes in this matter are well understood by the competent French authorities."[42]

A reply in a similar vein to a letter of protest, dated July 14, 1943, from the Jewish Labor Committee, was made public by Secretary of State Cordell Hull on August 1, 1943. This letter indicated clearly a change in the attitude of the State Department, which previously had disposed of criticism either by defending Giraud's policy or by referring critics to Giraud himself.

In this letter Mr. Hull explained that the United States previously had been unable to do anything about the abrogation of the decree because the French commanders in North Africa "quite unequivocally informed our military and civil representatives that they could not be responsible for the good will or — even now — aggression of the Arabs were the Crémieux Decree to be restored at the time that the

---

[42] American Jewish Committee, correspondence files of Overseas Department, "Crémieux Law" folder.

Vichy laws generally were repealed . . ." The behavior of the Arabs was important because "our military situation in Tunisia was at the moment far from secure . . . [but] the successful outcome of the battle for Tunisia has to some extent altered the military situation," making possible the disclosure of the Government's position on the issue. Mr. Hull also pointed out that the issue over the Crémieux Decree "is no longer one for a decision by General Giraud alone" and that "it is receiving careful study at the hands of the French Committee of National Liberation."[43]

With the establishment and increasing recognition of the French Committee of National Liberation under the leadership of General Charles de Gaulle, the Crémieux Decree was revalidated on October 21, 1943.

Invasion Proclamations and Armistice Agreements

The interest of the United States in the condition of the European Jews revealed itself in the invasion proclamations of its military leaders and in the Armistice Agreements which the American Government, as one of the United Nations, helped impose upon Italy, Finland, Bulgaria, Rumania and Hungary.

General of the Army Dwight D. Eisenhower's invasion message to the people of Sicily, made public on July 20, 1943, in addition to dissolving the Fascist organization of that island and all of its "appendages," declared that immediate steps would be taken to abolish all laws "which discriminate on the basis of race, color or creed."[44]

Likewise, one of the first acts of the Allied Military Government after the liberation of Rome (June 1944), was to rescind all anti-Jewish legislation, to release all Jewish and other political prisoners, and to begin the restoration to the Jews of their former homes and property.[45]

[43] For full text of Mr. Hull's letter, see *The New York Times*, August 21, 1943.

[44] For full text of General Eisenhower's message, see *The New York Times*, July 21, 1943.

[45] *Contemporary Jewish Record*, August 1944, page 410.

Of the Armistice Agreements, the most important, from the standpoint of the Jews, were those with Rumania and Hungary, which contained provisions specifically mentioning the Jews.

The Armistice Agreement with Hungary was concluded on January 20, 1945. The provisions in this Agreement which singled out the Jews for special mention were couched in almost the same words as the parallel provisions in the Agreement with Rumania. Article I, b, of the Hungarian Agreement, which provided that: "The Government of Hungary also undertakes to intern nationals of Germany," was modified by an Annex to Article I, which stated that this provision does not apply to German nationals of Jewish origin.[46]

Jews also benefited from Article IV of the Hungarian Agreement — and the analogous provisions in the Agreements with Rumania, Finland and Bulgaria — which provided for the immediate relase of all Allied prisoners of war and internees, and the provision of food, clothing, medical services, and means of transportation to their homes for Allied prisoners of war, internees, displaced persons and refugees.[47]

The most significant provision of the Hungarian Agreement was Article V which called for the immediate repeal of "all discriminatory legislation and difficulties arising therefrom." The Government of Hungary, under this provision, was required to "take all the necessary measures to insure that all displaced persons and refugees within the limits of Hungarian territory, including Jews and stateless persons, are accorded at least the same measure of security as its own nationals."[48] This article laid the basis for the restora-

[46] Department of State *Bulletin*, January 21, 1945, pages 83 and 85. (Italian Armistice Agreement made public on November 6, 1945, includes similar provisions.)

[47] *Ibid.*, January 21, 1945, page 83.

[48] *Ibid.*, January 21, 1945, pages 83–84. (Corresponding provisions were contained in Article VI of the Rumanian Agreement, Paragraph 21 of the Finnish Agreement, and Article V of the Bulgarian Agreement.)

tion to the Jews of Hungary — as did parallel articles in the agreements with Rumania, Finland and Bulgaria — of full legal equality. It was also intended to insure the safety of foreign Jews who had found refuge in Hungary and who might be exposed to hardships because of non-citizenship.

War Crimes

Even before the entry of the United States into World War II, in December, 1941, the American people and their leaders had voiced their horror at the unprecedented Nazi atrocities, especially the anti-Jewish extermination policy.[49] As a full ally in the war against the Nazis, the United States Government, through the Chief Executive, the State Department and Congress, on numerous occasions, voiced the resolve of the American people to punish all guilty of crimes against the civilian populations of the conquered countries.

These declarations were at first expressed in general terms. But as time went on, the American determination to punish the criminals was given more vigorous expression. War criminals were warned that machinery for collecting evidence had been set up, that neutral nations would be prevented from offering shelter to them, and that detailed methods for trying the guilty were being formulated. They were further told that crimes committed by a nation against its own nationals would not elude punishment by resort to legal technicalities, and that the whole of the German people who had looked on with indifference, and even approval, and continued to support the Government which was perpetrating these crimes, would be held equally responsible for them.

President Roosevelt in a statement of August 21, 1942, called attention to the declaration signed in London on January 13, 1942, by representatives of nine governments whose countries were under German occupation. This declaration had affirmed that acts of violence "perpetrated against civilian populations are at variance with accepted

[49] Documents on American Foreign Relations, Vol. IV, June 1941–July 1942, edited by L. M. Goodrich and D. P. Myers, page 662; Department of State *Bulletin*, October 25, 1941, page 317.

ideas concerning acts of war" and that "punishment, through the channel of organized justice of those guilty and responsible for these crimes, is one of the principal war aims of the contracting governments." The President noted that the American Government was keeping a file of information and evidence relating to war crimes, which would be available on the day of victory.[50]

On October 7, 1942, the president expressed the willingness of the United States Government to cooperate with the British and other governments in establishing a United Nations Commission for the Investigation of War Crimes:

I now declare it to be the intention of this Government that the successful close of the war shall include provision for the surrender to the United Nations of war criminals.

With a view to establishing responsibility of the guilty individuals through the collection and assessment of all available evidence, this Government is prepared to cooperate with the British and other Governments in establishing a United Nations Commission for the Investigation of War Crimes. The number of persons eventually found guilty will undoubtedly be extremely small compared to the total enemy populations. It is not the intention of this Government or of the Governments associated with us to resort to mass reprisals. It is our intention that just and sure punishment shall be meted out to the ringleaders responsible for the organized murder of thousands of innocent persons and the commission of atrocities which have violated every tenet of the Christian faith.[51]

As representative of the United States on the United Nations Commission for the Investigation of War Crimes, the President designated Herbert C. Pell, former American Minister to Portugal and to Hungary.

Towards the end of 1942, it became evident that the German Government had begun to take measures to carry into effect Hitler's oft-repeated intention to exterminate the Jews of Europe. Reports had been received that ghettos in Poland, established by the Nazis, were being systematically emptied of Jews and that those taken away were never heard from again. The number of victims were reckoned in

[50] Department of State *Bulletin*, August 22, 1942, pages 709–710.
[51] *Ibid.*, October 10, 1942, page 797.

many hundreds of thousands of innocent men, women and children. Jews from other occupied countries were also reported as having been transported in conditions of appalling horror and brutality to Eastern Europe.

In the hope of restraining the Nazis from going on with the execution of their horrible plans, the United States, on December 17, 1942, joined the Governments of Great Britain, Russia, eight other Allied nations and the Fighting French, in a declaration issued simultaneously in Washington, London and Moscow reaffirming the "solemn resolution" of the United Nations "to insure that those responsible for these crimes shall not escape retribution and to press on with the necessary practical measures to this end."[52]

Three months later, the Congress of the United States added its voice to that of the executive branch of the government and, in a joint resolution adopted on March 9, 1943, by the Senate and on March 18 by the House of Representatives condemned the inexcusable slaughter of innocent and helpless Jews and urged the just punishment of the guilty persons. The text of this resolution follows:

WHEREAS the American people view with indignation the atrocities inflicted upon the civilian population in the Nazi-occupied countries, and especially the mass murder of Jewish men, women, and children; and

WHEREAS this policy of the Nazis has created a reign of terror, brutality, and extermination in Poland and other countries in Eastern and Central Europe: Now, therefore, be it

RESOLVED BY THE SENATE (THE HOUSE OF REPRESENTATIVES CONCURRING), That these brutal and indefensible outrages against millions of helpless men, women, and children should be, and they are hereby, condemned as unworthy of any nation or any regime which pretends to be civilized:

RESOLVED FURTHER, That the dictates of humanity and honorable conduct in war demand that this inexcusable slaughter and mistreatment shall cease and that it is the sense of this Congress that those guilty, directly or indirectly, of these criminal acts shall be held accountable and punished in a manner commensurate with the offenses for which they are responsible.[53]

[52] Department of State *Bulletin*, December 10, 1942, page 1009.
[53] *Ibid.*, October 10, 1942, page 797.

Warnings that criminals could not escape punishment by claiming that they had merely been fulfilling orders imposed upon them by their superiors were given by the State Department which also put the blame upon the shoulders of the whole German nation.[54]

In a speech delivered before a mass protest meeting in Boston, Massachusetts, on May 2, 1943, Assistant Secretary of State Adolph Berle asserted: "The time has passed when we can pretend that this series of horrors constitutes the sole guilt of any small group of German rulers, or of any single party. No group of rulers, no party, could have conceived, organized and carried out a program of general civilian slaughter without at least the tacit acquiescence of a large part of the German people." What is true of the German Government and the German people is also true of the Governments and peoples of Rumania, Hungary and Bulgaria, added Mr. Berle. All who shared in the Nazi crimes will also share the same fate and retribution.

Another basis for the hope of escaping ultimate punishment was dissipated when President Roosevelt, on July 30, 1942, warned the neutral and satellite countries against sheltering war criminals. He stated that the government of the United States would regard such action "as inconsistent with the principles for which the United Nations are fighting and that the United States Government hopes that no neutral government will permit its territory to be used as a place of refuge or otherwise assist such persons in any effort to escape their just deserts."[55]

This warning to neutrals was repeated in a statement issued by the Secretary of State on September 28, 1944. This statement noted that the Department of State had formally apprised all the neutral nations of Europe and the Republic of Argentina of the July 30, 1943, statement of the President:

"The neutral governments were reminded that it was the intention of this government that the successful close of the war would

---

[54] *Ibid.*, May 8, 1943, pages 395–397.
[55] *American Jewish Year Book*, 1944–1945, pages 155–156.

include provision for the surrender to the United Nations of war criminals. They were advised that if they refused to admit Axis leaders and their henchmen and criminal subordinates to their territories problems between those governments and the United Nations could be avoided. . . . and that relations between the United States and the neutral governments concerned would be adversely affected for years to come should the Axis leaders or their vassals find safety in those countries."

Referring to the criticism that had been levelled against the War Crimes Commission in London for not having included the names of Hitler and other top officials in the list of war criminals compiled, the statement continued:

"The answer to any suggestion that they have been or are likely to be overlooked by the United Nations is found in the Moscow Declaration of 1943 on German atrocities, which, after stating that the perpetrators of atrocities in occupied territories will be brought back to the scene of their crimes and judged on the spot by the peoples whom they have outraged, specifically declares that the 'major criminals, whose offenses have no particular geographical localization . . . will be punished by the joint decision of the Governments of the Allies.' The omission of the names of these people from any particular list compiled by the War Crimes Commission is without any significance whatsoever from the point of view of what the Allied Powers have in mind in regard to them."[56]

An official United Nations statement on atrocities was given out at the conclusion of the Three Power Conference held at Moscow, October 19–30, 1943. The conference was attended by the Foreign Secretaries of the United States, Great Britain and Soviet Russia. The statement on atrocities, however, was signed by President Roosevelt, Prime Minister Churchill, and Premier Stalin. The full text of the statement follows:

The United Kingdom, the United States and the Soviet Union have received from many quarters evidence of atrocities, massacres and cold-blooded mass executions which are being perpetrated by the Hitlerite forces in the many countries they have overrun and from which they are now being steadily expelled. The brutalities of Hitlerite domination are no new thing and all the peoples or territories in their grip have suffered from the worst form of govern-

[56] Department of State *Bulletin*, October 1 ,1944, pages 339–340.

ment by terror. What is new is that many of these territories are now being redeemed by the advancing armies of the liberating Powers and that in their desperation, the recoiling Hitlerite Huns are redoubling their ruthless cruelties. This is now evidenced with particular clearness by monstrous crimes of the Hitlerites on the territory of the Soviet Union which is being liberated from the Hitlerites, and on French and Italian territory.

Accordingly, the aforesaid three allied Powers, speaking in the interests of the thirty-two United Nations, hereby solemnly declare and give full warning of their declaration as follows:

At the time of the granting of any armistice to any government which may be set up in Germany, those German officers and men and members of the Nazi party who have been responsible for, or have taken a consenting part in the above atrocities, massacres and executions, will be sent back to the countries in which their abominable deeds were done in order that they may be judged and punished according to the laws of these liberated countries and of the free governments which will be created therein. Lists will be compiled in all possible detail from all these countries, having regard especially to the invaded parts of the Soviet Union, to Poland and Czechoslovakia, to Yugoslavia and Greece, including Crete and other islands, to Norway, Denmark, the Netherlands, Belgium, Luxemburg, France and Italy.

Thus, the Germans who take part in wholesale shootings of Italian officers or in the execution of French, Dutch, Belgian or Norwegian hostages or of Cretan peasants, or who have shared in the slaughters inflicted on the people of Poland or in territories of the Soviet Union which are now being swept clear of the enemy, will know that they will be brought back to the scene of their crimes and judged on the spot by peoples whom they have outraged. Let those who have hitherto not imbrued their hands with innocent blood beware lest they join the ranks of the guilty, for most assuredly the three allied Powers will pursue them to the uttermost ends of the earth and will deliver them to their accusers in order that justice may be done. The above declaration is without prejudice to the case of the major criminals, whose offences have no particular geographical localization and who will be punished by the joint decision of the Governments of the Allies.

(Signed):   ROOSEVELT
                   CHURCHILL
                   STALIN[57]

[57] Department of State *Bulletin*, November 6, 1943, pages 310–311; *The New York Times*, November 2, 1943, page 14.

Until March 1944, the more than 800,000 Jews under Hungarian rule, while subjected to many types of legal and economic discrimination, had been permitted to live in safety. In the territories occupied by Hungary in the south and in the north, Hungarian army units had committed grave atrocities against the local non-Hungarian populations. But the Jews in the original pre-war territory of Hungary had dwelt unharmed, and in personal, physical security.

However, on March 17, 1944, in order to prevent the expected capitulation of the Hungarians to the Allies, the Nazi legions invaded Hungary and in a few days completed the occupation of the country. The Jews immediately suffered a fate similar to that of their Polish co-religionists.

In April 1944, the entire Jewish population of Carpatho-Ruthenia, a territory re-occupied by Hungary in 1940, some 60,000 to 80,000 people, were deported to extermination camps in German-occupied Polish Silesia. This action, a joint operation of the German and Hungarian military authorities, was the first chapter in an all-out extermination campaign. By the end of June it was reported that the number of Jews deported to the extermination areas of Poland had reached over 400,000. Parallel with the deportations, all Jewish property was confiscated and "Aryanized." Hundreds of thousands were deported to extermination camps in Poland; others were sent off for forced labor or imprisoned in ghettos.[58]

In a telegram to Secretary of State Hull, on March 23, the American Jewish Committee urged the leaders of the United Nations to issue a joint statement reaffirming the previous pledges of punishment of those guilty of inhuman treatment of civilians. The following day, March 24, President Roosevelt appealed to the peoples of Nazi Europe, particularly to those of Hungary and the Balkans, to assist the Jews and other persecuted persons to escape. He pledged continued rescue efforts by the United States and stressed

---

[58] *American Jewish Year Book*, 1944–1945, pages 254–261, gives a detailed account of the developments during these frightful days.

the determination of the United Nations "that none who participate in the acts of savagery shall go unpunished." The full text of the President's statement follows:

In one of the blackest crimes of all history — begun by the Nazis in the day of peace and multiplied by them a hundred times in war — the wholesale systematic murder of the Jews of Europe goes on unabated every hour. As a result of the events of the last few days, hundreds of thousands of Jews, who while living under persecution have at least found a haven from death in Hungary and the Balkans, are now threatened with annihilation as Hitler's forces descend more heavily upon these lands. That these innocent people, who have already survived a decade of Hitler's fury, should perish on the very eve of triumph over the barbarism which their persecution symbolizes, would be a major tragedy.

It is therefore fitting that we should again proclaim our determination that none who participate in these acts of savagery shall go unpunished. The United Nations have made it clear that they will pursue the guilty and deliver them up in order that Justice be done. That warning applied not only to the leaders but also to their functionaries and subordinates in Germany and in the satellite countries. All who knowingly take part in the deportation of Jews to their death in Poland, or Norwegians and French to their death in Germany, are equally guilty with the executioner. All who share the guilt shall share the punishment.[59]

This warning was followed on June 3, 1944, by a statement of the Senate Foreign Relations Committee which again condemned the threatened extermination of the Jews of Hungary and suggested to the non-Jewish population that they extend aid to the Jews and take no part in persecuting them. The text of both statements was broadcast by the Office of War Information to the Continent in a number of European languages. On June 21, a similar statement was issued by the House Foreign Affairs Committee.[60]

On July 14, 1944, Secretary Hull issued a further statement regarding Hungary which declared:

Reliable reports from Hungary have confirmed the appalling news of mass killings of Jews by the Nazis and their Hungarian

[59] Department of State *Bulletin*, March 25, 1944, page 277.
[60] *American Jewish Year Book*, 1944–1945, pages 156–157.

quislings. The number of victims of these fiendish crimes is great. The entire Jewish community in Hungary, which numbered one million souls, is threatened with extermination. The horror and indignation felt by the American people at these cold-blooded tortures and massacres has been voiced by the President, by the Congress, and by hundreds of private organizations throughout the country. It is shared by all the civilized nations of the world. This Government will not slacken its efforts to rescue as many of these unfortunate people as can be saved from persecution and death.

The puppet Hungarian government, by its violation of the most elementary rights and by its servile adoption of the worst features of the Nazi "racial policy," stands condemned before history. It may be futile to appeal to the humanity of the instigators or perpetrators of such outrages. Let them know that they cannot escape the inexorable punishment which will be meted out to them when the power of the evil men now in control of Hungary has been broken.[61]

Statements of warning to the Nazis were also issued by the military leaders of the United States. General Dwight D. Eisenhower, in a broadcast to Germany over the British radio on November 7, 1944, warned the German people not to harm persons in concentration camps or in forced labor battalions, "no matter what their religion or nationality may be." He declared that heavy punishment awaited those who harm or mistreat these people.[62]

In the beginning of 1945, public opinion in the United States became agitated over the apparent lack of progress of the United Nations War Crimes Commission. It was feared that legal technicalities would be allowed to impede punishment for excesses committed by enemy governments against their own nationals including Jews.

With the intention of r   uring public opinion that such crimes would not go unpunished, Joseph C. Grew, Acting Secretary of State, issued a statement on February 1, 1945, in which he reviewed the position taken heretofore by the United States and other Allied Governments on the question of war crimes. Concluding this review, he stated:

[61] Department of State *Bulletin*, July 16, 1944, page 59.
[62] *Contemporary Jewish Record*, February 1943, page 64.

Over the past months, officers of the State Department, in consultation with other departments, have worked out proposals ... as forthright and far-reaching as the objectives announced by the President, which they are intended to implement. They provide for punishment of German leaders and their associations for their responsibility for the whole broad criminal enterprise devised and executed with ruthless disregard of the very foundation of law and morality, including offenses wherever committed against the rules of war and against minority elements, Jewish and other groups, and individuals.[63]

The solemn vow "to bring all war criminals to just and swift punishment" was reiterated by the three major powers of the world, the United States, Great Britain and Soviet Russia, at the historic Crimea Conference in February 1945.[64]

At the Inter-American Conference in Mexico City, in February-March 1945, the American Government sponsored the resolution calling for the apprehension of war criminals who seek refuge in Latin America.[65] The resolution adopted recommended that the governments of the American republics "shall upon the demand of any of the United Nations ... surrender individuals charged with (war) ... crimes."[66]

Early in May, 1945, it was revealed that Judge Samuel I. Rosenman, representing President Truman, had suggested to the Russian, British and French delegations at the San Francisco Conference that the four great powers join in organizing an international military tribunal and in setting up of a procedure fo. the trial of major individuals and organizations accused of atrocities and war crimes in Europe. The heads of these delegations had agreed to submit these proposals to their respective governments.[66a]

On May 2, 1945, President Truman appointed Associate Justice Robert H. Jackson of the United States Supreme Court to act as chief counsel for the United States in the

[63] *The New York Times,* February 2, 1945, page 6; Department of State *Bulletin,* February 4, 1945, pages 154–155.
[64] *The New York Times,* February 14, 1945, page 10.
[65] *Ibid.,* February 26, 1945, page 11.
[66] *Ibid.,* March 9, 1945, page 12.
[66a] *Ibid.,* May 11, 1945.

prosecution of war criminals.[66b] A month after his appointment Justice Jackson presented to President Truman a report on Trials for War Criminals. This report, made public on June 7, 1945, became the basis of American policy on this matter.[66c]

Mr. Jackson divided war crimes into two major classes. First, crimes which were committed against a particular people or that could be localized; second, crimes which had no particular locale and would have to be punished by the joint decisions of all the allies.

Crimes of the first category would be dealt with on the spot by the Allied armies in accordance with military law. Traitors and criminals who managed to escape would be returned to the scenes of their crimes and punished by the individual countries as they saw fit. The proposed international military tribunal, however, would concern itself only with crimes and criminals of the second category.

On the basis of this classification, Justice Jackson recommended that the chief Nazi leaders be charged with three major categories of crimes:

(a) Atrocities or offenses against persons or property constituting violations of International Law, including the laws, rules, and customs of land and naval warfare. . . . such conduct as killing of the wounded, refusal of quarter, ill-treatment of prisoners of war, firing on undefended localities, poisoning of wells and streams, pillage and wanton destruction, and ill-treatment of inhabitants in occupied territory.

(b) Atrocities and offenses, including atrocities and persecutions on racial and religious grounds, committed since 1933. . . .

(c) Invasions of other countries and initiation of wars of aggression in violation of International Law or treaties.

These three categories Justice Jackson included under what he termed "the Nazi master plan . . . a grand, concerted pattern to incite and commit the aggressions and barbarities which have shocked the world."

[66b] *The New York Times*, May 3, 1945.
[66c] *Ibid.*, June 8, 1945.

The position of Justice Jackson was, on the whole, accepted by the other three major powers, and on August 8, the constitution and terms of reference of the International Military Tribunal were agreed upon.[66d] As formulated in this agreement, the three categories of crimes of which the Tribunal was to take cognizance were:

(a) Crimes against peace. Under this heading were included wars of aggression and wars in violation of international treaties, agreements, or assurances, and participation in a common plan or conspiracy for the accomplishment of such acts.

(b) War crimes, i.e., violations of the laws or customs of war.

(c) "Crimes against humanity, namely, murder, extermination, enslavement, deportation and other inhuman acts committed against any civilian population before or during the war; or persecution on political, racial or religious grounds in execution of, or in connection with, any crimes within the jurisdiction of the Tribunal whether or not in violation of the domestic law of the country where perpetrated."

The crimes committed in connection with the wholesale annihilation and spoliation of European Jews fell in the second and third categories, primarily the latter.

At the time of writing, (Summer 1945) the trials of the major war criminals had as yet not begun.

Latin America

The spread of the Nazi spirit in Europe after 1933 brought about a wave of anti-democratic action with its usual companion, anti-Semitic agitation, in the countries below the Rio Grande. While democratic doctrines had never become firmly rooted in Latin America, and anti-Semitism had existed before 1933, the Nazi rise to power emboldened the native fascist elements.

The people and government of the United States viewed these developments with apprehension. There was considerable pressure of public opinion for intervention on behalf of the democratic factions in the complex political struggles

[66d] *The New York Times*, August 9, 1945.

which were taking place in many of these countries. However, the President and State Department were restricted in a great measure by the "Good Neighbor" policy which implied that the United States would keep "hands off" the internal affairs of its American sister republics. Nevertheless, on several occasions, the United States Government condemned the actions of the Government of Argentina, and on one occasion, specifically rebuked it for an anti-Jewish act.

On June 4, 1943, the reins of government in Argentina were seized by a group of army colonels who transformed the country into a near-fascist state. Political parties were abolished, the press was muzzled, labor unions were largely broken up, and persons who dared to criticize the acts or ideology of the group in power were imprisoned without warrant or trial. This totalitarian disregard for democracy was soon followed by a series of anti-Semitic decrees and actions. One decree ordered the suspension on October 14, 1943, of the publication of newspapers in the Yiddish language.

This act evoked a sharp rebuke from President Roosevelt who, in a statement released to the press by the White House on October 15, 1943, described the arbitrary suppression of Yiddish newspapers as "of a character closely identified with the most repugnant features of Nazi doctrine." He further cited the resolution endorsed by Argentina at the Lima Conference in 1938, condemning "any persecution on account of racial or religious motives."

The following is the full text of President Roosevelt's statement:

"I have been informed that the Argentine Government has suspended the publication of Jewish newspapers, some of which have been in existence for many years. While this matter is of course one which concerns primarily the Argentine Government and people, I cannot forbear to give expression to my own feeling of apprehension at the taking in this hemisphere of action obviously anti-Semitic in nature and of a character so closely identified with the most repugnant features of Nazi doctrine. I believe that this feeling is shared by the people of the United States and by the people of the other American republics. In this connection I recall that one of the resolutions adopted at the Eighth International Conference of American States at Lima in 1938 set forth that 'any persecution on account of racial or religious motives which makes it impossible for a group of human beings to live decently, is contrary to the political and juridical systems of America.' "[67]

A few days later, Yiddish newspapers were permitted to resume publications, but were ordered to publish concurrently Spanish translations of their editorials.

However, this ostensibly favorable response to democratic pressure was short-lived. The regime continued its anti-Jewish policy. Jewish welfare and mutual aid groups were suppressed; raids were carried out on Jewish homes; anti-Jewish propaganda continued unabated in the press; Jewish school teachers were dismissed; and the compulsory teaching of the Roman Catholic religion was introduced into the schools.

The Argentine Government's anti-democratic excesses so strained diplomatic relations with the United States, that Norman Armour, United States Ambassador to Argentina, was recalled to Washington on June 27, 1944, although diplomatic ties were not severed.[68]

The influence of the United States was again made manifest in Latin America in the early part of 1945 at the Inter-American Conference on Problems of War and Peace, held at Chapultepec Castle in Mexico City. This Conference, called by the United States as a preliminary to the more important San Francisco Conference of the United Nations, which was scheduled to open April 25 of the same year, had as its purpose the improvement of the relations among the American republics, the strengthening of the organization of the Inter-American system, and the achievement of more effective cooperation of the American republics with the new world structure. Many of the resolutions adopted by

[67] Department of State *Bulletin*, October 16, 1943, page 264.

[68] For a chronological account of developments in Argentina with relation to Jews, from June 1943 to June 1944, see *American Jewish Year Book*, 1944–1945, pages 293–295.

the Conference, such as those concerning apprehension of war criminals who seek refuge in Latin America and freedom of the press and radio, were originally introduced by the United States delegation to the Conference.[69]

The Conference resulted in a number of significant agreements, important among which are the Act of Chapultepec — by which the American-Republics agreed to defend one another against aggression from any source —; the Resolution on Reorganization, Consolidation and Strengthening of the Inter-American System — revising and strengthening the functions of the Pan-American Union —; the Resolution on World Organization — reaffirming the desire of the American Republics to cooperate in the organization of a world system for the maintenance of peace —; the Economic Charter of the Americas — consisting of numerous resolutions on economic cooperation —; and the Declaration of Mexico — reaffirming the juridical equality of the American Republics and prohibiting any interference in the internal affairs of one State by another.

The Conference also adopted a number of other important resolutions, including one on the international protection of the essential rights of man, and one on racial and religious equality. The first of these resolutions (No. 40) called upon the American States to declare themselves in favor of a system of international protection of the rights of man, and charged the Inter-American Juridical Committee with preparation of a draft declaration of these rights to be submitted to all the governments of the Continent within the next six months.

The following is its text:

Whereas:

The Declaration of the United Nations has proclaimed the need for establishing the international protection of the essential rights of man;

In order to render such protection effective it is necessary to define these rights, as well as the correlative duties, in a declaration to be adopted as a convention by the states;

[69] *The New York Times*, February 24, 1945, page 7 and February 25, 1945; *New York Post*, February 27, page 5.

International protection of the essential rights of man would eliminate the misuse of diplomatic protection of citizens abroad, the exercise of which has more than once led to the violation of the principle of non-intervention and also of that of equality between nationals and aliens, with respect to the essential rights of man,

The Inter-American Conference on Problems of War and Peace Resolves:

1. To proclaim the adherence of the American Republics to the principles established by international law, for safeguarding the essential rights of man, and to declare their support of a system of international protection of these rights

2. To request the Inter-American Juridicial Committee to prepare a draft Declaration of the International Rights and Duties of Man, which shall be submitted through the Pan-American Union, to all the Governments of the continent, which in turn shall submit within a maximum period of six months, the comments they deem pertinent, in order that the Committee may prepare a final draft of such inter-American instrument

3. To request the Governing Board of the Pan-American Union, after the Committee has prepared this draft and others entrusted to it by the Conference to convoke the International Conference of American Jurists in order that the Declaration may be adopted as a convention by the states of the continent.

The text of the other resolution (No. 41) reaffirmed "the principle recognized by all American states of equality of rights and opportunities for all men, regardless of race or religion;" and recommended "to the governments of the American republics that, without prejudicing the freedom of the spoken or written word, they make in their respective countries every effort to prevent all acts which tend to provoke discrimination between individuals by reason of their race or religion."[70]

The Intergovernmental Committee on Refugees

American diplomatic action for the aid of Jewish victims of Nazism began even before the outbreak of the second world war.

[70] "The Final Act of the Inter-American Conference on Problems of War and Peace," D. F. Mexico, February 21 to March 8, 1945. (Provisional English translation of Spanish text, issued by the U. S. delegation, March 8, 1945; mimeographed.)

On March 24, 1938, it was announced that the Government of the United States had sent a note to twenty-nine countries proposing the creation of a special international committee to facilitate the emigration of political refugees from Germany and Austria. This conference met at Evian, France, on July 6 to seek a long-range solution of the refugee problem. Thirty-two nations were represented. The outcome of this meeting was the creation of the Intergovernmental Committee on Refugees, which carried on a number of activities in behalf of the refugees. It made efforts to coordinate the work of the private agencies engaged in refugee aid. It also conducted studies relating to the opening of new places for permanent settlement in many parts of the world.

One of the early activities of the Intergovernmental Committee was the unsuccessful attempt of its director, George Rublee, in the beginning of 1939, to negotiate with the German Government for the purpose of working out an orderly procedure of emigration of Jews. The terms of the German Government were unacceptable, because the Nazis were primarily interested in enlarging their holdings of foreign exchange and expropriating for themselves the possessions of Jewish emigrants.[71]

All efforts at further negotiations were halted by the outbreak of the war.

The outbreak of World War II, foreshadowed a refugee problem which threatened seriously to aggravate an already grave situation. In anticipation of the new problem, a special meeting of the Intergovernmental Committee was called at the White House in Washington D. C., on October 17, 1939. In extending his welcome to the delegates of the 32 participating governments, the President of the United States outlined the nature and scope of the new problem as he foresaw it. First, he explained, there was the problem of helping those individuals and families who were, at that

[71] J. H. Simpson, "Refugees — A Review of the Situation Since September 1938," London, 1939, pages 19–20; Arieh Tartakower, "The Jewish Refugee," New York, 1943, pages 416–419; *Annals of the American Academy of Political and Social Science*, May 1939, page 14.

time, in countries of refuge, having been compelled to flee before the outbreak of the war. This situation, which concerned probably not more than two or three hundred thousand persons — he said — presented a difficulty of comparatively small magnitude. These refugees had to be given an opportunity to settle in other countries where they could make permanent homes. The task had to be accomplished as quickly as possible, before the world as a whole would be faced with the new problem involving a great many more human beings, which would confront us when the present war is over. He therefore urged the Intergovernmental Committee to redouble its efforts. Since France and Great Britain were engaged in a major war, the burden of the task would fall upon the neutral nations. He prophetically estimated that "when this ghastly war ends there may be not one million but ten or twenty million men, women, and children belonging to many races and many religions, living in many countries and possibly on several continents, who will enter into the wide picture — the problem of the human refugee." He suggested that investigations be made of the possibilities of colonizing part of these refugees on the "many comparatively vacant spaces on the earth's surface." He announced that active steps had been taken to begin such actual settlement, "made possible by the generous attitude of the Dominican Government and the Government of the Philippine Commonwealth," which he hoped would be the "forerunner of many other similar projects in other nations."

In response to the President's appeal, the Intergovernmental Committee agreed to proceed with surveys of possible new areas of settlement. However, despite the sincere urging of the President and the well-intentioned statements made by the assembled delegations, the actual achievements of the Intergovernmental Committee have been quite modest. The two basic reasons for the meager results were the intransigence of the Nazi Government and the reluctance or inability of the member-governments to relax their immigration restrictions to any extent.

The one concrete colonization venture and that a modest

one, was the Santo Domingo project, which was first officially broached at the Evian Conference in July 1938.

When the Committee began to function in London, in August 1938, it received a specific proposal from the Dominican Government indicating that Santo Domingo might be prepared ultimately to receive as many as 100,000 refugees. This offer was investigated by the Refugee Economic Corporation of New York in collaboration with the President's Advisory Committee on Political Refugees.

A mission of agricultural experts, lent by the United States Government, carried out the study and submitted a favorable report in the spring of 1939. The responsibility for financing the scheme was assumed by the American Jewish Joint Distribution Committee and the American Jewish Joint Agricultural Corporation (Agro Joint), an organization known for its agricultural settlement work in the Ukraine and the Crimea. A series of meetings was then held with representatives of the State Department and with officers of the President's Advisory Committee on Political Refugees.[72] The first group of 37 settlers arrived in Santo Domingo in May 1940; by the end of 1941, the number of settlers exceeded 400 persons.[73]

The Philippine Commonwealth colonization project did

[72] This Committee had been set up by President Roosevelt with Mr. James McDonald as its head and Mr. George Warren as its Executive Secretary. Its function was to advise the Department of State with regard to intellectuals — authors, artists, journalists, statesmen, political leaders — who because of race, religion or political belief had incurred the enmity of the Nazis. The task of this Committee was to investigate these "political" refugees and submit recommendations concerning them to the Department of State.

[73] Department of State *Bulletin,* January 4, 1941, pages 15–16; Mark Wishnitzer, *Jewish Social Studies,* January 1942, pages 45–48. A comprehensive survey of the economic status and potentialities of the Dominican Settlement was made in 1942 by the Brookings Institution and published in a 410 page volume entitled "Refugee Settlement in the Dominican Republic." This survey, conducted under the direction of Dana G. Munro, director of the school of Public and International Affairs of Princeton University, presented a pessimistic picture of the possibilities of further absorption of refugees in the colony.

not fare as well. A scientific commission, consisting of experts from the United States Department of Agriculture and the United States Army, and financed by the Refugee Economic Corporation of New York, selected a site on the island of Mindanao. The Japanese invasion, however, interrupted the effort to establish a colony there. Nevertheless, prior to the invasion, over a thousand refugees — mainly Jewish — immigrated to the Philippines as individuals.[74]

It was not long before the prediction of President Roosevelt that the war would create a refugee problem unequalled in human history, became a reality. The successive Nazi invasions of Poland, Holland, Belgium, France, Greece, and Yugoslavia threw hundreds of thousands of persons, chiefly Jews, into headlong flight from a fate which meant slavery or death. In June 1940, most of France was occupied by the German armies. To avoid falling into the hands of the Nazis, thousands of persons, most Jewish, fled from the occupied into the unoccupied part of France.

In November, 1940, a note was received by Secretary of State Hull from Gaston Henri-Haye, French Ambassador to the United States, in which the latter requested the aid of the United States Government in solving the problem of the refugees, especially those of German origin, in unoccupied France. In this note, the French Ambassador cited the burden which lay upon the French Government to care for hundreds of thousands of these refugees. He requested that the countries of the Western Hemisphere be prepared to receive a share of them, particularly those of the Jewish religion. He further asked that, in view of the impossibility of holding a meeting of the Intergovernmental Committee, the United States Government study with the French Government ways and means of organizing emigration from France to the Western Hemisphere, and that the United

---

[74] *Survey Graphic*, November 1940, special section devoted to refugees, page 15; Refugee Economic Corporation, Annual Report, 1938, page 45 and President's Report of 1942, pages 3–4, 22–26.

States Government approach the other American governments with a view to enlisting their support of this project.

Secretary Hull's reply to this request, dated December 10, 1940, turned down the invitation of the French Government. Mr. Hull explained his action by citing two basic principles of the Intergovernmental Committee: (a) that no distinctions shall be made among refugees on grounds of race, nationality, or religion and (b) that no country shall be asked or is expected to receive a greater number of immigrants than is permitted by its prevailing practices and existing laws. He explained that, while his Government was doing its utmost under existing quotas to admit a maximum of refugees, the United States immigration laws did not admit of further liberalization at the moment. To accept the suggestion of the French Government, he asserted, would be tantamount to encouraging other governments to attempt to rid themselves of helpless and unwanted minorities. While the aim of the United States Government was to "bring order out of chaos in the migration of persons driven from their countries or countries of origin who must be resettled elsewhere—, it could not support or be a party to any measure which would encourage the spread from points outside the Western hemisphere of forced migration in which people in great numbers are intended to be driven anarchically upon the receiving states with unhappy consequences to the social and economic equilibrium of all."[75]

Mr. Hull also criticized sharply the French authorities for placing obstacles in the way of persons who had qualified for admission to the United States. "Many persons who have fulfilled the requirements for admission to the United States and have received visas have not been able to leave French territory owing to the fact that the French Government has been unwilling or has failed to grant the required exit permits with the consequence that these persons have not been able to proceed to the United States and remain on French terri-

[75] Department of State *Bulletin*, January 11, 1941, pages 57–59.

tory where they must be cared for and fed." The same, he observed, was true of refugees who had qualified for admission to other American countries.

The Bermuda Conference

Meanwhile, the mounting horror of public opinion in the United States and Great Britain at the wholesale extermination of the Jewish population in the Nazi-dominated countries made mandatory another attempt to rescue them from impending doom.

On March 3, 1943, the Department of State made public an invitation to the British Government to participate in a conference for a "preliminary exploration" of the problem of rescue. The American invitation was in response to an earlier British suggestion, in a note of January 20, 1943, that such a conference be called.

The note of the Secretary of State reiterated that "it has been, and is, the traditional policy of this country to seek every available means by which to extend to oppressed and persecuted peoples such assistance as may be found to be feasible and possible under the laws of the United States." The note reviewed the measures of assistance already afforded these peoples by the Government. These measures, it explained, consisted of official declarations condemning the policies and acts of the Axis Governments and their satellites; the appropriation of large amounts of public and private funds for the relief of persecuted persons; and the calling by the President of the United States of the first Intergovernmental Conferences at Evian and London in 1938 for the purpose of seeking a solution of refugee problems. Mr. Hull also observed that the Government had made efforts to persuade other countries to provide asylum for the refugees, as well as to find suitable places for colonization. He stated that the Government had applied the "immigration laws of the United States in the utmost liberal and humane spirit of those laws" and that from the advent of the Hitler regime in 1933 to June 30, 1942, the Government

had issued 547,775 visas to "natives or nationals of the
various countries now dominated by the Axis powers, the
great majority of which persons were refugees from Nazi
persecution. Of this number, 228,964 were issued in the
war years 1939–1942. Many more than that number of
visas were authorized during this latter period, the aliens
in whose behalf such authorizations were given having
been unable to depart from their places of foreign residence
to reach the United States. Yet, of the number actually
issued, practically all of the aliens who received them during
the war years 1939–1942 have actually arrived in the United
States and have remained here, many of them having
entered in a temporary status and not yet having departed."

The note also listed other activities of the Government
which, directly or indirectly, afforded relief to the oppressed
and persecuted peoples.

The purpose of enumerating the long list of rescue activities of the Government apparently was to discourage the
public from expecting drastic changes in the immigration
laws and rescue activities of the country. For, as Mr. Hull's
note emphasized, the Government felt, "in view of the
facts set forth above, that it has been and is making every
endeavor to relieve the oppressed and persecuted peoples.
In affording asylum to refugees, however, it is and must be
bound by legislation by Congress determining the immigration policy of the United States."

For these reasons, Mr. Hull suggested that the proposed
Conference should center its deliberations upon the following
points:

(a) That further efforts to solve the problem should "be
undertaken through the instrumentality already existing,
the Executive Committee of the Intergovernmental Committee on Refugees."

(b) "The refugee problem should not be considered as
being confined to persons of any particular race or faith."

(c) Whenever feasible, refugees should be granted temporary asylum "as near as possible to the areas in which those
people find themselves at the present time and from which

they may be returned to their homelands with the greatest expediency on the termination of hostilities."

(d) The neutral countries should be assured that, until the refugees are repatriated, funds for their support will be forthcoming from the United Nations; and the Governments-in-exile should give assurances to the neutrals that, upon the termination of hostilities, the refugees would be promptly permitted to return.

(e) The possibilities of temporary asylum "in countries other than neutral, and their dependencies," should be explored — with the understanding that the refugees would ultimately be repatriated.[76]

When this note was made public, Secretary Hull was subjected to severe criticism. Students of the problem pointed out that the figures he had cited regarding the number of visas issued were deceptive. The more than 300,000 visas claimed to have been issued before the outbreak of the war in Europe included those issued to persons outside of Germany. The figure of more than 225,000 visas claimed to have been issued since 1939, taken by itself, was also deceptive; for only 92,000 of the persons to whom visas were issued actually came to the United States. It was estimated that about 160,000 Jews had actually entered the United States between 1933 and 1942.

Because of Mr. Hull's statement, and a similar one of the British Government, the summoning of the Anglo-American Conference to be held in Bermuda was greeted with modest enthusiasm. Realizing that the scope of its deliberations would be narrow, people did not expect much from it.[77]

The Anglo-American Conference was held at Bermuda April 19–30, 1943, under the chairmanship of Dr. Harold Willis Dodds, President of Princeton University. No official report on the proceedings or decisions of the Bermuda Conference was issued at the conclusion of its sessions. Only

[76] For full text of the note, see Department of State *Bulletin*, March 6, 1943, pages 202–204.

[77] See editorials in *The New York Times*, April 21, 1943; *New York Post*, April 22, 1943: *New York World Telegram*, April 21, 1943.

a brief final communiqué was released to the press, which stated that "the delegates were unable to agree on a number of concrete recommendations which they are jointly submitting to their governments . . . Since the recommendations necessarily concern governments other than those represented at the Bermuda Conference and involve the military considerations, they must remain confidential."[78]

The "secret" decisions adopted by the Bermuda Conference were revealed several months later when testimony of Assistant Secretary of State, Breckenridge Long, presented to the Committee on Foreign Affairs of the House of Representatives, was made public.

Mr. Long's testimony had been given during hearings on concurrent resolutions introduced in both Houses of Congress proposing the establishment of a presidential commission to "effectuate the rescue of the Jewish people of Europe." The House Resolutions had been introduced on November 9, 1943, by Representative Will Rogers, Jr. (Democrat, Calif.), and Representative Joseph Baldwin (Republican, N. Y.). Mr. Long's testimony, presented before a closed session of the Foreign Affairs Committee, on November 26, was made public on December 10th.

According to Mr. Long, the most important decision made at Bermuda was to revitalize the Intergovernmental Committee on Refugees by widening its base and adding to its British director, an American co-director, Mr. Patrick Malin. Hitherto limited in its jurisdiction to assisting refugees from Germany, Austria, and the Sudetenland, the Intergovernmental Committee was to extend its efforts "to all countries from which refugees come — or in which they may find refuge." This included, he asserted, the authority to work "within and without Germany and the occupied territories." The United States and British Governments, through the Intergovernmental Committee, would continue efforts to secure the release of French refugees and other Allied nationals

[78] For full text of the joint communiqué, see Department of State *Bulletin*, May 1, 1943, page 388.

from Spain and transfer them for temporary residence to North Africa; would consult with the French National Committee to secure favorable consideration of a proposal to admit refugees to Madagascar; would ascertain the possibility of the reception of refugees into various overseas countries; and would urge all the Allied governments to adopt a joint declaration concerning the right of refugees to return to their homes after the war. Mr. Long also stated that the United States had admitted "since the beginning of the Hitler regime and the persecution of the Jews until today approximately 580,000 refugees."[79]

The testimony of Mr. Long was critically received by organizations actively interested in the refugee problem. The London headquarters of the Intergovernmental Committee denied on December 17th that it had been authorized to undertake direct negotiations with Germany. Mr. Long's figures on the number of refugees admitted since 1933, were vigorously criticized for giving the erroneous impression that the total immigration from 1933 to 1943 had been refugee immigration, and had all been occasioned by anti-Jewish persecutions. It was demonstrated on the basis of official data that, during the decade 1933–1943, a maximum of 160,000 Jewish refugees had been admitted to the United States, and all within the framework of the existing immigration laws.[80]

Nevertheless, Mr. Long's testimony caused the House Foreign Affairs Committee to hesitate in approving the Rogers-Baldwin resolution. Meanwhile, on December 20, the Senate Foreign Relations Committee approved the parallel resolution introduced by Senator Guy M. Gillette

[79] "Rescue of the Jewish and Other Peoples in Nazi-Occupied Europe." Hearings before the Committee on Foreign Affairs of the House of Representatives, 78th Congress, 1st Session, on House Resolutions 350 and 352, November 26, 1943, pages 24–29.

[80] For critical analyses of Mr. Long's statements, see article by Solomon Dingol, *Rescue Information Bulletin* of the Hebrew Immigrant Aid Society (HIAS), February 1944, pages 1 ff.; letter of Yiddish Scientific Institute (YIVO) to *The New York Times*, December 27, 1943; article by Victor H. Bernstein in the newspaper *PM*, December 14, 1943.

(D., Iowa).[81] Both House and Senate committees suspended further action on the resolution before them, when, on January 22, 1944, the President made public an executive order establishing the War Refugee Board.[82]

War Refugee Board

The War Refugee Board was created by President Roosevelt in response to an ever-growing public feeling in favor of adopting concrete measures to effect the rescue of as many as possible of the persecuted minorities in Nazi Europe. This growing public sentiment was a result of the increasing information received of the unexampled Nazi atrocities perpetrated against Jews and other helpless groups.[83]

The functions of the War Refugee Board, were to "include without limitations the development of plans and programs and the inauguration of effective measures for (a) the rescue, transportation and maintenance and relief of the victims of enemy oppression, and (b) the establishment of havens of temporary refuge for such victims."

The Executive Order made the War Refugee Board responsible directly to the President. It was to consist of the Secretaries of State, War and Treasury Departments, and was empowered to request the heads of other agencies and departments to cooperate with it in the obtaining of information, the provision of supplies, shipping and other forms of assistance. The Board was also authorized to accept the services or contributions of private organizations and foreign governments, and to cooperate with all the existing and future international organizations concerned with the problems of rescue and relief.[84]

The creation of the War Refugee Board was received enthusiastically by the American public generally and by

[81] *Contemporary Jewish Record,* February 1944, page 63.

[82] *Ibid., April* 1944, page 177.

[83] A survey of the steps leading to the creation of the War Refugee Board is contained in an article by Ilja Dijour, in the HIAS *Rescue Information Bulletin,* March–April 1944, pages 5 ff.

[84] For full text of the Executive Order, see Department of State *Bulletin,* January 22, 1945, pages 95–96.

the numerous private organizations engaged in related work.

The first executive director of the War Refugee Board was John W. Pehle, who had been, during the first years of the war, director of the Foreign Funds Control Division of the Treasury Department. Mr. Pehle immediately dispatched agents to Turkey, Portugal, Spain, Egypt, and Sweden. These agents were given the status of special attachés on refugee matters to the American embassies, legations, and consulates in these countries. From the outset, the War Refugee Board tried to establish contact with the underground organizations in the occupied countries and took other steps generally considered unconventional and off the beaten path of diplomacy. Among the activities of the Board were the conduct, through neutral channels, of negotiations with the Rumanian government regarding the return of 46,000 displaced persons from internment in Transnistria, with a view to their eventual emigration. With the aid of Laurence Steinhardt, United States Ambassador in Turkey, Mr. Ira Hirschman, agent of War Refugee Board in that country, succeeded in persuading the Turkish Government to permit refugees to pass through its territory. It was reported in October 1944 that the War Refugee Board in cooperation with the American Jewish Joint Distribution Committee and the Jewish Agency for Palestine had succeeded in rescuring and transporting to Palestine 8,000 Jews, 2,400 of them children, trapped in Hungary and several Balkan countries.[85]

General William O'Dwyer, who replaced Mr. Pehle as head of the War Refugee Board, initiated a program for feeding Jewish internees in labor and concentration camps.[86]

The full story of the rescue efforts of the War Refugee Board has not yet been made public.[87] While its achieve-

---

[85] *J.D.C. [American Jewish Joint Distribution Committee] Digest,* October 1944, page 2.

[86] *JTA* Daily News Bulletin, April 10, 1945, page 4.

[87] A brief account of the activities of the War Refugee Board is contained in an article by M. Frank, "A Yor Tetigkeit fun 'War Refugee

ments have been tragically modest, measured by the immensity of the problem it was created to handle, they constitute an additional significant chapter in the story of American activity in behalf of the oppressed and driven peoples of the world. The magnitude of its achievements becomes more evident when one considers that Allied arms were hard pressed on many fronts during much of the period of its activity, and all national efforts had to be devoted to prosecuting the war.

"Free Ports"

The adoption and implementation by President Roosevelt and the War Refugee Board of the "free port" idea also constituted a significant action in behalf of the refugees.

The plan, when first suggested, was quickly taken up and championed by many organizations and individuals. Resolutions favoring the creation of "free ports" were introduced in the Senate by Senator Guy Gillette (D., Iowa), on May 29, 1944, and in the House of Representatives by eight Congressmen during the following two weeks. Hearings on the various bills, were postponed due to the adjournment of Congress on June 23.[88] Although no further action with regard to them was taken by the legislative branch of the government, the President of the United States acted to carry out the humanitarian plan which the American public had taken up so enthusiastically.

On June 9, 1944, President Roosevelt announced that the United States would accept a total of 1,000 refugees located in Italy who would be brought to this country outside of the regular immigration procedure. These refugees would be placed in an "emergency refugee shelter" to be established at Fort Ontario, near Oswego, New York, where they could remain for the duration of the war. Responsibility for the execution of the program was to be vested in the War and Navy Departments, and in the War Relocation Authority,

Board' " (One Year's Activity of War Refugee Board), *Yivo Bleter*, March-April, pages 261–270.
    [88] *Contemporary Jewish Record*, August 1944, pages 401–402.

which would handle the actual administration of the camp. The Bureau of the Budget was to make arrangements for the financing of the project.

The same day, the White House released a cablegram which the President had sent to Ambassador Robert Murphy in Algiers, requesting him to make arrangements for the departure to the United States of 1,000 refugees to be placed in the first "free port." The cablegram explained the procedure to be followed and noted that "the procedure for the selection of the refugees and arrangements for bringing them here should be as simple and expeditious as possible, uncomplicated by any of the usual formalities involved in admitting people to the United States under the immigration laws." The cablegram, however, made clear that "it is contemplated that at the end of the war they will be returned to their homelands."[89]

The President formally notified Congress of his action in a message on June 12, 1944. He explained that Italy was overcrowded with refugees who, in view of the military situation, could not be cared for there, and who constituted "an additional and substantial burden for the military authorities." He again made it clear, however, that "upon the termination of the war they will be sent back to their homelands."[90]

The group of refugees consisted of 984 persons, including 918 Jews, 47 Roman Catholics, 14 Greek Orthodox, and 5 Protestants.[91]

United Nations Relief and Rehabilitation Administration (UNRRA)

Even before any territory held by the Axis Powers had been liberated or conquered, it was obvious that with victory would come many serious problems of relief and aid

[89] Department of State *Bulletin*, June 10, 1945, pages 532–533.

[90] *Ibid.*, June 17, 1944, pages 553–554.

[91] For a description of the Oswego camp, see the HIAS *Rescue Information Bulletin*, September 1944, pages 7–9.

to the liberated populations. Millions of refugees and Nazi slaves were far from their homes and all inhabitants of Nazi conquered territories had been living on a diet of slow starvation. Jews were receiving an amount of calories per day even lower than that given other Europeans.

The Department of State, therefore, established, in December 1942, the Office of Foreign Relief and Rehabilitation Operations (OFRRO). This agency, which was under the direction of Herbert H. Lehman, former governor of New York, made plans to provide and transport food, clothing and other basic necessities to war victims as they were liberated from enemy control. The British established a similar agency called the Middle East Relief and Refugee Administration (MERRA). The OFRRO and the MERRA opened camps in Tunisia where refugees were given food, clothing and shelter.

These two agencies were short-lived, however. They were soon absorbed by the United Nations Relief and Rehabilitation Administration (UNRRA), which was established on November 9, 1943, by the representatives of forty-four United and Associated Nations at a meeting in the White House, Washington, D. C.[92]

The purposes and the scope of UNRRA's task were defined as follows:

..... immediately upon the liberation of any area by the armed forces of the United Nations or as a consequence of the retreat of the enemy the population thereof shall receive aid and relief from their sufferings, food, clothing and shelter, aid in the prevention of pestilence and in the recovery of the health of the people, and that preparation and arrangements shall be made for the return of prisoners and exiles to their homes and for assistance in the resumption of urgently needed agricultural and industrial production of essential services . . .[93]

[92] Department of State *Bulletin*, November 23, 1943, pages 317–319.

[93] *Ibid.*, September 25, 1943, pages 211–216. For a detailed account of the organization and activities of UNRRA, see the *UNRRA Monthly Review*, Washington, D.C. (Published since August 1944); "UNRRA, Organization, Aims, Progress," Washington, D.C., 1944; Report of the Director General

Two days after the signing of the Agreement the UNRRA Council opened its first session in Atlantic City, New Jersey. On November 11, Herbert H. Lehman was elected Director-General and immediately assumed office. The Council then set to work to determine major policies by which the Administration was to be guided, and to outline the form of its administrative organization.

The UNRRA decided to enlist the services and use the experts of private voluntary relief organizations. In accordance with this policy, the staff and program of the American Jewish Joint Distribution Committee (JDC) were coordinated with the organization of the UNRRA. Similarly, Jewish experts were engaged to serve in communities which had large Jewish populations.

At the time of writing, December 1945, it is as yet too early to give a comprehensive account of the accomplishment of the UNRRA. There is no doubt, however, that it kept alive millions of unfortunates who otherwise would not have had the physical strength and the necessary morale to fight on. Millions of refugees were returned to their homes and were aided in their rehabilitation there. It must be added that by far the largest part of the budget of the UNRRA was supplied by contribution from the Government of the United States.

International Protection of Human Rights

Perhaps it is most appropriate to conclude our study of American diplomatic action affecting Jews, with a brief discussion of the international protection of human rights as envisaged in the United Nations Charter. This was the first time in human history that the principle of international protection of the rights of individuals in all countries was given formal recognition.

President Roosevelt and the heads of the other Big Three powers had on a number of occasions expressed their interest

to the Second Session of the Council of UNRRA, Washington, D.C., September, 1944 (Council II, Document I).

in such a project. In the Atlantic Charter and in the Teheran and Moscow Declarations, they had expressed their recognition of the need for protecting the basic freedoms indispensable to civilization. The Dumbarton Oaks Conference had adopted as one of the purposes of the General International Organization to be established, the intention "to achieve international cooperation in the solution of international, economic, social and other humanitarian" problems. It had envisaged an economic and social council "to facilitate the solution of international economic, social, and other humanitarian problems and promote respect for human rights and fundamental freedoms."

It was generally recognized that the violation of the rights of individuals and of minorities is a likely prelude to the violation of the rights of nations, and that aggression at home is likely to become aggression abroad. It was felt that an international guarantee of human rights would prove more effective than the minorities treaties imposed by the Paris Peace Conference after World War I, on the newly-created or enlarged states. The minorities treaties were recognized to have been a failure because, among other reasons, they had been imposed only upon some states — those newly created or enlarged. The state thus singled out felt that these treaties were a violation of their sovereignty. They feared, in some cases with good reason, the disruptive potentialities of the irredentist ambitions among their minorities. These treaties were frequently violated.

A different approach to the human rights problem was felt to be essential. The plan for an international bill of rights, accepted by all nations for all men, gained many adherents as the war drew to a close. Among the organizations most active in advocating this plan were the Federal Council of the Churches of Christ in America, the Carnegie Endowment for International Peace, the Congress of Industrial Organizations, and the American Jewish Committee. The proposal for an international bill of rights had been presented to President Roosevelt on March 20, 1945 by the

American Jewish Committee and had evoked from him a favorable response.

However, the fear was widespread on the eve of the United Nations Conference at San Francisco, held April–June 1945, that the delegates of the Great Powers would raise objections to any proposals which might threaten to lead to interference in their internal affairs. It was feared that the delegates would rest content with the vague clause in the Dumbarton Oaks Agreement. The Soviet delegation, it was feared, might see in the suggestion for a commission on human rights and an international bill of rights, an opportunity for anti-Soviet elements to charge the Soviet Union with violation of various fundamental freedoms. The British delegation might fear that nationalists in India and other British-controlled territories would be enabled to cause serious international embarrassment for Great Britain. The American delegation might fear that the establishment of the Commission would complicate efforts to win Senate ratification of the Charter, due, among other reasons, to the Negro issue.

It is agreed that much of the credit for the inclusion of the human rights provisions in the Charter is due to the consultants' group at San Francisco which represented forty-two organizations of citizens, including labor, farm, business, education, church, and veterans. These organizations had been invited by the Department of State to send representatives to San Francisco for the purpose of maintaining direct contact with public opinion.

On the morning of May 2, 1945, the American consultants were informed by Dean Virginia Gildersleeve of the American delegation, that the latter did not intend to go beyond the provisions of the Dumbarton Oaks Agreement and would not ask for the establishment of a commission of human rights.

The consultants were distressed. They were scheduled to meet that same afternoon with Mr. Stettinius at a meeting which would be their last chance to win over the American delegation to their views. Judge Joseph M. Proskauer, president of the American Jewish Committee, immediately drafted a petition to be presented to Secretary Stettinius, head of the American delegation. The petition was revised by Dr. James T. Shotwell, chairman of the group of consultants, by Jacob Blaustein, Clark Eichelberger and by other consultants. Twenty-two of the forty-two consultants — all who could be reached within the short time available — affixed their signatures to the petition before the scheduled meeting with Secretary Stettinius. The petition was presented to the Secretary by Dr. O. Frederick Nolde, representing the Federal Council of the Churches of Christ in America.

Mr. Stettinius agreed to bring the viewpoint of the consultants to the attention of the American delegation. Once the latter agreed, the acquiescence of the other delegations was secured.

As adopted by the United Nations Conference, the Charter contains many references to human rights. The preamble affirms faith in "fundamental human rights, in the dignity and worth of the human personality, in the equal rights of men and women, of nations small and large . . . ." The purposes of the United Nations Organization include the achievement of "international cooperation . . . in promoting and encouraging respect for human rights and for fundamental freedoms for all without distinction as to race, sex, language or religion . . . (Article 1, section 3). The Economic and Social Council is empowered to make "recommendations for the purpose of promoting respect for, and observance of, human rights and fundamental freedoms for all." (Article 62, section 3). It is required to "set up commissions in the economic and social fields, and *for the promotion of human rights* . . . ." (Article 68). A duty to promote the rights of the individual in trust territories is laid upon the Trusteeship Council. (Article 76, section C)

The one body envisaged in the Charter whose specific function is the protection of human rights, is the Commission on Human Rights. This Commission, whose creation is mandatory on the Economic and Social Council — in turn is responsible to the General Assembly. The Trusteeship Council is instructed (Article 91) to collaborate with the Economic and Social Council, and is also reponsible to the General Assembly. (Article 85).[94]

• As at present constituted, the authority of the Commission on Human Rights is qualified by the policy of non-intervention of the United Nations Organization in the domestic affairs of its member nations. Its powers may, however, be clarified and strengthened as the concept of international cooperation grows. As was stated by Mr. Stettinius, Secretary of State and Chief of the American delegation, to the UNCIO, on May 15, 1945: "We can here make only a beginning, but I believe it is a good beginning."

The hopes and expectations of the American people, as well as of the other peoples of the world, were voiced by President Truman on June 26, 1945, in his address before the final Plenary Session of the San Francisco Conference, when he said:

"Under this document we have good reason to expect the framing of an international bill of rights, acceptable to all the nations involved. That bill of rights will be as much a part of international life as our own Bill of Rights is a part of the Constitution. The Charter is dedicated to the achievement of 'observance of human rights and fundamental freedoms.' Unless we can attain those objectives for all men and women everywhere — without regard to race, language or religion — we cannot have permanent peace and security."[95]

[94] For a detailed account of the various problems handled at the San Francisco Conference, the different viewpoints espoused, and the principles finally agreed upon, see United States Department of State, "Charter of the United Nations: Report to the President of the Results of the San Francisco Conference," Washington, D.C., 1945.

[95] "A World Charter of Human Rights," published by The American Jewish Committee, 1945 [page 12].

APPENDIX

REPORT OF MINISTER ANDREW D. WHITE ON THE JEWISH
SITUATION IN RUSSIA[1]

Legation of the United States
St. Petersburg, July 6, 1893

SIR:

Your telegram, presumably of May 17, was received on the
morning of May 18, and answered at once.

Since telegraphing you I have made additional inquiries with
reference to your question, and am persuaded that there has been
no new edict banishing Israelites from Poland, as was stated in
some of the papers of Western Europe; but for some time past the
old edicts and regulations against them have been enforced in
various parts of the Empire with more and more severity.

Soon after my arrival at this post it was rumored that there was
to be some mitigation in the treatment of them, but the hopes
based on this rumor have grown less and less, and it is now clear
that the tendency is all in the direction of not only excluding
Israelites more rigorously than ever from parts of the Empire
where they were formerly allowed on sufferance, but to make life
more and more difficult for them in those parts of the Empire
where they have been allowed to live for many generations.

As you are doubtless aware, there are about 5,000,000 Israelites
in Russia, forming, as it is claimed, more than half of the entire
Jewish race, and these are packed together in the cities and villages
of what was formerly Poland and adjacent governments, in a belt
extending along the western borders from northwest to southeast,
but which for some years past has been drawn back from the frontier
about 40 miles, under the necessity, as it is claimed, imposed by
the tendency of the Israelites in that region to conduct smuggling
operations. In other parts of the Empire they have only been
allowed to reside as a matter of exceptional favor. This alleged
favor, under the more kindly reign of Alexander II, was largely
developed and matured into a sort of *quasi* right in the case of
certain classes, such as Israelites who have been admitted to the

---

[1] Foreign Relations, 1894, pages 525–35.

455

learned professions, or have taken a university degree, or have received the rights of merchants of the first or second guild, paying the heavy fees required in such cases. Certain skilled artisans have also been allowed to reside in certain towns outside the Jewish pale, but their privileges are very uncertain, liable to revocation at any time, and have in recent years been greatly diminished. Besides this, certain Israelites are allowed by special permits to reside as clerks in sundry establishments, but under the most uncertain tenure. This tenure can be understood by a case which occurred here about a month since.

At that time died an eminent Israelite of St. Petersburg, a Mr. ——————, who had distinguished himself by rescuing certain great companies from ruin by his integrity and skill in various large operations, and by the fact that, while he made large and constant gains for those interested in these companies and operations, he laid up for himself only a modest competence. He had in his employ a large number of Jewish clerks, and it is now regarded here as a matter of fact that at the expiration of their passes, say in a few months, all of them must leave St. Petersburg.

The treatment of the Israelites, whether good or evil, is not based entirely upon any one ukase or statute; there are said to be in the vast jungle of the laws of the Empire more than one thousand decrees and statutes relating to them, besides innumerable circulars, open or secret, regulations, restrictions, extensions, and temporary arrangements, general, special, and local, forming such a tangled growth that probably no human being can say what the law as a whole is — least of all can a Jew in any province have any knowledge of his rights.

From time to time, and especially during the reign of Alexander II, who showed himself more kind to them than any other sovereign had ever been, many of them were allowed to leave this overcrowded territory, and, at least, were not hindered from coming into territory and towns which, strictly speaking, they were not considered as entitled to enter; but for some time past this residence on sufferance has been rendered more and more difficult. Details of the treatment to which they have been subjected may be found in the report made by Mr. J. C. Weber and his associate commissioners entitled "Report of the Commissioners of Immigration Upon the Causes Which Incite Immigration to the United States," Government Printing Office. I must confess that when I first read this report its statements seemed to me exaggerated, or, at least, overcolored, but it is with very great regret that I say that this is no longer my opinion. Not only is great severity exercised as regards the main body of Israelites here, but it is from time to time brought to bear with especial force upon those returning to Russia from abroad. The case was recently brought to my notice of a Jewish woman who, having gone abroad, was stopped on her return at a frontier station, and, at last accounts, had been there three days, hoping that some members of her family in Russia might be able to do something to enable her to rejoin them.

Israelites of the humbler class find it more and more difficult to reenter Russia, and this fact will explain the case of Mrs. Minnie Lerin, referred to in Mr. Wharton's dispatch No. 60 (Foreign Relations 1893, page 536) as being refused a visa at the Russian consulate-general in New York, and it will also throw light on various other cases we have had in which the legation has been able to secure mitigation in the application of the rules.

On this latter point we have been successful in obtaining such mitigation in cases of many Israelites who have been subjected to annoyance by overzealous local authorities.

It may appear strange that any nation should wish to expel a people who, in other parts of the world, have amassed so much wealth. The fact is that but a very small fraction of them in Russia are wealthy; few even in comfortable circumstances. The vast majority of them are in poverty, and a very considerable part in misery — just on the border of starvation.

Nearly forty years ago, when, as an attaché of this legation, I was for seven days and nights on the outside of a post coach between St. Petersburg and Warsaw — there being then no railway to the frontier — I had ample opportunity to see something of these Israelites and of the region in which they live. They exist for the most part in squalor, obliged to resort to almost anything that offers, in order to keep soul and body together. Even the best of them were then treated with contempt by the lowest of the pure Russians. I myself saw two Israelites, evidently of the wealthier class and richly clad, who had ventured into the inclosure in front of the posthouse to look at the coach in which I was, lashed with a coach whip and driven out of the inclosure with blows by one of the postilions — evidently a serf.

A very few millionaire Israelites are to be found among the merchants of the first guild in some of the larger cities, but there is no such proportion of wealthy men among them as in the United States, Great Britain, France and Germany. In the smaller towns, in some of which they form the majority of the residents, their poverty is so abject that they drag each other down, making frequently a ruinous competition with each other in such branches of business as they are allowed to pursue. This is now even more the case than ever before, since recent regulations have swept the Israelites living in many rural districts into the towns.

A case was a few days since mentioned to me in which a small town of 8,000 or 10,000 inhabitants had recently received into its population nearly 6,000 Israelites from the surrounding country.

The restrictions are by no means confined to residence; they extend into every field of activity. Even in the parts of the Empire where the Israelites are most free they are not allowed to hold property in land, or to take a mortgage on land, or to farm land, and of late they have even been, to a large extent, prevented from living on farms, and have been thrown back into the cities and villages.

As to other occupations, Jewish manufacturers have at times, even under the present reign, been crippled by laws or regulations forbidding them to employ Christian workmen, but these are understood to be not now in force. They are relics of the old legislation which, in the interest of the servant's soul, forbade a Jew to employ a Christian servant under pain of death, and which, in a mitigated form, remained on the statute book until 1865, when it was abolished by Alexander II.

There are also many restrictions upon the professions considered more honorable. A few Israelites are allowed to become engineers, and they are allowed to hold 5% of the positions of army surgeons, but no more; and this in spite of the fact that from the middle ages until now their race has been recognized as having a peculiar aptitude for medicine and surgery. As a rule, also, they are debarred from discharging any public functions of importance, and even as to lesser functions a Jew cannot be elected mayor of a village or even member of its council.

Not more than one man in ten of those summoned to do jury duty can be a Jew, and even in the cities within the pale, where the Jews form the great majority of the population, they cannot hold more than one-third the places on a municipal council.

Perhaps the most painful of the restrictions upon them is in regard to the education of their children. The world over, as is well known, the Israelites will make sacrifices to educate their sons and daughters, such as are not made, save in exceptional cases, by any other people. They are, as is universally recognized, a very gifted race, but no matter how gifted a young Israelite may be, his chances of receiving an education are small.

In regions where they are most numerous, only 10 per cent of the scholars in high schools and universities are allowed to be Jews, but in many cases the number allowed them is but 5 per cent and in St. Petersburg and Moscow only three per cent. Out of seventy-five young Israelites who applied for admission to the University of Dorpat in 1887 only seven were allowed to enter. A few days since the case was brought to my notice of a well-to-do Israelite who wished to educate his son whom he considered especially gifted, but could not obtain permission to educate him in St. Petersburg, and was obliged to be satisfied with the permission to enter him at one of the small provincial universities remote from the capital.

To account for this particular restriction it is urged that if freely allowed to receive an advanced education they would swarm in the high schools, universities, and learned professions; and, as a proof of this, the fact is mentioned that some time since, in the absence of restrictions, at Odessa from 50 to 70 per cent of the scholars in sundry Russian colleges were Jews.

As to religious restrictions, the general policy pursued seems to an unprejudiced observer from any other country so illogical as to be incomprehensible. On one hand great powers are given to Jewish rabbis and religious authorities. They are allowed in the districts where the Israelites mainly live to form a sort of state within the state, with power to impose taxes upon their coreligionists and to give their regulations virtually the force of law. On the other hand, efforts of zealous orthodox Christians to proselyte Israelites, which must provoke much bitterness, are allowed and even favored. The proselytes, once brought within the orthodox Russian fold, no matter by what means, any resumption of the old religion by them is treated as a crime.

Recent cases have occurred where Jews who have been thus converted and who have afterwards attended the synagogue have been brought before the courts.

So, too, in regard to religious instruction it would seem to an unprejudiced observer, wishing well both to Russia and to the Israelites, that the first thing to do would be to substitute instruction in science, general literature, and in technical branches for that which is so strongly complained of by Russians generally — the instruction in the Talmud and Jewish theology. But this is just what is not done, and, indeed, as above stated, not allowed.

The whole system at present in vogue is calculated to make Talmudic and theological schools — which are so constantly complained of as the nurses and hotbeds of anti-Russian and anti-Christian fanaticism — the only schools accessible to the great majority of gifted young Israelites.

As to recent interferences of which accounts have been published in the English newspapers, and especially as to a statement that a very large number of Jewish children were, early during the present year, taken from their parents in one of the southern governments of Russia and put into monastic schools under charge of orthodox priests, this statement having been brought to my notice especially by letters addressed to me as the representative of the United States, I communicated with our consuls in the regions referred to and also obtained information from other trustworthy sources, and the conclusion at which I arrived was that the statement was untrue; it probably had its origin in the fact that much anxiety has recently been shown by certain high officials, and especially ecclesiastics, to promote education in which orthodox religious instruction holds a very important part.

In justification of all these restrictions various claims are made. First of all it is claimed that the Jews lend money to peasants and others at enormous rates of interest. But it is pointed out, in answer to this, that sundry bankers and individuals in parts of Russia where no Jews are permitted have made loans at a much higher rate than Jews have ever ventured to do; while it is allowed that 100 per cent a year has not infrequently been taken by the Israelites. There seems to be no doubt of the fact that from 300 to 800 per cent, and even more, sometimes, has been taken by Christians.

This statement seems incredible, but it is unimpeachable. In a general way it is supported by a recent report of a Russian official to Mr. Sagonof; and a leading journal of St. Petersburg, published under strict censorship, has recently given cases with names and dates where a rate higher than the highest above named, was paid by Russian peasants to Christian money lenders.

Those inclined to lenity towards the Jews point to the fact that none of them would dare to take any such rates of interest as Christians may freely demand; that to do so would raise against the Israelites in their neighborhood storms which they could not resist, and it is argued that, as their desire for gain is restricted in this way, their presence in any part of Russia tends to diminish the rate of interest rather than to increase it. On the other hand, it is claimed that they will not work at agriculture and, indeed, they will do no sort of manual labor which they can avoid.

As to the first of these charges, the fact is dwelt upon, which has so impressed Mr. McKenzie Wallace and other travelers, that the Jewish agricultural colonies founded by Alexander I, in 1810, and by Nicholas I, in 1840, have not done well.

But in answer it may be stated as a simple matter of history that, having been originally an agricultural people, they have been made what they are by ages of persecutions which have driven them into the occupations to which they are now so generally devoted; that in Russia they have for generations been incapacitated for agricultural work by such restrictions as those above referred to; that even if they are allowed here and there to till the land, they are not allowed, in the parts of the Empire which they most inhabit, to buy or even farm it, and thus the greatest incentive to labor is taken away.

As to other branches of manual labor, simply as a matter of fact, there are very large bodies of Jewish artisans in Poland, numbering in the aggregate about one-half of the entire adult male

Israelite population. Almost every branch of manual labor is represented among them, and well represented. As stone masons they have an especially high reputation, and it is generally conceded that in sobriety, capacity, and attention to work they fully equal their Christian rivals.

Complaint is also made that they, as far as possible, avoid military service. This is doubtless true, but the reasons for it are evident. For the Jewish soldier there is no chance of promotion, and when he retires from the service he is, as a rule, subject to the same restrictions and inflictions as others of his race. In spite of this fact the number of them in the conscription of 1886 was over 40,000.

I find everywhere, in discussing this subject, a complaint that the Israelites, wherever they are allowed to exist, get the better of the Russian peasant. The difficulty is that the life of the Israelite is marked by sobriety, self-denial, and foresight; and whatever may be the kindly qualities ascribed to the Russian peasant — and there are many — these qualities are rarely, if ever, mentioned among them.

It is also urged against the Israelites in Russia that they are not patriotic, but in view of the policy pursued regarding them the wonder is that any human being should expect them to be patriotic.

There is also frequent complaint against Jewish fanaticism, and recently collections of extracts from the Talmud have been published here as in western Europe, and even in the United States, to show that Israelites are educated in bitter and undying hate of Christians, and taught not only to despise but to despoil them; and it is insisted that the vast majority of Israelites in Russia have, by ages of this kind of instruction and by the simple laws of heredity, been made beasts of prey with claws and teeth especially sharp, and that the peasant must be protected from them.

Lately this charge has been strongly reiterated, a book having appeared here in which the original Hebrew of the worst Talmudic passages, with translations of them, are placed in parallel columns. It seems to be forgotten that the Israelites would be more than human if such passages did not occur in their sacred writings. While some of those passages antedate the establishment of Christianity, most of them have been the result of fervor under oppression and of the appeal to the vengeance of Jehovah in times of persecution; and it would be but just to set against them the more kindly passages, especially the broadly and beautifully humane teachings which are so frequent in the same writings.

An eminently practical course would be to consider the development of Judaism in the United States, Great Britain, and other countries, where undeniably those darker features of the Talmud have been more and more blotted out from Jewish teaching, and the unfortunate side of Talmudic influence more and more weakened.

But this charge of Talmudic fanaticism is constantly made, and Russians, to show that there is no hatred of Israelites as such, point to the fact that the Koraites,* who are non-Talmudic, have always been treated with especial kindness.

To this the answer would seem to be that the Koraites* are free from fanaticism because they have been so long kindly treated, and that this same freedom and kindness which has made them unobjectionable to Russian patriotism would, in time, probably render the great mass of Israelites equally so.

There is no need of argument, either in the light of history or of common sense, to prove that these millions of Israelites in Russia are not to be rendered less fanatical by the treatment to which they are at present subjected.

To prove that the more bitter utterances in the Talmud complained of do not necessarily lead Israelites to hate Christians, and indeed to show that the teachings which the Israelites receive in countries where they have more freedom lead them to a broad philanthropy of the highest type, I have been accustomed, in discussing the subject with Russians, to point to such examples of the truest love for human kind as those shown by Judah Tours** in the United States, Sir Moses Montefiore in England, Nathan de Rothschild in Austria, James de Rothschild and Baron Hirsch in France, and multitudes of other cases, citing especially the fact of the extensive charities carried on by Israelites in all countries, and the significant circumstance that the first considerable contribution from the United States to the Russian famine fund came from a Jewish synagogue in California, with the request that in the use of it no discrimination should be made between Jews and Christians. Cases like these would seem to do away effectually with the idea that Jewish teachings necessarily inculcate hostility to people of other religious beliefs.

There is also a charge closely connected with the foregoing which undoubtedly has much to do with the present severe reaction. It is constantly repeated that, in spite of the fact that the late Emperor Alexander II had shown himself more kindly towards the Israelites than had any of his predecessors — relaxing the old rules as to residence, occupation, education and the like, and was sure, had he lived, to go much farther in the same direction, probably as far as breaking down a mass of the existing barriers, and throwing open vast regions never before accessible to them — the proportion of Israelites implicated in the various movements against him, espe-

* Misspelling for "Karaites."
** Misspelling for "Touro."

cially in the Nihilistic movement, and in the final plot which led to his assassination, was far beyond the numerical proportion of their race in Russia to the entire population. This feeling was certainly at the bottom of the cruel persecutions of the Israelites by the peasants just after the death of the late Emperor, and has no less certainly much to do with the prejudices of various personages of high influence as well as of the vast mass of the people which still exist.

The remarkable reaction at present dominant in Russia is undoubtedly in great measure, if not entirely, the result of the assassination of Alexander II; it is a mere truism to say that this event was the most unfortunate in its effects on well-ordered progress that has occurred in this Empire; but, so far as the Israelites are concerned, the facts at the bottom of this charge against them can be accounted for, without imputing anything to the race at large, by the mass of bitterness stored up during ages of oppression, not only in Russia, but elsewhere. The matter complained of must certainly be considered as exceptional, for it can not hide the greater fact that the Jews have always shown themselves especially grateful to such rulers as have mitigated their condition or even shown a kindly regard for them.

I was myself, as minister at Berlin, cognizant of innumerable evidences of gratitude and love shown by the entire Jewish population toward the Crown Prince, afterwards the Emperor Frederick III, who, when Jew-baiting was in fashion, and patronized by many persons in high positions, set himself quietly but firmly against it. And this reminiscence leads me to another in regard to the oft-repeated charge that the Israelite is incapable of patriotism, is a mere beast of prey, and makes common cause with those of his race engaged in sucking out the substance of the nation where he happens to be. It was my good fortune to know personally several Israelites at Berlin, who as members of the Imperial Parliament showed their patriotism by casting away all hopes of political advancement and resisting certain financial claims in which some of their coreligionists, as well as some leading and very influential Christians, were deeply engaged. There is nothing nobler in recent parliamentary history than the career of such Israelites as Lasker and Bamberger during that period, and at this moment no sane man in Germany hesitates to ascribe to the Israelite Simson all the higher qualities required in his great office, that of chief justice in the highest court of the German Empire.

The same broad and humane characteristics have been shown among the vast majority of Israelites eminent in science, philosophy, literature, and the arts. Long before the Israelite Spinoza wrought his own ideal life into the history of philosophy, this was noted, and it has continued to be noted in Russia. During my former residence here there were two eminent representatives of the proscribed race in the highest scientific circles, and they were especially patriotic and broad in their sympathies; and today the greatest of Russian sculptors, Antokolski, an Israelite, has thrown into his work not only more genius, but also more of profoundly patriotic Russian feeling, than has any other sculptor of this period. He has revived more evidently than has any other sculptor the devotion of Russians to their greatest men in times past, and whenever the project of erecting at St. Petersburg a worthy monument to the late Emperor shall be carried out, there is no competent judge who will not acknowledge that he is the man in all Russia to embody in marble or bronze the gratitude of the nation. This is no mere personal opinion of my own, for when recently a critic based an article against Antokolski's works, evidently upon grounds of race antipathy, a brilliant young author, of one of the oldest and most thoroughly Russian families in the Empire, Prince Sergius Wolkonsky, wrote a most cogent refutation of the attack. It is also charged that in Russia, and, indeed throughout Europe, an undue proportion of Jews have been prominent in movements generally known as "socialistic," and such men as Ferdinand Lasalle and Karl Marx are referred to.

When this statement has been made in my hearing I have met it by the counter statement of a fact which seems to me to result from the freedom allowed in the United States, namely, the fact that at the meeting of the American Social Science Association in 1891, in which a discussion took place involving the very basis of the existing social system, and in which the leading representatives of both sides in the United States were most fully represented, the argument which was generally agreed to be the most effective against the revolutionary and antisocial forces was made by a young Israelite, Prof. Seligman, of Columbia University, in the city of New York. Here, again, results are mistaken for causes; the attitude complained of in the Israelites is clearly the result of the oppression of their race.

But there is one charge which it is perhaps my duty to say that I have never heard made against Israelites even by Russians most opposed to them — the charge that they are to be found in undue or even in any considerable proportions among inebriates or criminals. The simplest reason for this exception in their favor is found in the official statistics which show that, in the Governments where they are most numerous, diseases and crimes resulting from the consumption of alcoholic drinks are least numerous, and that where the number of Israelites is greatest the consumption of spirits is least. It is also well known, as a matter of general observation, that the Russian Israelites are, as a rule, sober, and that crimes among them are comparatively infrequent.

Yet, if in any country we might expect alcoholism to be greatly developed among them it would be in this Empire, where their misery is so great and the temptation to drown it in intoxicating beverages so constant; and if in any country we might expect crime to be developed largely among them it would be in this Empire, where, crowded together as they are, the struggle for existence is so bitter. Their survival under it can only be accounted for by their superior thrift and sobriety.

It would be a mistake to suppose that religious hatred or even deeply religious feeling is a main factor in this question. The average Russian believes that all outside the orthodox Greek Church are lost; but he does not hate them on that account, and though there has been of late years, during the present reaction, an increase of pressure upon various Christian organizations outside the established church, this has been undeniably from political rather than religious reasons; it has been part of the "Russifying process," which is at present the temporary fashion.

The rule in Russia has always been toleration, though limited by an arrangement which seems to a stranger very peculiar. In St. Petersburg, for example, there are churches for nearly all the recognized forms of Christian belief, as well as synagogues for Hebrews, and at least one Mohammedan mosque; but the only proselytism allowed is that between themselves and from them to the established church; in other words, the Greek Church may proselyte from any of them, and, within certain limits, each of them may proselyte from its unorthodox neighbors, but none of them can make converts from the Greek Church.

This regulation seems rather the result, on the whole, of organized indifference than of zeal, its main purpose being undoubtedly to keep down any troublesome religious fervor. The great body of the Russian peasantry, when left to themselves, seem to be remarkably free from any spirit of fanatical hostility toward religious systems differing from their own, and even from the desire to make proselytes. Mr. Mackenzie Wallace, in his admirable book, after showing that the orthodox Russian and the Mohammedan Tartar live in various communities in perfect peace with each other, details a conversation with a Russian peasant, in which the latter told him that just as God gave the Tartar a darker skin, so he gave him a different religion; and this feeling of indifference, when the peasants are not excited by zealots on one side or the other, seems to prevail toward the Roman Catholics in Poland and the Protestants in the Baltic provinces and Finland. While some priests have undoubtedly done much to create a more zealous feeling, it was especially noted during the fierce persecutions of the Jews early in the present reign that in several cases the orthodox village priests not only gave shelter to Israelites seeking to escape harm, but exerted themselves to put an end to the persecutions. So, too, during the past few days the papers have contained a statement that a priest very widely known and highly esteemed, to whom miraculous powers are quite generally attributed, Father John, of Cronstadt, has sent some of the charity money, of which he is almoner, to certain Jewish orphanages under the control of Israelites.

The whole present condition of things is rather the outcome of a great complicated mass of causes, involving racial antipathies, remembrances of financial servitude, vague inherited prejudices, with myths and legends like those of the Middle Ages.

But, whatever may be the origin of the feeling toward the Israelites, the practical fact remains that the present policy regarding them is driving them out of the country is great masses. The German papers speak of large numbers as seeking the United States and the Argentine Republic — but especially the former — through the northern ports of that Empire, and, as I write, the Russian papers state that eight steamers loaded with them are just about leaving Libau for America.

It is, of course, said in regard to these emigrants that they have not been ordered out of the country, that they can stay in Russia if they like, and that Russia has simply exercised her right to manage her own internal affairs in her own way; but is none the less true that the increasing severity in the enforcement of the regulations regarding the Israelites is the main, if not the only, cause of this exodus. In order that this question may be understood in its relations to the present condition of political opinion in the Empire, there is need to make some additional statement.

There has never been a time, probably, when such a feeling of isolation from the rest of the world, and aversion to foreign influence of every sort, have prevailed in Russia as at present; it is shared by the great majority from the highest to the lowest, and it is echoed in the press. Russia has been, during the last ten years, in a great reactionary period, which now seems to be culminating in the attempted "Russification" of the Empire, involving such measures as increasing pressure upon Poland, increasing interference with the Baltic provinces and the German colonies, in the talk of constitutional changes in Finland, in the substitution of Russian for German names of various western towns, in the steadily increasing provisions for strengthening the orthodox Russian Church against all other religious organizations, in the outcry made by various papers in favor of such proposals as that for transferring the university at Dorpat into the Muscovite regions of the interior, for changing the name of St. Petersburg, and for every sort of Russifying process which the most imaginative can devise.

In this present reaction, connected as it is with bitter disappointment over the defeat of Russian aspirations in the Berlin treaty and since, reforms which were formerly universally considered honorable and desirable for Russia are now regarded with aversion; the controlling feeling is for "Russification."

Peter the Great is now very largely regarded by Russians as having taken a wrong road, and, while monuments are erected to Alexander II, his services as emancipator of the serfs are rarely alluded to, and the day formerly observed in remembrance of the emancipation has ceased to be publicly noticed. This reaction shows itself in general literature, in paintings, in sculpture, in architecture, in everything. Any discussion regarding a change in the present condition of things is met by the reply that strangers do not understand Russian questions, and that these questions are complicated historically, politically, economically, and socially to such a degree that none but those having personal experience can understand them. If the matter is still further pressed and the good effects of a different policy in the United States, Great Britain, and elsewhere are referred to, it is answered that in those countries a totally different state of things exists, and that no arguments can be made from them to Russia. Any continuance of the discussion is generally met by the statement that Russian questions are largely misrepresented by the press of western Europe; that there is a systematic propaganda against Russia in England, Germany, Austria, and Italy; that England does or allows worse things in her Irish evictions and in her opium traffic, and the United States in lynch law proceedings and treatment of the Chinese, than any done or allowed in Russia; that, in short, Russia is competent to take charge of her own internal policy, and that other powers will do well to mind their own business. This feeling is closely akin to that which was shown sometimes in the United States before the civil war toward foreign comments upon our own "peculiar institution," when representations by such philanthropists as the Duchess of Sutherland, George Thompson, M. P., and others were indignantly repelled.

This condition of opinion and the actions resulting from it are so extreme that it naturally occurs to one who has observed Russian history that a reaction can not be long deferred.

The progress of Russia thus far has been mainly by a series of reactions. These have sometimes come with surprising suddenness. In view of that which took place when the transition was made from the policy of restriction followed by the Emperor Nicholas to the broadly liberal policy adopted by Alexander II, of which, being connected with this legation at that time, I was a witness, a reaction at present seems by no means impossible or even improbable. It is by no means necessary that a change of reign should take place. A transition might be occasioned, as others have been, by the rise of some strong personality bringing to bear upon the dominant opinion the undoubted fact that the present system of repression toward the Israelites is from every point of view a failure, and that it is doing incalculable harm to Russia.

This dispatch ought not, perhaps, to close without an apology for its length; the subject is one of great importance, and it has seemed to me a duty to furnish the Department, in answer to the Secretary's question, with as full a report regarding the present stage in the evolution of the matter concerned as my opportunities have enabled me to make.

I am, etc.,

ANDREW D. WHITE

INDEX

Aarifi Pasha, 45.

Abdullah, Akhund Mullah, 11.

Adams, John Quincy, President, favors restoration of Judaea, 42.

Adee, Alvey A., Acting Secretary of State, 245, 251; dispatch quoted, 245–46, 251–52.

Adler, Cyrus, corresponds with State Department regarding equal rights in Balkan countries, 135; aids in relief of Polish Jews, 143; confers with President Wilson regarding anti-Jewish excesses in Poland, 153; receives report of executions of Jews at Pinsk, Poland, 155; attends conferences on passport question at White House, 282; signs memorandum on conference sent to President Taft, 284; confers with Secretary Hull on Nazi anti-Jewish excesses, 365 ff.

Advisory Committee on Political Refugees, 436.

Alexander, Mr., 44.

Alexander I, Czar, 196, 394.

Alexander II, Czar, 197, 203, 389 f., 392, 396 f., 401.

Algeciras Act, 40.

Algeciras Conference, 36–40; motion regarding treatment of non-Moslems in Morocco, quoted, 39, 408; intent of resolution, 408–409.

Algeria, Crémieux Decree abrogated in, 411; Jews protest loss of citizenship in, 412–413. See also Crémieux Decree.

Alien Immigration Commission, 133.

Allenby, Edmund H. H., General, 68.

Alliance Israélite de Maroc, 26.

Alliance Israélite (Hamadan), 18.

Alliance Israélite Universelle, letter, quoted, 40, 113.

Alsatian Jews, 304, 307 f., 315.

Amar, Isaac, case of, 25.

American-British Convention regarding Palestine, 82, 86, 87, 91, 95.

American Council for Judaism, 400.

American Federation of Labor, 394, 400.

American Israelites, Board of Delegates of, 5, 20, 24, 26, 100.

American Jewish Committee, 10; relief in Palestine, 64; rights of Jews in Rumania, 135; its activity in bringing about the termination of the Russo-American Treaty of 1832, 278, 281 f., 285; representatives at White House conferences on passport question, 282; memorandum of conference of May 25, 1910, 282–84; 364 ff.; memorandum by, urging repeal of British White Paper, 394; correspondence with State Department, protesting exclusion of American Jews from immigration to Palestine, 394–395; in joint protest over *Struma* incident, 396; urges free entry of Jews into Palestine, 400; asks State Department to aid French Jews, 406–407; correspondence on discriminatory laws in Morocco, 408–409; urges abrogation of Crémieux Decree, 414, 415; efforts of, to help European Jews to escape, 424; advocates international protection of human rights, 450–451, 452.

American Jewish Congress, 375, 396, 407, 412.

American Jewish Congress, Women's Division of, 373 ff.; addressed by Mayor LaGuardia, 373 f.; attacked in *Der Angriff*, 374 f.

American Jewish Joint Agricultural Corporation, 436.

American Jewish Joint Distribution Committee, 18, 69, 70, 72, 436, 445, 449; activity in Poland, 141–47, 162.

American Palestine Committee, 394.

American Red Cross, aid to Jews in Turkey, 67.

American Relief Administration, 148.

American Zionist Emergency Council, 393, 396.

American Zionist Medical Unit to Palestine, 69, 72.

Anglo-Jewish Association, 26.

Anglo-Russian Treaty of Jan. 12, 1859, 201.

Anti-Semitic league, in Germany, 357 ff., 361.

Anti-Semitism, in Germany, 348; dispatch on, by Andrew D. White, 354–62; in German universities, 358, 360; opposition to, 358; in Nazi Germany,